Contents

Preface

The continued expansion of ISIS in Iraq and Syria, kidnappings by Boko Haram in Nigeria, the uncertainty caused by the Houthi insurgency in Yemen, and persistent attacks by al-Qaeda affiliates in Africa are stark reminders that terrorism continues to pose a threat to the international community. The threat, however, is not only from organized groups abroad. As recent attacks in Australia, Paris, and the United States indicate, the threat of homegrown terrorism may also be on the rise. Inspired by propaganda on the Internet and the ever more sophisticated use of social media, young men and women from the United States and other Western democracies have been inspired and recruited by violent extremist groups abroad. While some have traveled overseas to join these groups, others have chosen to carry out attacks in their home countries. So far none of these attacks have been on the scale of the attacks on the World Trade Center and the Pentagon in 2001. Nevertheless, the Boston marathon bombing in April 2013, which killed 3 people and injured more than 200 and the Charlie Hebdo attacks in January of 2015, in which 12 people died and 11 were injured, are brutal reminders that terrorism and political violence can occur anywhere and at any time.

While daily reports of death and violence from countries like Iraq, Syria, Yemen, Afghanistan, Nigeria, and Libya rarely make the headlines in the U.S. media, we need to remember that one major attack or catastrophic terrorist event can quickly propel the topic of terrorism back to the top of the agenda. History teaches us that when it comes to terrorism, periods of relative quiet are, at best, temporary phenomena. As a Provisional Irish Republican Army spokesman proclaimed in a 1984 statement released after the Brighton bombing, terrorists live by the creed " . . . we only have to be lucky once. You have to be lucky always." While some terrorist attacks may be prevented, it is impossible to prevent all terrorist attacks. No one is lucky 100 percent of the time.

Despite hundreds of billions of dollars spent on global military interventions and domestic security over the past decade, the threat of terrorism continues and will continue to affect our lives well into the twenty-first century. Political, economic, social, ethnic, and religious strife, fueled by the availability of weapons, advances in technology, and the increased accessibility of social and traditional media, provide fertile ground for the continue growth of violence and terrorism. No matter what we do, there will always be individuals who will resort to violence and terrorism in order to seek redress for issues, real or imagined.

As terrorism will inevitably continue to affect our lives, the only real defense against terrorism is to try to understand it.

Annual Editions: Violence and Terrorism continues focus on fundamental questions: Who are the terrorists? Why does terrorism occur? What tactics do they use? How can or should governments respond? This anthology provides a broad overview of the major issues associated with political violence and terrorism. The selections for this 15th edition of *Annual Editions: Violence and Terrorism* were chosen to reflect a diversity of issues, actors, and perspectives. This revision incorporates a significant number of new articles that reflect the changes that have occurred since the previous edition was published. While, as always, influenced by recent events, this volume endeavors to maintain sufficient regional and topical coverage to provide students with a broad perspective as a basis for understanding contemporary political violence. Articles for this introductory reader were chosen from a variety of sources and reflect diverse writing styles. It is our hope that this broad selection will provide accessibility at various levels and will thus stimulate interest and discussion. In addition to the aforementioned considerations, elements such as timeliness and readability of the articles were important criteria used in their selection.

It is our hope that *Annual Editions: Violence and Terrorism* will introduce students to the study of terrorism and serve as a stimulus for further exploration of this vital topic. I would like to thank the many scholars who provided feedback and submitted suggestions for articles to be included in this volume. I would also like to thank Mikhaila Calice who has worked with me as a research assistant for the past four years. She helped identify and select articles for inclusion in this anthology and helped coordinate and collate the work of other members of the research team. As a key member of the reseach team, she kept everyone on track and moving forward. I am also grateful to a group of undergraduate students at Randolph-Macon College who volunteered their time to worked with me on this 15th edition. Amanda Binion, Nicole Fote, Thomas Lewis, Olof Nordin, and Marcelo Roman helped review the numerous articles that were identified for consideration. They provided valuable insights and, above all, a critical students' perspective, which made the job of selecting articles for this edition much easier. I hope that you, the reader, will continue to provide us with feedback so we can continue to, with your help, improve future editions.

Thomas J. Badey

Editor

Thomas J. Badey is a professor of Political Science and the director of the International Studies Program at Randolph-Macon College in Ashland, Virginia. He received a BS in Sociology from the University of Maryland (University College) in 1986 and an MA in political science from the University of South Florida in 1987. In 1993 he earned his PhD in political science from the *Institut für Politische Wissenschaft* of the *Ruprecht-Karls Universität* in Heidelberg, Germany. From 1979 to 1988, he served as a security policeman in the United States Air Force and was stationed in the United States, Asia, and the Middle East. Dr. Badey teaches courses on International Terrorism and on Terrorism and Homeland Security and has published a number of articles on the subject. He is also the editor of the McGraw-Hill Contemporary Learning Series *Annual Editions: Homeland Security*.

Academic Advisory Board

Members of the Academic Advisory Board are instrumental in the final selection of articles for the *Annual Editions* series. Their review of the articles for content, level, and appropriateness provides critical direction to the editor(s) and staff. We think that you will find their careful consideration reflected in this book.

Andy Alali
California State University Bakersfield

Dean C. Alexander
Western Illinois University

Kristian Alexander
Zayed University, U.A.E.

M. Jennifer Brougham
Arizona State University

Robert Cassinelli
American River College

Cynthia C. Combs
University of North Carolina-Charlotte

Jeffery B. Cook
North Greenville University

Arthur I. Cyr
Carthage College

William F. Daddio
Georgetown University

Sofia Dermisi
Roosevelt University

Wilton Duncan
ASA College

Vanessa Escalante
LA College

Michael T. Eskey
Park University

Christian Fossa-Andersen
DeVry University

Paul Fuller
Knoxville College

Patricia Furnish
Blue Ridge Community College

David Gray
Fayetteville State University

Michael M. Gunter
Tennessee Technological University

Don Haider-Markel
University of Kansas

Vincent Henry
Long Island University

Edward M. Jankovic
Fairfield University

Linda Jasper
Indiana University Southeast

Lloyd Klein
St. Francis College/Hostos Community College

Natalie Kozelka
Northeast Iowa Community College

Bud Levin
Blue Ridge Community College

Charles Loftus
Arizona State University

Steve Mabry
Cedar Valley College

Daniel Masters
University of North Carolina, Wilmington

Jane D. Matheson
Northeastern University

George Michael
University of Virginia's College, Wise

Randall K. Nichols
Utica College

Richard Pearlstein
Southeastern Oklahoma State University

Ruth Pellow
University of Arkansas, Monticello

Kelly E. Peterson
South Texas College

Todd Sandler
University of Texas, Dallas

Donna M. Schlagheck
Wright State University

Chris Sharp
Valdosta State University

Stephen Sloan
University of Central Florida

Brent Smith
University of Arkansas, Fayetteville

Darren Stocker
Cumberland County College

David D. Van Fleet
Arizona State University

Paul Wallace
University of Missouri, Columbia

Mark Wintz
SUNY-Brockport

Unit 1

UNIT

Prepared by: Thomas J. Badey, *Randolph-Macon College*

What Is Terrorism?

Defining and conceptualizing terrorism is an essential first step in understanding it. Despite volumes of literature on the subject, there is still no commonly agreed upon definition of terrorism. The application of former Supreme Court Justice Potter Steward's famous maxim, "I know it when I see it," has led to definitional anarchy. The U.S. government, in its efforts to fight a Global War on Terrorism, has further confounded the definitional problem by a myriad of confusing statements and policies.

Terrorists have also exacerbated this problem. They often portray themselves as victims of political, economic, social, religious, or psychological oppression. By virtue of their courage, their convictions, or their condition, terrorists see themselves as the chosen few, representing a larger population, in the struggle against the perceived oppressors. The actions of the oppressor, real or imagined, against the population they claim to represent, serve as motivation and moral justification for their use of violence. Existing institutional mechanisms for change are deemed either illegitimate or are in the hands of the oppressors. Hence, the terrorists portray themselves as freedom-fighters and violence becomes the primary means of asserting their interests and the interests of the people they claim to represent.

While arguments among academics and policymakers about how terrorism should be defined continue, most would agree that terrorism involves three basic components: the perpetrator, the victim, and the target of the violence. The perpetrator commits violence against the victim. The victim is used to communicate with or send a message to the intended target. The target is expected to respond to perpetrator. Fear is used as a catalyst to enhance the communication and elicit the desired response.

Defining terrorism is an essential first step in the accumulation of statistical data. Definitions impact not only the collection and collation of data, but also its analysis and interpretation. Ultimately, definitions have a profound effect on threat perceptions and policies developed to counter terrorist activities.

The articles in this section explore different definitions of terrorism, as each author focuses on the elements he considers critical. The first article attempts to tackle the definitional problem. Eric Chase examines why a universally accepted definition of "terrorism" has not been developed. He suggests four steps that that the EU and NATO should take to address this issue. The second selection in this section takes an academic approach. Since the 1980s Alex P. Schmidt has advocated for a consensus on an academic definition of terrorism. While the long and rather complex result stemming from "three rounds of consultations among academics and other professionals," is not likely to be used by policymakers, it highlights critical components that most would agree differentiate terrorism from other types of violence. In the last article of this section, Fergal Davis argues that the confusion about what "terrorism" is may be overstated. He believes that the dilemma is more a function of politics than of linguistics or human understanding.

Article

Prepared by: Thomas J. Badey, *Randolph-Macon College*

Defining Terrorism: A Strategic Imperative

ERIC CHASE

Learning Outcomes

After reading this article, you will be able to:

- Identify the historical challenges that exist in defining terrorism.
- Discuss the necessity of a universally accepted definition.
- Determine the role international organizations can play in defining terrorism.

On September 11, 2012, a group of assailants, now believed to be part of, or affiliated with, the terrorist organization Ansar al-Sharia attacked the U.S. Consulate in Benghazi, Libya, killing the American Ambassador and three others. In the following weeks, U.S. political discourse focused on one question: was the event a terrorist attack or simply a spontaneous response to a viral internet video mocking the prophet Muhammad and the Islamic religion? For counterterrorism scholars and practitioners alike, the debate reaffirmed familiar challenges associated with studying terrorism or developing counterterrorism strategies. Namely, "terrorism" is a difficult concept to define.

Even if a video attacking the Muslim faith had in fact inspired a spontaneous attack on the Consulate, the Federal Bureau of Investigation (FBI) defines terrorism as "the unlawful use of force or violence against persons or property to intimidate or coerce a government, the civilian population, or any segment thereof, in furtherance of political or social objectives." This definition certainly seems applicable in such an instance. Nevertheless, applying the label "terrorism" or "terrorist" to any one event, person, or group conjures visceral emotions, incites ideological sparring, and stirs vociferous political debate that reverberate well beyond the initial application of the term.

This article recognizes that developing a universally accepted definition of terrorism is unlikely–if not impossible–when "universal" encompasses a stakeholder group, including nation-states, sub-state organizations, individual non-state actors, and scholars. Nation-states, sub-state organizations, and individual non-state actors frequently object to definitions which are

perceived to target their *modus operandi*. Indeed, these groups charge that "terrorists" are merely pursuing just ends with the only means available. Furthermore, scholars and political scientists are professionally inclined to push theoretical boundaries, test hypotheses, and question assumptions. Expecting academics to agree on a definition for an esoteric concept like terrorism might be a bridge too far. Rather, this analysis will demonstrate that terrorism *can and should be* defined for the discrete purpose of developing international counterterrorism strategies within an international framework bound by countries with common interests and shared objectives.

In these terms, developing an accepted definition for a limited group of stakeholders for a single purpose becomes feasible *and* useful. This argument is framed in three sections. The first section examines the historical and existent barriers that prevent individuals, organizations, and governments from defining terrorism in universally accepted terms. The second section argues that terrorism must be defined to provide governments, government agencies, and security practitioners a common reference point for developing effective counterterrorism strategy. The third section evaluates two illustrative international frameworks and definitions and proposes a recommended way-ahead.

"Not one, but many Terrorisms"

Walter Laqueur's observation that any attempt to define terrorism in specific terms "is bound to fail" for the simple reason that there is "not one but many terrorisms[1]" recognizes the multitude of factors, motivations, and activities considered when describing terrorism. The old adage, "one man's terrorist is another man's freedom fighter" succinctly captures a present-day challenge: a group's or individual's sympathies typically lie with either the "terrorist" perpetrator or the victim, and those sympathies unavoidably shape how the term's application is applied or rejected. Labeling actions simultaneously places on a moral judgment on those actions and is unavoidably shaped by the orientation of the definer and the receiver. "Terrorism" is a pejorative label. Characterizing an individual or organization with the term "terrorist" implies wrongdoing, and that reality has historically enticed governments, organizations, and individuals to indiscriminately apply the term to suit overtly political agendas.

Moreover, the meaning of the word "terrorism" has also changed over time. The term originated from the French Revolution "Reign of Terror" which associated terrorism with actions designed to restore order and deter counterrevolutionary critics.[2] In this context, French loyalists viewed state-sponsored terrorism—and the term's associated meaning—as a positive good supported by the generally accepted principle that state authority holds a monopoly on violence to maintain order. From this historical perspective, terrorism was considered a necessary and just application of the state's power to protect the civilian populace and to prevent a sub-state organization from resorting to violence to impose political change. During the next century, Europeans used the term to describe violence and intimidation directed against the state as opposed to the state's use—or threat—of violence. In this context, terrorism assumed the negative connotation it bears today.[3]

The meaning of the term continued to evolve over the centuries, describing anti-monarchical movements in the late 19th century, repressive tactics employed by authoritarian and fascist states like Russia and Germany during the 1930s, anti-colonial and nationalist movements during the next two decades, political extremists and disenfranchised minorities during the 1960s and 1970s, and religious extremists during the late 1980s. Each of these distinct "periods" witnessed different applications of violence to serve different ideological, political, and religious motivations. The dynamic nature of terrorism has left many to conclude that the only constant variable in terrorism is that it will change.

These historical challenges have convinced many counterterrorism thought-leaders that establishing a universal definition for terrorism is a futile effort. William Connolly argues that defining terrorism is problematic because the term is an "essentially contested concept"—an idea so internally complex that disagreements arise not only over the interpretation of the available evidence but also over the system of concepts and rules that make objective analysis possible.[4] Alex P. Schmid and Albert. J. Jongman highlight the inherent difficulty in defining terrorism in their 1988 study which presents 109 distinct definitions deconstructed into 21 commonly referenced definitional elements. Indeed, some scholars like Walter Laqueur conclude that "after thirty years of hard labor there is still no generally agreed definition of terrorism" and the debate does not contribute to the study of the subject.

"For without a Consensus of what Constituted Terrorism, Nations could not Unite Against It"

Conversely, there is broad consensus that there needs to be a universally accepted definition of terrorism for both analytical and practical purposes. Definitional elements shape the type of data collected to develop or disprove theories in the study of terrorism. Moreover, a universally accepted definition would influence domestic policy, international agreements, and global

strategies to counter terrorism. The challenge associated with classifying a singular event, like the Benghazi attack, under a universally agreed definition becomes even more complicated when the application of the term is part of national and international policy-making.

The U.S. Department of State (DOS), Bureau of Counterterrorism lists the Revolutionary Armed Forces of Colombia (FARC) as a Foreign Terrorist Organization (FTO).[5] While the FARC has remained a State Department designated FTO since 1997, Venezuelan president Hugo Chavez considers the group a legitimate rebel force and provides the organization with material aid and sanctuary for its leaders. The stark differences between how the U.S. and Venezuelan governments characterize the FARC is further evidence of the challenges associated with defining "terrorism" in universally (or internationally) accepted terms.

Although countries like Venezuela and their public leaders might publically condemn terrorism, agreeing on the specific definitional elements becomes problematic when they are intended to shape policy and influence behavior. Each of the State Department designated FTOs must either engage in "terrorist activities" or have the capability and intent to conduct "terrorist activities" as defined by the 1988 Foreign Relations Authorization Act. Moreover, the State Department outlines the desired effects for placing organizations on the FTO list, which include:

1. Supports efforts to curb terrorism financing and to encourage other nations to do the same
2. Stigmatizes and isolates designated terrorist organizations internationally
3. Deters donations or contributions to and economic transactions with named organizations
4. Heightens public awareness and knowledge of terrorist organizations
5. Signals to other governments our concern about named organizations[6]

Indeed, the United Nations (UN) recognized that "without a consensus of what constituted terrorism, nations could not unite against it." Nevertheless, eleven years after 9/11 the UN has been unable to agree on a definition of terrorism. The UN has generated numerous motions, resolutions, and committees to draft a comprehensive definition of terrorism. The Ad Hoc Committee to Eliminate Terrorism established in 1994 has been stifled by disagreements over how to address "freedom fighters," "national liberation movements," and "state sponsored terrorism." A transcript from a 2005 General Assembly meeting indicates that

> "some delegates also cautioned against identifying terrorism with a particular religion. The representative of Singapore said it was wrong 'to dignify the murders that these terrorists have committed around the world by associating them with any great religious faith of the world.' If measures to counter terrorism were to involve crude methods of profiling and targeting the followers of one

religion, that would be 'falling into the trap of the extremists who hope to sow divisions and provoke a clash of civilizations when no such clash needs to take place.'[7]

Even attempts to deconstruct terrorism into the term's most basic conceptual elements–means and ends–become problematic when the very concepts are contested. Ganor suggests that while different organizations may have similar strategic, political, or ideological ends, those organizations that choose to violate normative principles codified in international law and customs by willfully pursuing means that deliberately target noncombatants or civilians lose any claim to *jus ad bellum*. However, "just war" concepts and normative principles are not universal and are subject to moral debate, ideological perspective, and political interests. Instead, any "universal" interest in developing an accepted definition of terrorism must first focus on an alliance of international partners for the discrete purpose of developing a coherent, coordinated international counterterrorism strategy.

An International Framework for an International Problem

The urgent need to develop an international coalition committed to defining terrorism and developing counterterrorism strategies is manifest in the transnational nature present-day terrorism assumes. Terrorist organizations recruit, finance, and operate across, and between, internationally recognized boundaries. An international framework is necessary to defeat an international problem. While the UN Assembly readily admits there needs to be a consensus on a definition of terrorism, the international net the organization casts is far too large. The European Union provides an instructive example on how an internationally accepted definition can be used to combat terrorism. The Council Framework Decision announced on June 13, 2002 for combating terrorism established an accepted definition of terrorism and represents the cornerstone in EU counterterrorism policy and strategy. Article 1 of the Framework Decision on Combating Terrorism defines terrorism as any act that

> *"may seriously damage a country or an international organization where committed with the aim of: seriously intimidating a population; or unduly compelling a Government or international organization to perform or abstain from performing any act; or seriously destabilizing or destroying the fundamental political, constitutional, economic or social structures of a country or an international organization."*[8]

The Framework Decision also articulates the intent to "[harmonize] the definition of terrorist offenses in all Member States" to establish "jurisdictional rules to guarantee that terrorist offences may be effectively prosecuted."[9] The EU Framework Decision provides an excellent model for defining terrorism in an international construct to shape coordinated counterterrorism policy. However, the definition refrains from describing the political, ideological, or religious motivations that drive terrorism. The definition only describes the potential effects arising from terrorism. The overly broad definition prevents the narrow focus required to develop effective counterterrorism policies or strategies.

The North Atlantic Treaty Organization (NATO) defines terrorism as "the unlawful use or threatened use of force or violence against individuals or property in an attempt to coerce or intimidate governments or societies to achieve political, religious or ideological objectives."[10] However, unlike the EU definition, the NATO definition does not outline the strategic aim for defining terrorism in universal terms.

The nation-members of both the EU and NATO could and should work to establish an international coalition that will commit to 1) defining terrorism and 2) outlining clearly stated objectives for such an agreement. Each organization has already proven that this goal is possible and that the effort is urgently needed. A codified definition of terrorism agreed upon by a coalition from member nations of both organizations would create a strong international voice that 1) clearly identifies what constitutes terrorism, 2) unanimously condemns those activities, 3) enables a coordinated approach to developing international counterterrorism strategy, and 4) forces noncompliant states, sub-state organizations, and non-state actors to recalibrate the cost-benefit analysis of resorting to, or supporting, terrorism.

Notes

1. Walter Laqueur, *The New Terrorism: Fanaticism and the Arms of Mass Destruction,* New York: Oxford University Press (2000), p. 46.

2. Alison M. Jaggar, "What Is Terrorism, Why Is It Wrong, and Could It Ever Be Morally Permissible?" Journal of Social Philosophy, vol. 36, no. 2 (May 2005), 202.

3. Jaggar, 203.

4. Leonard Weinberg, et al., "The Challenges of Conceptualizing Terrorism," Terrorism and Political Violence, vol. 16, no. 4 (2004), 778.

5. "Foreign Terrorist Organizations," Department of State, Bureau of Counterterrorism, September 28, 2012.

6. Ibid.

7. "Agreed Definition of Term 'Terrorism' Said to be Needed for Consensus on Completing Comprehensive Convention Against It," 60th General Assembly, Sixth Committee , 4th Meeting, July 7, 2005.

8. Council Framework Decision on Combating Terrorism, Council of the European Union, Brussels, 18 April 2002, Art. 1.

9. *Amendment of the Framework Decision on combating terrorism and Evaluation report on the implementation of the Framework Decision on combating terrorism,* MEMO/07/448, Brussels, 6 November 2007.

10. NATO Glossary of Terms and Definitions, AAP-06 Edition 2012 Version 2.

Critical Thinking

1. Is there a need for a universally accepted definition of terrorism?
2. How does a definition of terrorism affect a state's policy making?
3. Why isn't the UN able to come to an agreement on the definition of terrorism?
4. What steps should international organizations take to address this issue?

Create Central

www.mhhe.com/createcentral

Internet References

UN Action to Counter Terrorism
www.un.org/terrorism/

EU Fight Against Terrorism
www.consilium.europa.eu/policies/fight-against-terrorism?lang=en

History of Terrorism
www.terrorism-research.com/history/

ERIC CHASE Captain Eric Chase is a former Intelligence Officer in the United States Marine Corps with multiple deployments to Iraq and Afghanistan. He currently commands Bravo Company, 1st Battalion, 24th Marines and he works at Toffler Associates as a consultant specializing in defense strategic planning and irregular warfare.

Chase, Eric. From *Small Wars Journal*, January 24, 2013. Copyright © 2013 by Small Wars Journal. Reprinted by permission.

Article

Prepared by: Thomas J. Badey, *Randolph-Macon College*

The Revised Academic Consensus Definition of Terrorism

ALEX P. SCHMID

Learning Outcomes

After reading this article, you will be able to:

- Develop an understanding of the need for an academic consensus definition of terrorism.
- Identify the key components of the academic consensus definition of terrorism.

The Definition of Terrorism

Terrorism is a contested concept. While there are many national and regional definitions, there is no universal legal definition approved by the General Assembly of the United Nations (the one proposed by the Security Council in Res. 1566 (2004) is non-binding, lacking legal authority in international law). The Ad Hoc Committee on Terrorism of the 6th (legal) Committee of the General Assembly has, with some interruptions, been trying to reach a legal definition since 1972—but in vain. In the absence of a *legal* definition, attempts have been made since the 1980s to reach agreement on an *academic* consensus definition. The latest outcome is the revised definition reprinted below. It is the result of three rounds of consultations among academics and other professionals. A description [of] how it was arrived at can be found on pp. 39–98 of Alex P. Schmid (Ed.), *The Routledge Handbook of Terrorism Research*, London and New York: Routledge, 2011. The same volume also contains 260 other definitions compiled by Joseph J. Easson and Alex P. Schmid on pp. 99–200.

Revised Academic Consensus Definition of Terrorism (2011)

Compiled by Alex P. Schmid

1. *Terrorism refers, on the one hand, to a doctrine about the presumed effectiveness of a special form or tactic of fear-generating, coercive political violence and, on the other hand, to a conspiratorial practice of calculated, demonstrative, direct violent action without legal or moral restraints, targeting mainly civilians and non-combatants, performed for its propagandistic and psychological effects on various audiences and conflict parties;*

2. Terrorism as a tactic is employed in *three main contexts:* (i) illegal state repression, (ii) propagandistic agitation by non-state actors in times of peace or outside zones of conflict and (iii) as an illicit tactic of irregular warfare employed by state- and non-state actors;

3. The physical *violence* or threat thereof employed by terrorist actors involves single-phase acts of lethal violence (such as bombings and armed assaults), dual-phased life-threatening incidents (like kidnapping, hijacking and other forms of hostage-taking for coercive bargaining) as well as multi-phased sequences of actions (such as in 'disappearances' involving kidnapping, secret detention, torture and murder).

4. The public (-ized) terrorist victimization initiates *threat-based communication processes* whereby, on the

one hand, conditional demands are made to individuals, groups, governments, societies or sections thereof, and, on the other hand, the support of specific constituencies (based on ties of ethnicity, religion, political affiliation and the like) is sought by the terrorist perpetrators;

5. At the origin of terrorism stands *terror*—instilled fear, dread, panic, or mere anxiety—spread among those identifying, or sharing similarities, with the direct victims, generated by some of the modalities of the terrorist act—its shocking brutality, lack of discrimination, dramatic or symbolic quality, and disregard of the rules of warfare and the rules of punishment;

6. The main direct *victims* of terrorist attacks are in general not any armed forces but are *usually civilians, non-combatants or other innocent and defenceless persons* who bear no direct responsibility for the conflict that gave rise to acts of terrorism;

7. The *direct victims are not the ultimate target* (as in a classical assassination where victim and target coincide) but serve as message generators, more or less unwittingly helped by the news values of the mass media, to reach various audiences and conflict parties that identify either with the victims' plight or the terrorists' professed cause;

8. Sources of terrorist violence can be individual *perpetrators,* small groups, diffuse transnational networks as well as state actors or state-sponsored clandestine agents (such as death squads and hit teams);

9. While showing similarities with methods employed by organized crime as well as those found in war crimes, terrorist violence is *predominantly political*—usually in its motivation but nearly always in its societal repercussions;

10. The immediate *intent* of acts of terrorism is to terrorize, intimidate, antagonize, disorientate, destabilize, coerce, compel, demoralize or provoke a target population or conflict party in the hope of achieving from the resulting insecurity a favourable power outcome, e.g., obtaining publicity, extorting ransom money, submission to terrorist demands and/or mobilizing or immobilizing sectors of the public;

11. The *motivations* to engage in terrorism cover a broad range, including redress for alleged grievances, personal or vicarious revenge, collective punishment, revolution, national liberation and the promotion of diverse ideological, political, social, national, or religious causes and objectives;

12. Acts of terrorism rarely stand alone but form part of a *campaign* of violence which alone can, due to the serial character of acts of violence and threats of more to come, create a pervasive climate of fear that enables the terrorists to manipulate the political process.

Critical Thinking

1. What are the main elements of the academic consensus definition of terrorism?
2. Why is there a need for an academic consensus definition of terrorism?

Internet References

Definition of Terrorism in the U.S. Code
http://www.fbi.gov/about-us/investigate/terrorism/terrorism-definition
Global Terrorism Database
http://www.start.umd.edu/gtd

Article

Prepared by: Thomas J. Badey, *Randolph-Macon College*

One Man's Freedom Fighter ...
Can We Ever Define Terrorism?

Fergal Davis

Learning Outcomes

After reading this article, you will be able to:

- Identify core principles of the term terrorism.

- Explain why using the word "terrorism" wields political power.

- Discuss why the word terrorism has not been defined.

Terrorism defies definition. We all know one man's terrorist is another man's freedom fighter; or in some cases, one man's terrorist is another's recipient of the Nobel Peace Prize. The use of the word "terrorist" by both sides of the current conflict between Hamas and Israel underline its ambiguity.

Indeed the perception that terrorism is too contentious to define has resulted in leading scholars, like Walter Laqueur, declaring:

> Disputes about a detailed, comprehensive definition of terrorism will continue for a long time and will make no noticeable contribution towards the understanding of terrorism.

Laqueur and others point to the failure of bodies such as the UN to define terrorism. The UN has been debating the meaning of terrorism in various committees since 1963. This matters—and not just because it makes terrorism research more difficult. In the aftermath of the terrorist attacks of 11 September 2001, the United Nations Security Council issued Resolution 1373 calling on member states to take co-operative legislative action against terrorism. Unhelpfully, Resolution 1373 left "terrorism" undefined.

However, the apparent confusion about what "terrorism" is may have been overstated. It is possible that while the word "terrorism" is politically divisive there is a commonly understood meaning of terrorism. After all if it looks like an elephant, sounds like an elephant and smells like an elephant it is unlikely to be a kangaroo.

A group of UNSW law scholars—of which I am part—are working as part of an Australian Research Council project on Anti-Terror Laws and the Democratic Challenge. In collaboration with a colleague in the UK we have identified a surprising amount of agreement in an area usually characterised by discord.

In 1988, two European scholars Alex Schmid and Albert Jongman produced one of the more robust definitions of terrorism. They did this by surveying 200 leading academics in the field of terrorism studies. The research asked each expert to define terrorism.

Schmid and Jongman received 109 responses. They identified 22 words or phrases which reoccurred across the definitions. They noted that on average the academic definitions included at least eight of these words or phrases.

This hinted at the possibility that a core understanding of terrorism might exist.

In our research we applied the same approach to seven legislative definitions of terrorism from six countries. We were expecting that the legislatures—each of whom defined terrorism after 11 September 2001—would have produced wildly different definitions from the academics. We thought we might discern some commonality across the legislatures themselves but we did not anticipate that they would correlate well with Schmid and Jongman. We were surprised.

In our work we discovered that the legislative definitions triggered on average 8 of the 22 words or phrases, the same level of correlation that the academics achieved. It is also important to say that the legislatures did not trigger the same 22 words—it couldn't be that easy. Still, we were able to extract the following modest proposal:

> Terrorism is some form of purposive and planned violence that has a political, religious, or ideological motivation. It is intended to coerce or intimidate and is targeted at civilians or government. Legislation prohibiting terrorism ought to have extra-territorial effect. Support for our definitions came from an unexpected quarter. Another colleague was recently giving a lecture in UNSW to a group of 14- and 15-year-old school kids. She asked them to define terrorism. They concluded that it was blowing stuff up; that it was aimed at terrorising the community; and that it was political.

It is difficult to argue that a bomb attack on a girl's school like this recent attack in Pakistan is anything but terrorism—however the attackers would justify it otherwise.

If academics, legislatures and Aussie school kids are all capable of defining terrorism with a fair degree of coherence and agreement why do international organisations struggle? Why does the Rome Statute, which established the International Criminal Court leave the crime of aggression undefined and the crime of terrorism unmentioned? The answer is politics.

The political power of a phrase such as terrorism stems from the fact that groups employ it to denigrate and undermine their opponents: the Irish Republican Army (IRA) frequently referred to the terrorism of the British government without hint of irony or self-awareness; both sides of the Arab-Israeli conflict throw it around; and the President of Iran, Mahmoud Ahmadinejad, is particularly fond of deploying the t-word.

States maintain this ambiguity because it enables them to utilise the phrase "terrorism" without having to clarify what it means. Simultaneously it allows states to avoid condemning behaviour which conforms to the definition of terrorism.

Agreeing on a definition of terrorism would restrain its use. It does not suit the purposes of many states to have terrorism defined: either because they do not want some actions to be defined as "terrorist"; or because they want to term something "terrorist", where in reality the word is inappropriate.

In the end, the dilemma is more a function of politics than it is of linguistics or human understanding. But any school kid could have told you that.

Critical Thinking

1. Why is the term terrorism politically divisive?
2. According to Fergal Davis, why are states hesitant to define terrorism?
3. How would you define terrorism?

Internet References

Country Reports on Terrorism 2013
    http://www.state.gov/j/ct/rls/crt/2013/index.htm
Institute for Economics and Peace: The 2014 Global Terrorism Index
    http://economicsandpeace.org/research/iep-indices-data/global-terrorism-index
The Changing Faces of Terrorism
    http://www.bbc.co.uk/history/recent/sept_11/changing_faces_01.shtml
What is Terrorism?
    http://www.aljazeera.com/indepth/opinion/2013/04/20134179548891867.html

Unit 2

UNIT

Prepared by: Thomas J. Badey, *Randolph-Macon College*

Terrorist Tactics

The tactics of terrorism appear to be universal. While ideologies and motivations vary, terrorist organizations in different parts of the world often use similar methods to instill fear and wreak havoc. It's unclear whether this is the consequence of increased communications among terrorist organizations, or the result of greater access to information in this age of global media. Some argue that terrorists simply tend to be conservative in their selection of tactics, often relying on tactics that have proven successful rather than risking potential failure by attempting to use new methods. Regardless of the underlying reasons, the tactics used by terrorist organizations have remained remarkably consistent.

While bombs have increased in size and sophistication, they are still the primary tool employed by terrorist organizations. Traditionally, bombs have been used in over two-thirds of all terrorist attacks around the world. However, because of their availability and the nature of ongoing conflicts in various parts of the globe, small arms have played an increasing role in terrorist attacks in the last several years Thus armed attacks of various types are becoming more frequent.

In addition to bombings and armed attacks, kidnapping, hostage taking, hijacking, and arson are tactics commonly employed by terrorist organizations. There have, however, been some attempts to integrate some new tactics into the existing terrorist arsenal. Video-taped executions, including beheadings and burnings of captives by ISIS in an effort to intimidate global audiences have sparked public outrage. While these tactics have captured public attention, it is unclear at this point whether they have been beneficial or detrimental to its cause.

To finance various activities terrorists are increasingly resorting to organized crime and drug trafficking, in some cases generating millions of dollars annually in revenue.

The articles in this unit highlight some of the more common contemporary terrorist tactics. In "Bomb Making for Beginners" Anne Stenersen examines efforts by on-line jihadists to create e-learning courses to teach bomb-making skills to on-line sympathizers. While she considers these courses at present a "marginal phenomenon," they appear to attract significant interest among online jihadists because they allow the participants to remain anonymous. Next, Ryan Lentz and Mark Potok of the Southern Poverty Law Center explore the "Rise of the Lone-Wolf." Focusing on terrorism in the United States, they conclude that the vast majority of attacks are conducted by "lone wolves" or small groups using the concept of "leaderless resistance." In the third selection, John Sullivan and Adam Elkus analyze the Charlie Hebdo attacks in Paris. They offer a set of questions for researchers and practitioners to consider when planning for, training to stop, and red-teaming urban siege scenarios. Next, John Cisar examines the nexus between drug trafficking and terrorism. He highlights the important role the drug trade plays in financing terrorist groups such as Hezbollah, FARC, and the Taliban. Finally, as we become increasingly reliant on the Internet, the fear of cyber-terrorism is growing. Peter Singer argues that while cyber-crime may be increasing, the threat of a cyber-terror attack has been greatly exaggerated.

Article

Prepared by: Thomas J. Badey, *Randolph-Macon College*

'Bomb-making for Beginners': Inside an Al-Qaeda E-Learning Course

Anne Stenersen

Learning Outcomes

After reading this article, you will be able to:

- Analyze the reasons for the trend toward individual jihad.
- Explain how jihadist e-learning courses have evolved.
- Discuss the benefits and drawbacks of learning bomb-making skills on the internet.

Introduction

This article discusses how the Internet may assist terrorists in learning how to manufacture explosives. Explosives remain the most common type of weapon for terrorist groups, with bombings accounting for about one-half of all terrorist attacks worldwide.[1] Previous studies of this kind have tended to concentrate on identifying the content of militant web pages, including what kind of "bomb recipes" are being circulated on these pages, and how technically accurate they are.[2] However, few studies have attempted to explain the actual learning process of terrorists who chose to rely on the Internet. How do real-life terrorists utilise online content to become proficient bomb-makers? What major obstacles and challenges do they face? And what efforts are being made by content producers (terrorist groups, forum administrators or "jihobbyists") to overcome these obstacles today?

The topic has become one of current interest as one of the world's most dangerous terrorist networks, Al-Qaeda, is increasingly trying to urge its followers to carry out terrorist attacks at their own initiative without first travelling to a foreign country for training, indoctrination and approval. Before 2001, it was relatively easy to travel to Al-Qaeda's training camps in Afghanistan. In fact, it was a central part of the Al-Qaeda leadership's training doctrine.[3] After 2001 and until today, it has become extremely risky, not only due to the risk of being compromised by security services, but also due to U.S. drone campaigns against known Al-Qaeda hideouts in the Afghan-Pakistani border areas as well as in Yemen. These drone campaigns have increased drastically since 2008 and have killed a number of high- and mid-ranking Al-Qaeda members. These include not only organisers and leaders of international terrorist operations, such as Hamza Rabia al-Masri and Saleh al-Somali. They also include bomb-makers such as Ibrahim al-Muhajir al-Masri, who helped build the bombs for the 1998 East African embassies bombings, and Midhat Mursi (aka Abu Khabab al-Masri), the Egyptian-born chemist who ran his own explosives training camp in Afghanistan during the Taliban's reign. He is believed to have continued this effort in the Tribal Areas of Pakistan after 2001 until he was killed in 2008.[4]

The study is divided into five parts. First, it discusses Al-Qaeda's strategic shift towards "individual jihad." Second, it explores how terrorists learn bomb-making skills more generally. Third, the article takes us inside an "e-learning course" which was held on *Shumukh al-Islam,* a well-known jihadi discussion forum, in April and May 2011. Fourth, the article discusses the evolution of Al-Qaeda's "e-learning tools" more generally, and fifth, it looks at a U.S. cell of would-be terrorists who sought to learn the art of bomb-making online.

Studies of jihadi discussion forums have several limitations. First, the members of a discussion forum are anonymous. All we know is their nickname as well as their status and activity on that particular forum. We do not know who they are and what their real life intentions might be. Second, we must assume that part of the course takes place through private correspondence, which is hidden to the outside observer. Nevertheless, there is much to learn from studying jihadi e-learning courses. The above-mentioned course included ten accessible lessons and more than 300 open comments, questions and suggestions from the participants. It gives us a good idea of the content and the dynamics of the course, as well as the obstacles faced by the participants.

Al-Qaeda's Shift towards "Individual Jihad"

Due to the extreme pressure on Al-Qaeda's current sanctuaries abroad, Al-Qaeda leaders seem to be expanding their strategy to include so-called "leaderless jihad." The concept is not new. The jihadi strategist Abu Mus'ab al-Suri wrote and lectured on the idea back in the 1990s, and held several lecture series to trainees in jihadi training camps. The strategic concept developed by al-Suri became known as *al-muqawama al-islamiyya al-'alamiyya,* "The Global Islamic Resistance."[5] He praised "lone wolf" terrorist attacks that were conducted by individuals that had no connection to Al-Qaeda Central, but who nevertheless carried out attacks supporting Al-Qaeda's global ideology. Individuals praised by al-Suri included El Sayyid Nusayr, an Egyptian-American who shot and killed the American-Israeli politician Meir Kahane in New York in 1990, and Ramzi Yusef, who carried out the first bombing of the World Trade Center in 1993.[6]

Al-Suri was never an official member of Al-Qaeda, but his publications are widely read by jihadists across the world, especially after the U.S. State Department announced a US\$5 million reward on al-Suri's head in November 2004.[7] Al-Qaeda's top leadership has later picked up on al-Suri's ideas. In June 2011, Ayman al-Zawahiri issued a video speech where he encouraged followers of Al-Qaeda to carry out "individual acts of jihad" in the countries in which they reside, rather than going to battlefields abroad.[8] The video states:

> "The door of jihad cannot be closed, and he who wants to launch in his midst with determination and honesty, should not stand [back] in the face of security restrictions nor the difficulty of reaching the fighting fronts, as he could make the place he is in one of the battlefields, and that would be through individual jihad . . . ."[9]

The video praises several individuals who carried out exemplary acts of "individual jihad" in the past, including Mohammad Bouyeri, who killed the Dutch filmmaker Theo van Gogh in Amsterdam in 2004, and Nidal Malik Hasan, who shot and killed fourteen U.S. soldiers at Fort Hood, Texas in 2009. The video acknowledges that such acts are regarded as more controversial than travelling to an occupied Muslim territory to fight so-called "classical jihad," and spends considerable time arguing that the two should go hand in hand.

The second part of the video contains brief operational guidance that focuses on the types of targets that should be attacked, including "the institutions that shape [the country's] economic joints," "influential public figures in the Crusader and Zionist government, industry and media," and "the headquarters of newspapers and the media outlets that mock our religion and prophet."[10] In addition, the video encourages disruptive activities by way of hacking, such as denial-of-service (DOS) attacks and hacking to disrupt electric power network systems.

With a few exceptions, the video does not instruct the would-be terrorist in how he should train or what weapons to use against the preferred targets. It suggests that jihadists based in the United States should attack with firearms, as these are assumed to be easily accessible. Apart from that, security awareness is the most specific operational guideline, and the video points to resources on the Internet:

> "[take] advantage of the wide range of resources available today on the Internet, particularly the various manuals, encyclopedias and course [sic] which deal with the Mujahideen's operational and electronic security, and security in general."[11]

The lack of detailed operational guidelines is probably intended–the fear and terror created by a campaign of "individual jihad" stems, in part, from not knowing who will attack, at what time and with what means. Al-Qaeda's video hints that the attacks should be simple–the "role models" presented all used knives, firearms, or, in one instance, homemade explosives (Ramzi Yusef in the 1993 World Trade Center bombing).

It is notable that Al-Qaeda discourages people from seeking training in foreign countries, even if such training increases the terrorists' chance of succeeding.[12] Instead, the operatives are to take advantage of opportunities in their home countries, such as procuring firearms legally, and to learn from literature on the Internet. Now and probably more so in the future, the Internet stands out as a crucial resource for Al-Qaeda to use to train its operatives without risking compromising their security, due to ease of access anywhere in the world, and the possibility of remaining anonymous.

An article published in 2008 argued that while there is an abundance of training literature on radical forums online, the Internet does not function as a "virtual training camp" for Al-Qaeda–mainly, because there is no organized effort on the part of Al-Qaeda Central to train people online. Others have argued that Internet training would never really replace real-life training because the Internet training can only transfer implicit but not tacit knowledge, i.e. the skills that can only come from hands-on experience.[13]

This paper argues that Al-Qaeda Central is still not making a determined effort to train followers online. However, online training courses organized by "jihobbyists" and forum administrators have become somewhat more professionalized over the past three years. The e-learning courses are more organized and include, to a greater extent than before, audio-visual learning materials as well as written compendiums. Their main weakness is their reliance on one or very few online instructors who are not always able to contribute on a regular basis, causing the interest to ebb away. It can be argued that if jihadi groups started using the Internet in a more systematic way, similar to commercial "remote learning" courses, the threat of individual terrorism would be greater than it is today. In principle, it should be possible. Academic literature argues that e-learning can be as effective as classroom teaching if conducted the proper way.[14]

How Do Terrorists Learn Bomb-Making Skills?

To discuss whether the Internet would be suitable for teaching bomb-making skills, we first need to establish how terrorists learn. More specifically, what are the conditions that need to be in place for a successful transfer of knowledge? In Al-Qaeda, as well as in other terrorist groups, knowledge has generally been transferred through direct contact, typically, in a training camp or similar settings. In the 1990s, Al-Qaeda started to record and compile knowledge in writing. The first, and most famous of such collections was the *Encyclopaedia of Jihad,* the purpose of which was to record all the experiences from the Afghan-Soviet jihad and to make sure the knowledge was not lost on future generations.[15] But written records are usually partial–they tell less than what is implicitly known by the practitioners of the craft.[16]

Al-Qaeda sought to transfer such knowledge directly, by establishing "explosives courses" that were taught in the training camps in Afghanistan by skilled experts. In the 1990s, Al-Qaeda's most famous bomb expert was not Abu Khabab al-Masri, as commonly thought (Abu Khabab was a "freelance trainer" for Al-Qaeda operatives, but was not directly involved in Al-Qaeda's major international operations). Al-Qaeda had as chief bomb-maker an Egyptian with the nickname Abu Abdul Rahman al-Muhajir (real name Muhsin Musa Matwakku Atwah), who constructed the bombs for the East African Embassy bombings in 1998; later he worked as a trainer and bomb-maker for Al-Qaeda in Afghanistan.[17]

Al-Qaeda's bomb-making experts transferred their knowledge to new recruits who could then take over their role as trainers in the future. A recruit named Tarek Mahmoud el-Sawah went to Afghanistan during the Taliban's rule and was hired as a bomb-trainer by Al-Qaeda. Having served in the Afghan-Soviet jihad as well as in Bosnia, he had previous experience with explosives. Nevertheless, once employed by Al-Qaeda, he was able to update and refine his skill, presumably, through

> "receiv[ing] specialized explosives training, including instruction in building improvised explosive devices (IEDs) and remote detonation devices, from Abu Abdul Rahman al-Muhajir. He went on to receive advanced explosives/electronics training from Abu Tariq al-Tunisi, learning how to make timers for IEDs using Casio watches as remote detonators. Then, from June 2001, he gave instruction in explosives and wrote a four-hundred-page bomb-making manual."[18]

After 2001, terrorist groups in Europe have preferred to go to a jihadi training camp, usually in Al-Qaeda's core areas in the Afghanistan-Pakistan border areas. For example, two of the London 7/7 bombers went to the Afghanistan-Pakistan border areas around 2004. Their training was organized by Al-Qaeda's then chief of "external operations," Hamza Rabia al-Masri. Yet these training courses were not necessarily run by Al-Qaeda members. Terrorists who attempted to carry out attacks in Europe or the U.S. were trained at various times by Pakistani militant groups (such as Tehrik-e-Taliban Pakistan, Lashkar-e-Tayba, etc.), the Uzbek-dominated Islamic Jihad Union, or by various local "freelancers." There are many reasons why would-be terrorists chose to go abroad to train–the prospect of receiving high-quality training is probably only one among several motivations. However, this aspect is beyond the scope of this paper, which focuses strictly on the process of transferring technical knowledge, not broader motivators and driving factors for radicalisation.

For Al-Qaeda's strategy of "individual jihad" to work, individuals are required to acquire the necessary bomb-making skills themselves, without going to a training camp. There are examples of terrorists who have learned how to make powerful

bombs based primarily on their own efforts and experiments. In 1995, Timothy McVeigh constructed a fertiliser truck bomb which demolished the Murray building in Oklahoma City, killing 168 people. McVeigh reportedly acquired the skills to make the bomb by picking up ideas from right-wing literature (among them *Hunter,* a William Pierce novel from 1989), and by conducting experiments on an abandoned farm.

In July 2011 the Norwegian Anders Behring Breivik constructed a bomb that partly demolished the Government's head offices in central Oslo, killing seven people. Thereafter he conducted a shooting massacre at a Labour Party youth camp at nearby Utøya, killing 77 more people. Like McVeigh, Breivik is assumed to have acquired the bomb-making skills by his own effort. As Breivik left a detailed diary of all his activities prior to the attack, his case provides rare insight into what it takes to acquire bomb-making skills at one's own effort, without previous training. Breivik's case illustrates that success requires more than simply downloading a bomb recipe from the Internet and buying the materials at the nearest grocery store. Rather, it is a meticulous process requiring high motivation, patience, and intelligence. Breivik claimed to have spent a total of 200 hours over two weeks to locate and study explosives recipes on the Internet, and two months to manufacture the explosives themselves.[19]

While the examples here are taken from the right-wing extremism, this is not to say that militant Islamists would also be capable of doing the same, if they have the necessary personal qualities. Jose Padilla is an example of an Al-Qaeda member who did not have the judgmental skills necessary to conduct such an attack alone: in 2001 he suggested to Khalid Sheikh Mohammed to build a nuclear bomb based on recipes found on the Internet. He was instructed to carry out a conventional attack with a better chance to succeed. His final attack plan was designed not by Padilla but by Mohammed Atef. Padilla's U.S. citizenship was probably the main reason why Al-Qaeda decided to use him–not his scientific knowledge.

Dhiren Barot, a U.K.-based Al-Qaeda member, proved more capable to conduct research and come up with a viable plan. Barot spent months doing research for his plan, the main component of which was to blow up limousines filled with gas tanks in underground parking areas. Many documents were later released by the British police, which give us insight in Barot's research methods. To devise a viable plan, Barot, like Breivik in Norway, researched multiple sources over a long period of time. Known sources to have been consulted by Barot included scientific articles, books and manuals found in the local library and on the Internet. Barot may have consulted jihadi training literature, but the main source of knowledge appears to have come from other open sources.[20]

This illustrates that a person who is dedicated to learn, and who has the ability to absorb and analyse the knowledge on his own, is not dependent on jihadi forums or Al-Qaeda-produced bomb manuals to find the necessary information. This article argues that the main strength of jihadi forums is not their technical content in itself, but the fact that they offer an interactive learning environment that may attract less dedicated would-be bomb makers–those who do not have the skills and patience to do extensive research on their own. Jihadi e-learning courses remove a major hurdle encountered by most hobbyist bomb-makers, namely, not knowing where to start.

Al-Shumukh's "Special Explosives Course for Beginners"

On 20 April 2011, a user with the nickname 'Adnan Shukri' started a new thread on the Shumukh al-Islam forum. Especially designed to attract newcomers, the thread's title read, "I am a beginner in the science of explosives and poisons, from where should I start? (Special course for the beginner *mujahid*)."[21] Over the next month, Shukri posted lessons, assigned 'homework' and replied to questions both openly on the forum, and through Personal Messaging (PM) with other forum members.[22]

Shukri's identity is unknown. On the forum, he claimed to be a middleman between the forum's members and Abdullah Dhu al-Bajadin, the main instructor of the course. Dhu al-Bajadin's identity is likewise unknown. The name has been used on various jihadi forums since at least 2006 by one or several people posing as self-proclaimed explosives experts. Dhu al-Bajadin is also known as the author of a number of jihadi bomb-making manuals that have been widely distributed on the Net.[23] Participants in the thread displayed great respect towards "Professor" Dhu al-Bajadin and his assistant Adnan Shukri. It increases the probability that the course is authentic because forum members are generally wary of impostors and 'spies' trying to infiltrate them. Another sign of authenticity is the fact that Shukri's thread was approved by one of Shumukh al-Islam's web administrators and granted "sticky" status on the forum over a period of several months.

The thread was active for six and a half months–from 20 April to 4 November, 2011. As of 11 November 2011 it had a total of 19,198 viewings and was by far the "most viewed" thread in al-Shumukh's sub-forum for explosives and preparation.[24] However, the actual course lasted little more than one month–from 20 April to 21 May, 2011. After this, Adnan Shukri disappeared from the forum, ending the organized part of the course. A total of ten lessons were posted–eight lessons in "Part One" and the two first lessons in "Part Two"–before the course was abruptly terminated.

During the first two weeks of the course, Adnan Shukri claimed to post lessons and answers to questions on behalf of Abdullah Dhu al-Bajadin. Then, on 5 May 2011, Shukri announced that Dhu al-Bajadin had lost his access to the Internet, for unspecified reasons, and that there would be a short break in the course. But posting of lessons resumed the next day, as Shukri decided he would carry on with the course on Dhu al-Bajadin's behalf. Forum members continued to show interest in the course and there was relatively constant activity until Shukri's departure in the end of May 2011.

By 21 May 2011, the thread had grown to 324 replies, including the comments and lessons posted by Adnan Shukri. A total of 58 forum members had been actively posting within the thread, but only nine out of them were active on a regular basis, i.e. having posted more than ten comments each; and only

six of them submitted answers to the "exam" that was given at the end of Part One of the course. Although the thread had been viewed more than 19,000 times in the end, the number of active participants in the course did not seem to exceed ten or twenty at most. This illustrates that jihadi e-learning courses is an extremely marginal phenomenon–on the other hand, they should not be regarded as insignificant. Al-Qaeda sympathisers are becoming more and more proficient at using modern communication technologies, especially for propaganda purposes. But since 2008, important improvements have been done in the field of e-learning as well.

The Evolution of Jihadi E-Learning Courses

The Al-Qaeda network has a long tradition of promoting remote learning courses, even before the age of the Internet. According to high-ranking Al-Qaeda member Fadil Harun, Al-Qaeda started to offer distant learning courses for new cadres already back in 1999-2000. The courses were part of a comprehensive program held within Afghanistan to educate future Al-Qaeda leaders. While practical skills were taught in training camps and at the Taliban's frontlines, some of the theoretical courses were offered through letter correspondence.[25] After 2001, training courses started to appear on the Internet–the "Al-Battar" series of Al-Qaeda on the Arabian Peninsula (first issued in January 2004) being a prominent example.[26] From around 2006, audio-visual training material started appearing on jihadi websites, including detailed instruction videos on how to manufacture explosives. However, these videos were not produced by the Al-Qaeda network's official media companies, but by individual jihadi sympathisers or Palestinian groups such as Hizbollah and Hamas. A study published by this author in 2008 concluded that Al-Qaeda was far from utilizing the full potential of the Internet in terms of training potential recruits.[27]

Since 2008, the number of instruction videos on jihadi web pages has increased, but producers and content are largely the same as before. An exception is the inclusion of two videos explaining how to build an improvised Explosively Formed Penetrator (EFP)–a weapon that appeared in the Iraq war after 2005. While most of the EFPs in Iraq were relatively sophisticated weapons–imported from Iran and used by Shia militias–there were attempts at using crude, home-made devices as well. At some point this production method was captured on tape–apparently by a Shia militia, since the salafi-jihadi version of the films refers to the producer as *hizb shaytan*–"The Party of Satan." The film eventually made its way to jihadi discussion forums, after being modified by members of the Al-Qaeda affiliated al-Fallujah forum.[28] It was first spotted by FFI researchers in February 2011.[29] The time lapse is worth noting: It took more than five years from when a jihadi group started developing the device on the ground in Iraq, until an instruction video on how to manufacture it appeared on a jihadi discussion forum. This may qualify the claim that the Internet plays an important role in transferring insurgent tactics and technologies between battlefields–at least for now–but this could rapidly change in the future, since the infrastructure for doing so is already in place. Most jihadi insurgent groups today have proven themselves capable of video-editing and rapid distribution via the Internet. It is probably a question of intention, rather than capability.

Returning to the topic of "e-learning courses" on jihadi forums the most visible development that has taken place since 2008 is the increased amount of courses being offered, as well as the integration of written and audio-visual learning aids. For example, al-Shumukh's "Special explosives course for beginners" which was offered in 2011 comprised a number of written compendiums in pdf-format–full of pictures and illustrations–in addition to video clips selected by the instructor to illustrate certain aspects of the lesson such as the effect of an explosion of a particular substance. Back in 2008, there were both audio-visual and written training courses offered on jihadi forums, but seldom a mixture of both. The development may not seem so significant, but at least it illustrates that certain efforts are being made at improving the effectiveness of such courses. Court cases against suspected terrorists in the West confirm that there is an interest among terrorists on the ground for accessing such e-learning material. This will be further detailed in the next section.

An Example of a Would-Be Jihadist Who Sought Online Training

The court case against Mohammad Zaki Amawi et al provides an example of how real-life militant islamists utilize the Internet for learning. Amawi was the leader of a three-member would-be "terrorist cell" in Ohio, USA. In 2004–2005, the cell tried to obtain militant training in the United States before going to Iraq to fight U.S. forces. They sought the assistance of a "trainer," the former Special Operations Forces soldier Darren Griffin, who in reality worked as an undercover agent for the FBI. The three members of the cell were convicted to lifetimes in prison in 2008.[30]

Amawi and one of his co-conspirators, Marwan El Hindi, were both active on jihadi forums on the Internet. Amawi had a large collection of propaganda films from Al-Qaeda, especially from Iraq. The cell's members met on several occasions and watched videos together. They also attempted to use the Internet to obtain training materials: In early 2005, Amawi downloaded the "Martyrdom operation vest preparation" instruction video (a video originally produced by Hizbullah). Al Hindi also downloaded the video, as well as a slide show entitled "The mujahidin in Iraq and the art of planting explosive charges," produced by the Islamic Army of Iraq. They also had other, unspecified training manuals on how to make explosives. They discussed the training materials with their "trainer" Darren Griffin, and they expressed interest in learning how to build IEDs.

In February 2005, El Hindi and Griffin visited the al-Ikhlas forum together. The website offered a "Basic training" and an "Advanced training" course. According to the court documents,

El Hindi helped Griffin to register for the basic training course. There is no further information as to whether El Hindi or his co-conspirators completed the course, but El Hindi was clearly familiar with its existence.

The case illustrates how real-life radicals may exploit online training material. It is worth noting that Amawi sought to join the jihad in Iraq for the first time between October 2003 and March 2004. It means that he was already radicalised at the time he downloaded the jihadi training materials and accessed the online e-learning course. The purpose of downloading the material was probably to get better prepared before attempting to join the jihad in Iraq a second time. In this case, the jihadi training manuals were not the initial radicalising factor, but they probably served as encouragement in later stages of Amawi's radicalisation process.

However, the case also indicates that the cell's members were not able to absorb the online training material on their own–indicated by the fact that they sought help from an external "trainer." Also, they were not able to judge the quality of the online training material. For example, El Hindi said he wanted to use the "Martyrdom operation vest preparation" video to train new recruits, but the instructions in the video are probably too advanced for a beginner with no experience in explosives.[31] Moreover, the video is not suitable if the purpose is to convince new recruits to become suicide bombers. It is strictly informative, and does not contain any of the emotional persuasion tools typical of Al-Qaeda-style recruitment videos (pictures of dead martyrs, images of paradise, religious hymns, etc.). In the end it was Griffin–the FBI infiltrator–who helped the cell's members receive proper firearms training by renting a commercial shooting range.[32]

Conclusion

Jihadi e-learning courses are a marginal phenomenon, yet they should not be ignored. While there are still very few active participants in such courses, they attract large interest among online jihadists. The quality of the courses has improved over the last few years, and there are dedicated people online who are interested in developing them further. As training in jihadi conflict areas has become difficult, more recruits are likely to try and obtain paramilitary skills before going abroad–or before attempting to carry out a terrorist attack at home. Some of these would-be jihadists might consider joining regular armed forces or private shooting clubs in their home country. A far less risky venture is to seek out jihadi training courses online, because they allow the participants to remain anonymous while conducting their training.

Notes

1. Adam Dolnik, *Understanding Terrorist Innovation: Technology, Tactics and Global Trends.* London: Routledge, 2007, p. 36.

2. See, for example, Anne Stenersen, "The Internet: A virtual training camp? *Terrorism and Political Violence* 20, no. 2 (2008), pp.215–33; see also Gabriel Weimann, *Terror on the Internet: The new arena, the new challenges* (Washington DC:

United States Institute of Peace, 2006), pp. 123–129, and Bruce Hoffman, *Inside Terrorism: Revised and expanded edition* (New York: Columbia, 2006), pp. 216–220.

3. Brynjar Lia, "Doctrines for jihadi terrorist training," *Terrorism and Political Violence* 20, no. 4 (2008): 526; Anne Stenersen, *Brothers in Jihad: Explaining the Relationship between Al-Qaeda and the Taliban, 1996–2001* Oslo: University of Oslo PhD Thesis, 2012, p. 281.

4. Abu Ubayda al-Maqdisi, *Shuhada fi zaman al-ghurba,* Place unknown: Al-Fajr Media Center, 2008. Accessed via *al-Ikhlas* on February 2, 2008, www.alekhlaas.net, 14–17; "Al-Qaeda confirms death of poisons expert in Pakistan," *The Guardian,* August 3, 2008; accessed on November 28, 2012, www.guardian.co.uk/world/2008/aug/03/alqaida.terrorism.

5. Brynjar Lia, *Architect of Global Jihad: The Life of Al-Qaeda Strategist Abu Mus'ab al-Suri.* New York: Columbia University Press, 2008, p. 102.

6. Abu Mus'ab al-Suri, *Da'wat al-muqawama al-islamiyya al-alamiyya* Place and publisher unknown, 2004, p. 1356.

7. "U.S. Offers $5 Million Reward for Information about Terrorist," *Global Security,* November 18, 2004; accessed November 28, 2012, www.globalsecurity.org/security/library/news/2004/11/sec-041118-usia01.htm.

8. "You are held responsible only for thyself–Part 1 & 2," *al-Sahab,* June 3, 2011. The quote is from an English translation of the video, posted on *Shabakat al-Jihad al-'Alami,* November 6, 2011, accessed October 13, 2011, www.aljahad.com/vb/.

9. "You are held responsible only for thyself–Part 1 & 2," *al-Sahab,* June 3, 2011.

10. "You are held responsible only for thyself–Part 1 & 2," *al-Sahab,* June 3, 2011.

11. "You are held responsible only for thyself–Part 1 & 2," *al-Sahab,* June 3, 2011.

12. Petter Nesser, "How did Europe's global jihadis obtain training for their militant causes?" *Terrorism and Political Violence* 20, no. 2 (2008): 234–56; Paul Cruickshank, "The Militant Pipeline: Between the Afghanistan-Pakistan border region and the West," *New America Foundation,* February 2010; accessed Nov. 28, 2012; http://counterterrorism.newamerica.net/sites/newamerica.net/files/policydocs/cruickshank.pdf.

13. Michael Kenney, "Beyond the Internet: Mētis, Techne, and the Limitations of Online Artifacts for Islamist Terrorists," *Terrorism and Political Violence,* vol. 22, no. 2 (2010), pp. 177–197.

14. See, for example, Barbara Means and Yukie Toyama et. al., "Evaluation of evidence-based practices in online learning: A meta-analysis and review of online learning studies," *U.S. Department of Education,* September 2010; accessed November 28, 2012, www2.ed.gov/rschstat/eval/tech/evidence-based-practices/finalreport.pdf.

15. The *Encyclopaedia* was compiled electronically by Khalil Said al-Deek (aka Abu Ayed al-Filistini), an American-Palestinian with a diploma in computer science from the U.S. Al-Deek's efforts ensured the *Encyclopaedia's* continued life on the Internet to this day. Ali H. Soufan, *The Black Banners: The Inside Story of 9/11 and the War against al-Qaeda.* New York: Norton, 2011, pp. 132–133.

16. Brian A. Jackson et al., *Aptitude for Destruction, Volume 1: Organizational Learning in Terrorist Groups and its Implications for Combating Terrorism.* Santa Monica: RAND, 2005, pp. 14–15.

17. Ali H. Soufan, *The Black Banners,* p. 78.

18. Ali H. Soufan, *The Black Banners,* pp. 480–481.

19. Andrew Berwick, "2083–A European Declaration for Independence," London, 2011, p. 990.

20. Anne Stenersen, "Nuclear Terrorism: Hype, Hoax, or Waiting to Happen?". In: Magnus Eriksson and Kari M. Osland (Eds.) *Nuclear Weapons in the 21st Century: Old Players, New Game–New Players, Old Game.* Oslo: NUPI, 2007, p. 118.

21. Adnan Shukri, "I am a beginner in the science of explosives and poisons, from where should I start? (Special course for the beginner *mujahid*) [in Arabic]," *Shumukh al-Islam,* 20 April 2011; http://180.235.150.135/~shamikh/vb.

22. Reference to Personal Messagings (PMs) were made in the public part of the discussion thread. This author has not had access to the PMs themselves.

23. Anne Stenersen, "The Internet: A virtual training camp?", op. cit., p. 217.

24. When the last updates to this article were done on 11 February 2013, the thread was still present on the al-Shumukh forum and it was still the "most viewed" training-related thread–with a total of 21,325 views.

25. Fadil Muhammad, *Al-harb ala al-islam: Qissat Fadil Harun, al-juz al-awwal.* Place and publisher unknown, 2009; accessed via *Ansar al-mujahidin* on May 4, 2009, www.as-ansar.com.

26. For more information on "al-Battar," see Bruce Hoffman, *Inside Terrorism,* op. cit., pp. 218–219.

27. Anne Stenersen, "The Internet: A virtual training camp?", op. cit., pp. 225–28.

28. This is apparent as al-Fallujah's logo has been superimposed on the instruction video.

29. This information was given to the author by FFI's Senior Research Fellow Brynjar Lia in November 2011.

30. "United States of America v. Mohammad Zaki Amawi, Marwan Othman El-Hindi, and Wassim I. Mazloum," Government's sentencing Memorandum, United States District Court, Northern District of Ohio, filed on October 5, 2009.

31. Anne Stenersen, "The Internet: A virtual training camp?", op. cit., pp. 220–221.

32. For more case studies of how U.S.-based jihadists used the Internet, see J. M. Berger, *Jihad Joe: Americans who go to war in the name of Islam.* Dulles: Potomac Books, 2011, pp. 177–201.

Critical Thinking

1. Why has Al-Qaeda shifted towards "individual jihad?"
2. How do terrorists learn bomb-making skills?
3. How have jihadist e-learning courses evolved?

Create Central

www.mhhe.com/createcentral

Internet References

www.nydailynews.com/new-york/al-qaeda-bomb-making-expert-publishes-magazine-detailing-explosives-article-1.1058969

http://centralasiaonline.com/en_GB/articles/caii/features/pakistan/2010/12/20/feature-02

ANNE STENERSEN *(M.Phil, PhD) is a research fellow at the Norwegian Defence Research Establishment (FFI), specialising on militant Islamism. E-mail: Anne.Stenersen@ffi.no.*

Article   Prepared by: Thomas J. Badey, *Randolph-Macon College*

Age of the Wolf

A Study of the Rise of Lone Wolf and Leaderless Resistance Terrorism

RYAN LENZ AND MARK POTOK

Learning Outcomes

After reading this article, you will be able to:

- Explain why a lone wolf attack is more likely to be successful.
- Discuss the findings from the SPLC survey pertaining to terrorist motivations, methods, and characteristics.
- Describe the benefits of terrorists operating in small cells.

At 2:22 A.M. on the morning after Thanksgiving, a man named Larry Steve McQuilliams, clad in a tactical vest and backpack hydration unit and armed with a semi-automatic AK-47, opened fire in Austin, Texas. He unleashed more than 100 rounds, first at a federal courthouse, then at the local Mexican consulate that he also tried to firebomb, and finally at the Austin Police Department headquarters.

Before he could harm anyone, the 49-year-old McQuilliams was killed by a near-miraculous pistol shot fired by an officer standing 312 feet away. When police searched his body and his van, they found another long gun, hundreds of rounds of ammunition, a map of 34 downtown buildings that appeared to be his targets, and a book and note indicating he saw himself as a "Phineas priest," a white supremacist who believes he's been personally called on by God to kill his enemies.

On his chest were the black-inked words, "Let Me Die."

McQuilliams' note said little more than that he was acting as a "priest in the fight against anti-God people." Because he had apparently spoken to no one about his plans and had no

help, it's unlikely that much more about him will be learned—beyond the fact that he was a "lone wolf," the very hardest kind of terrorist to stop.

"What keeps me up at night," said Austin Police Chief Art Acevedo, who called McQuilliams an "American extremist," "is these guys. The lone wolf."

The lone wolf. Going back at least to the 1980s, that concept—a person who carries out a terrorist attack entirely on his own—has taken root on the American non-Islamic radical right and even among many jihadists. In an age of instant communications and ever more tightly knit societies, the lone wolf style of attack is vastly more likely to be successful than the kind that was once literally planned in rooms full of men, sometimes by major group leaders. People who join criminal conspiracies today are more likely than ever to be caught. As a result, there has been a long-running trend toward the lone wolf and away from group action.

A major Southern Poverty Law Center (SPLC) study of domestic terrorism over the last six years confirms this trend in dramatic fashion. Surveying 63 incidents culled from academic databases and the SPLC's own files, 46 of them—fully 74%—were carried out by lone wolves, unassisted by others. And only one of the remaining 16 (in one case, the number of attackers is not known) was planned by a named organization. In most of those 16 cases, terrorists worked in pairs—a couple, a pair of friends, two brothers and a father and son, among them—with only six involving three or more. That means that 90% percent of the 62 cases where the number of perpetrators is known were the work of one or two people.

The Study

Analyzing terrorism comes fraught with pitfalls. There is no hard and fast agreement on what constitutes a terrorist action. What if the attack has a political dimension, but is carried out by someone who is clearly mentally ill? Is a rampage killing spree terrorism or simply an eruption of personal hatreds? Does the murder of three police officers responding to a domestic disturbance count, even if the killer does have a long history in the police-hating antigovernment movement?

To get a sense of the shape of contemporary domestic terrorism—both from the radical right and from violent Islamists—the SPLC scoured records maintained by Indiana State University and the University of Maryland's Global Terrorism Database, as well as SPLC's own roster of apparent domestic terror incidents. The survey included incidents that likely involved mental illness and arguably personal grudges, but that seemed to have an obvious political aspect. It covered terrorism inspired by antigovernment, Islamist and various forms of race or group hatred. And it encompassed both actual terror attacks and those which officials aborted.

The survey also included cases that were not terrorist plots per se, but major unplanned violence that occurred when authorities confronted volatile political extremists for any number of reasons—pulling them over for a traffic infraction or trying to serve a warrant, for instance. Less than a quarter of the incidents cited (a total of 14 cases) were unplanned and occurred after some unexpected run-in.

The time span covered is an important one—from April 1, 2009, a few days before the Department of Homeland Security issued a prescient but ultimately controversial study warning of a "resurgence in radicalization and recruitment" on the extreme domestic right, through February 1, 2015, press time. That span also very roughly corresponds to the period since Barack Obama took office in early 2009, a development that most analysts agree spurred rapid growth of the radical right.

One of the most noticeable results was the regularity of major violence or planned violence from domestic terrorists—one attack, on average, every 34 days. It's debatable how that compares to the 1990s, when the first wave of the antigovernment militia movement swept the country. One 2013 study, by West Point's Combating Terrorism Center, found that violence from the extreme right between 2000 and 2011 had surpassed that of the 1990s by a factor of four, but many experts agree that that seems exaggerated. What is certain is that domestic terrorism from all sources is endemic and shows no signs of abating.

The body count of victims during the 2009–2015 period is certainly less than that of the 1990s, but that is heavily skewed by Timothy McVeigh's murder of 168 people in the 1995 Oklahoma City bombing. If the Oklahoma victims are subtracted, it appears that the rate of killing has remained approximately the same throughout. The SPLC study found that 63 victims had been killed in 2009–2015 terrorist attacks, along with 16 assailants. Another recent study, from the public-private National Consortium for the Study of Terrorism and Responses to Terrorism, or START, counted 368 people murdered by far-right extremists between 1990 and 2013, including 50 law enforcement officers. Without the Oklahoma victims, the START study (which did not include jihadists) shows an average killing rate of almost nine victims a year, while the SPLC study (including jihadists) finds an annual rate of almost 11.

The impact of terrorist attacks, far more than that of most other crimes, goes way beyond the number of victims. Such attacks send shock waves through targeted communities—racial groups, sexual minorities, Jews, Muslims, police and so on—and also can result, as security is ramped up, in a real loss of daily freedoms.

Other findings that emerged from the SPLC survey:

- Almost half of the attacks during the period apparently were motivated by the ideology of the antigovernment "Patriot" movement, including "sovereign citizens," whose movement has been described by the FBI as "domestic terrorist." A little more than that (51%) came from ideologies of hate, ranging from white supremacy to misogyny to radical Islamism.
- Of the 61 incidents where the weapon used is known, 59% of attackers used firearms, while 25% used explosives, including such jury-rigged bombs as propane tanks. Five percent used both firearms and explosives. And 11% used other weapons, including arson fires and a private plane.
- Attackers were overwhelmingly male, with just seven female assailants.
- Attackers were much older as a group than most violent criminals. Various studies have shown definitively that males aged 15 to 24 are responsible for a vastly disproportionate share of violent crime. In the case of the perpetrators surveyed in this study, only about 33% of the 87 whose ages are known were under the age of 29, with the remainder over 30. Aside from the 20 to 29 age group, the offenders were clustered most heavily between 30 and 49 years of age, although a surprising number were older than that. This suggests that perpetrators spend many years on the radical right, absorbing extremist ideology, before finally acting out violently.

The very high percentage of lone wolf and leaderless attacks and the declining number of groups on the radical right might suggest to some that the importance of the larger radical milieu is declining. But in fact, the groups and their ideologues provide the essential ideology that motivates the lone wolves and others. Today, that ideology is far less likely to come in publications or at group meetings. Instead, it lives on the Internet, always available and always dangerous.

The Theory of Leaderless Violence

In April 1987, a federal grand jury in Arkansas indicted 14 of the best-known white supremacist leaders in the United States for conspiring to overthrow the federal government. The men were accused of plotting to kill a federal judge and establish an all-white nation in the Pacific Northwest. They were also accused of conspiring, during an Aryan World Congress in northern Idaho in 1983, to help launch The Order, a violent terrorist group composed of more than 20 people that was finally smashed in 1984, when its leader was killed by the FBI.

The 1988 trial was a fiasco. Most observers agreed that prosecutors had failed to prove a conspiracy, and in any event an all-white jury acquitted all 14 men in what amounted to a disaster for the government. The defendants emerged as heroes to the radical right—but one of them saw a critical lesson for the future.

Pondering the case later, Louis Beam, a violent Klansman and movement theoretician, republished an influential essay on "leaderless resistance" he'd written in 1983. In it, he advocated the end of large groups with a pyramid leadership structure, arguing that such organizations were too easy to infiltrate and destroy. In their place, he called for lone wolf action or leaderless resistance, by which he meant cells of no more than six men. The idea was these cells and individuals would act on their own, with no direction or contact with other radicals. In that way, he reasoned, even the destruction of a single cell would have little effect on the larger movement.

"As honest men who have banded together into groups or associations of a political or religious nature are falsely labeled 'domestic terrorists' or 'cultists' and suppressed," he wrote, "it will become necessary to consider other methods of organization—or as the case may very [sic] call for: non-organization."

Tom Metzger, a prominent neo-Nazi who long operated from California but now lives in Indiana, took up the leaderless banner after Beam, tirelessly promoting his ideas with such publications as his "Laws for the Lone Wolf," carried on his Resist.com website. Metzger advised fellow racists to avoid membership in groups, keep cash on hand for emergencies, and "never truly admit to anything."

"Never keep any records of your activities that can connect you to the activity," he wrote as part of a raft of suggestions.

"Keep in mind that repeated activity in one area will lead to increased attention to the area and possibly to you. The more you change your tactics, the more effective you will become."

Whether because of the admonitions of Beam, Metzger and others, or simply because the tactic makes obvious operational sense, there is little question that the vast majority of recent terror attacks in the United States have been by lone wolves or very small leaderless cells. There's also little question that the political violence is continuing apace and that little seems to have been effective in stopping it.

It may not have had to be this bad.

DHS Weighs In, Then Out

On April 7, 2009, the team of Department of Homeland Security analysts who study non-Islamic domestic terrorism issued a confidential report to law enforcement agencies entitled "Right-wing Extremism: Current Economic and Political Climate Fueling Resurgence in Radicalization and Recruitment." The report, which noted the effect the economy and the election of the nation's first black president was having on the radical right, was almost immediately leaked to the right-wing media.

There, it was pilloried, with right-wing pundits and groups like the American Legion falsely claiming that it attacked military veterans, conservatives and others on the political right. That was clearly not true—in fact, the report was remarkably accurate in its analysis and warnings (which included the assertion that the threat of lone wolves and small cells was growing)—but enough of a political firestorm was created that then-DHS Secretary Janet Napolitano renounced its findings. The team that wrote it and lead analyst Daryl Johnson were falsely accused of failing to follow DHS' procedures and were criticized by Napolitano and others in public.

But then undeniable reality began to kick in.

Even before the DHS report's publication—three days earlier, to be exact—the evidence was mounting. On April 4, 2009, Richard Poplowski, an extremist who believed the government was about to unleash troops against American citizens, ambushed and killed three Pittsburgh police officers responding to Poplowski's mother's call reporting a domestic disturbance at her home. Poplowski, who also had racist and anti-Semitic views, was eventually sentenced to death in the killings.

Three weeks later, a Florida National Guardsman named Joshua Cartwright, who had earlier expressed interest in joining a militia group and also was "severely disturbed" about Obama's election, shot two Okaloosa County sheriff's deputies to death as they attempted to arrest Cartwright on domestic violence charges.

About a month after that, on May 31—after Napolitano had withdrawn the April DHS report and apologized for its contents—an anti-abortion activist who had also been involved in the antigovernment "freemen" movement of the 1990s shot and killed Kansas abortion provider Dr. George Tiller in Tiller's church. A few days later, on June 10, an elderly neo-Nazi named James von Brunn opened fire at the U.S. Holocaust Memorial Museum and killed a guard. He clearly intended to get into the museum and kill many more, but was himself shot and later died.

From there, the roster of human carnage continued without pause. A nativist extremist murdered a Latino man and his 9-year-old daughter; a long-time white supremacist was indicted and later convicted of sending a mail bomb that injured a diversity officer in Arizona; an angry tax protester flew an airplane into an Austin IRS building, killing himself and an IRS manager and injuring 13 others.

The Federal Response

But by then, almost the entire DHS team led by Daryl Johnson had left, discouraged by their treatment and DHS' new reluctance to issue any reports because of the fear that they might become controversial. They were exhausted and perplexed by the criticisms of Napolitano, who accused them of violating vetting procedures. And Napolitano was not the only political figure that criticized Johnson and his colleagues. Then-House Minority Leader John Boehner (R-Ohio), for instance, described the DHS report as "offensive and unacceptable" and charged, without any basis, that DHS had abandoned the word "terrorist" to describe Al Qaeda and instead was using "the same term to describe American citizens who disagree with the direction Washington Democrats are taking our nation."

In the years since then, the DHS has held up or canceled a number of planned reports on domestic terrorism of various types. Even some law enforcement briefings were cancelled. At the same time, in the aftermath of the September 11, 2001, Al Qaeda attacks, the Justice Department's Domestic Terrorism Executive Committee was allowed to go fallow for more than a decade. But in the aftermath of the April 2014 murder of three people at two Kansas Jewish institutions, allegedly by a well-known neo-Nazi, Attorney General Eric Holder announced that he was bringing the committee back to life. It had held no meetings, however, as of press time.

Johnson's DHS unit was not a law enforcement agency, but it did play a key role in providing law enforcement with intelligence assessments. While it certainly could not prevent most terrorist attacks, the information it once produced was of high interest and importance to many police agencies. Former West Memphis, Ark., Police Chief Bob Paudert, whose police officer son was murdered by a father-and-son team of antigovernment extremists in 2010, has denounced the government for failing to brief police on such things as the "sovereign citizens" movement. His son's killers were sovereigns, who reject the laws of the federal government, and Paudert believes that if his son had been briefed on them he might have lived.

The FBI has taken up some of the slack left by DHS with occasional reports on extremism. And more than 70 fusion centers—regional centers where federal, state and local law enforcement agencies share information about threats—put out occasional papers and warnings to possible targets. But those who study terrorism are still deeply worried by the virtual dissolution of the DHS team. "It was a big mistake to take those people off the radar," said Mark Hamm, a criminologist at Indiana State University. "As soon as Barack Obama was elected, we could almost see it in the wind that there was going to be a revival of the radical right."

Still, there does seem to be some new activity on the part of the federal government, including the planned reactivation of the Domestic Terrrorism Executive Committee. The government is funding a number of studies on radicalization and other matters related to domestic terrorism. But it still remains to be seen if these initiatives and others really deal effectively with the threat.

For his part, Daryl Johnson, who warned in 2009 of the increasing move toward lone wolf and leaderless terrorism—criminal acts that are almost impossible to stop in advance because so few people are involved in their planning—worries that the government still concentrates too much on foreign Muslim extremists, and that the recent Charlie Hebdo attack in Paris could add to that bias. He says that another extreme-right attack on the order of Oklahoma City, which was facilitated by the fact that only four people knew of the plot in advance, is entirely likely.

"We're long overdue for a much greater attack from the far right," Johnson said as he weighed the prospects for violence by terrorists like Larry McQuilliams, who clearly intended to kill as many people as possible. "We are long overdue."

Critical Thinking

1. How do the findings from the SPLC study and the START study differ?

2. According to Louis Beam, why is the use of "leaderless resistance" more effective than traditional terrorist organization?

3. What types of groups are more likely to use these tactics?

Internet References

Foreign Policy: The Myth of the Big Bad Lone Wolf

http://foreignpolicy.com/2014/10/25/the-myth-of-the-big-bad-lone-wolf

The Heritage Foundation: Preventing the Next "Lone Wolf" Terrorist Attack Requires Stronger Federal–State–Local Capabilities

http://www.heritage.org/research/reports/2013/06/preventing-the-next-lone-wolf-terrorist-attack-requires-stronger-federalstatelocal-capabilities

Written testimony of DHS Secretary Jeh Johnson for a House Committee on Homeland Security hearing titled "Worldwide Threats to the Homeland"

http://www.dhs.gov/news/2014/09/17/written-testimony-dhs-secretary-jeh-johnson-house-committee-homeland-security

Article   Prepared by: Thomas J. Badey, *Randolph-Macon College*

Urban Siege in Paris: A Spectrum of Armed Assault

JOHN P. SULLIVAN AND ADAM ELKUS

Learning Outcomes

After reading this article, you will be able to:

- Analyze the *Charlie Hebdo* attacks.

- Explain why, according to Watts, the future of jihad is "inspired, networked, and directed."

- Discuss questions that both researchers and responders should consider when studying urban sieges.

In 2009, we laid out a conceptual model of terrorist "urban siege" based on the Mumbai attacks.[1] As noted by several observers, the recent terrorist attack in Paris on the *Charlie Hebdo* offices may have succeeded due to the unfortunate fact that security officials expected other attack modes (such as airline bombs), not a run and gun in the heart of an urban center.[2]

While it would be tempting to posit Paris as another bloody data point explained by our conceptual schema, Paris is in fact cause for broadening and expanding it. Unfortunately, the world faces urban security threats that span a spectrum of organization and lethality. Future threats may look like Mumbai (as has been seen in the Mumbai-like operation against the Westgate shopping mall in Nairobi) or they may resemble Paris.[3] And there is a large spectrum of threats that occupy the threat envelope in between.

Here we review the timeline of the attacks, analyze continuities and complications with urban siege schemas and relevant incidents, review relevant analysis that could inform a more robust analysis of urban siege, and close with a set of our own questions for researchers and practitioners about what assumptions we need to make in planning for, training to stop, and red-teaming urban siege scenarios.

Urban Siege in Paris

In France, the new year opened with a horrific urban siege. This latest installment of urban guerilla action involved armed assault and massacre, execution of police, a massive manhunt and two hostage-barricade situations. Three days of terror saw the deployment of 88,000 personnel from the French Interior Ministry—ranging from community police to specialized gendarmerie, augmented by a large military contingent.[4]

On Wednesday, 7 January, a car pulled up in front of the offices of *Charlie Hebdo,* a satirist magazine in Paris' 11th Arrondissement. Two men—the Kouachi brothers, Cherif and Said—got out of the car; they were dressed in black and carried automatic weapons. After making inquiries they made [their] way to the office and opened fire, killing one. When they arrived at the office they again opened fire killing the editor and 9 others including a police officer guarding the editor, as well as a police officer, Ahmed Merabat, the first responding officer to the scene.[5]

After the attack the self-styled Mujahideen fled the scene. The next day (8 January) they robbed a gas station near Villers-Cotterets. The same day a female police officer, Clarissa Jean-Phillpe was killed in Montrouge, a Paris suburb by Amedy Coulibaly (who has been linked to the Kouachi brothers. On 9 January, the Kouachi brothers robbed a car in northeast Paris. A few minutes later the Kouachi brothers took a hostage and the suspects were chased by helicopters in a massive manhunt. Area schools and businesses were put under lockdown and large numbers of officers from the National Police and Gendarmerie (including GIGN and RAID respectively) were deployed with support from the Army.[6] The suspects settled in for a hostage-barricade situation (the second siege) at a printers suite in Dammartin-en-Goele. The suspects boasted they would become martyrs.

A third incident at the Hyper Cacher, a kosher grocery, was conducted by Amedy Coulibaly to support the Kouachi brothers.[7] This siege, which resulted in the death of Couliby and four hostages, was terminated by a police counter assault. The counter assaults were coordinated, simultaneous actions with the taketown of the Kouachi brothers to limit risk to the hostages at the grocery since Coulibaly said he would execute them if police assaulted the Kouachis' location.

The aftermath of the assaults includes questions about intelligence failure, fear of follow-on attacks conducted by activated sleeper cells, threats to police, and the threat of attacks in The United Kingdom and United States.[8] Finally, the conflict has both physical and virtual dimensions as seen by a wave of attacks against French websites. Hackers, responding to the French public's defiance in the face of terror, hit 19,000 French websites with denial-of-service attacks.[9] A group of pro-Syrian regime hackers briefly commandeered the French newspaper *Le Monde*'s Twitter account, tweeting a message mocking the post-attack hashtag #JeSuisCharlie.[10]

Analyzing the Paris Urban Siege: Continuity and Complication

On one end of a spectrum of urban assault lethality and sophistication is the Mumbai attacks. The attackers belonged to a cohesive and organized terrorist organization and received guidance, direction, and real-time information support from an offsite handler. On the lowest end is a garden variety "active shooter" more akin to the Columbine school shooters—no training, no guidance, no resources, no contacts but nonetheless possessing a willingness to kill and die. The organized terrorist group type of attacker is obviously capable of waging urban siege. Operating in small squads, they can challenge police command and control and on-site response through dispersion, firepower, and entrenchment.

As David Kilcullen observed in an application of our work to the Westgate mall attack, the Mumbai attack also was terror by "remote control"—the attackers utilized Skype, cellphones, and satellite phones to connect to an offsite operations team in Pakistan monitoring social media and news reporting concerning the ongoing attack. The Nairobi attack exhibited similar characteristics.[11] Six suspects affiliated with al-Shabaab executed a hostage-barricade assault against the mall complex.[12] Multiple squads executed a coordinated attack and successfully entrenched within the mall complex for four days seventy-two people died before Kenyan security forces could retake the mall.

As with Mumbai, the Kenya attackers prepared for an entrenchment scenario, fused various weapons and teams, and thwarted a disorganized and bureaucratically disjointed security force response long enough to exact a gruesome toll. The attack, though novel in its ferocity, sophistication, and toll, was preceded by a drumbeat of urban terrorist attacks in which al-Shabaab demonstrated urban assault capabilities. The catastrophic impact of poor command and control cannot be overstated. An extensive *Guardian* report suggested that disputes over police and military command and control delayed response. Not only were attackers able to entrench and kill more victims, but a friendly fire incident also occurred and militants were able to foil a first joint police-army counterattack with sniper fire.[13]

Nor has Kenya been the sole instance of a suicide commando assault since Mumbai. In December of last year, the Pakistani Taliban launched a gruesome attack on a school for children of Pakistan army officers.[14] In a repeat of previous urban siege patterns, attackers provisioned for a long attack quickly pushed into the school. However, unlike in Beslan there would be no entrenchment and hostage situation. Pakistani forces responded within 15 minutes and killed all of the attackers. However, the security forces were too late to save the 132 children and 10 school staff slaughtered by the terrorists during the initial attack. Pakistani Taliban, Afghan Taliban, and al-Qaeda urban operations continue within urban centers in South Asia, a site C. Christine Fair has noted is one large "urban battlefield."[15]

While we do not suggest that older hostage and armed attack scenarios were simple, the operational challenges associated with these types of attacks dwarf the typical single-site, hostage-barricade assumptions seen in terrorist operations such as the 1970s Munich Olympics incident or the spate of aircraft hijackings seen during the wave of terror that preceded the current wave of radical Islamist terror. As J. Paul D. Taillon noted in his study of hijacking and hostages, successful counterterrorist operations involved forward base access, cooperation, and specialized units capable of dislodging attackers.[16] In contrast, modern urban sieges will require first responders to meet attackers head-on, regardless of sophistication and armament. Such direct police action is necessary to stop the 'kinetic momentum' and minimize casualties.[17]

For example, in June 2014, a team of heavily armed Pakistani Taliban militants assaulted the Jinnah International Airport in Karachi.[18] Attackers disguised themselves as airport personnel and were successfully held off by security personnel and finished off by military reinforcements. They were provisioned for a long siege, but failed to survive long enough to inflict major damage.[19] Whatever damage (material, human, and symbolic) they inflicted, it could have been far worse had airport security officers not immediately responded to the incident.

For police, responding to simple, single-site attacks requires a high degree of tactical proficiency. Larger, more complex, area-wide simultaneous assaults require a high degree of coordination and the employment of operational art. Urban operational art for the police demands integration of patrol, special operations (tactical response including SWAT, bomb squad, riot/crowd control, media/public information, detectives and investigation, and intelligence, as well as synchronization with the fire service, emergency medical services (EMS), emergency management, civil authorities, and potentially the military. Such coordination may be needed at multiple locations in a single jurisdiction or among authorities spread across multiple jurisdictions.

Our ability to comment on the Paris attacks is limited and based on details currently known in the open source. However, we can observe several important similarities and distinctions to the urban siege model we have outlined in prior work.

Some aspects of the Paris attacks had at least superficially to other observed urban terrorist attacks. While the main actual attack itself was relatively brief, the attackers themselves hid out in the Paris metropolitan area, lengthening the period of terror and fear. The incident reached a bloody climax when the assailants—seeking martyrdom and desiring a fight to the death—holed up in a small warehouse with a hostage and subsequently died at the hands of French law tactical responders.[20] Both gunmen received tactical training related to basic weapons usage, and one gunman may have visited Yemen to receive further instruction and financing.[21]

The distribution of the siege is also relevant. The *Charlie Hebdo* incident must be understood as an integrated whole, with the opening assault against the newspaper offices just one (high-profile) component. For three days, attackers went on a killing spree, distributing their attacks in time and space around Paris and its environs. During this time, the French security authorities were forced to deploy an enormous force to find, fix in place, and neutralize the suspects before they could accumulate a larger kill count. The attacks were synchronized to achieve maximum impact, and police faced enormous difficulties handling both situations simultaneously.

The Hyper Cacher hostage taker, for example, demanded that authorities cease their pursuit of the Kouachi brothers. While the police raid that broke the siege at the Hyper Cacher may seem improvised and amateurish to some observers, it was also conducted under extremely unfavorable conditions.[22] Both police raids had to be synchronized for hostages to survive. Moreover, coordinating a massive interagency response is complex and should be considered an operational success for the French security authorities given that difficulties in interagency coordination are an impediment to many operational responses and notably operational response to the Nairobi mall attack in 2013.[23]

While these elements may be familiar to those that respond to, cooand, or analyze urban siege, other elements of the attack were more novel. Analyzing the Paris attacks, Clint Watts argued that the future of jihad was "inspired, networked, and directed:"

> The jihadi movement may have finally become what its original luminaries always wanted it to be—and in Paris of all places. The amorphous connections between the Charlie Hebdo attackers, the Kouachi brothers—who attributed their actions to "al Qaeda in Yemen"—and kosher market attacker Amedy Coulibaly—who pledged **allegiance to the Islamic State in a recently released online video**—may reflect exactly what some early jihadi strategists intended: broad-based jihad via a loose social movement. . . . . Years ago, Bruce Hoffman rightly proposed a spectrum approach to understanding al, Qaeda **comprising of a core, affiliates, and locals.** His framework was appropriate but now needs some updates with the rise of the Islamic State. With two competing poles and a spectrum of adherents littered throughout at least five continents, jihadi plots and their perpetrators might best be examined through the blending of three overlapping categories: "directed", "networked" and "inspired". These three labels should not be seen as discrete categories but instead as phases across a spectrum—some plots and their perpetrators will bleed over these boundaries.[24]

Counterterrorism analysts have often argued over whether the future of jihad lies with centralized, hierarchal (if not completely top-down) groups capable of organized and lethal attacks or small groupings of alienated, mostly self-directed local attackers.[25] Watts suggests that this dichotomous understanding is ultimately misleading—it may be possible for an attack to feature such strange incongruities as terrorists belonging to two rival organizations (the Islamic State in Iraq and al-Qaeda) cooperating together.

Indeed, Islamic State supporter Coulibaly (with logistical support from other men that French authorities have detained) operated alongside al-Qaeda-identifying gunmen.[26] All three were part of a known network of French domestic extremists that orbited around a charismatic yet amateur and unofficial religious figure.[27] We leave discussion of what this means for the global terrorist threat landscape to counterterrorism specialists who will be informed by additional data. However, these debates, typologies, and considerations have practical meaning for operational authorities tasked with preparing for and countering urban attacks.

The three-day Paris siege complicates the assumptions of the conceptual schemas we and others have laid out regarding urban siege and urban terrorism.[28] Attackers did not belong to a single group—they were part of a common network that somehow received inspiration and possible direction from two ideologically opposed terrorist organizations. Investigators are still hunting for possible leads, but it is safe to say that the attacks were a "tangled" mess that involve uncertain connections between the attackers, local terrorist connections in Europe and external organizations in the Middle East.[29]

The threat of simultaneous attacks, follow-on attacks, and the tangled web of influence this situation involves complicates operational response. Police must assume from now on that attackers might derive logistical support, inspiration, funding, and/or direction from a diverse combination of local, regional, and extra-regional sources. Moreover, they cannot also assume that one large attack by an attacker group is all they must contend with—synchronized attacks may occur designed to augment the execution and impact of one attack mission. Campaigns containing multiple simultaneous (or near-simultaneous) and/or sequential attacks (including attacks or engagements during exfiltration and escape) must be accounted for and demand the development and employment of operational art for urban battle.[30]

While much of the urban sieges since Mumbai demonstrate continuity, complications and change suggest the need for new thinking, including full-spectrum policing, operational art, including operations-intelligence integration to support command.

Diagnosing Urban Siege: Toward a Spectrum of Armed Assault

Deriving problem classes of urban siege requires a look at both the organizational dimension of the attack and the actual means of operational preparation, planning, and execution.

As per Watts' typology of terrorist organization and influence, we believe that the organizational dimension of the attack matters a great deal in creating reasonable assumptions for training, response planning, and wargames/red-teaming efforts. We summarize his typology below. While we make no claims that Watts' typology is the only or necessarily the most accurate template for analyzing jihadist organization, we believe it at least illustrates many of the analytical challenges involved.

First, there is obviously the most traditional kind of attack organization. "Directed" attacks, Watts notes, assume a large degree of central organization by an external group and high lethality and capability. These attacks have become seemingly less likely as improved Western law enforcement, intelligence, and military efforts have made it difficult for attacks to be organized from the top-down. However, as Gartenstein-Ross and Leah Farall have noted, one should not count these attacks out.[31] Moreover, hierarchal organization does not necessarily assume a rigid, military-style command and control structure,

and Gartenstein-Ross has noted that our understanding of the global jihad remains too fragmented and incomplete to make sweeping judgments about the likelihood of directed attacks.

"Networked" attacks will assume fighters with some degree of training (perhaps derived from overseas conflicts) and some degree of connection to overseas terrorist organizations or communities of terrorist practice. But, in contrast to elaborately planned directed attacks, Watts notes, networked attackers will constitute a "swarm" that brings together operatives, resources, and perpetrators as needed. Key variables in networked attacks include the local strength of foreign fighter networks, availability of weaponry, and the Western security environment that jihadists must contend with. Watts has suggested elsewhere that the chain of foreign fighters and radicals being funneled to and from Western states to foreign battlefields may be modeled with the collective intelligence optimization technique known as ant colony optimization.[32]

Finally, "inspired" attacks feature "bungled plots and random violence" by "jihadi wannabees." While directed attacks and networked attacks demand a complex interagency operational response, "inspired" attacks may not typically fit the urban siege conceptual schema. Competent law enforcement should be able to handle it, as "inspired" but often incompetent jihadists are frequently just as much of a danger to *themselves* as they are to their targets. However, one cannot rule out that directed or network attacks may spawn copycat inspired attacks, complicating security response, intelligence, and investigation before, during, or after an urban siege scenario. It is possible that future "inspired" cells may develop sophisticated capacity on their own or through interaction with other cells over time (although it is expected that this is difficult to achieve).

Next, we summarize Gartenstein-Ross and Daniel Trombly's October 2012 report on the use of small arms by terrorists.[33] Gartenstein-Ross and Trombly note that the use of small arms figures highly in terrorist strategic thought and must be analyzed as a function of a larger jihadist war of attrition. Al-Qaeda documents outline a strategy for a war of attrition rooted in a combination of complex, multi-member operations and smaller attacks. Complex and large-scale missions force the target to expend significant resources to prevent future attacks of that type, while smaller operations create a constant threat stream and foster an atmosphere of fear and paranoia while driving up costs gradually.[34] A vehicle for this is the use of firearms and armed assault:

> For both large-scale and small-scale attacks, firearms figure prominently in al Qaeda's strategy. A considerable corpus of written works underlies the significant role given to small arms. For years, al Qaeda and other jihadi organizations have published documents on the value of

these weapons. In Abd al Aziz al Muqrin's *A Practical Course for Guerrilla War,* a book based on writings that first appeared in al Qaeda's online journal Mu'askar al Battar, multiple chapters describe tactical and operational planning for urban warfare. Techniques covered include assassination, hostage taking, attacking motorcades, assaulting and clearing fixed targets, and setting up ambush positions. Additional volumes cover the acquisition and maintenance of small arms.[35]

Having outlined the strategic aim behind al-Qaeda contemplation of armed assault, Gartenstein-Ross and Trombly create a typology of urban assault types. Assasination attacks involve terrorist targeting of a high-profile individual. Single-shooter attacks aim for a symbolic target or location of importance to the enemy. Two-shooter teams allow terrorists to conduct more sophisticated attacks over extended periods of time. Mass attacks and frontal assaults denote terrorist operations against fixed targets. Finally, complex urban warfare attacks include multi-man teams and hybrids of the aforementioned attacks. Terrorists may also mix hostage taking, robberies, and defensive siege combat with any one of these attack types.[36]

Both the Watts and Gartenstein-Ross and Trombly typologies address essential aspects of an urban siege scenario. The organizational capacity and style in one of the categories Watts outlines may dictate the nature of the small arms attack drawn from Gartenstein-Ross and Trombly's study. Moreover, as we have previously suggested, an attack of one Watts type may lead to follow-on and/or concurrent attacks featuring another Watts organizational attack type and multiple possible Gartenstein-Ross and Trombly small arms attack types.

Murky and ill-structured incidents like the Paris incident suggest the need for greater integration between the levels of analysis in both surveys. Both cover core elements of the problem—operational direction and mechanism of attack respectively—but understanding organizational capacity and the causation of attacks may help explain the overlaps between attack execution types that Gartenstein-Ross and Trombly note at the conclusion of their report. "With firearms attackers have great flexibility," Gartenstein-Ross and Trombly rightly note. Once an attack has begun, they can select new targets and counter law enforcement."[37]

This, when coupled with the potential for a more unpredictable attacker set composition, suggests that conceptual integration is of more than just academic or high-level policy relevance. It matters very much for operational preparation for countering armed assaults. In order to train, prepare, red-team, plan, and allocate resources properly *before* the attack, police and other security agencies need to have scripts, scenarios, and models of how an attack is organized, rehearsed, and executed.

Questions about Future Urban Siege

While we do not propose our own typology, the Paris attack and newer research and analysis by Watts, Garteinstein-Ross and Trombly, and others suggest some pressing questions for both researchers and operational responders to consider when pondering urban siege post-Hebdo. In pondering these questions, we hope that researchers and operational responders can grope towards some conceptual synthesis between the levels of analysis that Watts and Gartenstein-Ross and Trombly cover in their analyses. We list them below:

1. *What kind of organizational assumptions should we utilize when building urban terrorism scenarios?*

Both the Mumbai and Paris urban sieges had similar results—prolonged mayhem by multiple groups of attackers. However, in one operation (Mumbai) the terrorists belonged to one group distributed into multiple teams. During the Paris attack the terrorists belonged to a loose common network but only loosely coordinated their synchronized operations. This created two different kinds of command problems for the first responders. Of course, the police may not and likely won't know which type of adversary they are facing during the initial course of an actual attack sequence and must rely upon real-time intelligence and operational reports to develop situational assessments.

During the Mumbai operation first responders struggled to handle the command and control problem of countering a distributed operation. But in the Paris attack state capacity was high and this was not as grave of a challenge. Rather, the primary challenge was locating the perpetrators, connecting disparate incidents, and later during the hostage situations dealing with the new problem of an attacker that synchronized an attack to coincide with a main operation. This demanded synchronized police response, which was achieved.

The command implications most relevant for an urban siege problem will depend greatly on what kind of organizational assumptions we make about the connection between attacks in the urban terror scenario. But this question also pertains very much to the prevention of attacks before they happen.

A Mumbai-like scenario requires extensive preparation, planning, a forward base, and attack vector that might expose planners and operatives to vulnerability. The terrorist "kill chain" in this case may be amenable to detection and penetration. In contrast, a Paris-like scenario does not have to be analyzed by the familiar recourse to "intelligence failure" explanations—it is perfectly possible that an attack like Paris might occur absent the systemic intelligence-sharing and indications and warnings flaws observed after Mumbai.[38] Here the terrorist "kill chain" may be more obscure and difficult to penetrate.

2. *How should we weight maximum casualties and maximum disruption in the assumptions we make about terrorist mission planning?*

One issue that Gartenstein-Ross and Trombly implicitly raise is the dichotomy between disruption and casualties as objectives in an urban siege scenario. Certainly, killing a lot of people can induce disruption and disrupting a key site or system can lead to a substantial amount of casualties. But they ought not to be regarded as interchangeable. One can induce a substantial amount of disruption and fear without Mumbai or Peshawar kill counts—the toll of the Paris attack sequence was small compared to those incidents yet it also induced a massive mobilization of French security forces and led to fear, suspicion, and a backlash that may complicate future counterterrorism efforts.[39]

This raises some core questions about urban siege scenarios from the point of view of the attacker. Is there a tradeoff between casualties and disruption? How many casualties are necessary for disruption? Is one kind of objective easier to achieve than the other in an urban siege? Do attacker objectives change dynamically during the middle of an incident in response to new information? It should be noted that attackers themselves also may not see a distinction between casualties and disruption or heavily consider it in their planning. Enough casualties automatically suggest disruption, and disruption may be a primary objective with casualty count as a side effect.

All of these questions bear heavily on organizational assumptions and choice of attack tactics and weapons. As Gartenstein-Ross and Trombly note, firearms allow tremendous flexibility both prior to and during the prosecution of an urban siege. Police will be better able to model, red-team, and train for urban siege scenarios if they have a greater idea of how terrorists themselves view success and failure conditions for urban sieges.

3. *How should we think about social media information and operational security during urban sieges?*

We devote the most space to this issue due to the fact that operational security (OPSEC) in response has become more acute due to changes in the social media landscape since we last wrote on urban siege.

The issue of social media and OPSEC is by no means new. The Mumbai attacks were one of Twitter's first real-time crises, with both locals and foreigners giving contradictory and confused play-by-play as the event unfolded. However, the increasing saturation of social media platforms and the ubiquity of Twitter and other social media platforms are increasingly bringing uncertainties about social media and OPSEC to the fore.

In this attack sequence, social media played a significant role for police, the media, the community, and terrorist organizations alike. Jihadists and their supporters used social media to praise the attacks, and the #JeSuisCharlie meme went viral extremely quickly.[40] Additionally, Twitter became a tool for tracking terrorists and developing situational awareness (for all actors), and social media became a key operational security concern as the tactics, techniques, and procedures of security forces are now broadcast in real time by both new and conventional media and terrorists can track that presence as seen in the warning for police to keep a low profile on social media to minimize the potential for terrorist ambush.[41]

Both everyday citizens and major news media organizations maintain social media presences. Social media increasingly drives news during crises, and fusing social media information has grown easier over time due to the increasing maturation of third-party client applications. It has become easier for perpetrators of incidents to monitor feeds, as long as they have manpower to spare or are suitably entrenched in a manner that allows them to monitor feeds unimpeded.

While it is important to remember that attackers (if they successfully infiltrate) begin with the advantage of surprise and responders face an uphill challenge in sorting through contradictory information, so do attackers as well. More research and assessment needs to be done about cognitive and organizational limitations on how attackers receive, process, and utilize social media information during crisis scenarios.

The human factors and emergency response literature is replete with analysis about the incident commander's situational awareness challenges, but we know comparatively little about that of the attacker group.[42] It is plausible that information fusion and processing difficulties may be negated by external support and planning (like the Mumbai attack's handlers), but it also may just add yet another information channel to process as an extra burden. It is only by modeling the information processing challenges attackers face (and how technology may help or worsen them) that law enforcement organizations can gain a realistic idea of OPSEC considerations in future crisis scenarios and justify them to external audiences.

Conclusion: Are We Charlie?

The first question routinely asked after every major terrorist attack is "can it happen here?" Until more information is available about the *Charlie Hebdo* attacks, it is hard if not impossible to even offer informed speculation about the answer. Our own work is based on news reports and others' analyses and we will eagerly monitor how well they hold up as more detailed information continues to emerge about the attacks.

Our purpose in writing this piece, however, is not to argue about the potentials for urban siege. We know that armed assault and urban siege is likely to remain a dangerous threat in both the developed West and the developing world.[43] However, noting that the possibility for urban siege exists is no longer sufficient or useful. What increasingly matters is *how* the attack will occur, and we hope that our analysis and questions will spur others to move forward in intensely studying and wargaming the variations and permutations of urban siege.

We titled our first piece on urban siege: "Postcard from Mumbai: Modern Urban Siege." It is our sincere hope that, whatever the tangled aftermath of Paris, we do not see too many more lethal "postcards" of urban siege from any more cities.[44]

Notes

1. John P. Sullivan and Adam Elkus, "Postcard from Mumbai: Modern Urban Siege," *Small Wars Journal,* 16 February 2009, and "Preventing Another Mumbai: Building a Police Operational Art," 15 June 2009.

2. Shane Harris, "US Spies Expected Airline Bombs—and Got the Paris Attacks Instead," *The Daily Beast,* 17 January 2015, **http://www.thedailybeast.com/articles/2015/01/17/u-s-spies-expected-airline-bombs-and-got-the-paris-attacks-instead .html**

3. David Kilcullen, "Westgate Mall Attacks: Urban Areas Are the Battleground of the 21st Century," *The Guardian,* 27 September 2013.

4. *BBC,* "Charlie Hebdo Attack: Three Days of Terror," 14 January 2015. http://www.bbc.com/news/world-europe-30708237 and Pierre Bienaime, "France Has Mobilized 88,000 Personnel after the Paris Shootings," *Business Insider,* 8 Jan 2015. http://www.businessinsider.com/france-has-mobilized-88000-personnel-after-the-paris-shootings-2015-1

5. Emma Graham-Harrison, "Paris Policeman's Brother: Islam Is A Religion of Love. My Brother Was Killed by Terrorists, by False Muslims," *The Guardian,* 10 January 2015. http://www.theguardian.com/world/2015/jan/10/charlie-hebdo-policeman-murder-ahmed-merabet

6. *CBS News,* "The Special Forces Behind France's Rescue Operations," 9 January 2015. http://www.cbsnews.com/news/the-special-forces-behind-frances-rescue-operations/

7. Griff Whitte, "In a Kosher Grocery Store In Paris, Terror Takes a Deadly Toll," *The Washington Post,* 9 January 2015. http://www.washingtonpost.com/world/europe/paris-kosher-market-seized-in-second-hostage-drama-in-nervous-france/2015/01/09/f171b97e-97ff-11e4-8005-1924ede3e54a_story.html

8. Ray Sanchez, Laura Smith-Spark, and Hakim Almasmari, "Source: Terror Cells Activated in France," *CNN,* 11 January 2015, **http://edition.cnn.com/2015/01/10/europe/charlie-hebdo-paris-shooting/**, and Shashank Joshi, "Charlie Hebdo Attack: A French Intelligence Failure?" *BBC,* 10 January 2015. http://www.bbc.com/news/world-europe-30760656

9. Christian de Looper, "Post-Charlie Hebdo Attack, "Islamist Cyberattacks' Cripple French Media: About 19,000 Websites

KO'd," *Tech Times,* 19 January 2015. http://www.techtimes.com/articles/27228/20150119/post-charlie-hebdo-attack-islamist-cyber-attacks-cripple-french-media.htm

10. *AFP,* "Hackers Took Control of a French Newspaper's Twitter Account and Tweeted 'I'm Not Charlie'", 20 Jan 2015. http://www.businessinsider.com/afp-syrian-group-hacks-french-newspapers-twitter-account-2015-1

11. Kilcullen, ibid.

12. For an overview of that operation, see John P. Sullivan and Adam Elkus, "The New Playbook? Urban Siege in Nairobi," *Small Wars Journal,* 24 November 2013. http://www.isn.ethz.ch/Digital-Library/Publications/Detail/?lng=en&id=175657

13. Howden, ibid.

14. Sophia Saifi and Greg Botelho, "In Pakistan, Terrorists Kill 145, Mostly Children," *CNN,* 17 December 2014. http://www.cnn.com/2014/12/16/world/asia/pakistan-peshawar-school-attack/

15. C. Christine Fair, *Urban Battle Fields of South Asia: Lessons Learned from Sri Lanka, India, and Pakistan,* Santa Monica: RAND Corporation, 2004.

16. J. Paul D. Taillon, *Hijacking and Hostages: Government Response to Terror,* Westport: Praeger, 2002.

17. John P. Sullivan and Adam Elkus, "Preventing Another Mumbai: Building a Police Operational Art," *CTC Sentinel,* West Point: Countering Terrorism Center, 15 June 2009, https://www.ctc.usma.edu/posts/preventing-another-mumbai-building-a-police-operational-art

18. *BBC,* "Gunmen Kill 13 at Karachi's Jinnah International Airport," 8 June 2014. http://www.bbc.com/news/world-asia-27757264

19. Taimur Khan, "Karachi Attack Shows Pakistani Taliban Fighting to Re-Assert Itself," *The National,* June 2014. http://www.thenational.ae/world/pakistan/karachi-attack-shows-pakistani-taliban-fighting-to-reassert-itself

20. "Cornered French Suspects Vow to Die as Martyrs," *USA Today,* 9 Jan 2015. http://www.wusa9.com/story/news/nation/2015/01/09/report-hostages-taken-northeast-of-paris/21487097/

21. Scott Bronstein, "Cherif and Said Kouachi: Their Path to Terror," *CNN,* 14 Jan 2015. http://www.cnn.com/2015/01/13/world/kouachi-brothers-radicalization/Erich Schmitt, Mark Mazzetti, and Rukmini Callimachi, "Disputed Claims Over Qaeda Role in Paris Attacks," *The New York Times,* 14 Jan 2015. http://www.nytimes.com/2015/01/15/world/europe/al-qaeda-in-the-arabian-peninsula-charlie-hebdo.html

22. Some have snarkily compared the operation to the infamous "Leeroy Jenkins" raid in the computer game *World of Warcraft,* mixing the audio dialogue from the failed multiplayer mission with the video of the Hyper Cacher police assault. See, for example, https://www.youtube.com/watch?v=cKw65EN_JtE

23. Daniel Howden, "Terror in Westgate Mall: The Full Story of the Attacks That Devastated Kenya," *The Guardian,* 4 October 2013. http://www.theguardian.com/world/interactive/2013/oct/04/westgate-mall-attacks-kenya-terror#undefined

24. Clint Watts, "Inspired, Networked, and Directed: The Muddled Jihad of ISIS and Al-Qaeda Post-Hebo," *War on the Rocks,* 12 January, 2015. http://warontherocks.com/2015/01/inspired-networked-directed-the-muddled-jihad-of-isis-al-qaeda-post-hebdo/?singlepage=1

25. For an overview of the debate, see Daveed Gartenstein-Ross, "Is Al Qaeda a Global Terror Threat or a Local Military Menace?", *The Globe and Mail,* 28 May 2014, **http://www.defenddemocracy.org/media-hit/gartenstein-ross-daveed-debate-is-al-qaeda-a-global-terror-threat-or-a-local-military-menace/**

26. Maia de la Baume and Dan Bilefksy, "France Vows Forceful Measures against Terrorism," *The New York Times,* 21 Jan 2015. http://www.nytimes.com/2015/01/22/world/europe/amedy-coulibaly-paris-gunman-france.html

27. Griff Witte and Anthony Faiola, "Suspect in Paris Attack Had 'Long-Term Obsession' Carrying Out Terrorist Attack," *The Washington Post,* 8 January 2015. http://www.washingtonpost.com/world/europe/suspect-in-paris-attack-had-long-term-obsession-carrying-out-terror-attack/2015/01/08/b36f6c90-974e-11e4-aabd-d0b93ff613d5_story.html

28. See David Kilcullen, *Out of the Mountains: The Coming Age of the Urban Guerrilla,* Oxford: Oxford University Press, 2013, Anthony James Joes, *Urban Guerrilla Warfare,* Lexington: The University of Kentucky, 2007, and John Robb, *Brave New War: The Next Stage of Terrorism and the End of Globalization,* Hoboken: Wiley, 2007 for a sampling of academic and practitioner writings on urban guerrilla operations.

29. Mariano Castillo, "Following the Tangled and Treacherous Trail after France Terror Attack," *CNN,* 15 January 2014. http://www.cnn.com/2015/01/13/europe/france-charlie-hebdo-attack-trail/

30. The Boston Marathon Bombing Attack (2013) was followed by the shooting of an MIT police officer, carjacking, a manhunt, and firefight. See J.M. Hirsh, "Boston Bombing Overview: The Unfolding of a 5-Day Manhunt for Suspects," *Huffington Post,* 21 April 2013, http://www.huffingtonpost.com/2013/04/21/boston-bombing-timeline_n_3127079.html

31. Gartenstein-Ross and Farall's analysis is reviewed in Adam Elkus, "Leader of the Pack," *War on the Rocks,* 31 October 2013. http://warontherocks.com/2013/10/leader-of-the-pack/

32. Watts, "Foreign Fighters and Ants: How They Form Their Colonies," *Geopoliticus: The FPRI Blog,* June 2013, http://www.fpri.org/geopoliticus/2013/07/foreign-fighters-and-ants-how-they-form-their-colonies

33. Daveed Gartenstein-Ross and Daniel Trombly, *The Tactical and Strategic Use of Small Arms by Terrorists,* Washington, DC: The Foundation for Defense of Democracies, 2012.

34. Gartenstein-Ross and Trombly, 6.

35. Garteinstein-Ross and Trombly, 7.

36. Gartenstein-Ross and Trombly, 7–8.

37. Gartenstein-Ross and Trombly, 21.

38. Sebastian Rotella, James Glaz, and David E. Sanger, "In 2008 Mumbai Attacks, Piles of Spy Data, but an Uncompleted Puzzle," *ProPublica,* 21 December 2014. http://www.propublica.org/article/mumbai-attack-data-an-uncompleted-puzzle

39. Steven Metz, "The Paris Attacks and the Logic of Insurgency," *World Politics Review,* 16 January 2015, http://www.worldpoliticsreview.com/articles/14873/the-paris-attacks-and-the-logic-of-insurgency

40. Ben Hubbard, "Islamic Extremists Take to Social Media to Praise Charlie Hebdo Attacks," *The New York Times,* 10 January 2015. http://www.nytimes.com/2015/01/11/world/europe/islamic-extremists-take-to-social-media-to-praise-charlie-hebdo-attack.html?_r=0&gwh=DEF452EB18676C551C641B70B2D85FFF&gwt=pay

41. Noah Ryman, "How Twitter Tracked the French Terror Suspects," *Time,* 8 Jan 2015. **http://time.com/3659307/twitter-tracked-terror-suspects/** and Sanchez et al., ibid.

42. See, for example, Alexander Kott(ed), *Battle of Cognition: The Future Information-Rich Warfare and the Mind of the Commander,* Westport: Praeger, 2007, and Christine Owen (ed), *Human Factors Challenges in Emergency Management: Enhancing Individual and Team Performance in Fire and Emergency Services,* Farnham: Ashgate, 2014.

43. David Kilcullen "New terror paradigm after Charlie Hebdo raids," *The Australian,* 17 January 2015, http://www.theaustralian.com.au/in-depth/terror/new-terror-paradigm-after-charlie-hebdo-raids/story-fnpdbcmu-1227187609376

44. Postscript: As we completed this piece another urban siege attack transpired in Tripoli, Libya. This attack on 27 January 2015 involved a combined assault (car bomb and gun attack) against the Corinthia Hotel killing at least three and injuring a half dozen more. See UN News, "Terrorist attack on hotel in Libyan capital," *Scoop,* 30 January 2015, http://www.scoop.co.nz/stories/WO1501/S00251/terrorist-attack-on-hotel-in-libyan-capital.htm

Source

1. http://smallwarsjournal.com/author/john-p-sullivan
2. http://smallwarsjournal.com/author/adam-elkus
3. http://www.i24news.tv/en/news/international/europe/57338-150111-paris-supermarket-killer-swore-allegiance-to-islamic-state
4. http://www.rand.org/content/dam/rand/pubs/testimonies/2006/RAND_CT255.pdf
5. http://www.thedailybeast.com/articles/2015/01/17/u-s-spies-expected-airline-bombs-and-got-the-paris-attacks-instead.html

6. http://www.bbc.com/news/world-europe-30708237

7. http://www.businessinsider.com/france-has-mobilized-88000-personnel-after-the-paris-shootings-2015-1

8. http://www.theguardian.com/world/2015/jan/10/charlie-hebdo-policeman-murder-ahmed-merabet

9. http://www.cbsnews.com/news/the-special-forces-behind-frances-rescue-operations/

10. http://www.washingtonpost.com/world/europe/paris-kosher-market-seized-in-second-hostage-drama-in-nervous-france/2015/01/09/f171b97e-97ff-11e4-8005-1924ede3e54a_story.html

11. http://edition.cnn.com/2015/01/10/europe/charlie-hebdo-paris-shooting/

12. http://www.bbc.com/news/world-europe-30760656

13. http://www.techtimes.com/articles/27228/20150119/post-charlie-hebdo-attack-islamist-cyber-attacks-cripple-french-media.htm

14. http://www.businessinsider.com/afp-syrian-group-hacks-french-newspapers-twitter-account-2015-1

15. http://www.isn.ethz.ch/Digital-Library/Publications/Detail/?lng=en&id=175657

16. http://www.cnn.com/2014/12/16/world/asia/pakistan-peshawar-school-attack/

17. https://www.ctc.usma.edu/posts/preventing-another-mumbai-building-a-police-operational-art

18. http://www.bbc.com/news/world-asia-27757264

19. http://www.thenational.ae/world/pakistan/karachi-attack-shows-pakistani-taliban-fighting-to-reassert-itself

20. http://www.wusa9.com/story/news/nation/2015/01/09/report-hostages-taken-northeast-of-paris/21487097/

21. http://www.cnn.com/2015/01/13/world/kouachi-brothers-radicalization/Erich

22. http://www.nytimes.com/2015/01/15/world/europe/al-qaeda-in-the-arabian-peninsula-charlie-hebdo.html

23. https://www.youtube.com/watch?v=cKw65EN_JtE

24. http://www.theguardian.com/world/interactive/2013/oct/04/westgate-mall-attacks-kenya-terror#undefined

25. http://warontherocks.com/2015/01/inspired-networked-directed-the-muddled-jihad-of-isis-al-qaeda-post-hebdo/?singlepage=1

26. http://www.defenddemocracy.org/media-hit/gartenstein-ross-daveed-debate-is-al-qaeda-a-global-terror-threat-or-a-local-military-menace/

27. http://www.nytimes.com/2015/01/22/world/europe/amedy-coulibaly-paris-gunman-france.html

28. http://www.washingtonpost.com/world/europe/suspect-in-paris-attack-had-long-term-obsession-carrying-out-terror-attack/2015/01/08/b36f6c90-974e-11e4-aabd-d0b93ff613d5_story.html

29. http://www.cnn.com/2015/01/13/europe/france-charlie-hebdo-attack-trail/

30. http://www.huffingtonpost.com/2013/04/21/boston-bombing-timeline_n_3127079.html

31. http://warontherocks.com/2013/10/leader-of-the-pack/

32. http://www.fpri.org/geopoliticus/2013/07/foreign-fighters-and-ants-how-they-form-their-colonies

33. http://www.propublica.org/article/mumbai-attack-data-an-uncompleted-puzzle

34. http://www.worldpoliticsreview.com/articles/14873/the-paris-attacks-and-the-logic-of-insurgency

35. http://www.nytimes.com/2015/01/11/world/europe/islamic-extremists-take-to-social-media-to-praise-charlie-hebdo-attack.html?_r=0&gwh=DEF452EB18676C551C641B70B2D85FFF&gwt=pay

36. http://time.com/3659307/twitter-tracked-terror-suspects/

37. http://www.theaustralian.com.au/in-depth/terror/new-terror-paradigm-after-charlie-hebdo-raids/story-fnpdbcmu-1227187609376

Critical Thinking

1. How do armed attacks carried out by small terrorist cells challenge police response?

2. How do the Paris attacks challenge the conceptual schemas of urban siege?

3. What are the benefits and drawbacks of social media with regards to urban sieges?

Internet References

Georgetown Security Studies Review: The Threat of Urban Terrorism

http://georgetownsecuritystudiesreview.org/2015/03/22/the-threat-of-urban-terrorism/

Homeland Security Today: Charlie Hebdo's Jihadi Attackers Tied to AQAP; More Attacks May be Planned

http://www.hstoday.us/industry-news/general/single-article/charlie-hebdo-s-jihadi-attackers-tied-to-aqap-more-attacks-may-be-planned/86188f230f35c011700b6288b9b3c757.html

The Telegraph: Charlie Hebdo attack: what are the implications of the Paris shootings for counterterrorism policy in Europe?

http://www.telegraph.co.uk/news/worldnews/europe/france/11334326/Charlie-Hebdo-attack-what-are-the-implications-of-the-Paris-shootings-for-counterterrorism-policy-in-Europe.html

JOHN P. SULLIVAN is a career police officer. He currently serves as a lieutenant with the Los Angeles County Sheriff's Department. He is also an adjunct researcher at the Vortex Foundation in Bogotá, Colombia; a senior research fellow at the Center for Advanced Studies on Terrorism (CAST); and a senior fellow at *Small Wars Journal-El Centro*. He is co-editor of *Countering Terrorism and WMD: Creating a Global Counter-Terrorism Network* (Routledge, 2006) and *Global Biosecurity: Threats and Responses* (Routledge, 2010) and co-author of *Mexico's Criminal Insurgency: A Small Wars Journal-El Centro Anthology (iUniverse, 2011)* and *Studies in Gangs and Cartels* (Routledge, 2013). He completed the CREATE Executive Program in Counter-Terrorism at the University of Southern California and holds a Bachelor of Arts in Government from the College of William and Mary, a Master of Arts in Urban Affairs and Policy Analysis from the New School for Social Research, and a PhD, doctorate in Information and Knowledge Society, from the Internet

Interdisciplinary Institute (IN3) at the Open University of Catalonia (Universitat Oberta de Catalunya) in Barcelona. His doctoral thesis was "Mexico's Drug War: Cartels, Gangs, Sovereignty, and the Network State." His current research focus is the impact of transnational organized crime on sovereignty in Mexico and other countries.

ADAM ELKUS is a PhD student in Computational Social Science at George Mason University. He has published articles on international security and strategy at *The Atlantic, CTC Sentinel, Armed Forces Journal,* and other publications. He is currently a columnist at *War on the Rocks* and a contributor to CTOVision, AnalystOne, and other blogs.

Article   Prepared by: Thomas J. Badey, *Randolph-Macon College*

Narcoterrorism: How Drug Trafficking and Terrorism Intersect

JOHN CISAR

Learning Outcomes

After reading this article, you will be able to:

- Define narcoterrorism.

- Explain how Hezbollah, FARC, and the Taliban use the drug trade to fund their organizations.

- Discuss why governments have been unable to curtail narcoterrorism.

I n 2011, the U.S. State Department reported that 19 of 49 (39 percent) of designated foreign terrorist organizations (FTOs) have "confirmed links to the drug trade." This corroborated an earlier 2003 Drug Enforcement Administration (DEA) finding (Rollins & Wyler, 2013, p. 3). Criminals and terrorists often share similar tactics to reach their operational goals which include acts of terrorism and involvement in criminal activity for profit (p. 7). As such, the definition of what constitutes narcoterrorism gets muddied if one only looks at motives instead of acts or results. With international efforts to curtail traditional donor and state funding of terror organizations succeeding, many terrorist groups turn to criminal enterprises to replace that financing in order to survive and operate. For FTOs like Hezbollah, the Revolutionary Armed Forces of Colombia (FARC), and the Taliban, the drug trade provides a significant and lucrative means of support. Drug trafficking organizations (DTOs) like those in Mexico and Colombia use intense violence and murder to instill fear into government officials and the population to render that country's judicial systems ineffective thus allowing those groups to apply their trade with impunity. Despite international actions to control drug trafficking and terrorism, narcoterrorist groups like Hezbollah,

FARC, Taliban, and the Mexican DTOs use their involvement in the drug trade and their application of terror methods to survive and operate.

Literature Review
Defining Narcoterrorism

In order to effectively discuss narcoterrorism, one must first define narcoterrorism. Multiple organizations have diverse definitions of narcoterrorism based on different missions, agendas and viewpoints. The concept of "narcoterrorism" was introduced in 1983 by the Peruvian President Belaunde Terry to designate terrorist-like attacks against his country's drug enforcement police. Drug criminals utilized methods from political assailants to influence the politics of the country by causing terror and obstructing justice (Hartelius, 2008, p. 1). The Department of Defense (DOD) claims it is terrorism that is linked to illicit drug trafficking (2014, p. 181). The Department further articulates terrorism as the unlawful use of violence or threat of violence to instill fear and coerce governments or societies in pursuit of goals that are usually political (p. 266). The DEA more narrowly describes narcoterrorism as confined to violent acts by drug trafficking or terrorist groups that are designed to influence national-level, counterdrug policy (DEA, 1994, p. 1), while the U.S. Department of State uses the United States Code Title 22 Section 2656f legal meaning of terrorism as the premeditated, politically motivated violence perpetrated against non-combatant (civilians and military personnel who are not in a war-like setting) targets by subnational groups or clandestine agents (State, 2014, p. 317). The State definition focuses on the organization's motives (political change) instead of the societal behavior changes brought on by terror acts. Because of this, State would include the FARC, Hamas, and Taliban as narcoterrorist groups but exclude the Zetas, Sinaloa, and Medillin crime organizations even though these groups can equally produce societal changing fear in its target groups. Excluding these drug cartels would be a mistake. They too use violence and fear to accomplish their operational goals such as assassinating journalists and bombing newspaper buildings to discourage reporting of criminal operations and targeting government officials to render a country's judicial systems ineffective. For policy consideration and this paper, a much more useful definition of narcoterrorism is the unlawful use of violence or threat of violence to instill fear and coerce governments, societies, or peoples in pursuit of goals that are usually political and that violence is linked to illicit drug trafficking.

Hezbollah

As one of the world's largest non-state terror groups, Hezbollah is an Iranian-supported Shiite militia, political party, and social welfare organization that was created after Israel's invasion of Lebanon in 1982 (Harwood, 2013). They are on the U.S. State Department FTO list and are a specially designated terrorist group. Their highlights of terror attacks include suicide truck bombings targeting U.S. Marines and French forces in Beirut (in 1983 and 1984) and U.S. military forces in the 1996 Saudi Arabian Khobar Towers bombing. Hezbollah's cross-border operations from Lebanon into Israel have increased since the Israeli withdrawal to the 'Blue Line' in May 2000.[1] They actively support Palestinian terrorist groups targeting Israel (Levitt, 2005). Additionally, Hezbollah does conduct operations outside of the Middle East, Lebanon, and Israel. In 1992, a van bomb outside the Israeli embassy in Buenos Aires killed 29 people and injured 250. Two years later, another car bomb attack in Buenos Aires practically destroyed the Jewish-Argentine community center, killing another 87 individuals (Shelley & Picarelli, 2005, p. 60).

Hezbollah's annual operating budget ranges from 200 to 500 million USD (Cammett, 2011, p. 7). Iran reportedly contributes 100–200 million USD each year although some claim that Iranian financial support has steadily declined. This reduction of support suggests possible motives for seeking alternative and sometimes illicit sources of financing (p. 6). With Shiite Lebanese diaspora communities scattered throughout the Americas, Africa, and Europe, national security experts and government investigators have warned for more than a decade that terrorist financiers use these populations to remit significant funds back to Lebanon and into the coffers of Hezbollah (Harwood, 2013). While normally engaging in criminal activity often increases groups' vulnerability by exposing them to the scrutiny of law enforcement authorities, Hezbollah's reliance on fellow sympathizers and members of local expatriate communities minimizes that potential exposure (Levitt, 2005).

One such area of sympathetic expats is the Tri-Border Area of South America (see Figure 1) formed where the borders of Argentina, Paraguay, and Brazil meet. For many years, these three countries have been blaming each other for tolerating widespread crime activities in the Tri-Border Area. The lack of a concerted effort by all three governments allows criminal and terror groups to continue to operate almost unchecked. In this region, the short-term goals of criminals and terrorists converge with both benefiting from easy border crossings and networks necessary to raise funds through drugs and arms smuggling (Shelley & Picarelli, 2005, p. 61). The Paraguayan city of Ciudad del Este is a center of operations for several terrorist groups. With its lawlessness, the city has long allowed activities of malevolent non-state actors to flourish. Only since September 11 has Ciudad del Este come under closer scrutiny by security analysts and intelligence agencies (p. 60). In May 2002, Ali Assi, who ran a coffee shop in the Islamic Welfare Center in Ciudad del Este, was arrested at the Beirut airport with 10 kilograms of cocaine. Assi is the father-in-law of Ali Hassan Abdallah who is one of the key operatives of the Hezbollah financial network in the Tri-Border Area and also a business partner of Sobhi Mahmoud Fayad, a convicted Hezbollah lieutenant. Ali Hassan is believed to have ordered fund transfers to Islamic fundamentalist groups in the Middle East through an associate in Ciudad del Este (p. 62). The 2003 arrest of Bassam Naboulsi in Sao Paula revealed a cocaine smuggling ring operating from Ciudad del Este and Foz do Iguaçu. Lebanese criminal groups and Hezbollah terrorist cells within smuggling networks transported Colombian cocaine to the U.S., Europe, and the Middle East with about 400 to 1000 kilograms of cocaine shipped on a monthly basis through the Tri-Border Area on its way to Sao Paulo. Bassam's brother owned a store in the Page Gallery shopping mall in Ciudad del Este which is also partially owned by the Hezbollah financier Assad Ahmad Barakat who is related to both brothers (p. 63). Investigations into 1992 and 1994 Buenos Aires bombings discovered that that same mall was used as a front for Hezbollah's crime and funding operations (p. 64). Over all, as much as 261 million USD annually has been raised in the Tri-Border Area and sent overseas to support the terrorist activities of Islamic groups (p. 65).

In February 2011, the Treasury Department identified the Lebanon-based Lebanese Canadian Bank (LCB) for its role in money laundering activities of an international narcotics trafficking network with ties to Hezbollah, and imposed sanctions that effectively prohibited the bank from operating in the United States (Sullivan & Beittel, 2013, p. 24). The Treasury Department maintained that the network was involved in moving illegal drugs from South America to Europe and the Middle East via West Africa. In November 2011, the Department of Justice announced the federal criminal indictment of Lebanese

Figure 1   Tri-Border of South America.

From *Latin America: Terrorism issues* (p.23), by M.P. Sullivan and J.S. Beittel, 2013, Congressional Research Service.

citizen Ayman Joumaa for conspiring to coordinate shipments of cocaine from Colombia through Central America for sale to Los Zetas, one of Mexico's most violent drug trafficking organizations. The U.S. Treasury Department also designated Joumaa as a drug kingpin (SDNTs) and additionally identified him as a specially designated global terrorist (SDGT) in June 2012 (Rollins & Wyler, 2013, p. 14). An extensive DEA investigation revealed that Joumaa laundered hundreds of millions of dollars in drug trafficking proceeds from Europe, Mexico, the United States, and West Africa for cocaine suppliers in Colombia and Venezuela. His organization operates in Lebanon, West Africa, Panama, and Colombia, and launders proceeds from illicit activities and pays fees to Hezbollah to facilitate the transportation and laundering of the proceeds (Sullivan & Beittel, 2013, p. 24). He used trade-based money laundering (TBML)[2] schemes to help conceal and disguise the true source, nature, ownership, and control of the narcotics proceeds. As an example of these fees, Hezbollah was paid to safeguard and transport bulk cash[3] movements through Beirut International Airport (Rollins & Wyler, 2013, p. 14). U.S. Southern Command estimates that Islamist terrorist groups raise between 300 million and 500 million USD per year in the Tri-Border area and duty-free zones of Iquique, Colon, Maicao, and Margarita Island (Levitt, 2005).

Revolutionary Armed Forces of Colombia (FARC)

Revolutionary Armed Forces of Colombia (FARC) has been in operation since the 1960s and is one of the largest, oldest, most violent, and best-equipped terrorist organizations in Latin America (Rollins & Wyler, 2013, p. 19). As of 2012, the FARC concentrated on low-cost, high-impact asymmetric attacks which commonly included launching mortars at police stations or the military, explosive devices placed near roads or paths, sniper attacks, roadblocks, and ambushes. Attacks on infrastructure, particularly on oil pipelines and equipment, increased by 46 percent in 2013 compared to 2012 (State, 2014, p. 212). Although civilian casualties do occur the FARC mainly targets security forces and government facilities for attack. Government officials, civilians, and foreigners have also been kidnaped for ransom and held for years.

The organization's longevity is due in part to its involvement in the drug trade. The enormous profit opportunity that drug trafficking has provided to the FARC is widely viewed as the driving factor for its involvement in such criminal activity (Rollins & Wyler, 2013, p. 19). Political reform in Colombia and the fall of communism in Eastern Europe and the former Soviet Union have eroded the FARC's traditional bases of support

(DEA, 1994, p. 7). In need of money to support their revolutionary effects, the FARC first became involved in the drug trade in the 1980s by levying protection fees on coca bush harvesters, buyers of coca paste and cocaine base, and cocaine processing laboratory operators in territory under FARC control (Rollins & Wyler, 2013, p. 19). FARC fronts demanded "taxes" from cocaine traffickers which ran about $30 or more for each kilogram of cocaine produced in or transported through their area. In addition, FARC units would extract a 20 percent tax on every kilogram of opium gum sold from farmers involved in opium poppy cultivation. Some FARC groups have negotiated de facto "service contracts" with drug traffickers, and in exchange for money or weapons these units provide security for drug crops, cocaine laboratories, and clandestine airstrips (DEA, 1994, p. 7). When the Colombian government, with help from the United States, began a campaign to eradicate the big drug cartels, the FARC seized the opportunity to take over a larger share of the country's cocaine trafficking. In the beginning, the FARC had a tempestuous relationship with its Colombian drug cartel partners, but later the FARC became a major competitor of the drug cartels (Cardenas, 2013, p. 64). Over time, the FARC took a more direct role in drug production and distribution. FARC's leaders began to eliminate what they perceived as middle-brokers from the narcotics trade and to take a more direct role in drug production and distribution. Farmers were forced to grow and sell coca to local FARC commanders, who then transported the raw material to FARC-controlled processing and refining facilities. By 2005, 65 of the FARC's 110 operational units were believed to be involved in the cultivation and circulation of cocaine (Rollins, Wyler, & Rosen, 2010, p. 18). Colombian Army Commander General Heman Guzman even stated that the FARC had become the "country's third drug cartel" (p.8). By the 2000s, the FARC had become the world's largest supplier of cocaine (Rollins & Wyler, 2013, p. 19).

The effect of this criminal activity as a revenue source was described by Rudolf Hommes, a former Colombian finance minister, when he stated that the main Colombian groups had doubled their funding between 1991 and 1994, with the drug business contributing 34 percent of income, extortion, and robbery 26 percent, and kidnappings 23 percent (Porteous, 1996). Now the organization receives approximately 50 percent of their funding from the drug economy (Rollins, Wyler, & Rosen, 2010, p. 18). What started out as a Marxist-Leninist organization has become a major narco-trafficking cartel reaping an estimated net profit from drug related crime of at least 300 million USD every year (Hartelius, 2008, p. 1).

Taliban

Across Afghanistan in 2013, Taliban insurgents conducted a significant number of large vehicle-borne improvised explosive device (VBIED) attacks that targeted Coalition Forces bases, military convoys, and Afghan government buildings. In addition, these insurgents employed a variety of tactics to target Afghan security personnel and Coalition Forces in both major cities and rural areas, seeking to expand their territorial influence and further disrupt civil governance. In major cities, attacks were often well-coordinated and complex with the intention of garnering media attention. Insurgents also assassinated several provincial Afghan leaders (State, 2014, p. 179). Major Taliban attacks included an assault on the Presidential Palace and nearby U.S. Embassy facilities, detonated VBIEDs in front of Afghanistan's Supreme Court building, an attack against the Afghan Intelligence Headquarters in Kabul city, and detonated a suicide VBIED outside a judicial building in Farah City, followed by an assault on the Farah Court Building killing 34 civilians and 12 security members forces with an additional 100 people injured (p. 180). These operations line up with the Taliban's goals of driving the Coalition Forces out of Afghanistan, overthrowing the central Afghan government in Kabul, and a return to national power.

To accomplish these ambitious goals, the Taliban needs the support of the people and an expansive source of funds. Although historically not always the case, the Taliban have turned to the lucrative opiate trade as a key source of funds. According to United Nations figures, Afghan opiates generated approximately 68 billion USD in worldwide proceeds during 2009 (Rollins & Wyler, 2013, p. 11). Of that, UN Office of Drugs and Crime (UNODC) estimates the value of opium plus its heroin and morphine derivatives produced by Afghanistan contributed nearly 3 billion USD or the equivalent of about 15 percent of Afghanistan's Gross Domestic Product (GDP) in 2013 (Sopko, 2014, p. 1). Approximately 98 percent of Afghanistan's opium is produced in seven provinces that are under Taliban control (Rollins, Wyler, & Rosen, 2010, p. 21). The Taliban reportedly obtains drug-related proceeds in several ways. Since 90 percent of transactions in Afghanistan go through the hawala system,[4] it is difficult to distinguish a legal transaction from an illegal one and is often used by drug traffickers and the Taliban to meld illegally acquired funds into the legal market to obscure where the funds originated (Curtis, 2013, p. 5).

With this in mind, Khan & Er try to make an accounting of the Taliban's drug related income. First, Taliban commanders collect agricultural tithes (ushr) from poppy farmers (Rollins & Wyler, 2013, p. 11). In addition to the profit the Taliban makes by taxing farmers, they apparently also have started growing poppy on their own which they do covertly and avoid portraying themselves as opium farmers. By this, Taliban netted an estimated 142 million USD from the 2011 opium crop alone (Khan & Er, 2013, p. 55). Next, the Taliban tax drug processors according to the amount of refined end product they produce.

In 2011, total heroin production in Afghanistan was estimated at around 467 metric tons with the Taliban controlling more than 50 laboratories within Afghanistan. They levy a tax of 250 USD for every kilogram of refined heroin manufactured (morphine base is taxed at a slightly lower rate) which allowed the Taliban to collect approximately 116 million USD from the refining process in 2011 (p. 56). The third and most profitable stage is the movement or shipment of heroin from the laboratory where the opium was processed to the point of sale. Three main routes are used for moving the product out of Afghanistan, and the Taliban either control these routes or provide protection and diversion tactics to ensure safe movement of the opium. Using a transport protection fee rate of 850 USD per kilogram and approximately 360,000 kg of product, the shipping phase income is calculated to be about 300 USD million annually (p. 57). The total revenue for Taliban from the cultivation, processing, and shipment of opium and heroin comes to approximately 530–570 million USD annually (see Figure 2).

Moreover, local Taliban commanders have at times directly engaged in drug trafficking activities to supplement their incomes (Rollins & Wyler, 2013, p. 11). Links between the Taliban and drug smugglers were highlighted in the case of Haji Bashir Noorzai, a major drug trafficker, who was convicted of smuggling 50 million USD worth of heroin into United States. His indictment alleged that he provided explosives, weapons, and personnel to the Taliban in return for protection of poppy crops and trafficking routes (Curtis, 2013, p. 4).

The Taliban leadership realizes opium remains Afghanistan's biggest cash crop and major income earner (Sopko, 2014, p. 3). Afghans who relied on poppy cultivation favored Taliban rule because it allowed them to continue growing opium (Curtis, 2013, p. 4). The Taliban saw the eradication polices hurt poor farmers while lining the pockets of the Afghan authorities (pp. 2–3). An opium ban threatened to cause widespread public

unrest and disrupt the Taliban's ability to consolidate control over the country (p. 3). Recognizing the lucrative nature of this drug trade, the Taliban began to manage and control this industry, allowing the group to guarantee order, security, and a measure of economic prosperity (p. 4). While they asserted that drug consumption was still illegal, the production and sale of opium would be allowed (p. 3). The Taliban's support of the drug trade became the key source of its political legitimacy in poppy-growing regions (p. 4). Thus, the Taliban embracing of the drug trade accomplishes the goal of obtaining public support for their movement while securing a lucrative stream of revenue to fund its operations.

Medillin Cartel

In adopting insurgent or terrorist techniques, drug trafficking organizations in Mexico, Central and South America use intimidation, assassination, and corruption to render the judicial system impotent to protect government officials, law enforcement and the people as a whole. The Medillin cartel offered judges, police, and officials the choice of 'plata o plomo' or the choice of taking financial bribes or a bullet (Roth, 2010, p. 53). Throughout the 1980s and into the early 1990s, the cofounder of the Medillin cartel, Pablo Escobar, was responsible for killing an estimated 1,000 Colombian judges and government officials and the bombing of an Avianca jet, murdering 110 people (p. 153). According to General Rosso Jose Serrano, former Chief of Colombia Nation Police Force, Escobar had 500 policemen killed in Medellin in just one year (Boettcher, 2003). His plan of intimidation and corruption paralyzed the Colombian government's efforts to bring Pablo Escobar and his group to justice for their many acts of murder and narcoterrorism. When Colombian President Gaviria ordered him transferred to a more secure facility Pablo just walked out and escaped his luxury prison, built just for him, in front of a brigade of armed soldiers. Gaviria's "demand for an intensified effort to capture Escobar" encouraged the use of all police methods in addition to military and extralegal means (Evans, 2008). Those extralegal means included an American-Colombian taskforce in which U.S. Army Delta forces trained and equipped a special unit of the Colombian National Police, called the Search Block, to hunt Escobar and used the U.S. Army Intelligence Support Activity's Centra Spike aircraft to provide intelligence and electronic triangulation position reporting of communications (Boettcher, 2003). Additionally, a vigilante group call Los PEPES (People Persecuted By Pablo Escobar) started using similar terrorist tactics to attack Escobar's family, friends, supporters and properties in an effort to isolate Pablo from his support structure (Boettcher, 2003). With these combined legal and extralegal efforts, the Search Block found and killed Pablo Escobar in December of 1993.

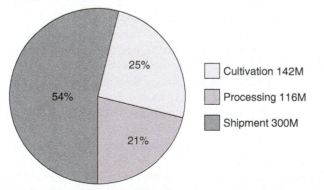

Figure 2 Annual Taliban Drug Revenue.

Created using data from "Cutting the link between illegal drugs and terrorists" by K.J. Khan and O. Er, 2013, *Combating Terrorism Exchange, 3*(3), pp. 55–57.

Mexican Drug Trafficking Organizations

In parts of Mexico, the same style narcoterrorism has been used to counter the Mexican government crackdown of the DTOs. "A number of indicators suggest the terror campaign is working, with police resignations and desertion from the military at record numbers" and newspapers censoring organized crime coverage (Roth, 2010, p. 54). From 2006 to 2013, 70 Mexican mayors and former mayors were killed, their murders bearing signs of organized crime killings (Heinle, Rodríguez Ferreira & Shirk, 2014, p. 34). In a sample of 4,380 organized crime murders[5] from 2006 to 2013 by the Memoria project, 680 (15.5 percent) of the bodies were accompanied by some kind of narco-message (narcomensaje) (p. 33). These types of messages are usually directed to government officials or rival cartels. The same survey sample also found that torture was identified in 710 cases (16.2 percent), decapitation in 456 (10.4 percent), and dismemberment in 349 (8 percent) (p. 34). The intimidation of public and police officials through violence or the threat of violence against their lives or their families' lives, is a much more widespread and effective tactic than just a trade for money, and likely accounts for a plurality of corrupt law enforcement officials in Mexico (Placido & Perkins, 2010, pp. 4–5). From 2006 to 2013, 91 journalist and media workers have been killed with many more suffering kidnappings, beatings, threats and other types of aggression (Heinle, Rodríguez Ferreira & Shirk, 2014, p. 36). This violence over the past decade makes Mexico one of the most dangerous places in the world for journalists. Often these attacks cause journalists to self-censor their work and news outlets to stop publishing or broadcasting stories on violent crime. Additionally, organized crime groups appear to be targeting citizens who use social media to report on the violence (Beittel, 2013, p. 27).

The brutal violence, military tactics, and powerful weapons such as hand grenades, rocket-propelled grenades, automatic rifles, and convoy ambushes employed by Mexican drug trafficking organizations far exceed acts normally committed by narcotics trafficking and organized crime in general, and more resemble armed conflicts and insurrections in other countries. The Zetas DTO was formed in 1998 by 14 former Mexican soldiers, some with American paratrooper training, and has grown to command more than 10,000 gunmen that operate from the Rio Grande border with Texas to deep inside Central America (Grillo, 2012). To counter this, the United States has extensively trained and supported special Mexican Marine units to hunt and capture/kill high-level DTO targets. This American cooperation with the Mexican Marines has been highly successful (Miroff & Booth, 2010). Reminiscent of other war zones where people fled for their safety, the Internal Displacement Monitoring Centre, an international non-governmental organization (NGO), estimated in 2011 that 230,000 persons were displaced due to the intense Mexican violence (Beittel, 2013, p. 32). Remarking on the situation in Mexico to the Council on Foreign Relations in 2010, then-U.S. Secretary of State Hillary Clinton said the organized criminal violence by the drug cartels may be "morphing into or making common cause with what we would call an insurgency"[6] (p. 5).

On August 25, 2011, 52 people lost their lives in a casino fire allegedly ignited by Los Zetas in retaliation against the owners leading Mexican President Calderón to decry this incident as the work of "true terrorists" (Beittel, 2013, p. 40). However, some claim these Mexican DTOs lack a discernible political goal or ideology and thus their acts do not fit the term of terrorism. In their ruthless pursuit of profit, they have a goal of challenging the Mexican government and other countries' state monopoly on the use of force and rule of law. As indicated in a 2012 message signed by the Zetas and hung from a bridge in Monterrey, "Even with the support of the United States, they [Mexican government] cannot stop us, because here the Zetas rule. . . The government must make a pact with us because if not we will have to overthrow it and take power by force" (Grillo, 2012). A Mexican Senate report detailed that 195 or 8 percent of Mexican municipalities were completely under control of organized crime and another 1,536 or 63 percent were infiltrated by organized crime (Beittel, 2013, p. 45). In addition, the report stated that criminal structures operate with logistical support from corrupt municipal police and politicians (p. 46). Organized crime groups like the Zetas seem to be achieving their goal of taking control of government functions. In light of the current situation, why does the U.S. State Department insist that "[t]here are no known international terrorist organizations operating in Mexico" (State, 2014, p. 217)? The acts of the Mexican DTOs are narcoterrorism as defined by this paper.

Control of Narcoterrorism

With the post 9-11 attention on terrorism, the international community fails to effectively control narcoterrorism. The FARC has evolved into a powerful drug cartel that was militarily decimated as an insurgency by Colombia. Yet, it remains extremely resilient despite being generally unpopular within Colombia as a whole and having very remote prospects for achieving its main ambition (Cardenas, 2013, p. 65). With more than two decades of international counternarcotics efforts, the FARC has refined its strategy and has seen its drug revenues rise to considerable levels to ably fund its terror and propaganda agenda. In Afghanistan, the Taliban has seen a robust resurgence even though they were almost completely exiled from the country by Coalition Forces. Again, years of international antidrug exertions have proven fruitless with Afghanistan providing more than 90 percent of the world's opiates. The Taliban's share of this drug trade has risen to over a half of a billion dollars which enables them to support a high level of attacks on government and Coalition Forces. Even with American government constraints, Hezbollah was able to deploy 10,000 rockets capable of penetrating well into Israel and could provide several millions of USDs of funding to al-Qaeda operatives and Palestinian terrorist groups in a year (Levitt, 2005). The Mexican drug trafficking violence has already spilled over into the United States and Mexican DTOs are present in more than 1,000 U.S. cities (Beittel, 2013, p. 6). Mexican drug cartels conduct murders all across America even in places far from the border like Oregon and Washington where mass execution style shootings and multiple bombings have been linked to Mexican drug traffickers (Zaitz, 2013b). Between January 2010 and April 2011, the Texas Department of Public Safety (DPS) reported that 22 murders, 24 assaults, 15 shootings and five kidnappings in Texas took place directly at the hands of Mexican cartels (McCaul, 2012, p. 23). American law enforcement officers are also becoming targets. Since 2007, violence against Border Patrol agents has increased by 35 percent to include 13 deaths (p. 24) and the Texas DPS records 58 incidents of shots fired at Texas law enforcement by Mexican cartel operatives since 2009 (p. 25). In Oregon, a Mexican drug trafficker associated with Zetas threatened to kill a DEA agent and his family who had worked to disrupt his drug trafficking operation. The former U.S. Attorney in the area proclaimed, "by threatening an agent's family, that was crossing a line that drug traffickers have not been willing to cross in the United States" (Zaitz, 2013a).

Despite the concentrated efforts of international agencies and governments, there is no evidence of success against narcoterrorism (Khan & Er, 2013, p. 61). Several factors may cause this. In drug-producing countries, the narcotics trade has the potential to provide drug friendly terrorist groups with an added bonus: recruits and sympathizers among impoverished, neglected, and isolated farmers who can not only cultivate drug crops but also popularize and reinforce anti-government movements (Rollins & Wyler, 2013, p. 10). Evidence of this terror group-farmer synergy can be found in Afghanistan where 89 percent of total poppy cultivation occurs in regions that have the strongest insurgent and criminal networks (Sopko, 2014, p. 5) and in Colombia where coca production thrived in areas under FARC control (Rollins & Wyler, 2010). Challenged strategic planning by American government agencies may create more favorable conditions for terror groups. The Special Inspector General for Afghanistan Reconstruction found in his last trip to Afghanistan that no one at the Embassy could convincingly explain to him how the U.S. government counternarcotics efforts were making meaningful impacts on the narcotics trade or how they will have a significant impact after the 2014 transition. In addition, he was astonished to find that the counternarcotics effort does not seem to be a top priority during this critical transition period and beyond (Sopko, 2014, p. 6). The terror-crime nexus creates risks to the American homeland. General Victor E. Renaults Jr, Commander of the U.S. Northern Command, stated that "drug cartels have developed a distribution system to rival the world's largest retailers." Terrorist networks could use their trafficking ties to facilitate the movement of personnel and harmful goods and material into the United States (Rollins, Wyler, & Rosen, 2010, p. 42). Neglected in the post 9-11 environment, international narcoterrorism prosecutions appear to have gained prominence since enactment of the USA PATRIOT Improvement and Reauthorization Act of 2005 (Rollins & Wyler, 2013, p. 27).[7] In spite of concentrated governmental efforts by Mexican President Calderón to attack the drug trafficking organizations, the country's violence rose to record levels with 60,000 organized crime-related homicides and another 26,000 Mexicans reported missing during his six year term. The level of homicides is expected to remain quite high in the near future (Beittel, 2013, p. 37). Even with international sanctions and counterterror efforts, Hezbollah, Taliban, FARC, and Mexican DTO groups have survived and continue to spread their violence and fear as the world continues to struggle to finds ways to control narcoterrorism.

Conclusion

A far more useful definition of narcoterrorism is the unlawful use of violence or threat of violence to instill fear and coerce governments, societies or peoples in pursuit of goals that are usually political and that violence is linked to illicit drug trafficking. As funding from traditional sources dry up, terror groups look at the billions of dollars generated by the worldwide drug trade for financial support. Hezbollah garners hundreds of millions annually through operations in the Tri-Border of South America and taxes on drug movements. The FARC is actually involved in the production and trafficking of cocaine which nets them about half of their annual revenue and the label of Colombia's third major drug cartel. The Taliban have tapped into Afghanistan's 93 percent of the world opium trade to earn a half of a billion and mount a resurgence. Through their links with and profits from the illicit drug trade, Hezbollah, FARC, and Taliban can be categorized as narcoterrorists, and their actions as narcoterrorism. With their extensive use of murder to instill fear in government officials and the public at large to further criminal activities, Mexican drug trafficking organizations and the Medillin cartel can too be considered narcoterrorists. Even though the international community has tried, they have yet to defeat these groups. Hezbollah, FARC, and Taliban still conduct their terror operations with funding supplied by the drug trade, and the Mexican crime organizations continue their murderous ways to sustain their lucrative drug enterprises.

References

Beittel, J. S. Library of Congress, Congressional Research Service. (2013). *Mexico's drug trafficking organizations: Source and scope of the violence* (R41576). Retrieved from http://fas.org/sgp/crs/row/R41576.pdf

Boettcher, M. (Performer) (2003). In *CNN PRESENTS: Killing Pablo*. Atlanta: Cable News Network. Retrieved from http://transcripts.cnn.com/TRANSCRIPTS/0305/25/cp.00.html

Cammett, M. U.S. House of Representatives, Committee on Homeland Security. (2011). *Hezbollah in Latin America—Implications for U.S. homeland security.* Retrieved from http://homeland.house.gov/sites/homeland.house.gov/files/Testimony Cammett.pdf

Cardenas, J. G. (2013). Human rights as a weapon of terrorists: A case study. *Combating Terrorism Exchange, 3*(3), 63–70. Retrieved from http://faculty.nps.edu/gsois/ctx/Vol_3_No_3_Final.pdf

Curtis, L. (2013, September 30). *U.S. counternarcotics policy: Essential to fighting terrorism in Afghanistan.* The Heritage Foundation Backgrounder, 2845, Retrieved from http://www.google.com/url?sa=t&rct=j&q=&esrc=s&source=web&cd=1&ved=0CB0QFjAA&url=http://www.heritage.org/research/reports/2013/09/us-counternarcotics-policy-essential-to-fighting-terrorism-in-afghanistan&ei=vYGkU7nDCZeXqAa2-YLoBg&usg=AFQjCNH08SinTc3tBeWmC6E8LCmyJNmZNA&bvm=bv.69411363,d.b2k

Department of Defense (DOD), (2014). *Dictionary of military and associated terms.* Retrieved from http://www.dtic.mil/doctrine/new_pubs/jp1_02.pdf

Evans, M. The George Washington University, National Security Archive. (2008). *Colombian paramilitaries and the United States: "Unraveling the PEPES tangled web."* Retrieved from http://www.gwu.edu/~nsarchiv/NSAEBB/NSAEBB243/

Grillo, I. (2012, May 23). Special report: Mexico's Zetas rewrite drug war in blood. *Reuters.* Retrieved from http://www.reuters.com/article/2012/05/23/us-mexico-drugs-zetas-idUSBRE84M0LT20120523

Hartelius, J. EastWest Institute and the Swedish Carnegie Institute, (2008). *Narcoterrorism.* Retrieved from http://www.google.com/url?sa=t&rct=j&q=&esrc=s&source=web&cd=1&ved=0CB0QFjAA&url=http://mercury.ethz.ch/serviceengine/Files/ISN/90550/ipublicationdocument_singledocument/7fcb6741-c9e0-4c69-8bbc-c3a195488fa4/en/2008-02-20_Narcoterrorism.pdf&ei=hzjIU4aXLYTJ8AGA54GYAw&usg=AFQjCNEgXzOTCk7QVml08LQ5riqVRgTeJg&bvm=bv.71198958,d.cGU

Harwood, M. (2013). Hezbollah's tri-border hub. *Security Management,* Retrieved from http://www.securitymanagement.com/article/hezbollahs-tri-border-hub-007779

Heinle, K., Rodríguez Ferreira, O., & Shirk, D. A. Justice in Mexico Project, (2014). *Justice in Mexico project: Data and analysis through 2013.* Retrieved from https://justiceinmexico.files.wordpress.com/2014/07/dvm-2014-final.pdf

Khan, K. J., & Er, O. (2013). Cutting the link between illegal drugs and terrorists. *Combating Terrorism Exchange, 3*(3), 54–62. Retrieved from http://faculty.nps.edu/gsois/ctx/Vol_3_No_3_Final.pdf

Levitt, M. The Washington Institute for Near East Policy, (2005). *Hezbollah finances: Funding the party of god.* Retrieved from http://www.washingtoninstitute.org/policy-analysis/view/hezbollah-finances-funding-the-party-of-god

Miroff, N., & Booth, W. (2010, December 4). Mexico's Marines team with U.S. DEA. *Washington Post.* Retrieved from http://www.washingtonpost.com/wp-dyn/content/article/2010/12/03/AR2010120307106_pf.html

Placido, A. P., & Perkins, K. L. U.S. Department of Justice, (2010). *Drug trafficking violence in Mexico: Implications for the United States.* Retrieved from http://www.drugcaucus.senate.gov/Joint-DEA-FBI-Placido-Perkins-5-5-10.pdf

Porteous, S. D. Canadian Security Intelligence Service, (1996). *The threat from transnational crime: An intelligence perspective.* Retrieved from http://www.opensourceintelligence.eu/ric/doc/The threat from transnational crime.pdf

Realuyo, C. B. Woodrow Wilson Center, Mexico Institute. (2012). *It's all about the money: Advancing anti-money laundering efforts in the U.S. and Mexico to combat transnational organized crime.* Retrieved from http://www.wilsoncenter.org/sites/default/files/Realuyo_U.S.-Mexico_Money_Laundering_0.pdf

Rollins, J., & Wyler, L. S. Library of Congress, Congressional Research Service. (2010). *International terrorism and transnational crime: Threats, policy, and considerations* (R41004). Retrieved from http://www.globalinitiative.net/wpfb-file/congress-research-service-international-terrorism-and-transnational-crime-security-threats-u-s-policy-and-considerations-for-congress-march-2010-pdf/

Rollins, J., & Wyler, L. S. Library of Congress, Congressional Research Service. (2013). *Terrorism and transnational crime: Foreign policy issues for Congress* (R41004). Retrieved from http://fas.org/sgp/crs/terror/R41004.pdf

Rollins, J., Wyler, L. S., & Rosen, S. Library of Congress, Congressional Research Service. (2010). *International terrorism and transnational crime: Threats, policy, and considerations for Congress* (R41004). Retrieved from http://fpc.state.gov/documents/organization/134960.pdf

Roth, M. P. (2010). *Global organized crime: A reference handbook.* Santa Barbara, California: ABC-CLIO, LLC.

Shelley, L. I., & Picarelli, J. T. (2005). Methods and motives: Exploring links between transnational organized crime and international terrorists. *Trends in Organized Crime, 9*(2), 52–67. Retrieved from https://www.ncjrs.gov/pdffiles1/nij/grants/211207.pdf

Sopko, J. F. Special Inspector General for Afghanistan Reconstruction, (2014). *Future U.S. counternarcotics efforts in Afghanistan.* Retrieved from http://www.drugcaucus.senate.gov/hearing-1-15-14/SIGAR John F Sopko.pdf

Sullivan, M. P., & Beittel, J. S. Library of Congress, Congressional Research Service. (2013). *Latin America: Terrorism issues* (RS21049). Retrieved from http://fas.org/sgp/crs/terror/RS21049.pdf

United Nations Interim Force in Lebanon (UNIFIL), (2014). *UNIFIL operations.* Retrieved from http://unifil.unmissions.org/Default.aspx?tabid=11580

United States Department of Homeland Security, Immigration and Customs Enforcement (ICE). (2013). *Trade-based money laundering.* Retrieved from http://www.ice.gov/cornerstone/money-laundering.htm

United States Department of Justice, Drug Enforcement Administration (DEA). (1994). *Insurgent involvement in the Colombian drug trade: Drug intelligence report* (DEA-94045). Retrieved from http://www2.gwu.edu/~nsarchiv/NSAEBB/NSAEBB69/col33.pdf

United States Department of State, Bureau of Counterterrorism. (2014). *Country reports on terrorism 2013.* Retrieved from http://www.state.gov/documents/organization/225886.pdf

Zaitz, L. (2013a, June 21). Drug cartels in Oregon: Violence in the Northwest. *The Oregonian.* Retrieved from http://www.oregonlive.com/pacific-northwest-news/index.ssf/2013/06/drug_cartels_in_oregon_violenc.html#/0

Zaitz, L. (2013b, June 23). Drug cartels in Oregon: Rise and fall of an Oregon kingpin. *The Oregonian.* Retrieved from http://www.oregonlive.com/pacific-northwest-news/index.ssf/2013/06/drug_cartels_in_oregon_rise_an.htm

Notes

1. While not an official border, the "Blue Line" is the "Line of Withdrawal" of Israel Defense Forces (IDF) from Lebanese territory in conformity with U.N. Security Council resolution 425 to roughly the 1978 pre-Israeli invasion of Lebanon troop positions. The Line separates Lebanese and Israeli controlled areas. A 15,000 member United Nations peacekeeping force monitors activities and the cessation of hostilities along the Blue Line (UNIFIL, 2014).

2. Trade-Based Money Laundering. This alternative remittance system allows illegal organizations the opportunity to transport and store illegitimate proceeds disguised as legitimate trade. Worth can be moved through this process by false-invoicing, over/under-invoicing, and over/undervaluing invoices and customs declarations on commodities that are imported or exported around the world. Global trade is frequently used by criminal organizations to move value around the world because of the complex and sometimes confusing documentation that is frequently associated with legitimate trade transactions (ICE, 2013).

3. Bulk cash smuggling entails physically transporting large quantities of cash and is designed to bypass financial transparency reporting requirements. Bulk cash smuggling does not actually constitute a money laundering mechanism as the cash remains in its original form (Realuyo, 2012, p.7).

4. Hawala is an informal system of money transfer that uses a third party and is mainly practiced in Islamic societies. A customer pays hawaladar (#1) in one place who authorizes an associate hawaladar (#2) in another place to pay the intended recipient. No actual cash is transferred between the customer and the recipient. Hawaladar #2 trusts that he will be eventually reimbursed by Hawaladar #1 in some way. The whole system is based on trust and leaves no written records thus the transfers are very hard for law enforcement to trace.

5. The criteria that the Mexican Government uses to classify murders as "Organized Crime Homicides": 1. Victim killed by high-caliber or automatic firearm typical of organized crime groups (OCG) (.50 caliber, AK- & AR-type). 2. Signs of torture, decapitation, or dismemberment. 3. Body was wrapped in blankets, taped, or gagged 4. Killed at specific location, or in a vehicle. 5. Killed by OCG within penitentiary. 6. Special circumstances (e.g., narco-message; victim OCG member; abducted, ambushed, or chased). (Heinle, Rodríguez Ferreira & Shirk, 2014, p. 17)

6. Insurgency defined as "the organized use of subversion and violence to seize, nullify, or challenge political control of a region" (DOD, 2014, p. 129).

7. Section 122 of the USA PATRIOT Improvement and Reauthorization Act of 2005 (P.L. 109–177) added a new prohibition against narcoterrorism with enhanced criminal penalties which [makes] it a violation of U.S. law to engage in narcotics-related crimes anywhere in the world while knowing, conspiring, or intending to provide support, directly or indirectly, for a terrorist act or to a terrorist organization (Rollins & Wyler, 2013, p. 27).

Critical Thinking

1. How does John Cisar define narcoterrorism?
2. What is the Tri-Border Area and how is it utilized by Hezbollah?
3. How did political reform in Colombia and the fall of communism affect FARC?
4. How does the Taliban use the drug trade to fund its organization?
5. Why have governments been unable to curtail narcoterrorism?

Internet References

Center for Security Policy: Los Zetas and Hezbollah, a Deadly Alliance of Terror and Vice
https://www.centerforsecuritypolicy.org/2013/07/10/los-zetas-and-hezbollah-a-deadly-alliance-of-terror-and-vice

Drug Enforcement Administration: Narcoterrorism News Releases
http://www.dea.gov/pr/top-story/Narcoterrorism.shtml

The White House: Strategy to Combat Transnational Organized Crime
https://www.whitehouse.gov/sites/default/files/Strategy_to_Combat_Transnational_Organized_Crime_July_2011.pdf

Article _____   Prepared by: Thomas J. Badey, *Randolph-Macon College*

The Cyber Terror Bogeyman

PETER W. SINGER

Learning Outcomes

After reading this article, you will be able to:

- Identify potential targets of a cyber-terror attack.
- Describe how terrorists are currently using cyberspace.
- Discuss the likelihood of a cyberterror attack on the United States.

We have let our fears obscure how terrorists really use the Internet.

About 31,300. That is roughly the number of magazine and journal articles written so far that discuss the phenomenon of cyber terrorism.

Zero. That is the number of people that have been hurt or killed by cyber terrorism at the time this went to press.

In many ways, cyber terrorism is like the Discovery Channel's "Shark Week," when we obsess about shark attacks despite the fact that you are roughly 15,000 times more likely to be hurt or killed in an accident involving a toilet. But by looking at how terror groups actually use the Internet, rather than fixating on nightmare scenarios, we can properly prioritize and focus our efforts.

Part of the problem is the way we talk about the issue. The FBI defines cyber terrorism as a "premeditated, politically motivated attack against information, computer systems, computer programs and data which results in violence against noncombatant targets by subnational groups or clandestine agents." A key word there is "violence," yet many discussions sweep all sorts of nonviolent online mischief into the "terror" bin. Various reports lump together everything from Defense Secretary Leon Panetta's recent statements that a terror group might launch a "digital Pearl Harbor" to Stuxnet-like sabotage (ahem, committed by state forces) to hacktivism, WikiLeaks and credit card fraud. As one congressional staffer put it, the way we use a term like cyber terrorism "has as much clarity as cybersecurity—that is, none at all."

Another part of the problem is that we often mix up our fears with the actual state of affairs. Last year, Deputy Defense Secretary William Lynn, the Pentagon's lead official for cybersecurity, spoke to the top experts in the field at the RSA Conference in San Francisco. "It is possible for a terrorist group to develop cyber-attack tools on their own or to buy them on the black market," Lynn warned. "A couple dozen talented programmers wearing flip-flops and drinking Red Bull can do a lot of damage."

The deputy defense secretary was conflating fear and reality, not just about what stimulant-drinking programmers are actually hired to do, but also what is needed to pull off an attack that causes meaningful violence. The requirements go well beyond finding top cyber experts. Taking down hydroelectric generators, or designing malware like Stuxnet that causes nuclear centrifuges to spin out of sequence doesn't just require the skills and means to get into a computer system. It's also knowing what to do once you are in. To cause true damage requires an understanding of the devices themselves and how they run, the engineering and physics behind the target.

The Stuxnet case, for example, involved not just cyber experts well beyond a few wearing flip-flops, but also experts in areas that ranged from intelligence and surveillance to nuclear physics to the engineering of a specific kind of Siemens-brand industrial equipment. It also required expensive tests, not only of the software, but on working versions of the target hardware as well.

As George R. Lucas Jr., a professor at the U.S. Naval Academy, put it, conducting a truly mass-scale action using cyber means "simply outstrips the intellectual, organizational and personnel capacities of even the most well-funded and well-organized terrorist organization, as well as those of even the most sophisticated international criminal enterprises."

Lucas said the threat of cyber terrorism has been vastly overblown.

"To be blunt, neither the 14-year-old hacker in your next-door neighbor's upstairs bedroom, nor the two- or three-person al-Qaida cell holed up in some apartment in Hamburg are going to bring down the Glen Canyon and Hoover dams," he said.

We should be crystal clear: This is not to say that terrorist groups are uninterested in using the technology of cyberspace to carry out acts of violence. In 2001, al-Qaida computers seized in Afghanistan were found to contain models of a dam, plus engineering software that simulated the catastrophic failure of controls. Five years later, jihadist websites were urging cyber attacks on the U.S. financial industry to retaliate for abuses at Guantanamo Bay.

Nor does it mean that cyber terrorism, particularly attacks on critical infrastructure, is of no concern. In 2007, Idaho National Lab researchers experimented with cyber attacks on their own facility; they learned that remotely changing the operating cycle of a power generator could make it catch fire. Four years later, the Los Angeles Times reported that white-hat hackers hired by a water provider in California broke into the system in less than a week. Policymakers must worry that real-world versions of such attacks might have a ripple effect that could, for example, knock out parts of the national power grid or shut down a municipal or even regional water supply.

But so far, what terrorists have accomplished in the cyber realm doesn't match our fears, their dreams or even what they have managed through traditional means.

But so far, what terrorists have accomplished in the cyber realm doesn't match our fears, their dreams or even what they have managed through traditional means.

The only publicly documented case of an actual al-Qaida attempt at a cyber attack wouldn't have even met the FBI definition. Under questioning at Guantanamo Bay, Mohmedou Ould Slahi confessed to trying to knock offline the Israeli prime minister's public website. The same goes for the September denial-of-service attacks on five U.S. banking firms, for which the Islamist group "Izz ad-Din al-Qassam Cyber Fighters" claimed responsibility. (Some experts believe the group was merely stealing credit for someone else's work.) The attacks, which prevented customers from accessing the sites for a few hours, were the equivalent of a crowd standing in your lobby blocking access or a gang of neighborhood kids constantly doing "ring and runs" at your front doorbell. It's annoying, to be sure, but nothing that would make the terrorism threat matrix if you removed the word "cyber." And while it may make for good headlines, it is certainly not in the vein of a "cyber 9/11" or "digital Pearl Harbor."

Even the 2007 cyber attacks on Estonia, the most-discussed incident of its kind, had little impact on the daily life of the average Estonian and certainly no long-term effect. Allegedly assisted by the Russian government, and hence well beyond the capacity of most terror organizations, the attacks merely disrupted public-facing government websites for a few days. Compare that with the impact of planes crashing into the center of the U.S. financial system, the London subway attacks or the thousands of homemade bomb attacks that happen around the world each year.

Even when you move into the "what if" side the damage potential of cyber terror still pales compared with other types of potential terror attacks. A disruption of the power grid for a few days would certainly be catastrophic (though it's something that Washington, D.C., residents have lived through in the last year. Does the Pepco power company qualify as a cyber threat?). But, again, in strategic planning, we have to put threats into context. The explosion of just one nuclear bomb, even a jury-rigged radiological "dirty bomb," could irradiate an American city for centuries. Similarly, while a computer virus could wreak havoc in the economy, a biological attack could

change our very patterns of life forever. As one cyber expert said, "There are [cyber] threats out there, but there are no threats that threaten our fundamental way of life."

Terrorists Online

Better than fixating on an unlikely hack that opens the floodgates of Hoover Dam, in assessing cyber terrorism we should look at how terror groups actually use the Internet. The answer turns out to be: pretty much how everyone else uses it. Yes, the Internet is becoming a place of growing danger and new digital weaponry is being developed. We must be mindful of forces that would use malware against us, much as we have used it in offensive operations against Iran. But the Internet's main function remains to gather and share information across great distances with instant ease.

For instance, online dating sites and terror groups alike use the Internet to connect people of similar interests and beliefs who otherwise wouldn't normally meet. Similarly, online voices—be they restaurant bloggers or radical imams—are magnified, reaching more people than ever. (Indeed, the Internet seems to reward the more extreme with more attention.) Al-Qaida, denied safe havens by U.S. military operations after 9/11, spent the next decade shifting its propaganda distribution from hand-carried cassette tapes to vastly superior online methods. The last video that Osama bin Laden issued before his death was simultaneously uploaded onto five sites. Counterterrorism groups rushed to take them down, but within one hour, the video had been captured and copied to more than 600 sites. Within a day, the number of sites hosting the video had doubled again, each watchable by thousands.

Beyond propaganda, cyberspace allows groups to spread particular knowledge in new and innovative ways. The same kinds of tools that allow positive organizations such as the Khan Academy to help kids around the world learn math and science has given terrorist groups unprecedented ways to discuss and disseminate tactics, techniques and procedures. The recipes for explosives are readily available on the Internet, while terror groups have used the Internet to share designs for IEDs instantly across conflict zones from Iraq to Afghanistan.

Online sharing has helped such groups continue their work even as drone strikes and other global counterterror efforts deprive them of geographic spaces to teach and train. And what terror groups value from the Internet is the same as the rest of us—reliable service, easy terms and virtual anonymity—which complicates the old way of thinking about the locale of threats. The Taliban, for example, ran a website for more than a year that released propaganda and kept a running tally of suicide bombings, rocket attacks and raids against U.S. troops in Afghanistan. And yet the host for the website was a Texas company called The Planet, which rented out websites for $70 a month, payable by credit card. The company, which hosted some 16 million accounts, wasn't aware that one of them was a Taliban information clearinghouse until it was contacted by U.S. authorities and shut the site down.

This gaining of knowledge is not just about the "how" of a terror attack, but even the "who" and the "where" on the targeting side. Groups have used cyberspace as a low-cost, low-risk means to gather intelligence in ways they could only dream about a generation ago. For example, no terrorist group has the financial resources to afford a spy satellite to scope out targets from above with pinpoint precision, let alone the capability to build and launch it. Yet, Google Earth filled in just as effectively for Lashkar-e-Taiba, a Pakistan-based terror group, when it was planning the 2008 Mumbai attacks, and for the Taliban team that planned the raid earlier this year on Camp Bastion in Afghanistan.

What this means when it comes to terrorism is that, much like in other areas of cybersecurity, we have to be aware of our own habits and uses of the Internet and how bad actors might take advantage. In 2007, when U.S. Army helicopters landed at a base in Iraq, soldiers reportedly used their smartphones to snap photos and upload them to the Internet. The geotags embedded in the photos allowed insurgents to pinpoint and destroy four of the helicopters in a mortar attack. The incident has become a standard part of experts' warnings. "Is a badge on Foursquare worth your life?" asks Brittany Brown, the social media manager at Fort Benning, GA.

A growing worry here is that groups might use social networking and Kevin Mitnick-style "social engineering" to seek information not just about hard targets, but human ones. After the bin Laden raid in 2011, an American cybersecurity analyst wondered what he could find out about the supposedly super-secret unit that carried it out. He was able to find 12 current or former members' names, their families' names and their home addresses. This information was acquired not as the result of leaks to the press, but rather through the use of social networking tricks (for instance, tracking people and their network of friends and family by their appearances in pictures wearing T-shirts with unit logos or through websites that mention BUDS training classes). In similar experiments, he uncovered the names of FBI undercover agents and, in one particularly saucy example, a pair of senior U.S. government officials who opened themselves up to potential blackmail by participating in a swinger site. The analyst uses the results of such exercises to warn his "targets" that there was more about them on the Internet than they realized—a useful reminder for us all.

Ultimately, in making a global risk assessment, we have to weigh an imagined future, in which terror groups unleash a cataclysm via computer virus, against the present reality, in which they use information flows to inform and improve their actions in the physical world.

So what does that suggest for cyber counterterror efforts?

A Double-Edged Sword

"It seems that someone is using my account and is somehow sending messages with my name," emailed one person who fell for an online trick. "The dangerous thing in the matter is that they [his contacts replying to what they thought was a genuine email] say that I had sent them a message including a link for download, which they downloaded."

We can all empathize with this fellow, whose story was captured by Wired magazine's Danger Room blog. Many of us have gone through the same experience or received similar warnings from friends or family that someone's hacked their account and to be aware of suspicious messages. The difference is that the person complaining about being hacked in this case was "Yaman Mukhadab," a prominent poster inside what was supposed to be an elite password-protected forum for radicals, called Shumukh. Before he sent out his warning to the forum, the group had been engaged in such activities as assembling a "wish list" of American security industry leaders, defense officials and other public figures for terrorists to target and kill.

Mukhadab's cyber hardships—induced, of course, by counterterrorism agencies—illustrate how technology remains a double-edged sword. The realm of the Internet is supposed to be a fearful place, perfect for terrorists, and yet it can also work for us. Some counterterror experts argue that instead of playing a never-ending game of Whac-a-Mole—trying to track and then shut down all terrorist use of the Internet—it might be better to take advantage of their presence online. "You can learn a lot from the enemy by watching them chat online," Martin Libicki, a senior policy analyst at the Rand Corp., told the Washington Post.

While the cyber era allows terror groups to easily distribute the playbook of potential terrorist tactics, techniques and procedures, it also reveals to defenders which ones are popular and spreading. If individuals and groups can link up as never before, so too do intelligence analysts have unprecedented abilities to track them and map out social networks. This applies both to identifying would-be cyber terrorists designing malware as well as those still using the bombs and guns of the present world.

In 2008 and 2009, U.S. intelligence agencies reportedly tried to attack and shut down the top terrorist propaganda websites on the anniversary of 9/11, to try to delay the release of a bin Laden video celebrating the attacks. In 2010, however, they took a different tack. As Wired magazine reported, "The user account for al-Qaida's al-Fajr media distribution network was hacked and used to encourage forum members to sign up for Ekhlaas, a forum which had closed a year before and mysteriously resurfaced." The new forum was a fake, the equivalent of an online spider web, stickily entangling would-be terrorists and their fans.

The following year, a similar thing happened to the Global Islamic Media Front, a network for producing and distributing radical propaganda online. GIMF was forced to warn its members that the group's own encryption program, "Mujahideen Secrets 2.0," shouldn't be downloaded because it had been compromised. More amusing was the 2010 episode in which al-Qaida in the Arabian Peninsula posted the first issue of Inspire, an English-language online magazine designed to draw in recruits and spread terror tactics. Excited terrorist readers instead found the pages replaced by a PDF for a cupcake recipe, reportedly put there by hackers for British intelligence agencies. One can imagine deadlier forms of information corruption, such as changing the online recipes of how to make a bomb, so that a would-be bombmaker blows himself up during assembly.

We can look at the digital world with only fear or we can recognize that every new technology brings promise and peril. The advent of reliable post in the 1800s allowed the most dangerous terrorists of that time, anarchist groups, to correspond across state borders, recruiting and coordinating in a way previously not possible, and even to deploy a new weapon: letter bombs. But it also allowed police to read their letters and crack down on them. So, too, today with the digital post. When it comes to cyber terrorism versus the terrorist use of cyberspace, we must balance chasing the chimeras of our fevered imaginations with watching the information flows where the real action is taking place.

Critical Thinking

1. Why have terrorists not used cyber-attacks against the U.S.?

2. What is the difference between cyber-warfare and cyberterrorism?
3. Will the likelihood cyberterrorism increase?

Create Central

www.mhhe.com/createcentral

Internet References

www.policymic.com/articles/24908/cyber-terrorism-will-be-the-greatest-national-security-threat-in-the-21st-century

http://news.yahoo.com/anonymous-hackers-bring-down-north-korean-websites-second-224016100.html

PETER W. SINGER Director, 21st Century Defense Initiative Senior Fellow, Foreign Policy @peterwsinger

Unit 3

UNIT

Prepared by: Thomas J. Badey, *Randolph-Macon College*

State Sponsored Terrorism

The role of states in international terrorism has long been the subject of debate. It is clear that states often support foreign groups with similar interests. This support can take a number of forms. States may provide political support, financial assistance, safe havens, logistical support, training, or in some cases even weapons and equipment to groups that advocate the use of political violence. State support for terrorist organizations, however, does not necessarily translate into state *control* over terrorism.

As Martha Crenshaw has noted, "while terrorists exclude no donors on principle . . . the acceptance of support does not, however, bind clients to the wishes of their patrons." Nevertheless, since the passage of the Export Administration Act of 1979, the U.S. government has sought to hold some states responsible for the actions of groups they support. Section 6 (j) of the Export Administration Act requires the publication of an annual list of state sponsors of terrorism and thus provides the basis for contemporary U.S. anti-terrorism and sanctions policy. It bans arms-related exports and sales, restricts exports of dual-use items, prohibits economic assistance, and imposes financial restrictions.

The list currently includes states such as Iran, Sudan, and Syria. Iraq was removed in 2004, Libya in 2006, and North Korea in 2008. Most recently, President Obama announced plans to finally remove Cuba from that list. Not surprisingly, this list includes and previously has included only states perceived to be, for a wide variety of reasons, a threat to U.S. interests. States in which the United States has significant political or economic interests, such as Saudi Arabia and Pakistan, are, regardless of their record on terrorism, deliberately excluded.

In the first article in this unit, Ramtanu Maitra asserts that the sudden emergence of the Islamic State of Iraq and Syria (ISIS) was not "sudden" at all. It was the direct result of Saudi and Qatari funded indoctrination and training of Salafi-Wahhabi jihadis. Next, Daniel Byman examines the changing dynamics of state-sponsored terrorism. He concludes that the biggest challenge the United States faces is preventing "passive sponsorship" of terrorist organizations by states like Saudi Arabia, Iran, Pakistan, and Lebanon. In "Terrorism of Bygone Era," Paul Pillar challenges conventional wisdom by arguing that state-sponsored terrorism has declined over the past two decades, because Iran has realized that terrorism is no longer critical for its survival, the Soviet Union has disbanded, and globalization has increased the opportunity costs of being a pariah state.

Article   Prepared by: Thomas J. Badey *Randolph-Macon College*

ISIS: Saudi-Qatari-Funded Wahhabi Terrorists Worldwide

RAMTANU MAITRA

Learning Outcomes

After reading this article, you will be able to:

- Identify the objectives of ISIS.

- Understand the role of Saudi money in creating foreign Wahabbi terrorists.

- Discuss the role of foreign fighters in ISIS.

August 25—The sudden emergence of another organized militant Islamist-terrorist group, the Islamic State of Iraq and Syria (ISIS), aka the Islamic State of Iraq and the Levant (ISIL), or simply IS, along the Iraqi-Syria borders, was not really "sudden" at all. A series of West-organized military actions, particularly the Iraq invasion of 2003, invasion of Libya in 2011, and arming and facilitating the passage of Islamists and terrorists, in the garb of freedom fighters, to Syria to dismantle the Assad regime, has served to bring together thousands of hard-core Islamic terrorists, from as many as 50 countries, who have for years been funded and indoctrinated by the Saudis, Qataris, and Kuwaitis, with the "kill them all" Wahhabi-Salafi vision of Islam, to establish what ISIS calls the Islamic State.

That state currently encompasses a swath of land stretching from the outskirts of Baghdad in the east, to the outskirts of Aleppo in Syria, bordering Lebanon and Turkey, in the west. Estimates of the number of fighters that might be affiliated with ISIS vary from more than 10,000, to as many as 17,000.

While many policy errors have contributed to creating this horror, there is one center of evil with the *intention* of spreading such brutal sectarian warfare, which destroys civilization and nation-states alike. This center is in London, often dubbed "Londonistan," for its role as a center for incubating international terrorists. As we review the history of the creation of ISIS, keep in mind the reality that we are dealing here with a *London* imperial project being carried out through Saudi Arabia, other Gulf States, and sundry British tools.

Setting Up Sectarian War

Although this large group of Wahhabi-Salafi terrorists in Iraq and Syria, who are killing Shi'as, and grabbing large tracts of land for setting up a Wahhabi-Salafi Caliphate, has been much better organized and trained over the decades, it is not altogether different from the London-organized, Saudi-funded, and Pakistan-trained mujahideen in the 1980s, who showed up in Afghanistan to drive out the invading Soviet military. While the objective of the mujahideen brought in by Western powers was to drive the Soviets out of Afghanistan, and then become terrorists-for-hire, ISIS is busy setting up a Caliphate in Southwest Asia.

It is perhaps because of this distinction that the chairman of the U.S. Joint Chiefs of Staff, Gen. Martin Dempsey, told reporters on August 24, on his way to Afghanistan, that he believes ISIS is more of a regional threat, and is not currently plotting attacks against the U.S. or Europe. He also pointed out that there is no indication, as of now, that ISIS militants are engaged in "active plotting against the homeland, so it's different than that which we see in Yemen." In Yemen, al-Qaeda in the Arabian Peninsula (AQAP) has attempted attacks against Western countries.

There is no doubt that the threat that ISIS poses, as observed by General Dempsey, is a regional threat, and is primarily directed against Iran, Iran's allies, and Shi'as in general. But it also poses a serious threat to all Arab monarchies and countries such as Lebanon.

The objective of ISIS became evident from its actions in Iraq and Syria. It is clear that the staunchest promoters of anti-Shi'a ideology, which is aimed at undermining Shiite Iran, are the Saudi monarchy, the Qatari monarchy under the al-Thanis, and the Kuwaiti monarchy under the al-Sabahs. These monarchies are exporters of the Salafi-Wahhabi version of Sunni Islam, which does not accept Shi'as as Muslims, and considers them to be heretics who should be annihilated in order to purify Islam.

Saudi Fears and Coverups

Nonetheless, the rise of the ISIS and its military prowess, seen in its securing a large tract of land not too-distant from the Saudi Arabian borders, has evoked an existential fear in the House of Saud. In addition, the presence of thousands of Western jihadi fighters who could raise hell upon their return to their home countries, has also made the Americans, the British, the French, and some other European governments—friends of the Saudi-Qatari-Kuwaiti axis—a bit uneasy. In order to assuage their Western friends' fears, the Saudis have begun a propaganda campaign to convince others that they do not fund ISIS.

The West, with its vested interest in Saudi Arabia and other Sunni Gulf nations, has continued to defend Saudi Arabia; U.S. Secretary of State John Kerry went on record praising the Saudi Kingdom for donating $100 million to the UN Counter-Terrorism Centre. Riyadh is also spewing out the lie that the ISIS militants are not adherents to Wahhabism. In a statement to the August 23 London-based Saudi news daily *Asharq al-Awsat,* a spokesperson for the Royal Embassy of the Kingdom of Saudi Arabia in London said:

> Saudi Arabia wants the defeat and destruction of ISIS and other terrorist networks. Terrorist networks are as abhorrent to the government and people of the Kingdom of Saudi Arabia as they are to the governments and peoples of the rest of the world. . . . There have been suggestions that ISIS followers are members of some sort of Wahhabi absolutist sect. Indeed, certain UK media outlets often refer to Muslims within Saudi Arabia as Wahhabists. The unsubstantiated use of this invented connotation must end because it is untrue. Wahhabism is not a sect of Islam.

"Muhammad [Ibn] Abd Al-Wahhab was a scholar and jurist of the 18th century who insisted on the adherence to Qur'anic values and the teachings of the word of God as revealed to the Prophet Muhammad," the statement added. The Saudi spokesperson criticized Western media attempts to draw comparisons between Wahhabism and extremist ideology.

But some Western news media are not buying these denials by Riyadh and Washington about the Saudi-Qatari-Kuwaiti connections to ISIS. The British weekly *The Spectator,* on August 21, alluded to the common ideology of the Saudi and ISIS Wahhabists:

Saudi Arabia is a close ally of Britain and a keen customer of our killing machines, and like most of the Arab states is hostile to lunatic elements like ISIS and Hamas. Yet they are part of the problem; like many Islamists, including those in Britain, the Saudis are happy to condemn ISIS in what they do but not their basic ideology, largely because it mirrors their own.

The article pointed out that "the Saudi hostility to ISIS could even be described in Freudian terms as the narcissism of small differences. ISIS is dangerous to them because for those raised in the Saudi version of Islam, the Islamic State's even more extreme interpretation is not a huge leap."

Wahhabi "Peaceniks" of Yesteryear and Today's ISIS

In 1744, Muhammad ibn Saud and Muhammad ibn Abd al-Wahhab swore a traditional Muslim oath, in which they promised to work together to establish a state run according to Islamic principles. Until that time, the al-Saud family had been accepted as conventional tribal leaders whose rule was based on longstanding, but vaguely defined, authority. Ibn Abd al-Wahhab labeled all those who disagreed with him heretics and apostates, which, in his eyes, justified the use of force in imposing both his beliefs and his political authority over neighboring tribes. This in turn led him to declare holy war (jihad) on other Muslims (neighboring Arab tribes), an act which would otherwise have been legally impossible under the rules of jihad.

In 1802, the Wahhabis captured Karbala in Iraq, and destroyed the tomb of the Shi'ite Imam Husayn. In 1803, the Wahhabis captured the holy city of Mecca. The Ottoman Turks became alarmed, and in 1811, dispatched Muhammad Ali, the Ottoman ruler of Egypt, to challenge the Wahhabis. He succeeded in re-imposing Ottoman sovereignty in 1813. Nearly a century later, in 1901, with Wahhabi help, Saudi emir Abd al-Aziz al-Saud recaptured Riyadh. Al-Saud's sovereignty over the Arabian peninsula grew steadily until 1924, when his dominance became secure. At that point, the Wahhabis went on a rampage throughout the peninsula, smashing the tombs of Muslim saints and imams, including the tomb of the Prophet's daughter Fatima. Saudi Arabia was officially constituted as a kingdom in 1932.[1]

In *Newsweek* July 8, Lucy Westcott wrote,

The Islamist militant group ISIS has been destroying Iraq's Shiite mosques and religious shrines as it continues to put pressure on the country and further its extreme agenda. The AFP reported that four shrines that commemorated Sunni Arab or Sufi figures have been destroyed, while six Shiite mosques were demolished. The destruction seems to have been limited to Iraq's northern Nineveh province, including militant-held Mosul. One local resident told Al-Arabiya that members of the group had also occupied the Chaldean cathedral and the Syrian Orthodox cathedral, both in Mosul, removing their crosses and replacing them with the black flag of the Islamic State.

There is another hallmark that ties Wahhabism with ISIS like an umbilical cord. Human Rights Watch reported recently that Saudi Arabia has beheaded 19 people since the beginning of August. Some confessions may have been gained under torture, and one poor defendant was found guilty of sorcery. Beheading of *Kafirs* (in Arabic, a slur to describe non-believers) is also the high-profile act of both ISIS and al-Qaeda under Sheikh Osama bin Laden, another group that was a beneficiary of Saudi money and wide-ranging Gulf support.

ISIS beheaded the American journalist James Foley recently in Iraq; while another American journalist, Daniel Pearl, was beheaded in 2002 in Pakistan. In both cases, videos of the beheadings were widely circulated to rev up emotions among the Wahhabis.

The Financing of ISIS

In 2011, in Syria, when President Obama, Prime Minister David Cameron, and President François Hollande joined forces to remove Syria's elected President Bashir al-Assad from power, and thus deal a body blow to the Russians and the Iranians, who acknowledge Assad's legitimacy, not-so-militant groups within were bolstered by attaching them to well-trained Salafi-Wahhabi terrorists from a number of countries. While the Western countries were quite generous with arms, and worked with the neighboring countries to facilitate entry of arms into Syria, the bulk of the money came from the Salafi-Wahhabi bastions of Saudi Arabia, Qatar, and Kuwait.

Despite denials issued from Riyadh and Doha to quiet gullible Westerners, the funding of various Sunni groups seeking to establish Salafism and Wahhabism in a number of countries has long been well-documented. Sen. John McCain (R-Ariz.), for example, who is keen to see Assad, and the Russian influence over Syria, vanish altogether, praised the Saudis and Qataris for financial help lent to the Syrian "rebels," in a discussion on CNN, in January 2014,

"Thank God for the Saudis and Prince Bandar, and for our Qatari friends," the Senator repeated at the Munich Security Conference in late January. McCain praised Prince Bandar bin Sultan, head of Saudi Arabia's intelligence services and a former ambassador to the United States, for supporting forces fighting Assad in Syria. McCain and Sen. Lindsey Graham (R-S.C.) had previously met with Bandar to encourage the Saudis to arm Syrian rebel forces.[2]

But McCain was a bit off the mark. At the time he was bloviating on CNN, the "rebel" power in Syria was already firmly in the hands of ISIS—now an enemy of the U.S. Indeed, in Syria, where the moderate Friends of Syria (those who, according to what the White House conveyed to the American people in 2011–13, were the recipient of arms thanks to American and other Western largesse), Jabhat al-Nusra (a faction of al-Qaeda), and ISIS worked together in the early stages of the West-orchestrated and Saudi-Qatari-Kuwaiti-funded anti-Assad militancy. These groups used to carry their flags together during militant operations against Damascus; but that changed, and the Salafi-Wahhabis, having seized arms and ammunition from their earlier collaborators, became the powerhouse.

Now, it is evident that ISIS has enough killing power to loot and extort funds to sustain itself, and even grow.

How Saudi Money Created Foreign Wahhabi Terrorists

In 2010, Britain's news daily *The Guardian* citing Wikileaks, December 5, 2010, quoted U.S. Secretary of State Hillary Clinton saying that Saudi Arabia is the world's largest source of funds for Islamist militant groups such as the Afghan Taliban and Lashkar-e-Taiba (LeT)—but the Saudi government is reluctant to stem the flow of money. Both the Afghan Taliban and the LeT espouse the Wahhabi version of orthodox Islam. "More needs to be done," wrote *The Guaridan,* "since Saudi Arabia remains a critical financial support base for al-Qaida, the Taliban, LeT and other terrorist groups, says a secret December 2009 paper signed by the US secretary of state. Her memo urged US diplomats to redouble their efforts to stop Gulf money reaching extremists in Pakistan and Afghanistan."

"Donors in Saudi Arabia constitute the most significant source of funding to Sunni terrorist groups worldwide," she said.

Three other Arab countries are listed as sources of militant money: Qatar, Kuwait, and the United Arab Emirates. The cables highlight an often ignored factor in the Pakistani and Afghan conflicts: that the violence is partly bankrolled by rich, conservative donors across the Arabian Sea whose governments do little to stop them. The problem is particularly acute in Saudi Arabia, where militants soliciting funds slip into the country disguised as holy pilgrims, set up front companies to launder funds, and receive money from government-sanctioned charities.

In other words, a small fraction of the Saudi money may have gone directly to ISIS, but it is definitely Saudi money that armed and trained terrorists in Russia's Chechnya, Dagestan, North Ossetia, Ingushetia; in Pakistan; along the Afghanistan-Pakistan borders; in the Kyrgyzstan-Uzbekistan belt in Central Asia and also in Europe, particularly in Britain's Londonistan.

These militants have come in droves to the Syrian theater with their expertise to boost ISIS's killing power.

In short, the Saudis have shipped money, sermons, and volunteers to Afghanistan, Bosnia, and Russia's North Caucasus, just as they're doing now in Syria. In Chechnya, Saudis such as Ibn al-Khattab, Abu al-Walid, and Muhannad (all *noms de guerre*) indoctrinated, armed, and trained militants who mired the Chechens in an endless war that killed some 160,000 people, while forcing Chechen women into Saudi-style isolation, and throwing Chechnya, Dagestan, Ingushetia, and North Ossetia into turmoil. Many of these jihadis are now on full display in the Syria-Iraq theater on behalf of ISIS.

In Afghanistan, Saudi money, and the Pakistani military, backed by Saudi money and support, have created a relatively small, but hardcore, Wahhabi capability in a number of provinces. Although these Afghan Taliban were not notably visible in either Syria or Iraq, they have helped facilitate movement of Saudi-funded Wahhabi terrorists coming down from the north to participate in the Caliphate-formation war in Iraq and Syria.

In Pakistan, myriad Saudi-financed Wahhabi and anti-Shi'a terrorists are growing in strength, and trying to establish inroads into the Pakistani military; while in Afghanistan, the Saudi- and opium-funded Taliban, spewing Wahhabi venom, are trying to seize power again. In addition, Saudi money is also being distributed to build bases in several nations for recruitment and training of jihadis for future operations. It is evident that such a widespread operation cannot be carried out in stealth for years; it is therefore fair to assume that such base-building is done in collaboration with the targeted nation's intelligence community. These recruits remain available for use by the mother-nation. This became visible when the Libyan Islamic Fighters Group (LIFG) was used to dismantle the Libyan state and kill Colonel Qaddafi. Pakistan and Britain are two important centers where the Saudis operate hand-in-glove with those nations' intelligence apparatus.

Britain in the Spotlight

Take, for instance, the recent beheading of the American photo-journalist James Foley by a British jihadi working with ISIS. Whether the British jihadi actually carried out the execution, or not, it was evident that ISIS was keen to project its strength, boasting that it has muscle in developed countries, such as Britain. And, indeed, it has.

The identified British jihadi was a product of the East London Mosque, situated at the heart of Londonistan, in the borough of Tower Hamlets in East London. Londonistan is a world unto itself, where British intelligence recruits and trains Saudi-funded radical and criminal Sunni Muslims to kill and assassinate, and then deploys them wherever needed to serve the "Empire's interest."

Tower Hamlets is where the Shi'a-hating radical Saudi cleric and head Imam of Mecca, Sheikh Adel al-Kalbani (who last year was refused entry into Britain) went to meet local council leaders for a "private meeting" in 2008. He was the guest of the Mayor of Tower Hamlets, Lutfur Rahman, a fanatic Islamist who heads the Saudi-funded Jamaat-e-Islami in Britain. According to a Bangladeshi journalist, Tower Hamlets has been converted into the "Islamic Republic of Tower Hamlets" under the mayor. That statement was right on the mark.

On August 9, *The Guardian* reported that some 20 Asian youths had gathered around the Tower Hamlets gates, where a black flag, resembling that of ISIS, was hoisted. The flag was subsequently taken down by a Catholic nun.

Tower Hamlets is one of many centers where the Saudis breed their Wahhabi recruits. In 2013, when Sheikh al-Kalbani was denied entry to the U.K., followers of radical hate preacher Anjem Choudary, spokesman for the Islamist group Islam4UK, led a demonstration in London in May against Shi'a Muslims, three years after Islam4UK was officially proscribed, on January 14, 2010, under the U.K.'s counter-terrorism laws. In other words, the proscription of Islam4UK is a paper job to cover up that group's activities.

It is also evident that the Saudi funding for Wahhabi-indoctrinated jihadi fighters has not gone to waste. Among the ISIS foreign fighters, the Londonistan-created jihadists are the largest and most dominant group. *The Telegraph,* in an August 21 article, "More British Muslims fight in Syria than in U.K. Armed Forces," cited Khalid Mahmood, the Member of Parliament from Birmingham, another recruiting and training center of Londonistan, saying that "1,500 British Muslims have gone to wage jihad since 2011, as opposed to the 400–500 the government estimates and the 650 serving in the British armed forces."

The Saudi Role in 9/11: Hidden in the 28 Pages

Aug. 26—The most efficient means to root out the evil behind the so-called "Islamic State" (IS/ISIL/ISIS), is to bring out the truth about the pivotal Saudi role in the Sept. 11, 2001 terrorist attacks against the U.S. In recent weeks, coverage of the fight to declassify the suppressed 28 pages from the Congressional Joint Inquiry into 9/11 has been expanding, and repostings of *EIR/LPAC* material, posts from the new website 28 pages.org, and other sites, are becoming much more common.

The initiative taken in Congress by Rep. Walter Jones (R-N.C.) provides the means to force President Obama to declassify the material. House Concurrent Resolution 428 currently has 11 co-sponsors, and the campaign for getting it passed is getting increasing coverage. Notable new items are:

- Walter Jones has stepped up his campaign to get the suppressed 28 pages declassified and released to the public. In addition to an Aug. 18 interview on the Ron Paul Channel, Jones posted another short video on his Congressional website and on his Facebook site, urging people to get their Representatives on board. Jones has posted at least four Facebook messages, plus a number of Twitter messages, over the past week. In his video message, he states:

  "I deserve to know the truths hidden in the 28 classified pages of the Joint Inquiry Report on 9/11, and you do too. Please contact your member of Congress and ask them to join us in declassifying this information, by co-sponsoring our bill, H. Res. 428. Join Ron Paul's hashtag #declassify campaign and make your voice heard."

- Ron Paul. In addition to the interview with Jones, the former Congressman has posted an interview conducted with himself by a staff member, about the U.S.-Saudi relationship, and the 28 pages, on his "Voices of Liberty" website. Paul describes how he was astounded that a group of Saudis was allowed to fly out of the United States within days of the 9/11 attacks, without even being questioned by the FBI, and before anyone else was allowed to fly. The Saudis "are not exactly our best friends," Paul said, adding that some day this relationship will have to change, perhaps when we get a hold of the 28 pages of the 9/11 report.

- Patrick Cockburn. In his new book, *The Jihadis Return: ISIS and the New Sunni Uprising,* Patrick Cockburn, Middle East correspondent for *The Independent,* treats the Saudi relationship to IS, al-Qaeda, and other terrorist groups, at some length. An excerpt published in Tom Dispatch and Truthout,

notes that almost every significant element in the 9/11 attacks leads back to Saudi Arabia, but 9/11 investigators were repeatedly blocked when trying to get this information. In spite of this, Cockburn continues, "President George W. Bush apparently never even considered holding the Saudis responsible for what happened. . . . Most significant, 28 pages of the 9/11 Commission Report about the relationship between the attackers and Saudi Arabia were cut and never published, despite a promise by President Obama to do so, on the grounds of national security."

Notes

1. Ted Thornton, "The Wahhabi Movement, Eighteenth Century Arabia," *Islam Daily,* Dec. 7, 2004.
2. Steve Clemons, "Thank God for the Saudis: ISIS, Iraq, and the Lessons of Blowback," *The Atlantic,* June 23, 2014.

Critical Thinking

1. Compare the motives of ISIS with the motives of the Mujahedeen.
2. How does Saudi money fund ISIS?
3. What is the most efficient way to deter ISIS?

Internet References

IMF: Anti-Money Laundering/Combating the Financing of Terrorism
https://www.imf.org/external/np/leg/amlcft/eng/aml1.htm

The Washington Institute: Saudi Funding of ISIS
http://www.washingtoninstitute.org/policy-analysis/view/saudi-funding-of-isis

US Department of the Treasury: Terrorist Finance Tracking Program (TFTP)
http://www.treasury.gov/resource-center/terrorist-illicit-finance/Terrorist-Finance-Tracking/Pages/tftp.aspx

Article   Prepared by: Thomas J. Badey, *Randolph-Macon College*

Iran's Support for Terrorism in the Middle East

Daniel Byman

Learning Outcomes

After reading this article, you will be able to:

- Understand how Iran uses terrorism to further foreign policy interests.

- Identify the factors that make Iran more likely to support terrorism.

- Analyze the complex relationship between Iran and Hezbollah.

Chairman Kerry, Ranking Member Lugar, members of this distinguished Committee, and Committee staff, thank you for the opportunity to testify today.

Iran has long been one of the most important and dangerous sponsors of terrorism in the world. Although the Islamic Republic's motivations have varied over the years, its leaders have consistently viewed ties to and support for a range of terrorist groups as an important instrument of national power. Disturbingly, Iran's support for terrorism has become more aggressive in recent years, motivated by a mix of fear and opportunism. Iran could become even more aggressive in the years to come, exploiting the perceived protection it would gain if it developed a nuclear weapon or, if thwarted through military force or other means, using terrorists to vent its anger and take revenge. However, under current circumstances Tehran still remains unlikely to carry out the most extreme forms of terrorism, such as a mass-casualty attack similar to 9/11 or a strike involving a chemical, biological, or nuclear weapon.

The United States should work with its allies to continue and expand an aggressive intelligence campaign to thwart Iran and its terrorist surrogates. After 9/11, the United States engaged in a comprehensive campaign against al-Qa'ida: a similar global approach is needed to combat Iranian-backed terrorism. However, as the United States is already exerting tremendous pressure on Tehran via sanctions and diplomatic isolation because of Iran's nuclear program, there are few arrows left in America's quiver and thus the United States will find it hard to place additional pressure on Iran due to terrorism.

In this statement I first lay out Iran's motivations for supporting an array of terrorist groups. I then offer explanations for how, and why, Iran is becoming more aggressive in its use of terrorism in response to a rapidly changing region. I then detail the dilemma regarding terrorism and Iran's nuclear program: allowing Iran to get the bomb is dangerous in and of itself and may make Tehran more aggressive in supporting terrorists, but a military strike to destroy the program is likely to lead Iran to use terrorism to take revenge. I conclude by presenting implications and recommendations for U.S. policy.[1]

Iran's Motivations for Supporting Terrorism

Since the 1979 Islamic revolution that toppled the Shah's government, Iran's clerical leadership has worked with an array of terrorist groups to advance its interests. Over 30 years later, this use of terrorism has continued and remains an important foreign policy instrument for Iran in its confrontation with its neighbors and with the United States. In his 2012 testimony, Director of National Intelligence (DNI) James Clapper warned that Iran continues "plotting against U.S. or allied interests overseas."[2]

Iran's most important, and most well-known, relationship is with the Lebanese group, Hizballah. Iran helped midwife Hizballah and has armed, trained, and funded it to the tune of well over $100 million a year—perhaps far more, depending on the year and the methodology used for the estimate. Iran's military aid included not only small arms and other typical terrorist weapons, but also anti-tank guided missiles, anti-ship cruise missiles, and thousands of rockets and artillery systems, making Hizballah one of the most formidable sub-state groups in the world. Iranian personnel and Hizballah operatives have even done joint operations together.

Although Hizballah was long subservient to Iran, this relationship has gradually evolved. Increasingly, Hizballah is a partner to Tehran—its leader, Hassan Nasrallah, has considerable stature in the Arab world, and the group's military resistance to Israel is widely admired. Hizballah makes its own decisions with its own interests in mind.

Despite the increasing parity in the relationship, Tehran continues to work closely with Hizballah's leaders, and its intelligence and paramilitary personnel are tightly integrated with Hizballah's external security apparatus. Hizballah officials see their organization as Iran's ally, and Tehran's considerable financial and military support give it considerable clout with its friends in Hizballah.

Iran, however, has also backed a wide range of other groups. In Iraq it has worked with an array of Shi'a factions. Tehran also has ties to Sunni groups including Iraqi Kurdish organizations, Palestine Islamic Jihad, and Hamas. Perhaps most striking, Iran has even allied at times with al-Qa'ida and the Taliban even though these groups are often violently anti-Shi'a and see Iran's leaders as apostates.

One motivation for backing many of these groups is and remains ideological. At the creation of the Islamic Republic, Iran's leaders made no secret of their desire to extend Iran's revolution throughout the Muslim world. Iran's first Supreme Leader and founding ideologue, Ayatollah Ruhollah Khomeini, declared that Iran "should try hard to export our revolution to the world."[3] Khomeini's goal is embedded in Iran's constitution and the charter documents of key organizations such as the Islamic Revolutionary Guard Corps (IRGC).

To this end, Iran worked with a variety of Shi'a groups, most successfully the Lebanese Hizballah but also Shi'a militants in Iraq, Bahrain, Pakistan, Afghanistan, and elsewhere, organizing them against rival groups and often against their host governments. Iran did this in part because it wanted to spread its revolutionary ideology, and it found some receptive adherents among embattled and oppressed Shi'a groups throughout the Muslim world, particularly in the years immediately after the revolution when the charismatic Ayatollah Khomeini was able to inspire many Shi'a communities to support his leadership, or at least admire his new regime.

As its revolutionary fervor has worn off, Tehran increasingly employed terrorists for an array of strategic purposes. These include non-Shi'a terrorist groups with whom it gains little ideological sympathy. In addition, Iran has used even its closest terrorist allies, such as the Lebanese Hizballah, for strategic purposes. These purposes include:

- *Undermining and bleeding rivals.* Iran has regularly used terrorist groups to weaken governments it opposes. This has included bitter enemies like Saddam Hussein's Iraq and also lesser foes like the rulers of Kuwait and Saudi Arabia. Tehran also backs a wide array of insurgent groups that also use terrorism in places like Iraq and Afghanistan. These groups may advance Iran's interests in key countries or, at the very least, undermine the position of rivals.

- *Power projection and playing spoiler.* Tehran has a weak military and only limited economic clout. Its ideological appeal at the height of its revolutionary power was limited, and today it is paltry. Nevertheless, Iran's regime sees itself as a regional and even a world power, and working with terrorists is a way for Iran to influence events far from its borders. Iran's support for the Lebanese Hizballah, Palestine Islamic Jihad, and Hamas make Iran a player in the Israeli-Palestinian and Israeli-Arab disputes. This in turn gives Iran stature and sway in the broader Middle East. Iran has supported groups whose attacks disrupted Israeli-Palestinian and Israeli-Syrian peace negotiations—a victory for Iran, which sees the negotiations as a betrayal of the Muslim cause and as a means of isolating the clerical regime. Tehran has also repeatedly assassinated opponents of the regime who lived in exile in Europe or in other supposedly safe areas, using its own operatives and those of terrorist allies like Hizballah to do so.

- *Gaining a voice in opposition councils.* For Iran, it was often important not just that an enemy regime lose power or be weakened, but that particular strands within an opposition get stronger. So in Lebanon, Iran undermined Amal, a Shi'a militia, because it did not share Iran's ideology and interests. Tehran helped found Hizballah to replace it—a risky gamble that paid off but could have easily backfired on Iran. In general, Iran has used weapons, training, money, and other support to try to unify potential militant allies and otherwise improve its position among the opposition.

- *Deterrence.* By having the ability to work with terrorists and to subvert its enemies, Iran is able to press them to distance themselves from the United States or to refrain from joining economic or military efforts to press Iran. Such efforts, however, often backfire: because these states see Iran as meddling in their domestic affairs and supporting violence there, they often become more, not less, willing to support economic or even military pressure directed at Tehran.

- *Preserving options.* As a weak state—one with little ability to coerce via military or economic pressure—in a hostile region, Tehran also seeks to keep its options open. Iranian leaders recognize that in Iraq, Afghanistan, and other turbulent countries, those in power today may be on the sidelines tomorrow and vice versa. In addition, they may want cordial relations with a neighbor at present but understand that circumstances may change in the future. So Iran courts and supports a range of violent groups even when it does not seek to exploit their capabilities under current circumstances. These groups can then be employed should Iran want to ratchet up pressure or punish an enemy.

Because Tehran's logic is often more strategic than ideological, Iran is willing to work with avowed enemies, though mutual mistrust limits the closeness of any relationship. So although many al-Qa'ida supporters loath Iran, and some of them have killed Shi'a in Iraq, Pakistan, Afghanistan, and elsewhere with abandon, Iran has worked with al-Qa'ida, at times allowing its operatives to transit Iran with little interference. Tehran has also given some al-Qa'ida operatives a limited safe haven, though at the same time it often curtails their movements and has even turned some over to the custody of their home governments. Using a similar logic, Tehran at times work with the Taliban, with which Iran almost went to war in 1998, because they have mutual enemies and to preserve Iran's options.

By working through terrorist groups like Hizballah or using its own operatives in a clandestine way, Tehran has been able to distance itself from attacks and thus often evade responsibility. Even in cases like the 1996 Khobar Towers bombing, where Iran was ultimately found to be responsible, the time involved in proving Iranian culpability made it far harder to gain political and diplomatic support for a robust response. So deniability also makes terrorism an attractive option, allowing Iran to strike back but avoid the consequences of open aggression. So Iran is less likely to use mines and anti-ship cruise missiles to try to close the Strait of Hormuz, but could instead use terrorist attacks [that] can be hard to trace directly to Tehran.

Although it is always tempting to attribute a strategic motive to all of Iran's behavior, Iran's leaders have at times used terrorism simply to take revenge on their opponents. Tehran struck at France and the Gulf states in the 1980s, for example, because they supported Baghdad during the Iran-Iraq war. Similarly, some Iranian attacks on Israeli targets may in part be spurred by Iran's belief that Israel is behind the killing of Iranian nuclear scientists—Iran's actions may be as much about revenge as they are about any putative deterrence. Hizballah, Iran's close ally has also vowed revenge for the killing in Damascus in 2008 of the leader of its operations wing, Imad Mughniyah, believed to be at Israeli hands.

How and Why Iran Is Changing

Iran aggressively supported an array of terrorist groups in the 1980s, especially the Lebanese Hizballah. Since the 1990s, Iran also championed Palestinian groups like Palestine Islamic Jihad and Hamas, supporting their efforts to carry out attacks in Israel and in the Palestinian territories. Tehran also worked with anti-U.S. insurgent groups in Afghanistan and Iraq. In terms of support for terrorism outside these theaters, however, the last Iranian-organized anti-U.S. attack was the 1996 strike on Khobar Towers, which killed 19 Americans. Yet Tehran has shown a renewed emphasis on terrorism outside the Israel/Lebanon/ Palestine theater or war zones like Iraq and Afghanistan in the last year. Israel has been a particular focus, but Saudi Arabia and the United States also appear to be in Iran's sights:

- On July 18, 2012, a suicide bomber blew himself up on a bus carrying Israeli tourists in Bulgaria, killing five Israelis, the driver, and himself and wounding over thirty. Israeli officials blamed Iran, though investigations to determine culpability are still underway;
- Several days before the Bulgaria attack, a Lebanese Hizballah operative was arrested in Cyprus, where he was believed to be planning attacks on Israeli targets;
- In 2012, Iranian plots against Israel were thwarted in Thailand, Georgia, and Azerbaijan;
- In 2012, Iran carried out bombings in India and Georgia. In New Delhi, an explosion wounded the wife of the Israeli defense envoy and other passengers in her car;
- Kenya authorities arrested two Iranian men believed to be IRGC members in June 2012. The men admitted they were planning attacks. Possible targets included American, Israeli, Saudi, or British personnel and facilities;
- In October 2011, the United States disrupted a plot to kill the Saudi Ambassador in Washington by bombing the restaurant where he often ate lunch. According to U.S. officials, the planned bombing was orchestrated by Iran. Had the bomb gone off as planned, it would also have killed many U.S. citizens dining at the restaurant;
- Israeli security officials claim that in the last two years Iran and Hizballah have plotted attacks in more than twenty countries.

The aggressive pace of attacks against Israel, taken together with the plot against the Saudi Ambassador in Washington, indicates that Iran's use of terrorism is becoming more aggressive. In the past, Iranian-backed groups like Hizballah did not strike in the United States, seeing it instead as a place to raise money and gain valuable specialized equipment, such as night-vision goggles. Now, however, Iran appears willing to risk this access as well as the wrath of the United States. As DNI Clapper contended, "The 2011 plot to assassinate the Saudi Ambassador to the United States shows that some Iranian officials—probably including Supreme Leader Ali Khamenei—have changed their calculus and are now more willing to conduct an attack in the United States in response to real or perceived US actions that threaten the regime."[4]

A mix of fear and opportunism are driving Iran. As with other countries in the Middle East, the Arab spring shook Iran. At first, Tehran tried to portray the revolution as a victory for Islamist and anti-U.S. forces, given that key allies of the United States like Mubarak fell during the turbulence. The new movements, however, evince little sympathy toward Tehran though some new leaders want to normalize relations to a greater degree. Indeed, some of the Islamist movements that are rising to power are exceptionally critical of Iran's form of Islamic governance.

Most important to Iran, however, has been the crisis in Syria where, slowly, Bashar al-Asad's regime has been pushed to the wall. Tehran has few allies in the Arab world, and indeed in the world in general, but Syria is a true friend. The loss of Syria would be a huge blow to Iran, reducing its ability to meddle in Lebanon and in the Israeli-Palestinian and Israeli-Arab arenas. From Iran's point of view, the campaign against Syria is also part of the broader campaign to weaken Iran. Iranian and Hizballah officials have made repeated statements blaming the United States and Israel for the unrest in Syria, though it is not clear how much they believe their own rhetoric.

Palestinian politics have also shifted markedly and for the worse from Tehran's point of view. After Hamas' founding in 1987, the relationship between Iran and Hamas was polite but limited. Hamas received money, arms, and training from Iran and Hizballah, but Hamas kept Tehran at arms' length, as its leaders were determined to avoid dependence on foreign sponsors, which had often doomed other Palestinian organizations. Ties became far stronger when Hamas seized power in Gaza in 2007 and, facing international isolation, sought more aid from Iran as well as weapons systems. Now this relationship has frayed. Open ties to Iran, always unpopular among many Sunni Islamists, are further tarnished because of Tehran's support for the regime oppression in Syria. Hamas' leadership has largely left Syria, going to Egypt and other countries. Some Hamas leaders have also criticized the Asad regime's crackdown and, in so doing, implicitly criticized Iran's support for Damascus. So Iran has lost influence with its most important Palestinian partner and lost support among Palestinians in general.

Tehran also sees Israel and the United States as on the offensive. The killing of Iranian nuclear scientists, explosions that destroyed Iranian missile facilities, the cyber attack that set back Iran's nuclear program, and other aggressive, but covert, measures are considered part of a low-level but nevertheless real war that the United States and Israel are engaged in—one that has escalated in recent years. From Iran's point of view, its own violence is a response to the war that is already being waged against the clerical regime.

The impressive sanctions the United States and its allies have orchestrated against Iran have hit the regime hard. Regime officials have admitted that the sanctions are causing Tehran serious economic problems, a rare public confession that U.S. policy is having an impact, as opposed to the usual rhetoric of defiance. In addition, the cutback in oil purchases from Iran's important customers has led to a plunge in the price and volume of Iran's most important export and lifeblood of the Iranian economy. Beyond the economic impact, the success of these measures also reinforces Tehran's sense of diplomatic isolation.

Yet even as Iran feels the pressure, it also believes that it can fight back. Iranian officials see the United States as on its heels given its withdrawal from Iraq and the coming drawdown in Afghanistan. In both instances, the United States initially vowed to transform the country and isolate pro-Iranian voices. In Iraq, Iran today is the most influential outside power, particularly in Shia areas though Iran also has sway in the Kurdish north. Iran is less powerful in Afghanistan, where Pakistan is the dominant force backing anti-U.S. and anti-regime elements. However, there too the United States is leaving without achieving its proclaimed objectives, and anti-U.S. forces may fill the void. In both cases, the violence in these countries—supported in part by Iran—was a major factor influencing U.S. decisions to reduce its commitment. So from Iran's point of view, the lesson is simple: hit the United States hard and persistently, and it will back down.

A shift in domestic politics may also explain Tehran's more aggressive policies. Since the early 1990s, it has been common to divide the complex Iranian political scene and describe it as a battle between "hardliners" and "pragmatists." And during the tenure of President Mohammad Khatami (1997–2005) and the so-called Green Revolution (2009) there was hope that Tehran would reform and embrace a more moderate foreign policy or even that the clerical regime as we know it would collapse. In crushing the reformist movement and the Green Revolution, Iran's hardline camp has narrowed the Iranian political scene. Within elite ranks, there are fewer voices that question the value of ties to terrorists. In recent years hardliners from the IRGC have entered politics in greater numbers and assumed more important positions in the national security bureaucracy. For the most part these individuals are not fanatical, but they have a worldview that sees revolutionary violence as valuable for its own sake and an important tool of state.

The Nuclear Dilemma

From a counterterrorism point of view, the question of how to respond to Iran's nuclear program is fraught with problems. The so-called shadow war between Israel and Iran, as the Bulgaria attack may indicate, has created a retaliatory dynamic, with Iran feeling compelled to respond to what it sees as Israeli aggression. This sentiment comes from a desire to prove to the Iranian population at large that its government is responding, anger within key elite audiences (particularly the IRGC) and a sense of humiliation, and a strong belief in revenge. So as long as Israel and other states use low-level attacks on Iran and maintain a high degree of economic and political pressure, Iran is likely to attempt terrorist attacks as a response.

If Israel and/or the United States did a direct military strike on Iran's suspected nuclear facilities, the Iranian terrorist response would be considerable. Because Iran supports terrorists in part to keep its options open, now would be the time for Tehran to call in favors. We could expect attempted terrorist attacks around the world—Iran and Hizballah have shown a presence in every inhabited continent. Tehran would also try to call in favors from groups like al-Qa'ida, Palestine Islamic Jihad, and others with whom it has relationships, though these groups would be far less dependable and their personnel are less skilled than those of Hizballah. In addition, Iran would be particularly likely to step up support for anti-U.S. forces in Afghanistan and elsewhere in its neighborhood. The scope and scale of the response would depend on the level of casualties from any attack and the political circumstances of the regime in Tehran at the time the attack occurred. However, Iran would be likely to attempt multiple attacks, and it would also consider strikes on the American homeland as well as American diplomatic, military, and civilian institutions worldwide.

Should Iran acquire a nuclear weapon, however, the picture is likely to change considerably. To be clear, Iran acquiring a nuclear weapon is bad for the United States and its allies in a host of ways, and preventing this should be a top goal of any U.S. administration. If U.S. policy fails and Iran does acquire a nuclear weapon, it is difficult to predict how Tehran would behave. Some scholars have argued the theoretical point that, in general, nuclear weapons make states more cautious as they fear the potentially catastrophic escalation that a nuclear crisis could bring about. Thus Iran, more secure due to the nuclear weapons and more cautious because of the associated risks, would be more restrained in its foreign policy.[5] More likely, though hardly inevitable, is that Tehran might become emboldened by a nuclear weapon. Currently the threat of U.S. conventional retaliation is an important check on Iranian behavior, as Tehran recognizes that its forces are no match for the United States. A nuclear weapon, however, would give Tehran the ability to threaten a devastating response should it be attacked with conventional forces. This "umbrella" would then enable Iran to be more aggressive supporting substate groups like Hizballah or opposition forces against various Arab enemies. The model here would be Pakistan: after acquiring a nuclear capability, and thus it believed a degree of immunity from India's superior conventional forces, Islamabad became more aggressive supporting various insurgent and terrorist groups in Kashmir and fighting New Delhi in general.

The silver lining is that Iran is not likely to pass a nuclear weapon to terrorist groups except under the most extreme circumstances. Tehran would not be likely to trust such a sensitive capability to a terrorist group—too much could go too wrong in too many ways. In addition, even a more emboldened Tehran would recognize that the United States and Israel would see such a transfer as a grave threat and would dramatically escalate their pressure on Iran, perhaps including significant military operations. In addition, the United States might be able to gain international support as almost all states, including China and Russia, fear such transfers. Moscow and Beijing have their own terrorism problems. While deniability might stay the U.S. hand from retaliation for a limited conventional attack, this would not be so for a more dramatic chemical attack, to say nothing of a catastrophic nuclear one. After an attack using unconventional weapons, all bets would be off. One indication of Iran's caution on this score is that it has not transferred much less lethal and controversial chemical weapons to Hizballah, despite having these in its arsenal for over 25 years. Groups like Hizballah, for their part, would fear the consequences of going nuclear, recognizing that this could lead to U.S., Israeli, and other countries' military actions that could threaten its position in Lebanon. In addition, these groups have proven quite capable in using rockets, explosives, and small arms to achieve their objectives.

However, should the clerical regime believe itself to be facing an imminent threat of regime change from the United States and its allies—a situation comparable to what Saddam Hussein faced in 2003 say—then the calculus would change dramatically. From Tehran's point of view, the United States and others would have already escalated beyond the point of no return. Tehran would have nothing to lose, and at least a chance of intimidating or deterring the United States, by such transfers. They might also fear that preemptive U.S. strikes would stop them from being able to launch their deterrent so transferring some items to a terrorist group would enable them to keep open the threat of a response even if much of their country were occupied. In addition, Iranian leaders may seek revenge or simply want to vent their rage and use terrorists to do so.

Policy Recommendations

Because Iran's use of terrorism often follows a strategic and rational logic, U.S. policy can affect Tehran's calculus on whether to support groups, and on how much to do so.

A first U.S. step is to expand efforts with allies to fight Iranian-backed terrorism, including by Hizballah. Too often Hizballah has gotten a free pass with U.S. allies because it also engages in political and social welfare activity, leading some states to try to distinguish between its "legitimate" and "illegitimate" sides. By making it clear that any use of or support for terrorism by Hizballah is illegitimate, allies would push the Lebanese organization toward ending or at least reducing its use of violence.

In addition, the intelligence and police campaign against Hizballah and Iran could be ramped up, leading to more investigations, arrests, and disruptions that make it far harder for the group and for Iranian officials to conduct successful attacks. Allies should also be encouraged to reduce the size of the Iranian diplomatic mission, as in some countries many of its true activities are related to intelligence gathering and support for militant organizations.

The United States has long made Iran's subversive networks and ties to Hizballah an intelligence priority. However, given the global reach of this adversary, a global response is necessary. This requires working with allies around the world, just as the United States has done against al-Qa'ida. Indeed, these friends are often, though not always, the same allies who are partners against al-Qa'ida, but it is vital to ensure—with financial and other support as appropriate—that they are also targeting Hizballah and other Iranian-backed groups. Hizballah, however, is seen as legitimate by many governments, or at the very least is not loathed by all as is al-Qa'ida. So it will be hard to conduct as comprehensive a campaign without considerable and sustained efforts.

Making the challenge harder, the United States has relatively few additional means of pressure to deploy directly against Iran because it is already using most of them to stop Iran's nuclear programs. Sanctions—targeted and broad—are already implemented against an array of Iranian targets. They have been expanded dramatically under the Obama administration and this effort should continue, but it will be hard to do much more under current political circumstances. Any terrorist actions or aggressive ones on the nuclear front, however, should be leveraged for the other issue. So when a terrorist attack does occur, Washington should press for more to be done on the nuclear front, as such actions create an opportunity for political engagement.

The United States must also set clear "red lines" regarding terrorism. For example U.S. officials should emphasize that attacks on the American homeland will meet with a severe response. Vital to the success of this, however, is deciding in advance what a response would be if a red line were crossed and then having the will and ability to carry out the response should this happen. On Iran's nuclear program and on its actions in Iraq and Afghanistan, Tehran repeatedly crossed U.S. red lines in the last decade with relatively few consequences, reducing the credibility of future U.S. threats. If the United States is not serious about a response, it is better not to threaten at all.

Another priority is trying to sever the links between Iran and al-Qa'ida. In contrast to Hizballah, al-Qa'ida is not ideologically close to Tehran and does not appear to have done joint operations. On the other hand, al-Qa'ida is far more willing to conduct large-scale indiscriminate attacks, including the use of chemical, biological, or nuclear weapons should they ever fall into the hands of Zawahiri's organization. At the same time, Iran has become more important to al-Qa'ida in recent years as regime pressure on the organization there has eased and the drone program in Pakistan has made that country a more difficult haven. Tehran, however, has largely gotten a free pass on the significant al-Qa'ida presence in its borders.

Limited military strikes, which often fail against terrorist groups or quasi-states like the Taliban's Afghanistan, have more of a chance of succeeding against countries like Iran, that have a real military and economic infrastructure. Demonstrative uses of forces, such as the 1987 and 1988 U.S. operations (Nimble Archer and Praying Mantis, respectively) that sank part of the Iranian navy, can reinforce U.S. deterrence if Iran crosses red lines. Because of Iran's severe economic difficulties, even the threat of such strikes would be taken seriously by Iranian leaders.

The fall of the Asad regime in Syria is desirable and would reduce Iran's influence, but it would not dramatically change Tehran's support for terrorism and may even increase Iran's reliance on substate groups. Although Hizballah would lose an important patron should the regime in Damascus change, and it would be harder to ship weapons to Lebanon via Syria, the importance of Hizballah would grow for Iran. It remains relatively easy to send weapons to Lebanon without transiting Syria, and Hizballah's role in the Lebanese government (and control of Beirut's airport) makes it almost impossible to stop the flow of weapons there. So Iran may end up doubling down on substate groups if it loses its main regional ally.

In the end, Iran's lack of strategic options and desire to respond to what it sees as a hostile world will lead Tehran to continue to work with a range of terrorist groups and selectively use violence. Successful U.S. policy can reduce the scope and scale of Iranian violence, but it is not likely to end it altogether.

Notes

1. This testimony draws extensively on two of my books: *Deadly Connections: States that Sponsor Terrorism* (Cambridge,

2005) and *A High Price: The Triumphs and Failures of Israeli Counterterrorism* (Oxford, 2011). Also relevant to my testimony and to this hearing are my articles, "Iran, Terrorism, and Weapons of Mass Destruction," *Studies in Conflict and Terrorism* Vol. 31 (2008), pp. 169–181 and "The Lebanese Hizballah and Israeli Counterterrorism," *Studies in Conflict and Terrorism,* Vol. 34 (2011), pp. 917–941.

2. James Clapper, "U.S. Intelligence Community Worldwide Threat Assessment," January 31, 2012. http://www.cfr.org/intelligence/clappers-testimony-worldwide-threat-assessment-january-2012/p27253

3. As quoted in Anoushiravan Ehteshami, *After Khomeini* (Routledge, 1995), p. 131.

4. Clapper, "U.S. Intelligence Community Worldwide Threat Assessment."

5. See most prominently Kenneth N. Waltz, "Why Iran Should Get the Bomb," *Foreign Affairs* (July/August 2012), http://www.foreignaffairs.com/articles/137731/kenneth-n-waltz/why-iran-should-get-the-bomb

Critical Thinking

1. Where do Hezbollah's and Iran's interests converge?
2. How have Iran and Hezbollah used Africa as a platform to further their goals?
3. What steps should be taken to prevent Iran's sponsorship of terrorism?

Internet References

Council on Foreign Relations: State Sponsors: Iran
http://www.cfr.org/iran/state-sponsors-iran/p9362

The Jerusalem Post: The Iran-Hezbollah terror connection: What must be done?
http://www.jpost.com/Opinion/Op-Ed-Contributors/The-Iran-Hezbollah-terror-connection-What-must-be-done-319577

United States Institute of Peace: Understanding the Iran-Hezbollah Connection
http://www.usip.org/publications/understanding-the-iran-hezbollah-connection

Daniel Byman, "Iran's Support for Terrorism in the Middle East," United States Senate Committee on Foreign Relations, July 25, 2012.

Article   Prepared by: Thomas J. Badey, *Randolph-Macon College*

Terrorism of a Bygone Era

PAUL R. PILLAR

Learning Outcomes

After reading this article, you will be able to:

- Identify examples of state-sponsored terrorist attacks.

- Explain the political, economic, and military costs of state sponsorship.

- Discuss the future of state-sponsored terrorism.

After peaking in the 1980s, the practice has declined since the fall of the Soviet Union.

The death of Abdel Basset Ali al-Megrahi in Libya means the departure of a living link to an era of terrorism that was much different from what we see today. The 1980s was the peak of modern state-fomented international terrorism. The decade began with American diplomats being held hostage in Tehran. The next few years saw lethal terrorism carried out directly by several states. Iran conducted a sustained campaign of assassination of exiled Iranian dissidents. Syria attempted to blow up Israeli airliners. North Korea blew up a South Korean airliner and conducted a bombing in Burma intended to kill the visiting South Korean president. The Libyan regime of Muammar Qaddafi was active in terrorism on multiple fronts, including the bombing of a night club in Berlin frequented by U.S. servicemen. And it was Qaddafi's regime that killed 270 people by bombing Pan Am flight 103 in 1988—a crime for which Megrahi was the only person ever convicted.

State-sponsored international terrorism declined precipitously over the subsequent two decades. Some of the reasons were specific to particular states that had been leading practitioners, such as the survival of the Islamic Revolution in Iran and the subsequent realization of rulers in Tehran that constant assassinations and subversion in neighboring states were not critical to keeping their regime alive. Two other factors had more general application. One was the end of the Cold War and demise of the Soviet Union, which had been an important source of aid to a state such as Syria—aid substantially greater than what Russia provides today. The other, related, factor was globalization and the escalation of opportunity costs of being a pariah state. Those costs, political as well as economic, provided the motivation for Qaddafi to get out of international terrorism (as well as out of the making of unconventional

weapons) later in the 1990s, making this one of the most successful uses of international sanctions. The explicit demand associated with the sanctions was for Libya to surrender the two main Pan Am 103 suspects, Megrahi and Al Amin Khalifa Fhimah (who was tried along with Megrahi in a Scottish court but acquitted), which it did in 1999. This quickly led to secret talks with the United States that culminated four years later in a formal agreement between Libya and both the United States and United Kingdom.

Megrahi was a low-ranking figure who did not initiate anything significant but whose case exemplified some larger patterns in international terrorism. Little fish who execute plans and expose themselves to leaving evidence and getting caught tend to get caught more often than the big fish who are the true initiators of an operation. Megrahi performed acts that involved the killing of many innocent victims; he was deserving of punishment for his role in terrorism. There always was an element of artificiality in his prosecution, however, in that he was an employee of a state and following orders from others. Megrahi's release and return to Libya also exhibited some of the trade-offs and tensions involved in counterterrorism. The justification for his release was humanitarianism in light of the metastatic prostate cancer that was said to be weeks away from killing him, although he would live for another three years. Accusations were made at the time—and denied by British officials—that a desire for oil deals with the Libyan government had something to do with letting him go.

The Pan Am 103 operation demonstrated some other realities about international terrorism. One is how much the success of a terrorist plot, and whether it is discovered either before or after it is executed, depends on small accidental details. The timer on the bomb that Megrahi planted in luggage was set to go off while the plane was over the Atlantic, with the intention that the physical evidence would be lost in the ocean. A late departure of the flight meant that the plane came down instead on land, providing the scraps that enabled a long and painstaking investigation to tie the bomb to Libya. If the departure had been even later and the bomb detonated while the plane was on the ground or well below cruising altitude, it probably would have killed no one—and there still would have been the evidence to implicate the Libyans.

Another lesson concerns what would stimulate even a government as warped as Qaddafi's regime to do something as horrible as taking down that airliner. The bombing of Pan Am 103 was very likely Qaddafi's response to the U.S. aerial assault on Libya in 1986.

Critical Thinking

1. What effect did the fall of the Soviet Union have on state-sponsored terrorism?
2. Has state sponsorship of terrorist organizations declined?
3. What are the potential benefits and drawbacks for states that sponsor terrorist organizations?

Create Central

www.mhhe.com/createcentral

Internet References

www.state.gov/j/ct/list/c14151.htm
www.vice.com/vice-news/sofex-the-business-of-war-part-1

Unit 4

International Terrorism

UNIT

Prepared by: Thomas J. Badey, *Randolph-Macon College*

International Terrorism

International terrorism has changed significantly over time. Simply said, it has become more complex. Increased organizational complexity, improved communications, and an increased willingness to cause mass casualties, pose new challenges for the international community.

Individuals and small groups dominated international terrorism in the 1970s. Larger groups and organizations played an important role in international terrorism in the 1980s. More complex terrorist networks emerged in the 1990s. Some of these operational networks have been replaced by what some experts describe as ideological networks spawning regional affiliates and inspiring small independent groups and individuals throughout the world. These small groups, sometimes referred to as B.O.G.s (Bunch of Guys) have emerged to carry out attacks in cities like Madrid, London, Boston, and Paris in support of the broad ideological goals of new global movements.

Today's terrorists appear to operate at all levels of organization. From ideologically affiliated individuals carrying out "lone Wolf" style attacks on local targets to large scale insurgencies such as Boko Haram and ISIS controlling significant territory in a number of countries, terrorists are carrying out attacks around the globe. Sometimes they act locally or regionally to pursue independent agendas. At other times they take advantage of cross-national links to obtain greater access to weapons, training, or financial resources. On occasion, they may temporarily set aside local interests and objectives to cooperate within loosely connected international networks to support broader ideological objectives. At a given point in time international terrorists can be engaged in activities at all levels, posing unique challenges to those engaged in the study of, and struggle against, international terrorism.

Modern communications technologies have also changed the way international terrorists operate. The cell phone and the laptop computer have become as important as the bomb and the AK-47 in the terrorist arsenal. The Internet and social media have provided terrorists with instant access to a global audience and have enhanced their ability to exchange information and an effective vehicle to rally their supporters. Almost all major international terrorist organizations operate their own websites and communicate via the Internet and social media.

A particularly disturbing trend in contemporary international terrorism is the increasing willingness by some terrorists to cause mass casualties. While, the potential causes of this trend are subject to debate, this trend has elevated terrorism to the top of the international agenda. While, over the past several decades, the number of international terrorist incidents has declined, the casualties caused by international terrorism have steadily increased. More importantly, this trend has focused international attention on terrorist methods deemed unlikely only a few years ago. Potential threats posed by biological, chemical, or radiological weapons are again at the forefront of international concern.

The selections in this unit reflect some of the diversity in international terrorism. The first article in this section focuses on the probability of the occurrence of another catastrophic terrorist event like 9/11. While he believes the occurrence of such an event is empirically unlikely, he concedes that American political leaders are likely to continue to overcommit resources to counterterrorism, because of inherent human and political tendencies of risk aversion. In the next article, Alex Waterman looks at ISIS' mentoring of jihadist groups in North Africa. While he believes that the financial, military, and political growth of ISIS will lead to closer ties with groups in North Africa, he argues that ISIS' expansion in North Africa has been limited by its goal to establish regional dominance in areas where groups are fighting local conflicts. In the third article of this section, Mahmood Ahmad Muzafar explores the root causes of terrorism in South Asia. He argues that in order to find a lasting solution for terrorism in South Asia, it is necessary to find and address the root causes of terrorism in this region. Finally, Philip K. Abbott examines the decades long conflict between the FARC and the Colombian government. He argues that a resolution of the ongoing conflict is unlikely because the length of the conflict in Colombia has created social-psychological barriers on both sides. He asserts that the conflict is so deeply rooted that instead of being resolved it is likely to be passed on to the next generation.

Article   Prepared by: Thomas J. Badey, *Randolph-Macon College*

Transnational Terrorism

STEPHEN KRASNER

Learning Outcomes

After reading this article, you will be able to:

- Understand the statistical likelihood of a terrorist attack.

- Explain reasons for the large allocation of resources committed to counterterrorism.

- Discuss the role of public opinion in political decision-making on counterterrorism.

The 9/11 attack was a stunning event with long-term consequences for stability in the Middle East and even the global order that have yet to play themselves out. Almost from the outset, the attacks generated two very different interpretations of the state of the world and the threat that transnational terrorism posed for the United States. The first is the position adopted by the Bush administration and echoed in President Obama's statements about the need to degrade ISIS/ISIL that transnational terrorism poses an existential threat to the security of the United States. The second is that transnational terrorism does not pose a security threat and that it should be treated as a crime. The appropriate response should not go beyond intelligence and policing.

Developments since 9/11 strongly support the second interpretation. The two figures below show the groups responsible for terrorist attacks in the United States, the casualties and fatalities resulting from these attacks, and the number of attacks.

Several points are evident. First, the total number of attacks has declined and the absolute numbers are very low. Second, almost all the attacks have been carried out by domestic rather than transnational groups. Third, the fatalities resulting

Table 1 Groups Responsible for Most Terrorist Attacks in the United States, 2001–2011

Rank	Organization	Number of Attacks	Number of Fatalities
1	Earth Liberation Front (ELF)	50	0
2	Animal Liberation Front (ALF)	34	0
3	Al-Qa'ida	4	2,996
4	Coalition to Save the Preserves (CSP)	2	0
4	Revolutionary Cells-Animal Liberation Brigade	2	0
5	Al-Qa'ida in the Arabian Peninsula (AQAP)	1	0
5	Ku Klux Klan	1	0
5	Minutemen American Defense	1	2
5	Tehrik-i-Taliban Pakistan (TTP)	1	0
5	The Justice Department	1	0

Note: These are all groups attributed responsibility for attacks in the GTD between 2001 and 2011. If responsibility for an attack was attributed to more than one group, then both are listed. The total number of attacks with attributed groups is 90. Seven of those attacks list a second perpetrator, resulting in 97 attributions of responsibility.

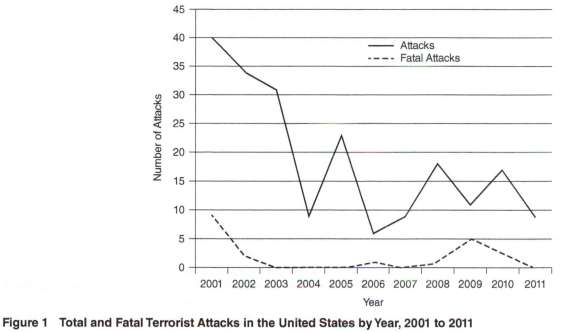

Figure 1   **Total and Fatal Terrorist Attacks in the United States by Year, 2001 to 2011**

Note: There were 208 total attacks and 21 fatal attacks in the United States between 2001 and 2011.

from terrorist attacks have been very low except for 9/11. An American's chance of being killed by a terrorist attack is de minimis about 1 in 20 million, about half the chance of being killed by lightning.

Given the experience of the past decade, why has American policy continued to be seized by the dangers posed by transnational terrorism, especially jihadist groups from the Moslem world? Why are the successes of ISIS/ISIL treated as a security threat rather than a humanitarian concern? Could American leaders redeploy assets—military, economic, and rhetorical—toward other policy objectives?

There are at least three reasons why the position taken by American leaders since 9/11, treating transnational terrorism as an existential threat, is inescapable: black swans, potential destruction, and risk aversion.

Nassim Taleb defines black swans as events that have three characteristics:

- High improbability
- High impact
- Explicable only after the event

Terrorist attacks designed to impose mass casualties are black swans. They are highly improbable; 9/11 is the most dramatic case in all of human history and had a huge impact, killing nearly three thousand people. But it also altered the course of history. The Bush administration had entered office with the intention of focusing on domestic policy. The administration's

most gripping foreign policy event before 9/11 was the collision of American and Chinese planes over the South China Sea and the subsequent emergency landing of the US EP-3 on Hainan island where it was dismantled and eventually returned in pieces by the Chinese. After 9/11 the United States attacked and removed the Taliban regime in Afghanistan and then invaded Iraq. For black swans, history does not provide guidance. That there has been no repetition of 9/11 (the Boston marathon bombing, which killed three people and injured more than two hundred, is a pale reflection) does not mean there will be no successful attack in the future.

The second reason that transnational terrorism has been treated as an existential security threat is that the level of destruction resulting from such an attack could approximate that seen in war. Criminal activities might kill scores of people. A terrorist attack could kill tens or hundreds of thousands or more. Actors with limited capabilities, both state and nonstate, can now secure weapons that could wreck havoc even on the most powerful states. The two obvious candidates are nuclear bombs and biological agents. Nuclear bombs are hard to obtain, very hard. Nevertheless, it takes little imagination to tell a story about how such a weapon might fall into the hands of transnational terrorists: governance in Pakistan might collapse or rogue elements in the military committed to a jihadist agenda might provide weapons to such a group; North Korea might sell a weapon if it were confident that its origins could not be detected or even, if it had enough weapons, if it were unconcerned about detection; or Iran could succeed in making nuclear weapons that it might provide to Hezbollah or another associated group, if the regime were facing a threat to its survival. Biologics, however, are a more likely threat for the future. The ability to develop biological weapons is becoming more widespread. In August 2014 a laptop that had belonged to an ISIL fighter from Tunisia was discovered in northern Syria. The fighter had been trained in chemistry and physics at two universities in Tunisia. On the laptop were files describing how to weaponize the bubonic plague from infected animals. The document stated that "the advantage of biological weapons is that they do not cost a lot of money, while the human casualties can be huge." The laptop also contained a file with a fatwa from a Saudi cleric stating that if unbelievers could not be defeated in any other way it was legitimate to use weapons of mass destruction "even if it kills all of them and wipes them and their descendants off the face of the Earth." (http://www.foreignpolicy.com/articles/2014/08/28/found_the_islamic_state_terror_laptop_of_ doom_bubonic_plague_weapons_of_mass_destruction_exclusive).

A successful mass destruction terrorist attack by a transnational terrorist group would upend norms and behavior in the international system. If such an attack originated in, or was associated in some way, with a country that would not or could not effectively suppress such a group, sovereignty, which has provided the principles for organizing political life at a global level, would be thrown out the window. No fig leaf of state approval would be required for kinetic strikes against suspected terrorist targets. Questions of proportionality—assessing the potential military gain against collateral damage to civilians—would become meaningless. National police forces or militaries would act freely within the boundaries of states unwilling or unable to suppress terrorist groups. Trusteeships or mandates—colonialism in one form or another—would become legitimated. The costs of such a transformed international environment, of more or less unconstrained interventionism, would be extremely high not only for the targets (weak or malevolent states) but also for the initiators (most obviously the United States).

Finally, transnational terrorism will continue to be treated as an existential threat rather than a criminal activity because of the way in which human beings, not only leaders but also electorates, confront low probability but potentially large loss events. Human beings are not naturally rational thinkers. Human behavior is more driven by what Daniel Kahneman has termed type 1 thinking (emotive, intuitive, nonreflective) than by type 2 thinking (rational and calculating). The following is a quote from Kahneman's recent book Thinking Fast and Slow:

I visited Israel several times during a period in which suicide bombings in buses were relatively common—though

of course quite rare in absolute terms. . . . For any traveler, the risks were tiny, but that was not how the public felt about it. People avoided buses as much as they could. . . .

My experience illustrates how terrorism works and why it is so effective: it induces an availability cascade. An extremely vivid image of death and damage. . . . The emotional arousal is associative, automatic, and uncontrolled. The emotion is not only disproportionate to the probability, it is also insensitive to the exact level of probability.

A successful mass terrorist attack would, as 9/11 did, dramatically alter people's subjective sense of security. The political costs for an American leader of such an event could be extremely high. The Bush administration was castigated for not connecting the dots but escaped political punishment by acting forcefully in Afghanistan and Iraq. No American president could risk taking the position that precautions against a mass casualty terrorist attack had been limited because the probability of such an attack was extremely low to vanishing. Although the rational course of action—the policy that would maximize expected utility ex ante (conforming with type 2 thinking)—might be to commit resources only to the measures that were thought to be most efficient in reducing the probability of a mass casualty terrorist attack, the policy that would be most politically judicious (conforming with type 1 thinking) would be to do everything reasonably possible to prevent such an attack. Kahneman captures this problem in Figure 13 of his book.

	Gains	**Losses**
High Probability	95% chance to win $10,000 Fear of disappointment RISK AVERSE Accept an unfavorable settlement	95% chance to lose $10,000 Hope to avoid loss RISK SEEKING Reject favorable settlement
Low Probability	5% chance to win $10,000 Hope of large gain RISK SEEKING Reject a favorable settlement	5% chance to lose $10,000 Fear of large loss RISK averse Accept unfavorable settlement

(Daniel Kahneman, Thinking Fast and Slow, Figure 13)

A mass casualty terrorist attack falls into the bottom-right-hand cell, except the probability is lower than 5 percent and the loss greater than $10,000. Under these conditions human beings are risk averse. They will accept policies that are unfavorable from a purely rational, utility-maximizing perspective because of the fear of a large loss. They will be willing to spend more on avoiding a large loss than a purely utility maximizing approach would dictate, and they will punish political leaders who, from their type 1 intuitive emotive thinking, do not take these threats seriously enough.

To sum up: The empirical evidence—the absence of a mass terrorist attack against the United States since 9/11 and the very low probability of such an attack taking place again—would suggest that the American government is devoting too many resources to counterterrorist activities. No American leader, however, will endorse such a conclusion. A mass terrorist attack would be a black swan. The cost of such an attack in terms of lives lost and instability at the global level would be extremely high. An inherent human tendency toward risk aversion with regard to large losses will continue to provide a base of political support for overcommitting (from a utility-maximizing perspective) resources to prevent such an attack.

If there is an argument that the United States has chosen the wrong path, it would have to rest on the proposition that the vigorous measures that the United States has taken to combat transnational terrorist organizations, most notably conducting kinetic attacks against Islamic jihadist organizations, ranging from drones to the invasion of Iraq, have made matters worse rather than better and have increased the number of individuals willing to join jihadist organizations rather than reduced them.

Critical Thinking

1. On what grounds is current counterterrorism spending too high?
2. Why is there an over commitment to counterterrorism?
3. What is the importance of a Black Swan?

Internet References

Countering Terrorism in the Digital Age
http://www.state.gov/p/io/rm/2014/234988.htm

Evaluating Counterterrorism Spending
http://object.cato.org/sites/cato.org/files/articles/mueller-stewart-journal-economic-perspectives-summer-2014.pdf

The Black Swan: The Impact of the Highly Improbable
http://www.nytimes.com/2007/04/22/books/chapters/0422-1st-tale.html?pagewanted=all

STEPHEN KRASNER is a senior fellow at the Hoover Institution. He is also a member of the political science department at Stanford University, where he holds the Graham H. Stuart Chair in International Relations and is a senior fellow in the Freeman Spogli Institute. He is widely known in academic circles for his work on international political economy and sovereignty.

Article

Prepared by: Thomas J. Badey, *Randolph-Macon College*

The Impact of ISIS' Mentoring of North Africa's Jihadist Groups

ALEX WATERMAN

Learning Outcomes

After reading this article, you will be able to:

- Understand the impact of the financial, political, and military power of ISIS.

- Determine the ways support is provided in local conflicts by ISIS.

- Discuss the likely increased ties and support amongst Jihadist groups.

The key jihadist insurgencies in North Africa are choosing to pledge allegiance to the Islamic State of Iraq and Syria (ISIS). The Islamic fundamentalist group that had declared an Islamic State, or caliphate, in territories its soldiers have captured in Iraq and Syria has inspired tactics and propaganda of the African insurgencies it is mentoring, and also provides practical support by training and giving experience to fighters who then carry out in Africa what they learned on the battlefields of the Middle East. ISIS' goal in North Africa is to assist insurgency groups to establish Islamic states in their respective countries. These states would then become part of a larger Islamic caliphate that, as envisioned by ISIS, would dominate the globe in time. North African Islamic states would be strategic allies to ISIS as it controls its own state from the remnants of Iraq and Syria.

Born out of the former Al Qaeda in Iraq (AQI) affiliate group, incubated in the Syrian Civil War and having swept into Iraq to exploited dissatisfaction of the alienation of Sunni tribes, the Abu Bakr al-Baghdadi-led ISIS insurgent organisation at the end of October 2014 controlled a belt of territory from Kobane, a Syrian town on the Turkish border, to the outskirts of Baghdad, Iraq. Notorious for its brutality and executions of

Western hostages, ISIS has also gained concerned notice in the Western world for its ability to recruit members from Western countries such as Britain, Australia and the US. Considering the instability that has swept across much of North, West, and East Africa in recent years and the economic and military power of ISIS in comparison to its rival al-Qaeda, ISIS is a formidable security threat to the North African region.

Factional power struggles and infighting between jihadists sworn to IS and more conservative al-Qaeda affiliates fuelled a rivalry exacerbated by al-Qaeda's disavowal of ISIS militants in Syria in February 2014. The resulting global power struggle between al-Qaeda and ISIS that resulted offers an opportunity for ISIS to deepen ties with insurgents on the African continent if they continue to pursue a policy of wooing these groups in 2015.

Using North Africa as an 'Incubator' for Likeminded Jihadists

North Africa has proved to be an ample supplier of ISIS fighters. Huge flows of foreign fighters who are willing and enthusiastic volunteers from Egypt, Tunisia and elsewhere to join ISIS in battle in Syria have had the inevitable effect of engendering closer ties between local jihadist groups and ISIS. Tunisian government sources, for example, have released their findings that 2,560 of their own citizens have fought in Syria. Of these fighters, 80% are believed to have been recruited into ISIS. Given Tunisia's distance from Syria, that number is surprising, and is higher than the number of Saudi Arabian and Jordanian citizens fighting in Syria. More alarming for the Tunisian government is the fact that, firstly, these official estimates are likely on the conservative side. Estimates from other sources suggest that up to 5,000 Tunisians have joined ISIS. Secondly, steps to cut off emigration to the Middle East by suspected ISIS fighters have resulted in 9,000 Tunisians having been prevented from travelling to Syria, presumably to fight. Not just Tunisia is providing ISIS fighters. Algeria and Morocco have also witnessed large numbers of their own citizens leaving to fight with ISIS.

In a related development, North Africa provides fertile recruiting ground for the Algerian group Soldiers of the Caliphate in Algeria, a former faction of al-Qaeda in the Islamic Maghreb (AQIM). In September 2014, the group broke away from AQIM and declared allegiance to ISIS after AQIM's leader, Abdel Malek Droukdel, renewed AQIM's allegiance to al-Qaeda and in so doing rejected ISIS' vision for an Islamic Caliphate. The Soldiers of the Caliphate in Algeria, led by Gouri Abdelmalek, declared in a statement that it was "following the orders of (ISIS) caliph Abu Bakr al-Baghdadi" when, on 24 September, 10 days after pledging its allegiance to ISIS, its fighters seized and beheaded a French citizen, Herve Goudel. The group justified the killing as retaliation for French participation in the aerial campaign against ISIS. In fact, the act was a duplication of the type of gruesome publicity-seeking beheadings that as a particularly grisly gimmick has given ISIS a windfall of attention it seeks.

However, repeating a pattern of internal struggles and group rivalries played out within and between ISIS and al-Qaeda, and which are so at odds with the ideal of a unified caliphate existing under Islamic Law, pro-ISIS groups in Tunisia and Algeria also engaged in power struggles. During the closing months of 2014, public feuding and even skirmishes occurred between al-Qaeda's Syrian affiliate, the al-Nusra Front, and ISIS-affiliated jihadists. As 2015 dawned over North Africa, momentum amongst rival jihadist groups seemed to favour the younger, more vibrant ISIS supporters who might eventually supplant the old guard of al-Qaeda comrades in AQIM. However, the feuding is a distraction from what should be the main preoccupation of the jihadists, which is the overthrow of North African governments in preparation of the Islamic caliphate. North African governments and civilians who are targets of terror activities are relieved to be spared the ravages of fully focused terror groups. Further, the power struggles between the two jihadist groups inspire little confidence in the groups' leadership abilities and competency to govern.

Gauging the Threat Posed by Libya and Egypt's Local Jihadists

Libya has served as part of a widespread arms trafficking route linking the Sahel, West Africa and the Middle East that supplies jihadists. The activity has flourished since the fall of the Gaddafi regime in 2011 and has also provided a potential weapons resource for jihadists continent-wide. The 2012 Benghazi US Embassy attack underlined the presence of Islamist militias in the country. Subsequent instability in Libya throughout 2013 and 2014 allowed Islamist groups such as Ansar Al Sharia and the Libyan Revolutionary Operations Room (LROR) to establish themselves. While claims linking these Islamist groups to al-Qaeda have remained unproved and perhaps spurious, Ansar al Sharia's declaration of a caliphate in Benghazi, and the Ansar-backed Shura Council of Islamic Youth's (SCIY) pledge of allegiance to the ISIS, suggest that the Libyan groups are strongly inspired by and may be developing ties with al-Baghdadi's ISIS organisation. Furthermore, there is evidence to suggest that Ansar al Sharia has sent fighters to engage in combat alongside ISIS. A Libyan militia known as the al-Battar Brigade fought alongside IS in Syria. Reports circulated in October 2014 that the al-Battar Brigade in fact returned from Syria at that time, having experienced combat, and established itself in Benghazi. The reports suggest that Islamist groups in Libya are directly benefitting from these veterans made battle-hardened by ISIS. Evidence also points to a degree of operational cooperation, although the extent of this coordination is yet to become clear.

The case of jihadist groups in Egypt, particularly Ansar Bayt al Maqdis in the Sinai Peninsula, is perhaps indicative of the broader impact that ISIS is currently having on African jihadism. The ISIS influence upon Sinai jihadists bears marked similarities to the way in which Boko Haram has endorsed and 'copies' ISIS in Nigeria, including embracing ISIS tactics. However, while Boko Haram may release ISIS-like videos declaring the establishment of a caliphate in north-eastern Nigeria, as the group did in September 2014, there is no significant contact between the geographically distant groups. ISIS is a source of inspiration for Boko Haram in the same way that ISIS inspires Egypt's Sinai jihadists—at a distance. For example, Ansar Bayt al Maqdis, which unleashed a violent response to the ouster of Muslim Brotherhood President Mohamed Morsi in 2013, has increasingly engaged in 'copycat' violence modelled after the ISIS example. The ISIS beheading on video gimmick was copied by Ansar Bayt al Maqdis when it decapitated four Egyptians suspected to be Israeli 'spies' and posted the video on YouTube in October 2014. The group also engaged in ongoing violent attacks against government targets as a demonstration of supposed strength. Although Ansar Bayt al-Maqdis formally pledged its allegiance to ISIS, there exists tactical differences between the ways in which the group seeks to obtain its goals. Unlike ISIS, Ansar Bayt al-Maqdis is reluctant to target civilians.

Meanwhile, the Soldiers of the Caliphate in Egypt in September 2014 declared its allegiance to ISIS and expressed its intention to attack US interests. However, no subsequent action has been taken against US interests. Evidence is lacking that operational ties have developed between ISIS and any of the Egyptian insurgent groups. Non-tactical support in the form of the inspiration ISIS offers is plentiful.

Ideation Will Not Be Enough to Make ISIS Affiliates Effective in Their Jihadist Goals

If ISIS appears to have primarily influenced African jihadists on an ideational rather than operational level, this is primarily due to the nature of the conflicts in which the North African jihadists are engaged. The groups are essentially fighting in local conflicts, whereas ISIS' end-game is to establish a regional dominance. However, the significant financial, military and political growth of ISIS and the cases of its developing ties with Algerian, Egyptian, Libyan and Tunisian Islamic militants show closer and practical ties are likely to develop between ISIS and these groups in the near future. If ISIS, itself a former al-Qaeda affiliate, is able to supplant al-Qaeda as the Middle East's paramount jihadist organisation, then ISIS may develop relations with the emergent 'Sons of the Caliphate' groups in a similar fashion to the way in which al-Qaeda provided financial, spiritual and logistical support to such African affiliate groups as AQIM in Algeria and al-Shabaab in Somalia. AQIM statements condemning the US airstrikes against ISIS may suggest that al-Qaeda is in fact already being supplanted by its rival ISIS. Attempts are being made by al-Qaeda to stem an exodus of defections of former affiliated groups across Africa. In 2014, though, the tide turned in ISIS' favour, with more pledges of allegiance from former al-Qaeda affiliates and more slavishly violent 'copycat' acts emerging.

While rivalries between terror groups may seem good news to North Africa's governments and potential civilian victims of their terror acts, a shift from radical extremists to extreme extremists is a troubling development for the region and international partners with stakes in North Africa. Violently bloody as is al-Qaeda's terror playbook, the group's acts are motivated by the rationale of its political beliefs. ISIS seems motivated by publicity-seeking and the acquisition of territory to empower a dictatorial leadership. ISIS' professed goal of a state of religious purity is sought through a wanton disregard of human life and a lack of empathy toward human suffering that characterises the psychopath. The December 2014 release of an ISIS manifesto that approves of the rape and enslavement of underage girls who are 'nonbelievers' is typical. North African states and their allies must devise a rational programme to counter the ISIS cruelty-laced challenge.

Critical Thinking

1. What factors enabled ISIS's rapid growth?
2. What is ISIS's goal, and why is mentoring local groups vital for achieving it?
3. What is keeping ISIS from expanding its Caliphate?

Internet References

ISIS Governance in Syria
http://www.understandingwar.org/report/isis-governance-syria
Woodrow Wilson Center: The Diversity of North Africa's Islamists
http://www.wilsoncenter.org/islamists/article/the-diversity-north-africas-islamists
World Affairs: North Africa: Beyond Jihadist Radicalization
http://www.worldaffairsjournal.org/article/north-africa-beyond-jihadist-radicalization

ALEX WATERMAN is a Research Associate with CAI's Conflict and Terrorism unit with a focus in insurgencies, civil wars and counterinsurgency strategy.

Article   Prepared by: Thomas J. Badey, *Randolph-Macon College*

Terrorism in South Asia: Anatomy and the Root Causes

Mahmood Ahmad Muzafar

Learning Outcomes

After reading this article, you will be able to:

- Identify four broad categories of political violence and terrorism in South Asia.

- Describe the potential root causes of terrorism in South Asia.

- Discuss how laws to address terrorism can lead to more terrorism.

Introduction

South Asia is a group of countries with common colonial past, long history of conflict, war, terrorism and trans-boarder ethnicity. Nationalism, ethnicity and religion are powerful factors that contribute to terror. These countries, including India, at best are developing and far from achieving the status of developed countries. India, Pakistan and Sri Lanka should be considered developing, the remaining are least developed. The technological threshold is low despite claims of high technology. Over 40 percent of total population are illiterate. There is human rights abuse, unemployment and uncontrolled corruption. The political class often ignores the aspiration of the people who vote them in. There is no bar in criminals becoming politicians and ministers. Ethnicity is double edged, it is used to germinate and spread terrorism and yet the same platform is used for communication and resolution of disputes.

It is said that, "South Asia has had more than its share of crises and wars, their causes ranging from national identity and irredentism to mutual interfering in each other's politics, the unfinished business of a botched partition, and conflicting territorial claims. Also notable, few of the major clashes were of a bilateral nature." These and other factors make for a complicated crisis history marked by an assortment of events, political violence and terrorism.

Any discussion of terrorism in South Asia cannot ignore its wider influences and ramifications for the rest of the world. The issue of terrorism has been discussed by analysts and policy makers extensively from diverse and multiple perspectives, depending upon the specific context and requirement at a given point of time. Diverse political experiences, ideologies, ethnic identities and economic conditions across and within the states pose significant challenges, for conflict/crisis management in the region. As in the case of many other regions, South Asia has been increasingly overwhelmed with what has been termed "non-traditional security threats" such as ethnic and ethno-nationalistic insurgencies that undermine the ability of state institutions to manage conflict. As the problem is transnational, coordinated approach is lacking due to continuous mistrust and rivalry between different countries of the region.

Most of the countries in South Asia have insurgency movements. The level of violence is variable, but several of these conflicts have been classified as high intensity. The separatist Tamil Tiger movement in Sri Lanka is one example, where an ethnic group seeks territorial withdrawal from the state entity. The Kashmir dispute feeds on and exacerbates political instability in both India and Pakistan. India faces further challenges in its north-eastern regions. The Maoist movement in Nepal impedes effective government in a similar way, and over the past few years commentators have expressed concern about the possible Talibanization of Pakistan. Afghanistan easily qualifies to be one of the foremost strategic challenges that the international community faces today. Even the western powers are contemplating the withdrawal of their troops from this war-torn southern Asian country; the situation in Afghanistan is nowhere close to stability. It is therefore no doubt that Afghanistan has the potential to adversely affect the stability in the Asian region and beyond. With these threats to political stability and territorial integrity, South Asia remains a region with a high potential for violence and conflict. Nepal has been much in the news in the past couple of years or so, in part because of the palace massacre of the royal family, but mainly because of the ferocity and intractability of the Maoist insurgency. Weakened states and enfeebled political institutions and leaderships are increasingly incapable of dealing with domestic crises in South Asia, which, in turn, breed inter-state conflicts. Cross-country migration and refugee flows, as well as the issue of treatment of one's own nationals in neighbouring countries, have the potential to trigger inter-state conflict.

South Asia is the most terror affected area of the world. Each country suffers varying degree of insurgency and terror. In fact all countries are intertwined as far as terror networking is concerned. The major conflicts in the region between India and Pakistan keep the resolution of terror problem elusive. Pakistan continues to pursue its policies of exporting terror in its neighbourhood and the world over the state policy. Pakistan is central to cause of terror problem in South Asia. AlQaeda, Taliban and a large number of other terror groups operate in concert with anti-west, anti-Jew and anti-India agenda.

As everybody knows, terrorism and political violence are not new challenges in South Asia. They have long been used by groups espousing a wide variety of causes, including national self-determination or separatism, both right- and left-wing politics, and militant religious extremism. In many instances, the fragility of relatively young political systems and nascent democracies has also generated a permissive environment for the use of political violence. In addition, militant religious groups are exploiting local grievances and drawing on international events to promote radical and extremist causes, though the underlying objectives of many of these groups remain the capture of state power and the transformation of systems of government.

Terrorism is not a problem of only one state in South Asia. It is however, the transnational nature of terrorism that is playing a significant role in transforming the rhetoric and the challenge in South Asia. The ferocity and organization of the attacks in Mumbai testify to the potential of terrorism to not only challenge national security but threaten regional and international peace. Not only this, major states of India are continuously under the threat of Terrorism. Same is the case with Pakistan, Bangladesh and rest of countries in South Asia. The tribal belt of Afghanistan and Pakistan becomes the new and the hottest battle ground for the proxy war. These developments have eventually weakened both India and Pakistan as in their endeavour to bleed each other, they have become hostage to a variety of terrorist organizations and now the handle is finally in hands of

these groups who, through a repeat of Mumbai assembly attack in Jammu and Kashmir, and the Parliament attack in India or the recent attack on educational institutions and minorities like the Ahmadiya community in Pakistan, [and other] like adventures, can at any time ignite a round of hostilities between different neighbours.

The stability of South Asia, and the success and failure of initiatives for the resolution of existing conflicts will in the twenty-first century depend on the exploration of new ideas, ideologies and strategies that provide concrete and effective alternative to violence as a means to political ends; and these alternatives must appeal, equally, to the establishment and to the alienated groups that currently believe that violence is only a method to secure some relief within the prevailing system.

The Anatomy of Terrorism in South Asia

In modern times, humanity is facing a challenge of a different kind of war. Here the enemy is not visible and battlefield nowhere. But the entire globe is in the grip of destruction. No one is safe. The name of this new war is terrorism. It seems to have become endemic to modern society. It continues to be generated by recurrent social crisis, arising from the increasing fear of marginalisation of some sections of society caused by the indiscriminate spread of Capitalism and free economy, through much publicised globalisation which may be perceived as another dimension of religious fanaticism. The point can further be elaborated by stating that colonialism was common cause that eventually contributed to secessionism. Ethnically discriminatory practices followed by the British in favour of the Tamils [were seen] as the root cause of conflict in Sri Lanka. Another point is that violence—social, political or economic, or physical—perpetrated by the state or the agents of the state against other states or its own people also generates terrorism to a great extent.

Taking South Asia, the conceptualization of terrorism does not differ basically as the anti-terrorist legal measures adopted by each country suggest. For India, terrorism means 'intentions to threaten the unity, integrity and security of India or strike terror in people or any section of the people by using bombs, explosive substances, firearms or other lethal weapons'. For Pakistan, 'Terrorism is to strike terror or create disturbances by using bombs, explosives firearms or inflammable substances. It also includes an act of gang rape, child molestation, or robbery coupled with rape'. For Sri Lanka, terrorism means causing the death of any specialized person, committing any other attack upon such persons, which would be punishable with death or imprisonment for seven years. Nepal considers terrorism as 'any act or plan of using any kind of arms, grenades, or explosives with the objective of hurting the sovereignty or the security and law and kingdom of Nepal.

In order to understand terrorism in South Asia, four broad categories of political violence and terrorism may be identified; (A) Ethno-nationalist separatism; (B) Left ideological; (C) Religious extremism/sectarian and (D) Externally organised. These four categories of terrorism have been found in different countries of South Asia. The war for a Tamil homeland by the LTTE in Sri Lanka; insurgency in the Baluchistan province of Pakistan and in India's Northeast for separate identity and statehood, all fall into the ethnic category. The Maoist movement in Nepal, although monarchy has been overthrown, the Maoists along with other political forces are trying to draft a Constitution for the country. The left-extremism raging in India's so called 'red-corridor' (across Maharashtra and Andhra to Orissa, Jharkhand, Chhattisgarh, West Bengal and Bihar) is the representative examples of ideologically led political violence and terrorism. As of June 2010, Indian Government has identified 83 districts in nine states as Naxal hit in central and eastern parts of the country. The Naxalites, however, claim to operate in 182 districts. Moreover; religious extremism has also become the main cause in fuelling terrorism in South Asia. Examples like mujahideen, Jihadists, Hindu fundamentalists and so on have tried to influence their co-religiosities in neighbouring countries to adopt the path of violence against the established governments. The utilization of Al-Qaida, Lashkar-e-Toiba (LeT), Jamait-ul-Dawa and Islamic extremist groups of this genre by Pakistan to launch attacks into Afghanistan and India could easily escalate into inter-State conflicts and Terrorism. In the Af-Pak region and within Pakistan, jihadi terrorism driven by Islamic extremism and aimed at promoting a 'purist' Islamic state is being confronted by the international community, in collaboration with Pakistan and Afghanistan.

Lastly, there is 'cross-border' terrorism against India inspired and organised by Pakistan. This cross-border terrorism goes beyond fuelling political unrest in India's Jammu & Kashmir to reinforce Pakistani claims on this region, and extends to whole of India with the purpose of weakening its economy and sabotaging its political and social stability. The Kashmir conflict has clearer external factors in its origin, due to which terrorism became a distinctive factor in the mid-1980s.

In Sri Lanka the Tamil movement was transformed from a relatively peaceful one until the 1960s into an extraordinarily violent struggle with regional ramifications in the 1980s. Assassinations and suicide bombings became central means of terror. A similar central trait is the marginalization of the so-called moderates. It is argued by some that the major locus of international terrorism has shifted to South Asia. Terrorist acts are committed in relation to both internal and inter-state conflicts, and the level of violence is alarming. Allegations are also frequently made that governments may support cross-border terrorism to undermine neighbouring states. The latest disclosures with regard to the Mumbai terror attacks in November 2008 clearly reveal the character of externally organised terrorism in South Asia. Analysts also point out that India's involvement in the Tamil insurgency in its early stages, or Bangladesh's support and sheltering of India's Northeast insurgents or China's support for the first phase of Naxal insurgency in India during the late sixties and early seventies also can be taken as examples of externally organised political violence and terrorism in South Asia.

It can be no doubt, but the critical difference between all these examples and that of the Pakistani 'cross-border' terrorism against India is that all the former cases of political violence had their basic roots within the country of their manifestations and the neighbours exploited the turmoil and conflicts for limited strategic and foreign policy goals. Many other places in India is a category in itself, wherein terrorism is used as a systematic instrument of strategic policy, of confronting and weakening India, of waging a war by other means. The above categories however are not rigid. There is considerable overlap and spill-over among them. Take for instance, the extremist left ideological groups, the Maoists, in India and Nepal. The ethnic component in these insurgencies is clearly visible. The Nepal Maoists mobilised the marginalised ethnic groups like Magars, Gurungs, Limbus, Kirats, Thakalis, and Tamangs, etc. This has added the powerful agenda of meeting the aspirations of these 'nationalities' to the ideological programme of the Maoists. In case of Indian Maoists, the tribal's from the backward eastern region are the mainstay of the insurgency. There are also other regional identities enmeshed in the movement that are reflected even at the leadership levels and in the strategies being pursued by the insurgents. Similarly, in the predominantly Tamil ethnic insurgency of Sri Lanka, various militant groups were divided along ideological lines. The Eelam Peoples Revolutionary Liberation Front (EPRLF) with its strong Marxist orientation had a perpetual ideological discord with the LTTE. Even with the religion driven terrorist groups with allegiance to Islamic extremism, sectarian (Shia-Sunni) and ethnic divisions cannot be ignored. Besides the ethnic and ideological overlap in the categories of insurgent and terrorist groups in South Asia, the groups also have logistic and ideological supportive linkages, even across the borders.

Belief in militancy and sympathy for the militants gradually raised among the Tamils after the ethnic riots of 1983. With the massive exodus of Sri Lankan Tamil Nadu after the 1983 roits, India could not remain unaffected by the events. New Delhi offered its good offices to resolve the conflict to ensure its national security interests and stability in the region. At the same time, the Indian intelligence agencies provided military training to prominent Tamil militant groups. This encouraged the militants to take on Sri Lankan forces with more confidence in what is known as 'Eelam Wars'. Reports are also there that, LTTE in Sri Lanka consistently tried to link up with Indian and other insurgent groups to promote their commercial interests (selling arms and explosives, providing training, etc.) as also to forge a common front against the Indian state. Reports of the LTTE'S links with the Andhra Maoist groups and northeast ethnic insurgents have appeared in Indian media. The nature and extent of ideological and logistic linkages between the Nepal Maoists and the Indian left-extremist groups have been debated in the Indian media for a very long time. The South Asian Maoists groups forged an institutional relationship in July 2001 by establishing a Coordination Committee of the Maoist Parties of South Asia (CCOMPOSA). This committee meets periodically and adopts resolutions in support of 'revolutionary struggles' in South Asia. Also the terrorist outfits in India like Indian Mujahedeen's are suspected to have linkages with jihadi groups in Pakistan and even Al Qaeda. The links between Al Qaeda and the Pakistani Taliban and jihadi groups are well established. There is a tendency among the policy makers and political leaders to project the terrorist and insurgent groups as coherent organisations. This is far from the ground-reality of these groups. The diverse and differentiated natures of these organisations become evident, on closer scrutiny of their various layers and tiers.

Root Causes of Terrorism in South Asia

The basic concept of the root causes of terrorism is that certain conditions provide a social environment and widespread grievances that, when combined with certain precipitant factors; result in the emergence of terrorist organizations and terrorist acts. These conditions—such as poverty, demographic factors, social inequality and exclusion, dispossession, and political grievances—can be either permissive or direct. The idea suggests, for example, that "human insecurity, broadly understood, provides the enabling conditions for terrorism to flourish." What is the relationship between root causes and patterns of terrorism? Can this relationship be systematically explained; can a theory be developed that incorporates root causes and that has general explanatory value as to where and why terrorism occurs? Do root cause explanations have greater utility in explaining certain types of terrorism? If root causes are key determinants of support for terrorist groups, for the emergence of terrorist groups, and for the occurrence of terrorist activities, what are the implications for the war on terror and contemporary counterterrorism policy?

When we look towards this critical subject i.e., the root causes of terrorism, the general explanations tend to identify poverty, the lack of democracy or history as prominent factors causing terrorist violence. In debates on terrorism, we quite often come across abstract notions, such as poverty causes terrorism or democracy is the antidote to terrorism. However, a closer look at the ground reality reveals that this is not always the case. Africa is mostly poverty ridden and politically authoritarian and the western world is rich and democratic, yet the latter has seen more terrorism than the former. Democracy may be an antidote to terrorism, but its lack or absence in a country or a region cannot be construed as a principal cause of terrorism. Poverty plays an indirect role in terrorism also becomes clear when we critically analyse the case of madrassas in Muslim countries like Pakistan afflicted with terrorist violence.

The structure of societies and polities together with continued exploitation of people by the designated members of the upper caste, class, and political elites is taken as the factor responsible for terrorism. For, these elites have not been able to transform themselves into new, progressive elites regardless of the nature of political systems. As a result, steeped in tradition of disparity and exploitation, South Asian region in general inherits a peculiar mixture of socio-economic and political structures in addition to producing new breeding grounds for modified parochialism such as the rise of religious and sectarian factors which also contribute to violence and terrorism.

Although protracted conflicts have been prevalent in South Asia for more than 50 years, there is hardly any cause of terrorism which is uniformly applicable to all South Asian countries. Yet, some critical variables can be identified. These include, persistace of poverty and accompanying deprivations like unemployment, low levels of literacy, limited access to health services, years of misgoverance, which have made violence the only means of bringing about a change and alienation of whole cultural or ethnic-groups brought about by threat to life by frequent communal violence and destruction of means of livelihood. There are also other issues like territorial disputes inherited from colonial past, water disputes and Intra-State conflicts involving ethno-linguistic and religious groups with cross border affiliations. Conflicting economic interests—these and other factors are also said to have created terrorism, generating conflicts and spilling over national boundaries.

One of the key elements that sustain terrorism in a particular situation has been the role of external support. This has been widely discussed. There are growing knowledge bases on this as the very nature of terrorism has grown into massive conglomerate with an intrinsic international network. There are various ways that the phenomenon of external support to a terrorists movement or a group has been recorded. In Pakistan, free education provided by madras or religious schools has attracted a large number of people. And at least some schools clearly inculcate extremism and violence in the younger minds as reflected in the orientation of formations like the Taliban. There are a number of reports that the LTTE raises money through external agencies and drug trafficking.

There are two pertinent examples of support for terrorists from hostile neighbours. Firstly, India's support to Tamil militants in Sri Lanka is a widely known fact. And the second example is that of Pakistan's involvement in assisting terrorism in Jammu and Kashmir in India. Though India maintains that its support was essentially guided by its changing threat perception and security concerns emanating from Sri Lanka, it did provide initial boost and substance to Tamil's militant activities.

Another feature of the phenomenon is continuous intervention and financial aid policies of big powers like United States which has also added to the problem. US approach to south Asia had been given a position of priority. Clincton had already given more importance to this region than had the earlier presidents. After September 11, the coming together of the new threats to US and the new policy meant that South Asia rose to first position in US foreign policy priorities. The War on Terror policy of United States has resulted into a situation of anarchy in Pakistan as major drone attacks of US and NATO armies is said to be the challenge for Pakistan Sovereignty and internal security. Hundreds of people have left their homes and migrated, and majority of homeless young people have joined Pakistani Madrasas, that are fuelling terrorism continuously. US intervention in Pakistan and Afghanistan has resulted into a war like situation in South Asia instead of creating a secure environment for which US claims its presence.

Not only this, terrorism also impacted the domestic political structures in South Asian countries in a negative way. It has encouraged militarism, chauvinism and a distinct tilt towards right wing extremism. It has been used as an excuse for undermining democracy. Though the LTTE as an organization was set up to voice the legitimate demands of Tamil population in Sri Lanka, its degeneration into a terrorist outfit gave the Sri Lankan state the excuse to use brute force and follow militaristic policies and it finally succeeded into obliterating the LTTE. While this was welcomed, it also led to a massive upsurge in Sinhala nationalism, which is coming in the way of a political settlement between the Tamil population and Sinhala-dominated Sri Lankan government.

Terrorism in relation with South Asian cannot be treated with a single or a broad brush. Needless to say, terrorism or violence by non state actors in pursuance of particular political objectives is not a new phenomenon for this region. However, the fact is that the attention this issue has received at this juncture is linked with global developments post-9/11. The new definition of terrorism that is being pursued by the west sees terrorist activities primarily as violence pursued by networks like Al Qaida. These networks do not necessarily have a regional or national agenda even though such organizations operate in parts of South Asian region as well. The United Nations has also paid less attention towards the political issues of this region which has resulted into a war like situation in South Asia. Though several developmental programs have been started by United Nations in different countries but development alone cannot end the crisis in this region.

The convergence of limited response capacities of governments and law-enforcement agencies with grievances about widespread corruption, under-development, socioeconomic marginalization, and the sometimes problematic role of the state, make South Asia an attractive operating base for a wide array of violent groups whose empty talks and actions can have an impact on ethnic and ideological kin across political borders.

The South Asian Association for Regional Cooperation (SAARC) has made several attempts to forge regional responses to common challenges, including drugs, small arms, and counterterrorism. Its efficacy is often held hostage to the relationship between India and Pakistan. In recognition of the difficulties of political engagement, SAARC has consequently focused primarily on regional economic development rather than on political questions. A wariness of international intervention and encroachments on territorial and political sovereignty, engendered by the history of colonialism in the region, adds an additional obstacle to regionalization and the development of any supranational regional organization. Along with that strategic partnership between Pakistan and China, political instability in Afghanistan, religious extremism in Bangladesh also acts as barriers for regional cooperation to combat terrorism in South Asia.

In future, terrorism might endanger the existence of human kind as a whole, since its fanatical forms do not know any limits and would not stop before anything. If we have to understand the underlying principles of terror and terrorism. We have to get acquainted with it, just the same as with any other social phenomenon, in its historical development and context. The international community is already considerably awakened to dangers and inhuman phenomenon of terrorism. What is needed to curb and eliminate the evil is to unite and fight terrorism in all forms and manifestations. States sponsoring terrorism must be isolated by international community and forced to abandon the weapon of terrorism. Nations must not distinguish between friends and foes when it comes to identifying terror sponsoring states. Such states must face the united might of humanity to save itself from scourge.

Conclusion

Terrorism is a disease which needs to be treated rather than fought. We are not fighting an enemy but mentally sick and misguided who must be brought on course by looking in to their grievances and aspirations. A tooth for tooth strategy is counterproductive and has never succeeded. No effort is being made to defend the actions of terrorists; their actions are not being approved, nor encouraged. However, the states must follow the law and not retaliate indiscriminately. Negotiations should be the hallmark. Terrorism cannot be tackled by state terrorism. Despite actions by armed forces of the states, the menace of terrorism has increased.

Terrorism which itself is an amorphous term and its activity is not easy to address either by the state or by other domain of civil society. In some countries, terrorism originates from religious bigotry and in some others, the issue of identity, the desire to have an honourable and secured life or the objective of a democratic system and freedom becomes the motivating factor for resorting to extreme forms of actions that are characterized by violence, killing, extortion and crimes of various kinds. When other channels fail or are perceived to have failed by involved actors, conveniently branded as terrorists by the opposite side, the former use coercive intimidation to further their goals.

The introduction of special or extraordinary laws to address terrorism can be particularly detrimental to the protection of human rights, as they can lead to long-term institutionalization of oppression and foster a culture of impunity within state security forces and agencies. Widespread human rights abuses by security and law enforcement officials seriously undermine relations between security services and minority populations which have further contributed to cycles of violence across much of the subcontinent. In India, for example, the current government repealed the 2002 Prevention of Terrorism Act (POTA) after a parliamentary review committee found that of 1,529 people detained under its provisions, which allowed the government to detain terrorist suspects for up to 180 days without charges, "the cases of 1,006 did not meet prima facie standard-rights" groups noted that the law was "often used against marginalized communities such as Dalits (so-called untouchables), indigenous groups, Muslims, and the political opposition. The Armed Forces Special Powers act, which is operative in Jammu and Kashmir has resulted into human rights violations to a great extent where 2010 alone witnessed hundreds of deaths without any charge sheet and action on part of the State Government.

The cooperation between different governments and establishment of regional intelligence unit can help to a great extent, cooperation between Bangladesh and India to fight terror is noteworthy. This has also produced significant results and dealt a major blow to Islamist groups as well as Northeast insurgents. Though this cooperation is admirable, it has still not reached a level seen in the case of India and Bhutan, where security forces of both countries launched coordinated assault against the terrorists in their respective territories leaving little room for terrorists to escape. However, the cooperation with Bangladesh should not be underestimated.

Combating terrorism is not a easy task in South Asia, as there are number of issues which act as barrier for cooperative effort, but India, said to be the hegemon of the region, can play a crucial role. Along with that, all the countries of the region should realize that continuous rivalry can prove dangerous in long run. A regional, technically focused counterterrorism mechanism which may be complementary but not formally related to SAARC should be established to stimulate practical cooperation at the functional level. Among other things such a mechanism could provide a platform for counter terrorism training and other capacity building activities, facilitating the exchange of expertise and information among government officials, which is essential for building the trust needed for effective cross border cooperation as well as the sharing of good national implementation among the countries of the region.

References

Brig V. P Malhotra, *Terrorism and Counter-Terrorism in South Asia and India.* (New Delhi: Vij Books India Pvt Ltd, 2001), p-142.

P. R. Chari, Pervaiz Iqbal Cheema, Stephen P. Cohen, *Four Crises and a Peace Process: American Engagement in South Asia.* (Washington, D.C.: Brookings Institution press, 2007), p-13.

S. D. Muni, Beyond Terrorism: Dimensions of Political Violence in South Asia, in Anand Kumar Ed, *The Terror Challenge in South Asia and Prospect of Regional Cooperation.* (New Delhi: Pentagon Security International, 2012), p-19.

Shiva Hari Dhal, Gazdar Haris, Keethaponcalan S. I. and Murthy Padmaja, Internal Conflict and Regional Security in South Asia. (Geneva: United Nations Publications 2003), p-4.

United Nations, South Asia in the world: Problem solving perspectives on security, sustainable development, and good governance, by: Ramesh Thakur and Oddny Wiggen (New York: United Nations press, 2004), p-5–6.

Happymon Jacob, *Afghanistan needs good neighbours,* Greater Kashmir, January 29, 2012, p-8.

United Nations, South Asia in the world: Problem solving perspectives on security, sustainable development, and good governance, by: Ramesh Thakur and Oddny Wiggen (New York: United Nations press, 2004), p-6.

Brig V. P Malhotra, *Terrorism and Counter-terrorism in South Asia and India.* (New Delhi: Vij Books India Pvt Ltd, 2001), p-142–143.

Eric Rosand, Flick Naureen Chowduary and Ipe Jason, *Countering Terrorism in South Asia: Strengthening Multilateral Engagement.* (New York: International Peace Institute 2009), p-3 http://www.ipinst.org/publication/policy-papers/detail/77-countering-terrorism-in-south-asia-strengthening-multilateral-engagement.html

Ibid, p-3.

Umbreen Javaid, Urgency for Inter-state Dialogue for Fighting Terrorism in South Asia, *Journal of Political Studies,* Department of Political Science, University of Punjab, Lahore, Vol. 18, Issue 1, p-2.

Darvesh Gopal, Terrorsim in South Asia, in Dipankar Sengupta and Sudhir Kumar Singh, Ed, *Terrorism in South Asia.* (Delhi: Authorspress, 2004), p-36–37.

Sheikh Saleem Ahmed, Dimensions of Terrorism and Religious Extremism: Two sides of the same coin, in Mahavir Singh, ed. *International Terrorism and Religious Extremism: Challenges to Central and South Asia.* (New Delhi: Anamika Publishers and Distributers(P) LTD, 2004) p-37–39.

Baral Lok Raj, Responding to Terrorism: Political and Social Consequences in South Asia, in S.D. Muni ed. *Responding to Terrorism in South Asia* (New Delhi: Manahor publishers, 2006), p-302.

S.D. Muni, Beyond Terrorism: Dimensions of Political Violence in South Asia, Anand Kumar, Ed. *The Terror Challenge in South Asia and Prospect of Regional Cooperation.* (New Delhi: Pentagon Security International, 2012), 21.

Sri Lanka has successfully managed to eliminate the LTTE. However, it remains to be seen how the situation is managed by the Sri Lankan government from here on, so that no such group emerges there in future.

Anand Kumar, Ed. *The Terror Challenge in South Asia and Prospect Of Regional Cooperation.* (New Delhi: Pentagon Security International, 2012), 3.

Brig V. P Malhotra, *Terrorism and counter-terrorism in South Asia and India.* (New Delhi: Vij Books India Pvt Ltd, 2001), p-144.

Though Islam condemns all forms of Terrorism and violence. But extremist groups have misinterpreted the teachings of Islam.

P. R. Chari, Armed Conflicts in South Asia: The Emerging Dimensions,in D. Suba Chandran and P. R. Chari Ed. *Armed Conflicts in South Asia 2011: The Promise and Threat Of Transformation,* (New Delhi, U.K: Routledge, 2012). 6.

S. D. Muni, Beyond Terrorism: Dimensions Of Political Violence In South Asia, Anand Kumar, Ed. *The Terror Challenge In South Asia And Prospect Of Regional Cooperation* (New Delhi: Pentagon Security International, 2012), 21–22.

United Nations, South Asia in the world: Problem solving perspectives on security, sustainable development, and good governance, by: Ramesh Thakur and Oddny Wiggen (New York: United Nations press, 2004), p-5–6.

S. D. Muni, Beyond Terrorism: Dimensions Of Political Violence In South Asia, in Anand Kumar, Ed. *The Terror Challenge in South Asia and Prospect of Regional Cooperation.* (New Delhi: Pentagon Security International, 2012), 21–22.

Ibid, p-22.

N. Manoharan, With Lions and without Tigers: Conflict Transformation and the Search for peace in Sri Lanka", in D.Suba Chandran and P. R. Chari, Ed. *Armed Conflicts in South*

Asia 2011: The Promise and Threat of Transformation. (New Delhi, U.K: Routledge, 2012). 212.

S. D. Muni, "Beyond Terrorism: Dimensions Of Political Violence In South Asia", The Terror Challenge In South Asia And Prospect Of Regional Cooperation Ed. *Anand Kumar* (New Delhi: Pentagon Security International, 2012). p-22–25.

Edward Newman Exploring the "Root Causes" of Terrorism, Studies in Conflict & Terrorism, 29, no.8, (2006):750, accessed February 10, 2014, URL: http://dx.doi.org/10.1080/10576100600704069

Ishtiaq Ahmad,Terrorism: A Conceptual Framework, in Updesh Kumar and Manas K. Mandal, Ed. *Countering Terrorism: Psychosocial Strategies,* (New Delhi: SAGE Publications India Pvt Ltd, 2012), 15–16.

Ibid, p-17.

Lok Raj Baral, Responding to Terrorism: Political and Social Consequences in South Asia, in S. D. MUNI, Ed. *Responding to Terrorism in South Asia,* (New Delhi: Monohar Publishers, 2006), p-303–304.

V. R. Raghavan, "Role of Third Parties in Resolving Terrorism-generating conflicts," in S. D. MUNI, Ed. *Responding to Terrorism in South Asia,* (New Delhi: Monohar Publishers, 2006), p-360–361.

Mahendra P. Lama, Political Economy of Terrorism: Sustenance Factors and Consequences, in S. D. MUNI Ed. *Responding to Terrorism in South Asia,* (New Delhi: Monohar Publishers, 2006), p-401–402.

Ibid, p-402.

I. P Khosla, South Asia And the US forward presence, in Omprakash Misra and Sucheta Ghosh, Ed. *Terrorism and Low Intensity Conflict in South Asian Region,* (New Delhi: MANAK 2003), p-149.

Anand Kumar, *The Terror Challenges in South Asia and Prospect of Regional cooperation,* (New Delhi: Pentagon Security International Press:2012), p-2.

Ayesha Siddiqa, Terrorism in South Asia, in S. D. Munni ed. *Responding to Terrorism in South Asia.* (New Delhi: Manohar publishers, 2006), p-337.

Eric Rosand, Flick Naureen Chowduary and Ipe Jason, Op. cit, p-3.

Ibid, p-3.

Darvesh Gopal, Terrorsim in South Asia, in Dipankar Sengupta and Sudhir Kumar Singh ed. *Terrorism in South Asia,* (Delhi: Authorspress, 2004), p-37.

Brig V. P Malhotra, Terrorism and counter-terrorism in South Asia and India. (New Delhi: Vij Books India Pvt Ltd, 2001), p-148.

Baral Lok Raj, Responding to Terrorism: Political and Social Consequences in South Asia, in S. D. Muni ed. *Responding to Terrorism in South Asia* (New Delhi: Manahor publishers, 2006). p-301.

Ibid, p-21.

Kumar Anand, Return From The Precipice, Bangladesh's Fight Against Terrorism (New Delhi: Pentagon Press, 2012), p-131.

Rosand Eric, Flick Naureen Chowduary and Ipe Jason, Op. cit, p-25.

Critical Thinking

1. What are the four categories of political violence and terrorism in South Asia?

2. What are the root causes of terrorism in South Asia?

3. Is terrorism is a disease? If so, how should it be treated?

Internet References

NBR: Counterterrorism Cooperation in South Asia: History and Prospects

http://www.nbr.org/publications/element.aspx?id=412

South Asia Assessment 2014

http://www.satp.org/satporgtp/southasia/index.html

South Asia: Battle Ground Between ISIS & al-Qaeda

http://www.foreignpolicyjournal.com/2014/11/07/south-asia-battle-ground-between-isis-al-qaeda

Terrorism in Southeast Asia

http://www.history.navy.mil/research/library/online-reading-room/title-list-alphabetically/t/terrorism-in-southeast-asia.html

Article   Prepared by: Thomas J. Badey, *Randolph-Macon College*

The Intractable Conflict: Why Colombia's War Against the FARC Eludes Resolution

PHILIP K. ABBOTT

Learning Outcomes

After reading this article, you will be able to:

- Explain the underlying causes of the conflict in Colombia.
- Identify U.S. foreign policy objectives in the region.
- Discuss continuing divisions that exist in Colombian society.

Introduction

Through qualitative analysis, it is the author's view that the country of Colombia has evolved into what can be coined as an intractable conflict with the Revolutionary Armed Forces of Colombia-People's Army (FARC-EP). This conflict has remained unresolved for such a long period of time and at such a high level of intensity and destructiveness, that each side views the seemingly rigid position of the other side as a threat to its very existence. Intractable wars are often perceived as a controversial concept, particularly among academicians. Even so, this particular dispute is not impossible to resolve nor should it be misconstrued as a statement to undermine everything President Juan Manuel Santos and the FARC leadership are attempting to do in bringing peace to this war-torn-nation. It is simply an opportunity to acknowledge root and proximate causes of this conflict and to further analyze both positive and negative intervening factors. As is true with any breakdown in social behavior, there are many contributing elements that make analysis and resolution extremely challenging despite the

heroic efforts by government officials, military leaders, and the overwhelming application of military power.

The story line of this conflict straddles between expectations and political power, and there is an underlying fear of never reaching a win-win resolution. This is perceived as compromising on endearing values or as demonstrating a sign of weakness. Apparently, anyone showing the courage to change for the good of Colombia (or anyone appearing to placate the status quo challenger) faced real risks. Unfortunately, history shows that all efforts to suppress the FARC's illegal approach to dissent from the state have been unsuccessful.

Not surprisingly, with few exceptions, insurgencies do not successfully end by military action but by social, economic and political change.[1] It seems that governments defeat themselves more often than they are defeated by a dominant insurgency like FARC. This is true because governments tend to address the root causes half-heartedly, fail to extend credible control of rural areas, overly depend on military means to solve social problems, and become too dependent on fickle sponsors burdened with sustaining domestic support.[2] This is further compounded by the seemingly belligerent and ambiguous U.S. foreign policy. Therefore, unless there is a fundamental change in how Colombian society views and manages this conflict, we can be assured these differences will stalemate or elude a resolution for decades to come.

This essay will portray the necessity in moving beyond military solutions, unsubstantiated propaganda, and negative imaging, which for so many years has dominated the Colombian narrative. Moreover, it is the author's intention to summon the reader to the social-psychological dimension that permeates all aspects of this intractable conflict. History, perceptions and identity are not only inherently present in the escalation of Colombia's conflict with the FARC; they are also intrinsic in managing this conflict and contributing to a sustainable peace. In order to gain a more equitable perception of reality, it is important to acknowledge history, learn empathy, and to recognize fear and its according legitimacy. These efforts will help formulate policies and strategies that are coherent and accurately address these realities.[3]

Acknowledging Colombia's Violent History

So what are the underlying causes of this destructive and intractable conflict? Clearly they have been ignored and grossly blurred over Colombia's past fifty years. Conflict analysis requires not only learning history, but actually acknowledging the progression of events, conflicts, and the related eruption of violence. In viewing this narrative, understanding how history and critical junctures shaped Colombia's path of economic and political institutions enables us to have a more complete theory of the origins of differences between poverty and prosperity.[4] Besides gaining insight of the root causes of this prolonged struggle, it also offers the necessary perspectives for effective conflict management.

The inheritance of the Iberian Crowns' *caste system,* a way to exercise political and economic control over colonial Latin America, has a profound place in Colombian history.[5] Arguably, benevolent autocracy and legitimized cruelty also had enduring effects on Colombian society. During the 16th century, Spain carried the stamp of absolutism where military prowess, religious purity and subordination to the Spanish Crown were above commerce, identity, and material gain.[6] After independence from Spain, land became available, ostensibly for both the Colombian working class and elite.[7] The sudden opening of this valuable frontier led to further divergence, shaped by the existing institutional differences, especially those concerning who had access to the land.[8] This created an egalitarian and economically dynamic country, where land was allocated to the politically powerful and those with wealth and contacts, making such people even more powerful.[9] Consequently, the revolutionary movement failed to open the political system to a broader cross section of Colombian society, and prevented more inclusive economic institutions. The growing fear of unmet expectations provoked social unrest, but neither armed hostilities nor the resulting peace agreements laid the necessary foundation or basis to resolve these long-standing grievances for political and agrarian reform.[10] Now a decade into the 21st century, Colombia remains replete with symptoms of the same deep-rooted tensions between the governing elite and the land-less poor.

As played out before in history, when socially and ideologically different worlds collide, those who adhere to a particular social order often demonstrate very little empathy for opposing views, and are therefore unwilling to compromise on their opinions or world views. The Colombian ruling elite's lack of addressing political injustice, and the growing socio-economic disparity and humiliation further fomented social unrest. The Colombian government tried to suppress the resistance by belligerent means. Despite its futility, once the Colombian government legitimatized their monopoly of violence as a "justifiable" measure to counter the opposition, it sent a clear signal to the FARC regarding their "natural right" to do what it must to stay alive.[11]

Colombian history also shows how internal conflicts are not always independent of their domestic context. Although the social, economic, and political conditions may have been set internally since the independence movement, its trajectory has been greatly affected by a multitude of external factors of varying scope and impact. A major external factor influencing Colombia's domestic context was a set of other global conflicts that became superimposed or impinged upon the growing unrest over social injustice. Indeed, the Cold War had immense effect on Colombia's seemingly manageable internal dispute. During this period, the Soviet Union, the United States, and their proxies routinely sustained regional alliances.

As marginalized segments of Colombian society unsuccessfully sought changes within the traditionally unfair political, social and economic structures; the threatened, poor, working class fled to remote areas of Colombia to seek refuge and create meaningful living arrangements. Many also began to organize under the Colombian Communist Party (PCC), which was perceived as a feasible and democratic way to leverage social and economic reform.[12] Notwithstanding the growing consternation and seemingly legitimate claims for unfulfilled human needs, this once tractable conflict quickly escalated. Tangible issues became increasingly more embedded within a larger set of values, beliefs, identities, and cultures.[13] Over time, the actual genesis of this conflict became more diluted and progressively less relevant. Three distinct phases of U.S. foreign policy began shaping Colombia's internal security environment, often at the expense of conflict resolution.

During the second half of the 20th century, U.S. foreign policy aimed at defeating communism. This ideology had an important role in foreign policy formulation, "for within ideologies lie many of the values that inform the definitions of national interest."[14] However, ideologies can also contain highly generalized and abstracted interpretations of history. They often narrowly focus on the world as it is becoming and should become, rather than a realistic appreciation of the world as it actually is.[15] "To invert the medical metaphor, ideology is like a powerful medicine of which a drop will cure but a teaspoon will kill."[16]

Unlike President Eisenhower, Kennedy's initial response to the perceived danger of communism spreading in Latin America was drawn from the premise; "those who make reform impossible will make revolution inevitable."[17] Kennedy believed that in order to safeguard security interests, the United States must address the poverty and oppression that seemed a fertile breeding ground for communism.[18] Notwithstanding the well-intended *Alliance for Progress* initiative—a sort of *Marshall Plan* for Latin America—aimed at reducing revolutionary pressure by stimulating economic development and political reform, it quickly ran out of political steam. In fact, by November 1963, the *Alliance for Progress* was essentially moribund.

A growing obsession with global communism further exacerbated domestic tensions. It made any substantial political changes to Colombian society increasingly harder to achieve and much more expensive than supplying military weapons and counterinsurgency training.[19] Similarly, the idea of creating self-sufficient communes or "communist enclaves" in the middle of the Andes Mountains was viewed as a threat to both Bogota and Washington. Meanwhile, Kennedy was ever sensitive to charges of appearing "soft" on communism and the bitter contention regarding his military leadership's role within a cold war context. He decided to fulfill his campaign promises by regaining the upper hand in this political debate.[20]

As the United States began to export militaristic anti-Communist policies throughout Latin America, the most important U.S. [anti-communist] ally became Latin American armed forces.[21] Under this strategic security arrangement, U.S. naval and air power would handle any communist invaders from outside the hemisphere, while "Latin American armies would turn their U.S. supplied weapons inward against the internal enemies of freedom: revolutionary organizers in factories, poor neighborhoods, and universities."[22] To this extent, while U.S. counterinsurgency strategy began to build momentum under *Plan Laso*,[23] the conflict in Colombia took on a more destructive and violent narrative. The creation of these "communist enclaves" provided the CIA and the Pentagon with their first foray into Colombia. In May 1964, after several years of planning by the CIA and U.S. Southern Command, *Operation Maquetalia* launched an estimated 5,000 Colombian army elite force, backed by U.S. helicopters and fighter planes dropping napalm to destroy the "*Independent Republic of Marquetalia*." Although initially praised as a successful mission, the joint U.S.-Colombian military operation to destroy *Marulanda's communists* failed to achieve its strategic objective, which actually helped catalyze the founding of the FARC.

With the collapse of the Soviet Union, the long-lived anti-communism policy was soon replaced by a war-against-drugs policy as the most important domestic issue in U.S. politics,

especially with regards to Colombia. By 1999, Colombia had surpassed Peru and Bolivia as the world's largest producer of coca and source country for over three-fourths of the world's cocaine supply.[24] The General Accounting Office (GAO) further reported that an estimated two-thirds of FARC units were engaged in drug activity.[25] GAO's quantifying charges of FARC involvement in drugs were perhaps less significant for the Colombian social elite than the FARC's involvement with extortion and especially kidnappings, which directly impacted their lives. Nonetheless, this made the FARC an easy target for Colombian society and a national scapegoat for all the ills that beset Colombia.

In preparing for the 1998 presidential elections, FARC leader, Manuel Marulanda, met with Conservative Party candidate Andres Pastrana, making it known that if Pastrana were elected, the FARC would negotiate for peace in good faith. On the basis of that understanding, the Colombian people, who were desperate for an end to the conflict, voted Pastrana into office as the "peace candidate." Pastrana was eager to fulfill his campaign promises, so he presented *Plan Colombia* to the U.S. Congress and requested assistance for judicial reform and socio-economic development. However, U.S. lawmakers were more concerned that Pastrana's emphasis on peace negotiations would distract Colombia's attention from a U.S. antidrug agenda. Characteristically, senior U.S. government officials exerted pressure on Pastrana to emphasize counternarcotics as a national priority.[26] From what was substantially envisaged a "*Marshall Plan*"[27] for peace and social development, *Plan Colombia* soon became the cornerstone to a U.S. regional counterdrug policy. To that end, U.S. Congress passed a resolution that would decertify Colombia, essentially cutting off all U.S. foreign assistance to Colombia, if Pastrana's peace initiatives—especially the proposed plan to grant the FARC a demilitarized zone—interfered with coca aerial eradication efforts in southeastern Colombia. The extreme variation in analyzing Colombia's security problem indicated a lack of clear strategic vision as to how U.S. policy should integrate with the fundamental goals of Colombia's internal security challenges and the ongoing peace process with the FARC. Moreover, this ambiguity reflects on the content of a strategic plan that went from a vision to complement the ongoing peace process with the FARC, to a U.S. inspired and controlled counternarcotics policy.

For their part, FARC leaders argued that the state had acted in bad faith by pretending to negotiate while continuing to work with paramilitary forces that massacred peasants in areas under FARC influence. The FARC further justified their distrust by pointing to the results of a previous round of peace negotiations with President Belisario Betancur in the mid-1980s. As a result of those talks, the Colombian government agreed to allow the FARC and the Colombian Communist Party to form the Patriotica Union (UP), a legal political party that was joined by other leftist leaders and movements. However, over the next decade paramilitaries, hired assassins, and state security agents killed an estimated three to four thousand UP members, including two presidential candidates. The near extermination of the UP not only strengthened the FARC's hardline military position, but also further diluted the true nature of the conflict and its complexity, from a popular insurgency seeking political and economic pluralism to a contemptuous narcoinsurgency.

The third U.S. foreign policy decision directly affecting conflict resolution in Colombia was a result of the September 11, 2001 attacks on the United States. Overnight, the FARC was suddenly branded a "terrorist" organization, as the *Global War on Terrorism* replaced a U.S.-backed counter-insurgency strategy. Under President Uribe's heighted security policy, *Plan Patriota's* counterterrorism strategy appeared to replicate *Plan Colombia's* counter narcotics strategy in that the majority of resources were still being used for military operations against the FARC and very little dedicated for social and economic development.[28]

As seen during *Plan Colombia,* the *War on Terrorism* further dehumanized the FARC, making it easier to enable the Uribe government to act more forcefully without constraint. Both the Colombian government and FARC came to perceive one another as dire enemies. Although a very common practice, once the enemy was considered to be less than human, it became psychologically "acceptable" to resort to increasingly more destructive means, which resulted in gross violations of human rights from both sides of the conflict.

The Impact of Empathy in Conflict Resolution

"I'm not a Chavista, but I understand where he is coming from with respect to the poor."[29] The callous indifference of the Colombian ruling elite and FARC slowly depleted humanity and civility out of those who participated in this seemingly endless struggle. In analyzing Colombia's violent history, it is increasingly more apparent that this intractable conflict will continue to be an indisputable fact of life well into the twenty-first century, unless there is a paradigm shift where both sides of the argument exercise their capacity for empathy.[30] Empathy has a reputation as a fuzzy, feel-good emotion that is often associated in some vague way with everyday kindness or civility. Therefore, its value is easily dismissed when defending national interests or seeking diplomatic and political solutions to ideological differences.[31] Interestingly, two wise South African leaders, Nelson Mandela and Desmond Tutu, are veritable examples of how they challenged South African citizens

to will a society in which justice and fairness became common practice. In this particular case, empathy played an integral role in achieving a peaceful resolution. Moreover, during the 2008 U.S. presidential primaries, voters were asked what they felt was most important in a presidential candidate. The majority regarded "empathy" as legitimate and highly relevant in determining the best president to lead the most powerful nation in the world.[32]

However, such an empathic society is only possible when individuals are conditioned to imagine themselves in other people's situations. Just as perceptions are formed early in life and passed down through generations, "empathy also shapes individuals, and in many ways, has the power to transform entire societies."[33] For a Colombian citizen to see through the eyes of a FARC member, or vice versa, this presupposes the fundamental corrigibility of human nature, whereby individuals can learn, grow and improve their behaviors. Unfortunately, the FARC and their affiliates live in a survivalist society imperiled by economic hardship and insecurities. In this kind of environment, self-expression is low and empathy rarely reaches beyond family bonds or kinship relations.[34] Indeed, the envy of many societies, Switzerland for example has developed a cultural ability to expose human beings to empathy at a very early age. Through generations this process sharpens its citizens' receptivity, tolerance, and their capacity to be nice to each other ["sind lieb miteinand"] in local Swiss dialect. Consequently, empathy becomes an essential component of this direct democracy built on consensus.[35]

Moreover, with empathy as part of a national identity, individuals develop the ability to humanize each other and bring greater understanding to differing ideological views and perceptions. How Colombia's prolonged conflict is managed will depend on a clear understanding and acknowledgment of their historical context. More importantly, their conflict may be a direct reflection on its willingness to reach beyond one's own narrow interpretation of reality.[36] As commonly seen in Colombia, perceptions are not always perfect images of reality. They tend to exploit deception and false information to gain a strategic advantage over the "enemy," which has led to a "good-versus-evil" dialectic.[37] Unfortunately, over time this has created a very destructive atmosphere, which is increasingly more difficult to reverse.

As shown in South Africa under Nelson Mandela, only when the Colombian society imagines the experience of people living outside of their ascribed social status, will they freely enter into a dialogue that would enable reconciliation of differences. Mendala's South Africa was an example of how empathy is important in solving socio-political problems. But empathy is not a panacea for solving Colombia's intractable conflict. Human beings generally withhold empathy from others because cultural and ideological narratives present them as irrevocably different, making it easier to portray the enemy as contemptible and therefore deserving of their misfortune.[38] What is meaningful, however, is that empathy serves as a powerful psychological guide for compassion and social responsiveness. Without it, the FARC and Colombian government are likely to remain cold toward each other and therefore unable to even know how to understand or make sense of the destructive predicament they face. Not only is Mandela's unique ability for forgiveness a valuable leadership lesson, his real genius lies in making the citizens of South Africa amenable to recognizing fear and seeing others as worthy or legitimate to be listened to and to negotiate with.[39]

Recognizing Fear and According Legitimacy

"It all began so innocently . . . all I wanted in life was to get married, get a job as a seamstress, and take care of my children."[40] The Colombian conflict has taken on increased symbolic significance over the past fifty years. The original argument—to create more pluralistic political and economic institutions for a broader cross section of society—has become less relevant as new causes and fears were generated. Both the Colombian government and FARC developed a mutual fear of each other as well as a profound desire to inflict as much physical and psychological harm on each other as possible.[41] This sense of threat and hostility has pervaded the lives of those directly and indirectly involved in this conflict, and seems to override their ability to recognize and legitimize any common concerns they may actually share.[42]

Arguably, fear can be viewed as both a cause and a consequence of Colombia's violent history, making conflict analysis and resolution more difficult. This intractable conflict involves interests and general values that both Colombia's ruling elite and FARC regard as worthy to fight over. The FARC faced a legitimate fear based on unfulfilled social, economic, and political needs and the consequences of losing one's identity and security. On the other hand, the Colombian government faced perceived security concerns regarding the spread of communism, the social scourge of drug trafficking, and most recently terrorism.

It is understandable for Colombia's ruling elite to view the FARC as nothing more than bandits, communists, and drug trafficking terrorists who are willing to destroy the country and restructure political and economic institutions in their favor. Brutal tactics and reliance on the cocaine business, as one source of illicit financing, further alienated the majority of the population outside of certain rural regions. The FARC

members were also responsible for countless atrocities against civilians including massacres, car bombings, mass kidnappings, and coerced recruitment of children. Their improvised explosive devices (IEDs)[43] killed and mutilated thousands of Colombian citizens and forced millions of innocent people to be internally displaced from their homes.

The FARC's involvement with drugs, extortion and especially kidnapping, only complicated the issue making them an even easier target for negative imaging and dehumanization. Once the FARC and their affiliates were considered less than human, it became psychologically acceptable to employ less than human practices—a perfect recipe for human rights violations. This is an extremely dangerous practice.

It is equally convenient for the FARC and their affiliates to question the legitimacy of the Colombian government and ruling elite as untrusting hegemons, full of selfish and corrupt practices to control political and economic power in their favor. It is the FARC's view that Colombian democracy has flaws, particularly when two-thirds of Colombians living in rural areas still suffer from "absolute poverty," as defined as the inability to properly feed and clothe themselves. Living in constant danger, one can ask, "How can violence be the solution when violence was the primary reason for poverty and inequality?"[44]

Like hundreds of thousands of deprived Colombians, Pedro Antonio Marin, *alias* Manuel Marulanda Velez, was also swept up by the maelstrom that followed Jorge Gaitans death,[45] which catapulted the country into a decade-long civil war, known as *La Violencia*, or The Violence.[46] Full of fear, poor peasants desperately fled to the remote mountains and organized into liberal and communist self-defense groups to protect themselves and their families against the rampages of the conservative government's paramilitary and police forces. Although most *communists, guerrillas* or *bandits,* as they were labeled, put down their weapons during the 1958 national-front government's amnesty, several demobilized leaders and hundreds of their followers were savagely murdered.[47] The communists were cautious because the Colombian government demonstrated an unwillingness to grapple with serious solutions concerning agrarian reform and the associated challenges of rural living.

Colombia's ruling elite harbored a profound distaste for centralized power, a tradition that dated back to the days of the Spanish Crown.[48] There was simply no appetite for political and economic inclusivity or a desire to create a consensus around solutions to ideological differences and social tension. The political agreement that finally ended *La Violencia* guaranteed a sixteen-year period in which liberals and conservatives would share power, leaving no electoral outlet for social reform. There seemed to be no effort to understand, legitimize or demonstrate empathy for any of the political concerns or social challenges facing the poor. It also appeared that Colombia defied solutions to social problems, a defining characteristic since independence, where each "spasm of bloodshed always seemed to be a continuation of the previous one."[49]

Conclusion

The sign outside the entrance to the cemetery reads; "Aqui somos todos iguales." In English, "Here we are all equals." But equality in the cemetery cannot ignore the violent experiences and deep-rooted perceptions that have polarized Colombia into two unequal worlds. Decades of revenge and attacks on areas of personal sensitivity have created an atmosphere of distrust, anger, and vulnerability. The adversarial relationship between the ruling elite and FARC is marked by such a long history of fear and mistrust that only when a paradigm shift in thinking happens can the true causes of this dispute be openly acknowledged and the rigidity of thinking pacified. Regrettably, violence in Colombia is rooted in complex social-political factors: poverty, ideological differences, social inequality, the government's shortcomings, the scourge of narcotics, and numerous other problems. These have led to the fact that in nearly two centuries since independence, Colombia has experienced only forty-seven years of peace.[50]

Revenge solves nothing according to former Colombian President Alvaro Uribe Velez who said, "We cannot lash out angrily at this violence and expect it to go away."[51] Nor should violence in Colombia be interpreted in moral terms as a confrontation between good and evil. The biggest obstacle to conflict resolution as pointed out by former FARC leader Marulanda "is the isolation of this fight. . . between you in the city, and us, here in the mountains. Your voices and our voices don't listen to each other; we rarely speak to each other. It's not the mountain across our paths that form[s] the obstacle. Among yourselves, it's the very little you know about us, among us, it's the very little we know of your history.[52]

Colombian society is as much divided today as it was fifty years ago because of these social-psychological barriers. There is still pro-FARC Colombians from rural areas who remain distrustful of a government they view as failing to deliver on past promises. "Historically, the government has never helped us, and with coca we helped ourselves economically. Now the government wants to help, but we are afraid it will ruin the economy we now depend on to survive."[53] There are also a majority of right-wing urban dwellers avidly defending the government who they associate with security, sound democratic practices, and economic prosperity. Over the past two decades, Colombia has emerged as a much safer and economically prosperous country. Unfortunately, absent some form of compromise and a clear understanding of the "enemy's narrative," the wishes of all Colombians cannot be simultaneously met or legitimized.[54]

How can Colombia bring better clarity to the seemingly blurred perspective regarding this conflict? Perhaps a Truth and Reconciliation Commission, as realized in South Africa could add value to the process of acknowledging history, learning empathy, and recognizing fear and its according legitimacy. In theory, a Truth and Reconciliation Commission would help facilitate open communications between the FARC and Colombian society as once suggested by Marulanda. This would also help disabuse prejudices and misconceptions. It would help dissolve the rigidity of thinking. It would help acknowledge history. It would help create an environment to share with each other the "enemy's world." It would help promote individual healing. It would help humanize the "enemy." It would help legitimize the once negative portrait of the "enemy." It would help unblock empathy. It would help encourage reconciliation of differences. In summary, it would help provide the necessary foundation for a peaceful resolution to this fifty-year conflict.

Changing Colombia's calcified understanding of life and people will not be an easy task. Anything worthwhile rarely is "easy." The danger with perceptions is that while they are drawn from reality, over time they actually create reality, as highlighted in Colombia's historical context.[55] Many of Colombia's ruling elite, as well as the FARC, operate far more from assumptions than from a genuine understanding of reality. Both groups have their own history and narrative about the conflict, as passed down from previous generations; however, few know very little about the narrative and history of the other. They are unable to reach beyond their own perspectives primarily due to the scarcity of interaction between them.

Maybe this is where the South African philosophy of humanism, as expressed under Mandela's leadership, could serve as a basic blueprint for conflict resolution. This could be the paradigm shift where civility replaces violence as the solution to Colombia's social problems. Surprisingly, this philosophy may have played out during the August 22, 2014 dialogue on humanistic conditions between General Javier Flórez, the former second-in-command of Colombia's armed forces, and FARC negotiators in Havana. It was one of the most dramatic moments in almost two years of ongoing peace talks between the Colombian government and the FARC because it enabled, as stated by senior FARC negotiator, Ivan Márquez, "the opportunity to talk warrior-to-warrior."[56] Regrettably, President Santos was emphatic during his recent meeting with United Nations Secretary General Ban Ki-moon, when he proclaimed that the Colombian government will have nothing to do with *Castro-chavismo*,[57] essentially telling the world that the Colombian government will not negotiate with the FARC any alternative options to current political and economic institutions.[58] All hope rests on signing a peace agreement in Havana, Cuba, but does this simply mean that Colombia's violence and ongoing social struggle will be bequeathed to the next generation?

Notes

1. Robert Taber, *War of the Flea: The Classic Study of Guerrilla Warfare,* (Washington, DC: Potomac Books, Inc., 2002) p. 170.

2. Ben Connable and Martin C. Libicki, *How Insurgencies End,* (Santa Monica, CA: Rand Corporation 2010), p. 152.

3. Maire A. Dugan, "Power Inequalities," *The Beyond Intractability Project,* Edited by Guy Burgess and Heidi Burgess (Colorado: The Conflict Information Consortium, University of Colorado, February 2004), http://www.beyondintractability.org/essay/power-inequalities.

4. Daron Acemoglu and James A. Robinson, *Why Nations Fail: The Origins of Power, Prosperity and Poverty,* (Great Britain: Profile Books, 2012) p. 101

5. John Charles Chasten, *Born in Blood & Fire: A Concise History of Latin America,* (New York: W.W. Norton & Company 2006) p. 83.

6. Robert Harvey, *Bolivar, The Liberator of Latin America: The War Against the Spanish Empire,* (United Kingdom: Skyhorse Publishing 2011), p. 37.

7. Albert Berry, "Has Colombia Finally Found an Agrarian Reform That Works?" http://www.peri.umass.edu/fileadmin/assets/pdfs/Berry-AGREF_1_.10.pdf.

8. Acemoglu and Robinson, p. 37.

9. Ibid, p. 37.

10. Karen Ballentine and Jack Sherman, editors, *The Political Economy of Armed Conflict: Beyond Greed and Grievance,* (A project of the International Peace Academy, 2003).

11. Thomas Hobbs, *Leviathan,* (Australia: The University of Adelaide, February 27, 2014 by eBooks @ Adelaide), Chapter 21.

12. Garry Leech, *The FARC: The Longest Insurgence,* (Halifax: Fernwood Publishing 2011), p. 7.

13. Michelle Maiese, "Causes of Disputes and Conflicts," *The Beyond Intractability Project,* (Colorado: The Conflict Information Consortium, University of Colorado, October 2003), http://www.beyondintractability.org/essay/underlying-causes.

14. Henry Kissinger, *Years of Upheaval,* (Boston, MA: Little, Brown & Co. 1982), pp. 465–467.

15. Terry L. Deibel, *Foreign Affairs Strategy: Logic for American Statecraft,* (Great Britain: Cambridge University Press 2007), p.118.

16. Ibid, p. 118.

17. John Charles Chasteen, p. 280.

18. Steven R. Robe, p. 7

19. Ibid, p.281.

20. Steven R. Robe, p. 703.

21. John Charles Chasteen, p.281.

22. Ibid, p.281.

23. In 1962, *Plan Laso* was the first U.S. initiative designed to pre-empt the spread of communism in Colombia. One of its primary objectives was to "eliminate the so-called independent republics" created by leftist insurgents and some bandit elements in the upper Magdalena Valley.

24. Cynthia J. Arnson, Introduction, *The Peace Process in Colombia and U.S. Policy,* (Latin American Program: Woodrow Wilson International Center for Scholars Number 246, May 2000), p. 11.

25. Ibid, pp. 6–18.

26. Ibid, p. 11.

27. The Marshall Plan, named after Secretary of State George C. Marshall, was launched by President Harry Truman (1945–1952) to reconstruct sixteen Western European countries after World War II. The total amount of support was estimated at thirteen billion dollars.

28. Garry Leech, *Beyond Bogota,* p. 173.

29. Interview with demobilized FARC members, Bucaramanga, Colombia, 2013.

30. Claudia Seymour, "Social Psychological Dimensions of Conflict," *The Beyond Intractability Project,* Edited by Guy Burgess and Heidi Burgess, (Colorado: The Conflict Information Consortium, University of Colorado, September 2003), http://www.beyondintractibility.org/essay/social-psychological.

31. Roman Krznaric, "Can Empathy Help Resolve Violent Conflict?", *Outrospection,* November 5, 2013.

32. Jeremy Rifkin, *The Empathic Civilization: The Race to Global Consciousness in a World in Crisis,* (New York: Penguin Group, 2009), p. 446

33. Anna Titulear, "The Power of Empathy in Conflict Resolution," *Peace and Conflict Monitor,* May 16, 2012.

34. Jeremy Rifkin, p. 449.

35. Philip K. Abbott, "Achieving a Peace Settlement between Abkhazia and Georgia: Lessons from Swiss Federalism", *Small Wars Journal,* May 6, 2011.

36. Anna Titulaer, The Power of Empathy in Conflict Resolution.

37. Claudia Seymour, Social Psychological Dimensions of Conflict.

38. Martha Nussbaum, *Upheavals of Thought: The Intelligence of Emotions,* (Great Britain: Cambridge University Press 2001), p. 327.

39. John Kane, *The Politics of Moral Capital,* (England: Cambridge University Press 2001), pp.329–300.

40. Interview with demobilized FARC members in Cali, Colombia, 2012.

41. Peter Coleman, "Intractable Conflict," *The Handbook of Conflict Resolution: Theory and Practice,* edited by Morton Deutsch and Peter Coleman, (San Francisco: Josey-Bass, 2000), p. 428.

42. Maiese, Michelle, "Causes of Disputes and Conflicts," *The Beyond Intractability Project,* Edited by Guy Burgess and Heidi Burgess, (Colorado: The Conflict Research Consortium, University of Colorado, October 2003), http://www.beyondintractability.org/essay/underlying-causes.

43. On an annual average from 2009 to 2013, there have been over 2,000 Colombian army soldiers wounded and over 500 killed in

action. The majority of these casualties are inflicted by FARC emplaced improvised explosive devices.

44. Alvaro Uribe Velez, *No Lost Cause,* (London: Penguin Books, 2012), p. 57

45. Jorge Eliecer Gaitan, the populist Liberal leader whose radical politics resonated with Colombia's excluded poor. His assassination on April 9, 1948 ignited an uprising in Bogota that changed the course of Colombian history. The uprising spread throughout the country, further igniting a decade-long civil war between Liberals and Conservatives known simply as *La Violencia,* in which more than 200,000 Colombians were killed.

46. Dennis M. Rempe, "Guerrillas, Bandits, and Independent Republics: US Counter-insurgency Efforts in Colombia 1959–1965," in *Small Wars* (Winter 1995). http://www.icdc.com/paulwolf/colombia/smallwars.htm.

47. In 1958, the National-Front government assumed power under the power-sharing agreement that called for the Liberal Party and Conservative Party to alternate the presidency every four years and split all government posts. This political arrangement lasted until 1974.

48. Alvaro Uribe Velez, p. 52.

49. Ibid, p. 51.

50. Alvaro Uribe Velez, p. 33.

51. Ibid, p. 33.

52. Arturo Alape, *Manuel Marulanda, Tirofijo Colombia: 40 Años de Lucha Guerrillera,* (San Isidro, Mexico: Txalaparta 1998), p. 54.

53. Interview with demobilized FARC member in Bucaramanga, Colombia in 2013.

54. *Beyond Bogota: Diary of a Drug War Journalist in Colombia,* (Boston, MA 2009), p. 217.

55. Claudia Seymour, Social Psychological Dimensions of Conflict.

56. The Americas, "The moment of truth: Colombia's peace process," *The Economist,* (August 30, 2014).

57. Castrochavismo is in reference to the economic option taken by Fidel Castro and Hugo Chavez whereby a centralized government plays a much stronger role in guiding the choice of each individual decision.

58. Politico, "No tenemos nada que ver con el castrochavismo," El Tiempo, http://www.eltiempo.com/politico/acciones, (22 de septiembre de 2014).

Links

1. http://smallwarsjournal.com/author/philip-k-abbott

2. http://www.beyondintractability.org/essay/power-inequalities

3. http://www.peri.umass.edu/fileadmin/assets/pdfs/Berry-AGREF_1_.10.pdf

4. http://www.beyondintractability.org/essay/underlying-causes

5. http://www.beyondintractibility.org/essay/social-psychological

6. http://www.icdc.com/paulwolf/colombia/smallwars.htm

7. http://www.eltiempo.com/politico/acciones

Critical Thinking

1. What are the underlying causes of the conflict in Colombia?

2. What is the impact of FARC's involvement with drugs, extortion, and kidnapping?

3. What role should the United States play in ongoing negotiations?

4. Will the conflict be passed down to the next generation?

Internet References

FARC, ELN: Colombia's Left-Wing Guerrillas
http://www.cfr.org/colombia/farc-eln-colombias-left-wing-guerrillas/p9272

CRS: Colombia: Background, U.S. Relations, and Congressional Interest
https://www.fas.org/sgp/crs/row/RL32250.pdf

Colombia's Coca Farmers Face Uncertain Future as FARC Negotiates Peace
http://www.npr.org/2015/01/20/378681784/colombias-coca-farmers-face-uncertain-future-as-farc-negotiates-peace

COLONEL PHILIP K. ABBOTT, U.S. Army, is currently the Combating Terrorism Portfolio Manager at the United States Southern Command in Miami, Florida. He received a B.A. from Norwich University, an M.A. from Kansas University, and an M.S. from the National Defense University. He served in various Command & Staff positions in Europe, the Pacific, and worked extensively throughout the Western Hemisphere as a Latin American Foreign Area Officer.

Unit 5

UNIT

Prepared by: Thomas J. Badey, *Randolph-Macon College*

Terrorism in the United States

Domestic terrorism remains a difficult topic for many in the United States. While Americans are willing to believe in "evil forces" with origins in other countries, many become uncomfortable at the thought of U.S. citizens as a source of political violence. Many refuse to believe that a system as free, open, and democratic as that of the United States can spawn those who hate and wish to destroy the very system that has bestowed on them tremendous individual freedoms, including the right to political dissent.

Public debate in the wake of the Boston marathon attacks echoes these sentiments. It is much easier to focus on potential foreign influences, on the Tsarnaev brothers, than to deal with the complex question of how two individuals, one of them an American citizen, who grew up in the United States and benefited from its freedoms, could so violently turn against their fellow citizens.

American reactions to domestic terrorists vary. While many Americans are outraged by domestic terrorism, some terrorists, like Eric Rudolph, responsible for four bombings, including attacks on the Olympics in Atlanta, two women's clinics, and a bar, have achieved cult-hero status, with bumper stickers and T-shirts popularizing Rudolph's near-legendary flight from law enforcement officials. Groups like the Animal Liberation Front (ALF) and the Earth Liberation Front (ELF) continue to attract apologists searching for ways to justify or explain the violent behavior of otherwise "good Americans." Even the case of Timothy McVeigh, who was prosecuted and executed for the Oklahoma City bombing, has attracted some that continue to believe in an international conspiracy with origins in the Middle East, despite evidence to the contrary. This apparent schizophrenia is echoed in media reporting, public opinion, and public policy.

While the media demonizes the foreign terrorist, it often tends to humanize those who are "just like us." Thus, media reporting about American terrorists often emphasizes a human-interest perspective. Stories about Minnesota's middle-class soccer mom, Jane Olson, or the young, idealistic, and obviously misguided "American Taliban," John Walker, or even the psychologically unbalanced log-cabin recluse, Ted Kaczynski, make good copy and are designed to elicit sympathy or empathy in a larger audience. In its efforts to explain how or why "good" Americans have gone "bad," the violence and victims are sometimes ignored. An apology to veterans groups a few years ago by the Secretary of Homeland Security for a DHS report that indicated that some veterans were attracted to or active in right-wing militia groups indicates that the topic of domestic terrorism is still a political minefield.

Public opinion and public policy are also subject to this apparent dissonance. While the American public and U.S. policymakers appear to care little about the legal rights or physical detention of foreigners suspected of association with terrorist organizations, the legal rights of domestic terrorist suspects are often the subject of intense public scrutiny and debate.

The selections in this unit look at the problem of terrorism in the United States. In the first article in this section Jonathan Masters offers an overview of four basic categories of militant extremists and briefly describes the domestic intelligence infrastructure developed to address this threat. Next, Mark Potok from the Southern Poverty Law Center in his annual report looks at "The Year in Hate and Extremism." His research indicates that after an all-time high in 2012, there has been a significant decline in the number of conspiracy-minded antigovernment groups in the United States. Potok posits that this decline may be the result of the co-opting of their issues by mainstream politicians, of an improving economy, and of law enforcement crackdowns. Finally, a study by the Anti-Defamation League reports a dramatic increase of Islamic extremist arrests in the United States. It attributes this trend to the increased role of social media in recruitment and attempts to categorize these cases.

Article   Prepared by: Thomas J. Badey, *Randolph-Macon College*

Militant Extremists in the United States

JONATHAN MASTERS

Learning Outcomes

After reading this article, you will be able to:

- Describe four "broad categories" of domestic extremists identified by the FBI.

- Identify the three primary groups involved in combating domestic extremism.

- Discuss the challenges that the US government faces in responding to this threat.

Introduction

The January 2011 shootings—in which a lone gunman killed six people at a Tucson, Arizona, shopping center—served as a reminder of the threat posed by militant extremism in the United States. Similar acts of violence in the last few years—such as the suicide plane crash into an IRS building in Texas and the 2009 shooting at the U.S. Holocaust Memorial Museum—have brought renewed attention to the dangers posed by fringe political extremism. Although the frequency of these types of attacks has decreased in recent years, "lone wolf" violence is on the rise. The FBI is particularly concerned by such threats because they are performed by individuals who are unaffiliated with any larger movement and are, therefore, hard to detect. As with the case of Tucson shooter Jared Lee Loughner, it is difficult for authorities to determine whether such an act of violence falls under the legal definition of "domestic terrorism," a determination that invokes much harsher sentencing guidelines. Some experts criticize a lack of consistency in the way U.S. domestic terrorism laws are applied, which can lead to dissimilar procedures and outcomes for similar cases.

Violent Extremism or 'Domestic Terrorism'?

Since September 11, the threat of internationally based Islamic extremist networks has dominated concerns of Homeland Security officials. And while authorities say the threats posed by homegrown Islamic extremism is growing, the FBI has reported that roughly two-thirds of terrorism in the United States was conducted by non-Islamic American extremists from 1980–2001; and from 2002–2005, it went up to 95 percent.

With the enactment of the Patriot Act in 2001, the legal definition of "terrorism" was expanded to include domestic as well as international terrorism. However, alternative definitions still exist at the FBI, Justice Department, Homeland Security Department, and Defense Department. Some descriptive terms (such as "sub-national," "pre-meditated," "noncombatant," etc.) are present in one definition and absent in others. Furthermore, many law enforcement groups, like the FBI, use the labels of domestic terrorism and violent extremism interchangeably. One consequence of this practice is a lack of uniformity in the way domestic terrorist activities are prosecuted. In an effort to improve federal terrorism laws, a Syracuse University-sponsored watchdog organization compared the number of terrorism cases listed by three entities—the courts (310), the prosecutors (508), and the National Security Division (253)—and found that from 2004–2009 only 4 percent of cases were classified as terrorism on all three lists. This suggests that the agency that made the designation, not the facts of the case, determined whether a suspect was prosecuted as a terrorist and, therefore, may have received a harsher sentence. The same report found "little public evidence that the Obama administration has launched a significant effort to deal with the continuing criminal enforcement flaws."

Alternative definitions [of what legally constitutes terrorism] still exist at the FBI, Justice Department, Homeland Security Department, and Defense Department.

A Spectrum of Militancy

The worst case of domestic extremist violence was the 1995 bombing of the Alfred P. Murrah Federal Building in Oklahoma City that killed 168 people. In the twenty-five years prior, the United States experienced an average of forty-eight such attacks per year. Since 1995, the average attacks per year declined to nineteen. However, the percentage of attacks perpetrated by individuals acting alone, characterized by law enforcement as "lone wolf" offenders, has increased roughly *five-fold*. Defending against these types of attacks is a daunting task for the FBI and police.

The FBI divides domestic extremists into four broad categories, including left-wing, right-wing, single issue groups, and homegrown Islamic. The lone offender phenomenon spans all categories, and the classifications have other overlapping characteristics as well.

Lone Offenders

Violence by lone offenders may pose the most immediate threat in the United States. According to an FBI report on terrorism, the lone wolf label refers to individuals "who commit acts of violence outside of the auspices of structured terrorist organizations or without the prior approval or knowledge of these groups' leaders." A Department of Homeland Security study found that attacks by individuals constituted one-third of all extremist acts of violence since 1995, up from just 6.5 percent in the twenty-five years prior. Recent high-profile cases of these attacks include those by Jared Lee Loughner, James von Brunn, and Abdulhakim Mujahid Muhammad. Because of their isolation from organized extremist groups, lone wolves are particularly hard to track for intelligence agencies. However, their independence often makes them less effective than members who are well connected to large networks.

Left-Wing Groups

The FBI states leftist extremist groups "generally profess a revolutionary socialist doctrine and view themselves as protectors of the people against the "dehumanizing effects" of capitalism and imperialism." From 1960 to the mid-1980s, most acts of extremist violence were committed by leftist factions like the Weather Underground. A wellspring of disaffected, radical youth with ideological roots in the civil rights, women's liberation, and anti-war movements provided these groups with much of their militant fervor. However, broad left-wing violence has been in a marked decline since the fall of the Soviet Union and a successful FBI infiltration campaign in the mid-1980s.

Single-Issue Groups

Single-issue extremists attack targets that embody distinct political issues like environmental degradation, abortion, genetic engineering, or animal abuse. These groups are usually composed of small, autonomous cells that are hard to infiltrate because of rigid secrecy. According to the FBI, so-called eco-terrorists and animal rights groups like the Earth Liberation Front have committed over two thousand crimes and caused losses of over $110 million since 1979. Ecological extremism gained particular notoriety in the 1990s, and in 2004 the FBI declared these groups the No. 1 domestic terrorism threat. Anti-abortion extremists are responsible for seven murders, forty-one bombings, and 173 acts of arson in the U.S. and Canada since 1977, according to the National Abortion Federation, an abortion rights group. While much of this violence peaked in the 1990s, the 2009 murder of Dr. George Tiller served as a reminder of the threat still posed by these factions.

Right-Wing Groups

The most recent swell of extremist violence began to emerge from right-wing militants in the late-1980s and 1990s. According to a 2005 FBI report on terrorism, these groups, which are "primarily in the form of domestic militias and conservative special interest causes, began to overtake left-wing extremism as the most dangerous, if not the most prolific, domestic terrorist threat to the country." Right-wing extremists champion a wide variety of causes, including racial supremacy, hatred and suspicion of the federal government, and fundamentalist Christianity. The Southern Poverty Law Center, which tracks the activities of hate groups, suggests militia groups declined every year since 1996 but have seen a dramatic resurgence since 2008.

Civil Liberties and Counterterrorism

Following the Church Committee hearings of 1975 and the exposure of several illegal U.S. intelligence programs, U.S. lawmakers instituted a number of legal reforms to safeguard civil liberties, including the 1978 Foreign Intelligence Surveillance Act or FISA. This legislation created strict procedures for reviewing government requests for the electronic surveillance of Americans and resident aliens, and sought to end the practice of warrantless wiretapping. It placed the legal burden of proof on the intelligence community to demonstrate that the subject of surveillance is "a foreign power or agent of a foreign power."

However, after the September 11 attacks, the FBI shifted its directive from law enforcement to terrorism prevention—returning its emphasis to proactive domestic surveillance. The public fear of another large-scale attack ushered in a new privacy-security paradigm, and with it came legislation aimed at broad national security reforms, such as the Patriot Act, the Homeland Security Act, the Intelligence Reform and Terrorism Prevention Act, and the 2008 FISA Amendment Acts. But despite this overhaul, CFR's Richard Falkenrath suggests, "The federal government has a quite limited domestic intelligence program and capability. The government does not have an unfettered right to collect information on Americans. It's a very complicated legal and executive order framework, which governs when and how the government can collect information of potential threats domestically."

The Domestic Intelligence Infrastructure

September 11 was a seminal event for U.S. intelligence culture. Prior to the attack, critical components of the intelligence infrastructure like the CIA, FBI, and NSA were not sharing essential information. The 9/11 Commission Report cited a number of reasons for this including structural barriers, divided management, lack of common practices, and excessive secrecy. In their effort to reform the system, lawmakers deemed terrorism prevention a national priority that required the integration of all elements of the intelligence infrastructure, including local and state entities as well as dedicated federal agencies like the FBI. To fulfill their new role, local police commanders promoted the adoption of "intelligence-led policing", a philosophy emphasizing future-oriented, risk-based intelligence.

The conventional wisdom from law enforcement officials is that prevention requires active, exploratory intelligence gathering. But despite the new emphasis, CFR's Falkenrath says the U.S. domestic intelligence system "is still really built around a framework that requires 'predication,' or evidence of a crime that has occurred or is about to occur. This framework works well in a criminal justice setting, but it really struggles when you know there are real threats that don't have clear predication."

In an open-source review for the Department of Homeland Security in 2009, the RAND Corporation mapped the domestic intelligence network to identify all the components "involved in the collection, analysis, and sharing of information about individuals and organizations in the United States." This study identifies three principle categories focused on domestic extremists:

- **Department of Homeland Security.** Formed in 2002, DHS is a cabinet-level department that performs a vast number of domestic intelligence activities and initiatives. The Office of Intelligence and Analysis is the core element of its intelligence function. DHS also operates the National Operations Center, which collects and fuses information from more than thirty-five public and private agencies. In addition, Information-Sharing and Analysis centers or ISACs are an assortment of public-private partnerships designed to protect critical physical and electronic infrastructure from terrorist attacks. For example, DHS launched a cybersecurity operation center in New York in November 2010.
- **Department of Justice.** The Federal Bureau of Investigation is the government's lead agency for domestic intelligence and counterterrorism, but the DoJ also includes the DEA, U.S. Attorneys Offices, U.S. Marshals Service, and the Bureau of Alcohol, Tobacco, Firearms, and Explosives. The FBI intelligence mission is managed at the National Security Branch which, among other things, manages the National Joint Terrorism Task Force and the Terrorist Screening Center.
- **State, Local, and Private-Sector Groups.** The FBI-led Joint Terrorism Task Force and the DHS-supported Fusion Center program are the most prominent federally directed, multiagency initiatives. Both programs use intelligence from multiple entities to leverage information-sharing potential. However, the FBI task force is always the lead agency for domestic terrorism investigations, as demonstrated in the the January 2011 MLK Day attempted-bombing in Washington state. On the other hand, fusion centers may be focused on any number of other concerns outside the realm of terrorism, such as organized crime, immigration, and natural disasters.

The Road Ahead

Militant extremism in the United States continues to provide grist for the national debate on a number of policy areas. The shootings in Tucson revived the issue of gun control once again, highlighting some of the nation's controversial firearm legislation—like the Arizona law allowing citizens to carry concealed weapons without a permit. In addition, public discussion continues over the legal definition of domestic terrorism and whether it is applied equitably. Questions also remain as to whether the United States has lessons to learn from the counterterrorism experiences of other countries. For instance,

should it create an independent domestic intelligence agency similar to Britain's MI-5, which does not incorporate a law enforcement function like the FBI?

> **"We're at a point where you have to start asking hard questions about changing the law, and/or the executive orders that interpret the law, to be more permissive"**
>
> —CFR Adjunct Senior Fellow Richard Falkenrath

Efforts to counter homegrown militancy will also continue to drive a conversation on civil liberties. Liberal groups like the American Civil Liberties Union advocate for stricter legal guidelines, "oppos[ing] the broad definition of terrorism and the ensuing authority that flows from that definition." On the other hand, proponents of assertive enforcement capabilities, like CFR's Falkenrath, raise concerns over potentially excessive regulation. "We're at a point where you have to start asking hard questions about changing the law, and/or the executive orders that interpret the law, to be more permissive."

Additional Resources

- "Are We Safer?" PBS Frontline Video (2010)
- "The Challenge of Domestic Intelligence in a Free Society", RAND Corporation (2009)
- "Congress and the Intelligence Community", Belfer Center, Harvard University (2009)
- "National Strategy for Homeland Security", Department of Homeland Security (2007)
- "Spying on the Home Front," PBS Frontline Video (2007)
- "Intelligence-Led Policing: The New Intelligence Architecture", DOJ (2005)

Critical Thinking

1. Which type of extremist poses the biggest threat? Why?
2. According to the 9/11 Commission Report, why did US intelligence agencies fail to share intelligence?
3. How can the United States more effectively address the threat of militant extremism?

Create Central

www.mhhe.com/createcentral

Internet References

The Dangers of the Lone-Wolf Terrorist
   http://nation.time.com/2013/02/27/the-danger-of-the-lone-wolf-terrrorist/
The Domestic Counterterrorism Enterprise
   www.heritage.org/research/reports/2012/10/domestic-counterterrorism-enterprise-time-to-streamline
Domestic Terror
   www.cnn.com/2012/09/16/us/domestic-terrorism

Article   Prepared by: Thomas J. Badey, *Randolph-Macon College*

The Earth Liberation Front: A Social Movement Analysis

MICHAEL LOADENTHAL

Learning Outcomes

After reading this article, you will be able to:

- Explain the ideological motivations of the Earth Liberation Front.
- Describe the organizational structure of the Earth Liberation Front.
- Discuss why the Earth Liberation Front has been successful in the United States.

The Earth Liberation Front is a radical environmental movement that developed from the ideological faction-alization of the British Earth First! movement of the 1990s. Its ideological underpinnings are based in deep ecology, anti-authoritarian anarchism highlighting a critique of capital-ism, a commitment to non-violence, a collective defense of the Earth, and a warranted feeling of persecution by State forces. In its current form, the Earth Liberation Front is a transnational, decentralized network of clandestine, autonomous, cells that utilize illegal methods of protest by sabotaging and vandalizing property. The small unit cells are self-contained entities that can operate without the support of external entities such as finan-ciers or weapons procurers. Tactical and operational knowledge is developed and shared through commercially available books written by the broader environmental movement throughout the last four decades, as well as inter-movement publications produced by the cells and distributed through numerous sym-pathetic websites. Membership can be understood as occurring on two levels, the covert cell level and the public support level, both of which operate in tandem to produce and publicize acts of property destruction. At the cell level, individuals conduct

pre-operational reconnaissance and surveillance, develop and construct weapons systems, carry out orchestrated attacks, and announce their actions to support groups and media while main-taining internal security and anonymity. At the aboveground level, support entities help to publicize attacks carried out by cells, respond to media inquiries and other public engagements, identify and coordinate aid to imprisoned cell members, and develop and distribute sympathetic propaganda produced by, and in support of affiliated individuals. This case study uses the history of the Earth Liberation Front's United States attacks as its unit of analysis, and seeks to outline the ideology, structure, context and membership factors that constitute the movement.

Introduction

October 14 is Columbus Day, a national holiday in the United States when citizens are reminded of their colonial roots. On this day in 1996, the Earth Liberation Front (ELF) leapt into action in the US state of Oregon. In one night, individuals car-ried out three simultaneous attacks targeting a Chevron station, a public relations office and a McDonald's restaurant. All three targets had their locks glued and their property painted with political messages including a three letter calling card, E.L.F. (Molland 2006, 55). For the US, this was the first salvo from the ELF, a clandestine, decentralized network of autonomous cells using sabotage and vandalism to cause financial hardship to tar-gets thought to be abusing the Earth. From this small action, less than ten years later, the US would declare the ELF "the most active criminal extremist element in the United States" (Lewis 2004) and the "number one domestic terrorist threat"[1] (Schuster 2005). While such rhetoric was mobilized with great strength in the decade following the millennium, the ELF remains active, transitory and for the most part, resistant to discovery and arrest.

The ELF is often discussed in tandem alongside other environmental and animal liberation/rights-focused movements as the main actors engaging in "eco-terrorism," defined as:

> The use or threatened use of violence of a criminal nature against innocent victims or property by an environmentally orientated subnational group for environmental-political reasons, aimed at an audience beyond the target, and often of a symbolic nature. (Eagan 1996, 2)

Broadly, this definition fails to define the ELF as it does not employ violence against "innocent victims." In the framing of "innocent victims" versus "property" noted above, one presumes that *victims* refers to *humans,* and as such, the ELF defies this definitional description as it has sought to damage property, not humans, and has managed to avoid injuring individuals accidentally (Borum and Tilby 2005, 212; Leader and Probst 2003, 44; Taylor 1998, 3, 8). As one scholar familiar with the "eco-terrorist" history writes, "While the ELF has caused millions of dollars worth of property damage, it has not yet intentionally (or even unintentionally) brought harm to anyone" (Ackerman 2003, 162). Such a casualty-free history should be noted as with nearly 300 attacks[2] claimed globally from 1996–2009 (Loadenthal 2010, 81), not a single human has been killed or injured (Loadenthal 2010, 98). In its 290 attacks claimed as the ELF, and its 69 attacks (Loadenthal 2010, 81) claimed jointly with the Animal Liberation Front (ALF), the target has always been property.

What follows is a case study analysis of the ELF movement as it operated (1996–2009) in North America. The majority of evidence presented is taken from centrist, state-affiliated, security-themed sources[3] whose purpose is to identify, locate and capture activists. While many of these sources make specious claims regarding activists' behaviors, they remain the most often quoted, 'authoritative' sources on the subject. For this reason the majority of the facts established herein will be adopted from such security-industry forces as to produce a descriptive social movement account that is both informed by a radical analysis, and triangulated with facts established by the State and its largess of resources and affiliated institutions.

Whereas the ELF is a global movement, with cells active in more than twenty countries, for the purpose of this analysis, cases will be limited to their North American attacks, the vast majority of which occurred in the continental US. Other affiliated radical networks and movements, such as the ALF and Earth First! (EF!) will be discussed as they relate to the history and developmental context of the ELF. This study is an attempt to paint a holistic picture of the ELF as a social movement, examining its ideology, structure, context, and multi-tiered membership that collectively constitute its ranks.

This study seeks neither to prove nor dispel a testable hypothesis, but rather to develop a detailed picture of the ELF's praxis as developed via its US activity. The study utilizes the US ELF movement as its unit of analysis (Yin 2008, 22–23), and seeks to explore the movement's philosophical underpinnings, networks, the context leading to its development, and the characteristics of its membership. The evidence presented herein is a synthesis of open source documentation, archival records and academic journals as well as numerous inter-movement publications authored by pro-ELF organizations. Whenever possible triangulation of data has been achieved and demonstrated through the multi-sourcing of findings via scholarly studies, government reports and inter-movement publications (Yin 2008, 91–92).

A Brief History

Beginning in the 1960s, a political movement emerged advancing a radically new critique of environmental and animal use practices. These new ideological tendencies were characterized by not only a shift in philosophical outlook, but also in language and collective practice. This time period is often associated with the founding of the *deep ecology* framework, authored by Norwegian philosopher Arne Næss in 1972 (Eagan 1996, 3), replacing the environmental protectionism of [the] past, as well as ideas of *animal liberation,* inspired by a 1975 book of the same title by Peter Singer. Just as Singer's notion of *liberation* replaced previously popular notions of animal *welfare* or *rights,* the groups which formed during this time replaced previously dominant strategies of collective popular protest with that of self-guided, autonomous units. These new revolutionary frameworks were quickly adopted by emergent groups, which began to utilize sabotage, vandalism, and arson.

1963 saw the formation of the Hunt Saboteurs Association, dedicated to physically disrupting hunting expeditions, often taking the form of sabotage and provocation. After working with a group of hunt saboteurs in the early 1970s, several activists decided to shift their tactical focus. In 1972, the Band of Mercy (BOM) formed in England as the outgrowth of desire for a new praxis that prioritized taking animals out of harm's way, as well as financially sabotaging companies and institutions contributing to animal exploitation. Within three years of its founding, the BOM morphed into what has historically been the most active, clandestine, direct action group, the ALF. Since its founding in England in 1976, the ALF has carried out thousands of attacks globally. Several years after the formation of the ALF, the movement witnessed a factionalization into smaller, more violence-prone splinter cells and experienced deterritorialization to over forty countries. By 1994, the ALF inspired the formation of an organizationally and tactically similar movement targeting institutions of *ecological* exploitation through methods of sabotage and vandalism—the ELF.

Throughout [the] thirty-eight years under examination, the BOM, ALF and ELF have further deterritorialized and [this has] led to the formation of at least three hundred similarly styled groups. This global movement of movements which opposes violence (toward animals and the environment) has garnered the label 'eco-terrorism' from governments, media, and elements of the academic community.

Political-Philosophical Ideology

In establishing the ELF's ideology, we examine movement literature produced through aboveground support networks, such as the North American ELF Press Office[4] (NAELFPO). In a 2001 pamphlet, the NAELFPO states that "if an individual believes in the ideology and follows a certain set of guidelines she or he can perform actions and become a part of the ELF" (North American Earth Liberation Front Press Office 2001, 3). In a similar fashion to the ALF, these "guidelines" are established by unknown persons and distributed through movement literature thus creating a discursive reality for subsequent action. While there is no central authority that then judges actions to be in agreement with or in violation of the guideline, movement debate and discussion serves as a vetting process. According to the NAELFPO pamphlet, "Frequently Asked Question About the Earth Liberation Front," (2001) the group's guidelines are:

1. To cause as much economic damage as possible to a given entity that is profiting off the destruction of the natural environment and life for selfish greed and profit,
2. To educate the public on the atrocities committed against the environment and life,
3. To take all necessary precautions against harming life.

Such broad-based guidelines serve a functional purpose allowing for great tactical and strategic diversity while avoiding the factionalizing function (Joosse 2007) of public debate regarding the legitimacy of every action taken under the ELF moniker. Thus as an action is carried out, it is up to the activists to decide to either adopt the ELF name or not.

The "ideology" of the ELF contains thematic trends collectively constituting a shared ethos. Firstly, "deep ecology," often termed biocentrism, that teaches all living entities, human and non-human, have equal worth and value and an *inherent right* to exist and prosper. It is through this lens that the ELF understands its position *vis-à-vis* those understood to be destroying the Earth. Some of this influence comes from the ELF's historical development alongside anarchism, and specifically its anti-civilization tendencies often termed Green anarchism, anarcho-primitivism or simply, Primitivism (Taylor 2003, 181). At this juncture, the *greening* of anarchism extends its typically anthropocentric analysis toward deep ecology (Ackerman 2003, 147; The Green Anarchy Collective 2009).[5]

Green anarchism advocates the creation of a collectivized, pre-industrial, "wild" civilization of loosely affiliated, village-sized communities, devoid of modern industry and technology (Eagan 1996, 3–4; Helios Global, Inc. 2008, 4–5; Leader and Probst 2003, 40). The ELF ideology borrows heavily from anarchism, and as such, a great number of anarchists fill the ranks of the movement (Borum and Tilby 2005, 208; Leader and Probst 2003, 40; Taylor 2003, 181). The philosophical teachings of anarchism and the ELF concur that all forms of oppression are inherently incompatible with human society and must be replaced with non-hierarchical, non-coercive methods of organization and collective responsibility (Ackerman 2003, 147; Leader and Probst 2003, 40). This philosophical understanding opposing hierarchal structures, is reflected in the ELF's organizational methods (Chalk 2001; Eagan 1996, 2; Trujillo 2005, 146). Closely linked, the ELF shares a great deal with the broad leftist movements often termed, "anti-corporate/globalization," or "anti-capitalist" (Ackerman 2003, 153; Leader and Probst 2003, 40; Trujillo 2005, 159). Radical environmentalists share ideology with these movements arguing that modern capitalism "represents the single most important threat to the . . . environment," (Helios Global, Inc. 2008, 5) and that Western-led individualism is *predicated* on the exploitation of the natural resources of the Earth. (Ackerman 2003, 146; Helios Global, Inc. 2008, 4)

Secondly, the ELF claims to act as the "voice of the voiceless," the "defender of the defenseless," arguing that the planet is the victim of attacks perpetuated by mankind, for which it cannot respond in voice nor action (Ackerman 2003, 146–147; Helios Global, Inc. 2008, 4). The inability of the Earth to speak for itself empowers the ELF to speak and act in its defense (North American Earth Liberation Front Press Office 2001, 4) despite such a anthropocentric protectionism being challenged[6] by critical activists. Thirdly, the ELF advocates non-violence as it relates to all forms of life, simultaneously denying that non-living entities such as the property of eco-offenders, corporations, governments, etc. also have an inherent protection from violence (Eagan 1996, 9; Leader and Probst 2003, 41; North American Earth Liberation Front Press Office 2001, 27–28). This understanding and consistent injury-free practice allows the ELF to frame its acts of property destruction as non-violent sabotage, as such actions fail to target living creatures (jones 2006, 324).

Lastly, ELF ideology is tinged with accusations of unjustified attack by law enforcement (Ackerman 2003, 146; Eagan 1996, 13). This theme is commonly cited in communiqués from ELF cells as many believe they are being maliciously persecuted by governments. Such accusatory posturing by the ELF in their criticism of the State is certainly deserved. Since the US began its Domestic War on Terrorism following the attacks of September 11, 2001, environmental and animal liberation activists have become the target of increased State repression (Loadenthal 2013; Lovitz 2010; Potter 2011; Slater 2011) in what activists have termed the Green Scare. Within this pursue to produce arrests, the State has utilized a host of repressive methods not typically deployed amongst non-violence social movements. Included in its arsenal targeting direct action animal and earth liberationists is the use of state[7] and federal-level legislation (e.g. Animal Enterprise Terrorism Act, Ag-Gag legislation), the placement of police informants and provocateurs (such as the case of Eric McDavid and Marie Mason), home raids and other militarized forms of overt policing, increased electronic surveillance, use of Grand Juries to coerce information, and the use of anti-terrorist prison facilities to house inmates (such as the case of Daniel McGowan, Andrew Stepanian, Stanislas Meyerhoff and Walter Bond).[8] The largess of the State's targeted repression of such activists has been well established in activist scholarship and as such is not the focus of this investigation.

Tactical Ideology

The ELF extends its framework establishing tactical methodology melding philosophy with practice, creating a radical, anti-State, anti-capitalist, environmental praxis. This praxis advocates "direct action," (Helios Global, Inc. 2008, 12) to "remove the profit motive from killing the Earth" (North American Earth Liberation Front Press Office 2001, 28). Direct action, a key component of the anarchist tradition, is seen as the only way to achieve the ELF aims as traditional methods of politicking and lobbying have failed to achieve rapid success (Trujillo 2005, 146). For the ELF, direct action constitutes the use of illegal means of political protest such as sabotage, arson and other manners of property destruction to economically damage entities established as its enemies. In this sense, the ELF's goal is the financially insolvency of its targets using economic sabotage. To this end, the ELF advocates the use of methods (termed "weapon technologies" in the Terrorism/Security Studies literature) that cause financial harm while avoiding harming humans, animals and the environment. The weapons socio-political groups choose to provide insight into their politics, as "the specific weapons technologies groups choose . . . [and] . . . define the scale and scope of their violence" (Jackson and Frelinger 2008, 583). For the ELF there is a focus on improvised incendiaries (Jackson and Frelinger 2008, 597–598) self-manufactured from modified, off-the-shelf items (Helios Global, Inc. 2008, 26), guided by instruction from movement publications distributed mainly through the Internet (109th Congress 2005, 44; Joosse 2007, 354). The decision to use incendiaries, as opposed to firearms or projectiles, reflects ELF's desire to damage property while avoiding casualties (Jackson and Frelinger 2008, 598).

The ELF's targeting ideology reflects its desire to cause financial hardship whilst avoiding casualties and generally chooses target such as "facilities and companies involved in logging, genetic engineering, home building, automobile sales, energy production and distribution" (Leader and Probst 2003, 43). Targets chosen by cells are understood to be *directly* damaging the environment. Also contributing to the ELF's targeting decisions is the amount of security their targets employ. The ELF tends to attack targets that are not hardened against attack such as those affiliated with commercial business, University research and residential housing as opposed to more heavily protected targets such as military sites, government facilities or heavy industrial or manufacturing facilities. Therefore homes under construction are targeted, not realtors (North American Earth Liberation Front Press Office 2009b).[9] Privately owned vehicles are targeted, not car manufacturers (North American Earth Liberation Front Press Office 2009c).[10] Genetically engineered organisms (GMO) are pulled from the ground, and research centers destroyed with fire (North American Earth Liberation Front Press Office 2009a).[11] In these examples, the targeting reflects the desire to *directly* target the perceived ills, not to remedy them through attacking intermediary or secondary target. When examined through a global incident-based, quantitative analysis, one discovers that the ELF's main target types are construction and industrial equipment (14%), model homes and homes under construction (13%), business properties (12%) and automobiles most often sport utility vehicles (10)% (Loadenthal 2010). Other target types include (in descending order of frequency) phone booths, private business vehicles, farms, ranches and breeders, GMU crops and government property including vehicles.

Structure—Organizational Network

The ELF functions as a networked movement, not as an organization. It is a decentralized collection of autonomously operating, small unit, clandestine cells without organizational hierarchy or command and control structure (Helios Global, Inc. 2008, 1, 8, 11). Thus, "ELF" is a name given to the sum total of attacks carried out by disconnected cells and "lone wolf" attackers. It is an adoptable moniker for whomever wishes to use it. Whereas ELF cells may share a basic philosophical-political critique, generally cells have no communication or cooperation amongst themselves. In some isolated cases, operation coordination, or at least communication has likely occurred between cells. For example, on May 21, 2001, two ELF cells carried out simultaneous arsons targeting the Jefferson Poplar Farms in Clatskaine, Oregon and the horticulture research laboratory of the University of Washington in Seattle, Washington. According to the Federal Bureau of Investigations (FBI), both ELF cells responsible for the arsons were part of a twenty person multi-cell unit of the ELF known as "the family." Eleven members of "the family" were arrested by the FBI during "Operation Backfire" in late 2005 and early 2006, and linked to seventeen attacks in Oregon, Wyoming, Washington, California, and Colorado. From open source information, it is impossible to determine how common such multi-cell entities are within the greater milieu of the ELF movement. Law enforcement have found cells extremely difficult to infiltrate (Helios Global, Inc. 2008, 11) reporting that most possess "sophisticated organization and operational security," (Ackerman 2003, 151) including knowledge of forensics, signals intelligence, computer security, cryptography, and police surveillance (109th Congress 2005, 44; FBI Counterterrorism and Cyber Divisions 2004, 2–4; Immergut et al. 2007, 5, 35, 102, 117, 123, 134; Leader and Probst 2003, 42; Trujillo 2005, 154–155, 163). Cells operate with no known external support structure, existing self-sufficiently, fulfilling their logistical, funding, intelligence, and weapons acquisition needs. Unlike traditional terrorist organizations and violent non-State actors, there is no need for ELF cells to receive financial support from nation-states or smuggle weapons through secretive networks. Attacks are self-funded from the cell members as their cost is low (Helios Global, Inc. 2008, 27). Additional tasks traditionally assigned to externals are self-managed including pre-operational surveillance and reconnaissance, training and weapons acquisition (Leader and Probst 2003, 42).

Beyond the level of the cell, the ELF is understood as a movement of "leaderless resistance," a style of decentralization popularized by Louis Beam (1992), an American white supremacist, who describes a leaderless resistance model as:

> . . . A fundamental departure in theories of organization . . . [wherein] all individuals and groups operate independently of each other, and never report to a central headquarters or single leader for direction or instruction, as would those who belong to a typical pyramid organization. (1992)

This leaderless resistance, with no centralized authority or command and control, is seen in the workings of the ELF. The structure has great advantages for resisting infiltration by law enforcement, and provides a simple means of cell replication. The decentralized, autonomous, non-hierarchical network structure is also familiar to new members as it is the common organizational method within anarchist movements where many ELF members are active (Borum and Tilby 2005, 212; Chalk 2001). Due to the autonomy of the ELF cells, cells are not aware of others, and existing cells cannot be joined (Dishman 2005, 243). Because of their self-contained nature, new recruits are encouraged to form their own cell (Joosse

2007, 354). This advice is given plainly in a NAELFPO (2001) pamphlet, wherein the author states:

> Individuals interested in becoming active in the ELF need to follow the above guidelines and create their own close knit anonymous cell made up of trustworthy and sincere people. Remember the ELF and each cell within it are anonymous not only to one another but also to the general public. So there is not a realistic chance of becoming active in an already existing cell. Take initiative, form your own cell and do what needs to be done to protect all life on the planet! (2001, 15)

The leaderless resistance structure provides the ELF with a number of benefits, besides operational security, most notably, the ability to avoid protracted ideological debate leading to stagnation and factionalization. Paul Joosse (2007) addresses this, writing:

> Leaderless resistance allows the ELF to avoid ideological cleavages by eliminating all ideology extraneous to the very specific cause of halting the degradation of nature . . . leaderless resistance creates an 'overlapping consensus' among those with vastly different ideological orientations, mobilizing a mass of adherents that would never [have] been able to find unanimity of purpose in an organization characterized by a traditional, hierarchical, authority structure . . . [individuals can] . . . 'believe what they will,' while mobilizing them to commit 'direct actions'. (2007, 352)

Leaderless resistance prevents factionalization, allowing divergent activists to appear unified despite ideological differences.

The independence of leaderless resistance contains the potentiality to damage the movement if cells act outside of stated policy. For example "a particularly militant splinter cell, a peripheral individual or . . . ad-hoc group" could carry out an attack attributed to the ELF but via means breaking from group tradition (Ackerman 2003, 153). The ELF movement lacks the ability to prevent cells from committing lethal actions and claiming them in the movement's name, (Leader and Probst 2003, 42) other than arguing that its guidelines call for the taking of "necessary precautions against harming life". Such a tension is of growing relevance with a sudden surge in eco-affiliated, primitivist-themed attacks in countries such as Mexico, where networks such as Individuals Tending Toward the Wild have reportedly killed and injured targets attacked do to their role in biotechnology and the larger "Techno-Industrial System." This potential conflict for the ELF has yet to be tested, but provides a challenge for the network in preserving its records of avoiding human causalities. Despite this risk, the ELF's structure allows cells and individuals to act independently to set the agenda for the larger transnational movement (Joosse 2007, 356), thus the global ELF campaign is simply the collection of attacks carried out by autonomous entities.

Structure—Organizational Learning

Due to the tendency for cells to act without support, the movement must uniquely develop tactical and operational skill sets. The ELF has addressed this, facilitating organizational learning through print text and Internet. Many texts were the product of radical environmentalist movements led by EF! preceding the ELF's founding. (Leader and Probst 2003, 38) From 1970-1980, numerous skills-based instructive texts, such as Ecodefense[12], emerged wherein readers were taught tactics utilized by the modern ELF including sabotage, arson, and internal security. (Eagan 1996, 8; FBI Counterterrorism and Cyber Divisions 2004, 2–4; Laqueur 2000, 203)[13] Following an increase in Internet access, the focus was shifted to online resources for cataloging technical and training material. In his report for RAND, Horacio Trujillo (2005) writes:

> Operational learning has been facilitated by . . . the movement's use of published material, first in print and now via the Internet, to disseminate and store knowledge . . . Advances in information technology, particularly the Internet, have significantly increased the reach of these organizations' materials and have provided the ELF with the ability to disseminate training and logistics information. (2005, 153)

The ELF's main (now defunct) aboveground website, NAELFPO,[14] formerly acted as a clearinghouse for individuals looking for links to sympathetic sites that host training materials. The NAELPO's site has been offline often for extended periods of time, but when active, receives a great deal of traffic partially due to heavy referencing in media accounts of attacks. Brigitte Nacos's (2006) discussion of terrorist groups' use of the Internet makes this claim stating:

> Overblown media reports about arson attacks on new housing developments or gas-guzzling sports utility vehicles by the Earth Liberation Front familiarized the American public with the motives of this by and large negligible 'eco-terrorist' movement . . . the mainstream media helped interested persons to find the group's Internet site that serves as a recruitment tool and a how-to-commit-terrorism resource. (2006, 43)

As of the time of writing, the NAELFPO website has been down for some time, but despite this barrier, movement communiqués can still be viewed at affiliated English language sites such as Bite Back Magazine[15], the North American Animal Liberation Press Office[16], and a host of direct action/insurrectionary anarchist themed websites such as 325,[17] War on Society[18], Act For Freedom Now! and Contra Info.[19] Through these websites and others in a host of foreign languages, individuals can access semi-centralized resources for publicizing attacks, reading communiqués from previous attacks, and learning operational skills such as security,[20] sabotage,[21] and weapons production.[22]

The weapons technology of the ELF, consists of off-the-shelf materials with dual usage[23] used to construct incendiaries. (Helios Global, Inc. 2008, 1, 26) Typical designs for improvised incendiary devices utilize widely available items such as alkaline batteries, kitchen/egg timers, basic electrical components, matches, road flares, model rocket igniters, filament light bulbs, alligator clips, granulated sugar, liquid hydrocarbon fuels (gasoline, diesel, oil, kerosene, etc.), paraffin, sawdust, incense sticks, sponges, tampons, plastic jugs, cigarette lighters, solder, and insulated wire. Through the guidance provided by online guides[24] the ELF can develop organizational knowledge, distribute member instruction, and adapt new technologies as developments improve.[25] Beyond technical training and development, the Internet also serves a variety of functions to establish a collectively crafted history of attacks, analysis and critique. This trend is not unique to the ELF as it is increasingly common for political movements to utilize the Internet as a source of intelligence and training. (Weimann 2006, 123–124)

Context

The ELF's development was the product of philosophical shifts in the environmental movement, and practical issues that emerged throughout EF! leading to its factionalization. While direct action, similarly styled animal liberation networks such as the BOM and the ALF began in the UK in the early 1970s, the environmental militancy found its focus a bit later. In 1992, following direct actions in England, EF! hosted a national meeting in Brighton. (Leader and Probst 2003, 38) At this meeting, segments of EF! expressed a desire for the movement to halt its use of illegal tactics, and it was decided that as EF!, the movement would refocus on demonstrations, in effect creating the ELF as a new entity to continue producing illegal actions. The ELF name was intentionally chosen because of its similarity to that of the ALF, as the new Earth movement hoped to borrow ALF structure, guidelines and tactics. (Molland 2006, 49)

The emergence of the ELF from EF!'s factionalization allowed it to embrace leadless resistance, while avoiding further ideological splits. It was understood as important to avoid EF!'s mistakes wherein, "factionalization progressed . . . [and] . . . energy was diverted towards debates about ideology and away from performing the direct actions . . . envisioned as being Earth First!'s *forte*" (Joosse 2007, 358). Four years after the ELF emerged in England, it became active in the US, which would quickly become the focal point of the movement's attacks. (Trujillo 2005, 151) On October 31, 1996, the ELF carried out arson, its first major US action after four years of carrying out small vandalisms.[26]

The ELF's emergence was made possible via the broader context of a growing radical environmental movement in Western Europe and North America. (Walton and Widay 2006, 97–99) Thus the emergence of the ELF can be seen as a reactionary movement combating issues such as deforestation and a loss of biodiversity at a time when government policies were seen as disregarding or ignoring the problem. (Ackerman 2003, 155) Following global acknowledgment of such issues, knowledge of GMO agriculture and climate change grew in prominence as well, leading the ELF to execute a number of attacks on GMO crops and research. (Leader and Probst 2003, 46) Similarly, the 1990s saw the emergence of a "sprawl" critique, criticizing the surge in construction of low-density, car-dependent, luxury, urban/suburban housing developments. (Sally and Peter 2006, 415–416) These larger conversations provided the context for an arson campaign targeting luxury home developments, and other large land uses including ski resorts and golf courses. (Ackerman 2003, 153) Following the arson of a "luxury home" under construction[27] an ELF communiqué addressing "sprawl" was released:

> Greetings from the front, The Earth Liberation Front claims responsibility for the torching of a luxury home under construction in Miller Place, Long Island on December 19th. Anti-urban sprawl messages were spray-painted on the walls, then accelerants were poured over the house and lighted . . . This is the latest in a string of actions in the war against urban sprawl. Urban sprawl not only destroys the green spaces of our planet, but also leads directly to added runoff of pollutants into our waterways, increased traffic that causes congestion and air pollution, and a less pleasing landscape . . . Unregulated population growth is also a direct product of urban sprawl. There are over 6 billion people on this planet of which almost a third are either starving or living in poverty. Building homes for the wealthy should not even be a priority. (Earth Liberation Front 2000)

The growing global environmental consciousness, with its critique of GMO-technology and sprawl, provided the context for the popularization of radical activism that drew support from the upsurge in complementary leftist movements that occurred in the late 1990s-2000s, following demonstrations opposing the World Trade Organization in Seattle. (Ackerman 2003, 154; starr 2006, 375; Trujillo 2005, 159)

Similarly the anti-globalization initiates of the Zapatista Army for National Liberation (EZLN) in the Mexican state of Chiapas, which peaked in 1994 with the passage of the North American Free Trade Agreement (NAFTA), served to inspire leftist radicals globally as the movement spoke out strongly against Western capitalism and promoted a collective initiate toward environmental protection and sustainability. (Becker 2006, 76–77; Garland 2006, 68)[28] Within this tradition, the ELF can be said to be enacting a form of revolutionarily defensive environmentalism advocated by the ELZN. For example, the establishment of the 1978 Montes Azules Biosphere Reserve by Mexican President Jose Lopez Portillo, expropriated 940,000 acres of the Lacandon Jungle from largely indigenous communities, and led to the radicalization and militarization of the EZLN. Self-defense structures were established when the State attempted to move these individuals and in 1989, a ban on wood cutting and the establishment of a State-aligned security force to implement such measures led to one of the first offensive strikes by the EZLN. In this incident in March 1993, EZLN fighters killed two members of the Mexican security forces who had come upon a clandestine sawmill located near the city of San Cristobal. Less than one year later, when the EZLN led a largely bloodless uprising following the passage of NAFTA, one of their first achievements was to expel thousands of oil workers employed by PEMEX, US Western Oil and Geofisica Corporation. For both the ELF and EZLN, the active defense of the ecological realm is not a matter of long-term campaigning, but immediate, reactionary, needs-based maneuvers. Both movements act within the logic of an ever-shortening timeline for appropriate measures and resultantly, shun reformist methods that offer State-involvement, compromised negotiations and further entanglement with the legislative process.

Membership: Clandestine

Establishing membership is a difficult endeavor amongst a movement that does not have members, and as individuals do not *join* the ELF, membership status is tricky to discern. (Helios Global, Inc. 2008, 9) There is a lack of open source material, provided by security services documenting or estimating numbers of ELF cells. (Helios Global, Inc. 2008, 3) The only known ELF members or cells are the relatively few that have been identified and arrested. (Ackerman 2003, 151) NAELFPO (2001) addressed the question, writing that "it is next to impossible to estimate the number of ELF members internationally or even country by country." The closest discernable figures concerning the size of the ELF may come from a 2001 estimate, reporting that the ALF, a similarly structured movement, has an estimated "100 hardcore members" (Helios Global, Inc. 2008, 2). Such a figure appears arbitrary and most likely erroneous. What is known however is that as activity has waned in the US in the latter part of the 2000s, it has resultantly risen in other countries such as Mexico, Russia, the UK and many parts of Western Europe and South America (Loadenthal 2010).

Despite the fact that the number of ELF members is unknown, a membership profile exists. From these records, the profile of the most typical ELF activist emerges indicating the individual is likely male, well educated, possessing a high technical capability (Ackerman 2003, 148, 151), under the age of twenty-five, Caucasian, middle to upper-middle-class, from an industrialized Western nation (Helios Global, Inc. 2008, 3), supportive of environmentalism and animal rights (Walton and Widay 2006, 99), active in larger activist movements (Ackerman 2003, 145), and disenfranchised with mainstream environmental protest (Joosse 2007, 356). Sporadic arrests over the last ten years have shown these findings to be generalizable despite the arrest of numerous females and individuals acting in a host of non-Western countries from Indonesia to Bolivia. Recruitment and incitement propaganda produced by ELF-affiliated entities may also consciously attempt to engage youth subcultures through a positive portrayal of the movements as 'instigators of violent action' (Joosse 2007, 360).

This characterization is not surprising as Gary Perlstein (2003) writes that the ELF receives "a great deal of moral and perhaps even financial support from politically liberal urban . . . [and] academic settings" (2003, 171–172). Thus US universities may be a 'recruitment' setting as many attendees would share demographics characteristics. Thus if a movement seeks to 'recruit' twenty-one year old, privileged, well educated, politically liberal individuals from the industrialized West, the university setting is ideal. This 'supportive' university environment can also be seen in events held on campus supporting radical environmentalism generally, and the ELF specifically. (Helios Global, Inc. 2008, 26; Jarboe 2002) For example, pro-ELF and ALF speakers have given presentations at numerous leftist conferences and gatherings including the National Conference on Organized Resistance, the Animal Rights conference, the Liberation Now tour, as well as the Primate Freedom Tour which featured former ELF spokesmen, Craig Rosebraugh. In 1998, Rosebraugh, and ELF arsonist Jonathan Paul, presented at the National Animal Rights Conference being held at the University of Oregon, urging unity between the ELF and the ALF.

From the available information, the most typical membership in the clandestine elements of the ELF would likely be filled by a Caucasian male between the ages of 18 and 25, from a middle/upper-middle class background, living in the US. He would likely be attending, or have graduated from post-secondary education, identify with anti-authoritarian leftist politics, and be involved in public, aboveground social change movements possibly related to environmentalism, animal rights or anti-globalization. Other indicators such as proficiency with computers or dietary choices may be instructive but are largely anecdotal.

Membership: Aboveground

Membership in the ELF is not limited to clandestine cells. A multinational, aboveground support structure exists to disseminate propaganda, support prisoners, publicize actions, provide legal support, and allow pro-ELF persons a venue to promote the aims of radical environmentalism. At present, there exists a host of explicitly pro-ELF print and online magazines in national distribution throughout the US. Two examples are *Bite Back* magazine,[29] (in print 2001-present) and *No Compromise* magazine,[30] (in print 1989–2006). Both magazines focus on the actions of the ALF but also provide coverage of ELF attacks and prisoners.

Bite Back and *No Compromise* deal primarily with the ALF, addressing the ELF as a supportive ally, but in 2009, an explicitly pro-ELF magazine was created entitled *Resistance: Journal of the Earth Liberation Movement*. Currently in its third issue, *Resistance* (2009) plans to publish four issues a year with the stated goal of providing "a vehicle to inform, inspire, and energize the earth liberation movement." Although *Resistance* appears to be a project independent of the NAELFPO, its former spokesman Craig Rosebraugh, is the founder of Arissa Media Group which is the journal's distributor. (Arissa Media Group 2009) Both *Resistance* and Arissa unequivocally embrace the ELF publicly, whereas *Bite Back* and *No Compromise* share tactical methods and a broad affinity. Additionally, there is *The Earth First! Journal* published since the early 1980s and often covering attacks associated with the ELF and other clandestine, pro-environment groups. Currently the *EF! Journal* is published six times a year containing:

> . . . reports on direct action; articles on the preservation of wilderness and biological diversity; news and announcements about EF! and other radical environmental groups; investigative articles; critiques of the entire environmental movement . . . essays exploring ecological theory . . . (*Earth First! Journal* 2009)

The journal's creators describe the periodical as "The voice of the radical environmental movement . . . [and] an essential forum for discussion" (2009) within the radical environmentalist movement.

Beyond these supporters there exist numerous periodicals that regularly praise radical environmentalism and green anarchism, often documenting ELF attacks. Examples published in the US include *Green Anarchy,*[31] (in print 1999–2008), *Fifth Estate,*[32] (in print 1965-present), and *Species Traitor*[33] (in print 2000–2005). In total, there are more than eight periodicals, regularly published in the US that document and promote the ELF and sympathetically publicize ELF-affiliated prisoners, in effect allowing these organizations to act as aboveground support networks facilitating the building and maintenance of a pro-ELF movement.

The aboveground support networks of the ELF extend beyond publications, and provide support to individuals arrested and imprisoned for attacks. This prisoner support network identifies and tracks ELF-affiliated prisoners around the world. (Anti-Defamation League 2005, 11; Helios Global, Inc. 2008, 26) This information allows supporters to learn about prisoners, and write letters to those incarcerated, broadening the public support network to peripheral, sympathetic individuals. At least four organizations are currently operating to meet the needs of ELF prisoners.[34] Additional aboveground support networks for the ELF include the North American Earth Liberation Front Press Office (currently offline) which anonymously receives ELF communiqués from cells and publicizes them globally. Though currently the NAELFPO has no aboveground individual speaking on its behalf, in the past both Craig Rosebraugh and Leslie James Pickering served as official spokesmen for the ELF through its Press Office. Rosebraugh and Pickering have also both authored books documenting the ELF.[35] Furthermore, Rosenbraugh's project, Arissa Media group (now managed by the Institute for Critical Animal Studies and not Rosebraugh) distributes books, magazines, and CDs promoting the ELF. In 2008, the National Lawyers Guild, established the "Green Scare hotline," in response to a series of arrests targeting ELF cells. The purpose of the hotline is to provide support to individuals arrested or accused of involvement with environmental or animal rights motivated attacks. The hotline will assist the individual in locating a lawyer. The Guild has also published a guide, entitled *Operation Backfire: A Survival Guide for Environmental and Animal Rights Activists* (2009), explaining activists' legal rights and anti-terrorism laws as they have been applied in prosecutions of ELF-ALF members.

The functions of aboveground support entities are crucial for clandestine members to function effectively. The separation allows cells to remain unseen and unheard while supporters act as their voice and promoters. In this model, the cells carry out attacks, and the supporters document and disseminate propaganda the movement creates but is not able to distribute for fear of discovery. (Joosse 2007, 353) Under this model, based on the leaderless resistance structure, both the clandestine and public actors are necessary participants as both operate within complementary spheres of involvement predicated on a shared ideology and divergent tactics.

Conclusion: Neo-Guerillas & New Social Movements

The ELF is a network of clandestine, autonomous cells, organized via a decentralized and broad ideology based in deep ecology, primitivist-themed anarchism, collective defense of the natural world, and a critique of environmental policy, genetic engineering, residential development, and globalized capitalism. The success of ELF cells avoiding discovery and arrest has limited the available data concerning the identity of participants, but a broad profile does exist as it pertains to sex, race, age, class, nationality, political affiliation and education. The ELF network emerged as support grew for the use of illegal protest tactics within the British radical environmental movement, modeling itself after the ALF as a leaderless resistance movement choosing sabotage, arson and vandalism as its main tactics. These attacks are carried out by tactically proficient, highly secure, small unit cells, using easily accessible weapons technologies and online instruction. This underground network of attackers is aided by aboveground support structures which help to promote and publicize the aims of the clandestine units.

The popularity and deterritorialization of the ELF in the US has served as a tactical and strategic inspiration to a host of movements who have drawn from the ELF's methods for a variety of goals. In this sense, the ELF, despite its decline in domestic activity, must be understood as an instrumental social movement in the post-millennial period of radical, direct action, anti-State politics. Its praxis of insurrectionary-styled direct attack and unmediated offensive strikes offers inspiration to activists; inspiration which is aided by the network's relative imperviousness to disruption, arrest and infiltration. Despite being established as a 'number one domestic terrorist threat' by the US intelligence community, and despite malicious prosecutions and egregious sentencing of activists, the network remains.

Since around 2007 when the so-called anti-globalization, counter-summit movement declined in the US, a large number of activists were left with a time vacuum. Hours that had once been dedicated to planning outreach, recruitment, logistical preparation and infrastructure building (e.g. housing, food, legal support networks) were now freed. While it is too early to make such determinations, it is entirely possible that with the decline of such mass-based protest movements, some individuals shifted their *modus operandi* toward what the military would term 'small unit tactics.' In other words, when regional and national mobilizations proved to be a resource-intensive, short victory producing avenue of resistance, attack histories such as that of the ELF may have led the charge for a multitude of movements to embrace lone wolf, leaderless resistance and urban guerilla tactics which had declined in domestic popularity with the disbanding of the United Freedom Front, George Jackson Brigade, Black Liberation Army (BLA), May 19th Communist Organization and others in the 1980s. Just as the decline of the anti-Viet Nam revolutionary groups (e.g. Weather Underground, Black Panthers) led to the establishment of the more vanguardist 'Peoples Armies' such as the BLA, so too may have the latter's decline left a void filled by the rise of clandestine property destruction networks in the early 1990s. In this sense, the ELF should be understood historically as an instrumental tactical and strategic tendency in North American protest as it offered a model of outright resistance at a time when aboveground movements were gaining publicity and momentum.

At present, in 2013, the North American environmental justice movement is once again experiencing a period of growth and diversification. Popular movements utilizing non-violence civil disobedience are prominent in their position of the transnational Keystone Pipeline for transporting oil and the more generalized use of hydraulic fracturing (often called hydro-fracking) for extracting natural gas and petroleum from subterranean areas. Continued logging campaigns in the Pacific Northwest have led to the reinvigoration of forest defense and encampment campaigns such as those being fought by Cascadia Forest Defenders. These movements, while adopting self-sacrificial civil disobedience (e.g. lockdowns, tree sits, tripods) as their main tactics, will also likely include the use of clandestine, ELF-inspired property destruction. Previous campaigns around the world have witnessed such a hybridized campaign, often with great success. To cite but one example, in 2010, activists in Scotland were able to derail the construction of numerous open cast coalmines (i.e. strip mines) through the use of forest defense in conjunction with the anonymous sabotage of machinery at sites like the Mainshill Solidarity Camp. The company building and managing the mines, Scottish Coal, financially collapsed in early 2013, likely pushed into ruin by the costly and frequent sabotages it experienced during the anti-open cast campaign. Following one particularly costly construction equipment sabotage by anonymous monkey wrenches, the activists released this statement to Scotland's *Indymedia*:

> In the early hours of this morning machinery at Mainshill open cast site was sabotaged. Two Caterpillar D9T's and a 170 tonne face scrapping earth mover, an O&K RH90, were targeted, both will be inoperable today, and will cost Scottish Coal greatly. . .The machinery at the Mainshill site, and any other coal site in Scotland, are extremely vulnerable. Sabotage against the coal industry will continue until its expansion is halted. This action was done by autonomous environmentalists in solidarity with the people of South Lanarkshire [Scotland] who are fighting to save their community and their health from the coal industry. This is also in solidarity with people around the world, including Columbia and India, who are fighting for their lives against the coal industry. (Anonymous 2010)

From this short communication one can see broad affinity with the ELF in its methods as well as its politics. The use of clandestine sabotage in defense of the Earth did not begin nor end with the ELF, but the network has been key in the invigoration of a sense of possible victory. The production of spectacular, multimillion-dollar strikes time and again has had a catalyzing effect on those that stand in the shadow of foreboding multinational giants such as Monsanto, Exxon and the likes.

Since the US made its largest arrests during Operation Backfire in 2005, it touted the end of the ELF with "key" members in custody and jailed. Despite this great loss to the movement, the international growth of the ELF since that time has been remarkable. What started as a small attack tendency in mid-90s Oregon is now a history of ELF-claimed attacks in a host of countries including Australia, Canada, Chile, Colombia, Iceland, Indonesia, Italy, Mexico, Netherlands, New Zealand, Russia, Sweden and the UK. In the past two years in particular the ELF name has been partnered in numerous attacks claimed by the Informal Anarchist Federation (FAI) and the International Revolutionary Front (IRF) in attacks throughout Europe, Asia and the Americas.

The ELF is not an organization in the traditional sense and is more akin to a movement of informal networks. Names such as the ELF, ALF, EF!, FIA, IRF are freely adoptable political markers providing little more than an articulation of a shared politic and recognizable name. The usage of such names to claim attacks allows disparate actors to present themselves as a global movement, linking isolated cells and individuals through a central meaning. Thus, the adoption of the ELF moniker in conjunction with newly established clandestine attack networks such as the FAI and IRF speaks to the draw of the ELF as an *idea* more than a collectivity of individuals or single, isolated actions. In the end, the ELF may die as a domestic network and live on as an idea—an idea to be included in the signatory line of communiqués claiming responsibility for attacks in perpetuity, serving to carry the ELF moniker far beyond its original horizons and into the annals of radical history.

References

Congress. 2005. "Oversight on Eco-Terrorism Specifically Examining the Earth Liberation Front ('ELF') and the Animal Liberation Front ('ALF')." http://epw.senate.gov/hearing_statements.cfm?id=237836 (April 2, 2012).

Ackerman, Gary A. 2003. "Beyond Arson? A Threat Assessment of the Earth Liberation Front." *Terrorism and Political Violence* 15(4): 143–70.

Anonymous. 2010. "Mainshill Coal Site Sabotage!" http://www. indymediascotland.org/node/18959 (January 1, 2013).

Anti-Defamation League. 2005. "Ecoterrorism: Extremism in the Animal Rights and Environmentalist Movements." http://www. adl.org/learn/ext_us/Ecoterrorism_print.asp (January 1, 2013).

Arissa Media Group. 2009. "About - Arissa Media Group, LLC." *Resistance Magazine.* http://www.arissa.org/about.html (December 20, 2009).

Auntie ALF, Uncle ELF and the Anti-Copyright gang. 2003. "Arson Around with Auntie ALF: Your Guide for Putting the Heat on Animal Abusers Everywhere." http://archive.org/stream/Arson-aroundWithAuntieAlf#page/n0/mode/2up (January 1, 2013).

Beam, Louis. 1992. "Leaderless Resistance." *The Seditionist* (12). http://www.louisbeam.com/leaderless.htm (January 1, 2013).

Becker, Michael. 2006. "Ontological Anarchism: The Philosophical Roots of Revolutionary Environmentalism." In *Igniting a Revolution: Voices in Defense of the Earth,* eds. Steven Best and Anthony Nocella. Oakland, CA: AK Press.

Borum, Randy, and Chuck Tilby. 2005. "Anarchist Direct Actions: A Challenge for Law Enforcement." *Studies in Conflict & Terrorism* 28(3): 201–23.

Chalk, Peter. 2001. "U.S. Environmental Groups and 'Leaderless Resistance'." *Jane's Intelligence Review [republished by RAND Corporation].* http://www.rand.org/commentary/2001/07/01/JIR. html (January 1, 2013).

Dishman, Chris. 2005. "The Leaderless Nexus: When Crime and Terror Converge." *Studies in Conflict & Terrorism* 28(3): 237–52.

Eagan, Sean P. 1996. "From Spikes to Bombs: The Rise of Eco-terrorism." *Studies in Conflict & Terrorism* 19(1): 1–18.

Earth First! Journal. 2009. "About the Earth First! Journal." *Earth First! Journal.* http://www.earthfirstjournal.org/subsection. php?id=5>. (December 20, 2009).

Earth Liberation Front. 2000. "Communiqué - 12.19.00." http://www. elfpressoffice.org/comm121900.html (December 20, 2009).

FBI Counterterrorism and Cyber Divisions. 2004. "Tactics Used by Eco-Terrorists to Detect and Thwart Law Enforcement Operations."

Fireant Collective. 2001. "Setting Fires With Electrical Timers: An Earth Liberation Front Guide." http://www.scribd.com/ doc/10523512/Setting-Fires-With-Electrical-Timers (January 1, 2013).

Frontline Information Service. n.d. "A Final Nail Exclusive: Electronically Timed Incendiary Igniter." http://www. animalliberation.net/finalnail/index.html.

———. 1998. "The Final Nail: Destroying the Fur Industry - A Guided Tour #2." http://www.animalliberation.net/finalnail/ index.html.

Garland, Davey. 2006. "To Cast a Giant Shadow: Revolutionary Ecology and Its Practical Implementation Through the Earth Liberation Front." In *Igniting a Revolution: Voices in Defense of the Earth,* eds. Steven Best and Anthony Nocella. Oakland, CA: AK Press.

Helios Global, Inc. 2008. "Ecoterrorism: Environmental and Animal-Rights Militants in the United States."

Immergut, Karin J., Kirk A. Engdall, Stephen F. Peifer, and John C. Ray. 2007. "Government's Sentencing Memorandum in the United States District Court for the District of Oregon [case Numbers CR 06-60069-AA, CR 06-60070-AA, CR 06-60071-AA, CR 06-60078-AA, CR 06-60079-AA, CR 06-60080-AA, CR 06-60120-AA, 06-60122-AA, 06-60123-AA, 06-60124-AA, 06-60125-AA, 06-60126-AA]."

Jackson, Brian, and David Frelinger. 2008. "Rifling Through the Terrorists' Arsenal: Exploring Groups' Weapon Choices and Technology Strategies." *Studies in Conflict & Terrorism* 31(7). http://www.rand.org/pubs/working_papers/WR533. (December 12, 2012).

Jarboe, James. 2002. "The Threat of Eco-Terrorism." http://www.fbi. gov/news/testimony/the-threat-of-eco-terrorism (April 4, 2012).

Jones, pattrice. 2006. "Stomping with the Elephants: Feminist Principles for Radical Solidarity." In *Igniting a Revolution: Voices in Defense of the Earth,* eds. Steven Best and Anthony Nocella. Oakland, CA: AK Press.

Joosse, Paul. 2007. "Leaderless Resistance and Ideological Inclusion: The Case of the Earth Liberation Front." *Terrorism and Political Violence* 19(3): 351–68.

Laqueur, Walter. 2000. *The New Terrorism: Fanaticism and the Arms of Mass Destruction.* Oxford University Press, USA.

Leader, Stefan H., and Peter Probst. 2003. "The Earth Liberation Front And Environmental Terrorism." *Terrorism and Political Violence* 15(4): 37–58.

Lewis, John. 2004. "Animal Rights Extremism and Ecoterrorism." http://www.fbi.gov/news/testimony/animal-rights-extremism-and-ecoterrorism (April 5, 2012).

Loadenthal, Michael. 2010. "Nor Hostages, Assassinations, or Hijackings, but Sabotage, Vandalism & Fire: 'Eco-Terrorism' as Political Violence Challenging the State and Capital." MLitt Dissertation. Centre for the Study of Terrorism and Political Violence, University of St Andrews.

———. 2012. "Operation Splash Back!: Queering Animal Liberation Through the Contributions of Neo-Insurrectionist Queers." *Journal of Critical Animal Studies* Special Edition: Intersecting Queer Theory and Critical Animal Studies.

———. 2013. "Deconstructing 'Eco-terrorism': Rhetoric, Framing and Statecraft as Seen through the Insight Approach." *Critical Studies on Terrorism* 6(1). http://www.tandfonline.com/doi/abs/1 0.1080/17539153.2013.765702.

Lovitz, Dara. 2010. *Muzzling a Movement: The Effects of Anti-Terrorism Law, Money, and Politics on Animal Activism.* Lantern Books.

Molland, Noel. 2006. "A Spark That Ignited a Flame: The Evolution of the Earth Liberation Front." In *Igniting a Revolution: Voices in Defense of the Earth,* eds. Steven Best and Anthony Nocella. Oakland, CA: AK Press, 47–58.

Nacos, Brigitte. 2006. "Communication and Recruitment of Terrorists." In *The Making of a Terrorist Volume 1: Recruitment,*

Training, and Root Causes, The Making of a Terrorist, ed. James J. F. Forest. Westport: Praeger Security International.

National Lawyers Guild. 2009. "Operation Backfire: A Survival Guide for Environmental and Animal Rights Activists." http://www.nlg.org/resource/know-your-rights/operation-backfire (January 1, 2013).

North American Earth Liberation Front Press Office. 2001. "Frequently Asked Questions About the Earth Liberation Front." http://www.elfpressoffice.org/elffaqs.html (December 18, 2009).

———. 2009a. "Earth Liberation Front Diary of Actions- 1999." http://www.elfpressoffice.org/actions1999.html (January 10, 2010).

———. 2009b. "Earth Liberation Front Diary of Actions- 2003." http://www.elfpressoffice.org/actions2003.html (January 10, 2010).

———. 2009c. "Earth Liberation Front Diary of Actions- 2006." http://www.elfpressoffice.org/actions2006.html (January 10, 2010).

Perlstein, Gary. 2003. "Comments on Ackerman." *Terrorism and Political Violence* 15(4): 171–72.

Potter, Will. 2011. *Green Is the New Red: An Insider's Account of a Social Movement Under Siege.* 1st ed. City Lights Publishers.

Resistance Magazine. 2009. "About - Resistance: Journal of the Earth Liberation Movement." *Resistance Magazine.* http://www.resistancemagazine.org/about.html (December 20, 2009).

Sally and Peter. 2006. "ELF Claims Vandalism Against New Housing Developments in Philadelphia Suburb." In *Igniting a Revolution: Voices in Defense of the Earth,* eds. Steven Best and Anthony Nocella. Oakland, CA: AK Press, 415–16.

Schuster, Henry. 2005. "Domestic Terror: Who's Most Dangerous?" *CNN.* http://www.cnn.com/2005/US/08/24/schuster.column/index.html>. (November 10, 2010).

Slater, Colin. 2011. "Activism as Terrorism: The Green Scare, Radical Environmentalism and Governmentality." *Anarchist Developments in Cultural Studies* (Ten Years After 9/11: An Anarchist Evaluation): 211–38.

Someone. n.d. "The Animal Liberation Primer [3rd Ed.]." http://www.animalliberationfront.com/ALFront/primer3.pdf (January 1, 2013).

starr, amory. 2006. "Grumpywarriorcool: What Makes Our Movements White." In *Igniting a Revolution: Voices in Defense of the Earth,* eds. Steven Best and Anthony Nocella. Oakland, CA: AK Press.

Taylor, Bron. 1998. "Religion, Violence and Radical Environmentalism: From Earth First! to the Unabomber to the Earth Liberation Front." *Terrorism and Political Violence* 10(4): 1–42.

———. 2003. "Threat Assessments and Radical Environmentalism." *Terrorism and Political Violence* 15(4): 173–82.

The Green Anarchy Collective. 2009. "Back to Basics Vol. #4 - What Is Green Anarchy: 'An Introduction to Anti-Civilization Anarchist Thought and Practice'." http://www.greenanarchy.org/index.php?action=viewwritingdetail&writingId=283 (December 18, 2009).

Trujillo, Horacio. 2005. "Chapter 6: The Radical Environmentalist Movement." In *Aptitude for Destruction: Case Studies of Organizational Learning in Five Terrorist Groups,* Arlington, VA: RAND Corporation.

Walton, Matthew, and Jessica Widay. 2006. "Shades of Green: Examining Cooperation Between Radical and Mainstream Environmentalists." In *Igniting a Revolution: Voices in Defense of the Earth,* eds. Steven Best and Anthony Nocella. Oakland, CA: AK Press, 415–16.

Weimann, Gabriel. 2006. *Terror on the Internet: The New Arena, the New Challenges.* 1st ed. United States Institute of Peace Press.

Yin, Robert K. 2008. *Case Study Research: Design and Methods.* 4th ed. SAGE Publications, Inc.

Notes

1. A lengthy analysis of the post-9/11 rhetoric of terrorism deployed against environmental and animal liberation activists is the subject of an article recently published by this author (Loadenthal 2013) entitled "Deconstructing 'Eco-Terrorism': Rhetoric, Framing and Statecraft as Seen Through the Insight Approach," appearing in the journal *Critical Studies on Terrorism,* Vol. 6, Issue 1.

2. All quantitative data of this variety are taken from a previously completed study (Loadenthal 2010) of the larger field of "eco-terrorism" completed in 2010 as part of the author's MLitt dissertation completed while studying at the Centre for the Study of Terrorism and Political Violence at the University of St Andrews. This research included an incident-based, quantitative analysis of 27,136 incidents of "eco-terrorism" occurring in over 40 countries from 1972–2010. Each incident was passed through a decision tree, and if included in the data set, coded for 22 variables and analyzed with the Statistical Package for the Social Sciences (SPSS) software program.

3. See for example (109th Congress 2005; Ackerman 2003; Anti-Defamation League 2005; Borum and Tilby 2005; Chalk 2001; FBI Counterterrorism and Cyber Divisions 2004; Helios Global, Inc. 2008; Immergut et al. 2007; Jackson and Frelinger 2008; Jarboe 2002; Taylor 2003; Trujillo 2005).

4. The NAELFPO has at times gone silent for large periods. After being established in 1999, it maintained an active web presence for years before going offline, and then reestablishing itself in 2008. At present, in 2013, the site is once again offline.

5. The politics and philosophy of anarcho-primitivism have been developed and popularized by writers such as John Zerzan, Kevin Tucker, Bob Black, John Moore, Derrick Jenson, and infamously by Theodore Kaczynski, better known as the "Unabomber."

6. See for example (Loadenthal 2012) wherein this author challenges the human-centric notion of protectionism offered by animal/earth liberation activists who claim to be speaking for the oppressed non-human animals and 'natural' world.

7. Such as Pennsylvania's "Ecoterrorism - 18 Pa. Cons. Stat. § 3311."

8. A detailed exploration of the methods employed in the Green Scare is the subject of a book chapter written by the author to be published in late 2013 entitled "The 'Green Scare' & 'Eco-Terrorism': The Development of US Counter-Terrorism Strategy Targeting Direct Action Activists." Published in *The Law Against Animals: A Challenge to the Animal Enterprise Terrorism Act.* Eds. Jason Del Gandio, et al. Forthcoming. Lantern Press, 2013.

9. September 19, 2003, an ELF cell burned down four luxury homes and damaged three others in San Diego, California's Carmel Valley neighborhood. A banner was left at the scene of the arson that read, "Development destruction. Stop raping nature. The ELFs are angry."

10. May 17, 2006 an ELF cell damaged six SUVs in Fair Oaks, California by slashing the vehicles' tires and using spray paint to write "ELF" on the vehicles.

11. December 31, 1999 an ELF cell severely damaged a research center at Michigan State University's Lansing campus because the University was conducting genetic engineering research in conjunction with GE-advocate Monsanto and the United States Agency for International Development. The fire caused $900,000 in damages.

12. A complete copy of the 3rd edition of Dave Foreman's book *Ecodefense: A Field Guide to Monkeywrenching,* is available online at http://www.omnipresence.mahost.org/inttxt.htm. In establishing the themes of this book, as discussed in the study, the text was accessed online, without page numbers, making item specific referencing impossible. The complete citation for the book can be found below:

    Foreman, Dave. *Ecodefense: A Field Guide to Monkeywrenching.* 3rd edition. Chico: Abbzug Press, 1993.

13. These skills-based texts of the time include *Ecodefense: A Field Guide to Monkeywrenching,* where readers are taught tactics utilized by the modern ELF including tree spiking, sabotage, arson, and internal security.Additional books also emerged at this time serving as guides to potential saboteurs including *The Black Cat Sabotage Handbook, EF! Direct Action Manual,Earthforce! An Earth Warrior's Guide to Strategy* and *Road Raging: Top Tips for Wrecking Roadbuilding.* A complete version of *Road Raging* is available at: http://www.eco-action.org/rr/

14. Available at: http://www.elfpressoffice.org/

15. http://www.directaction.info/

16. http://www.animalliberationpressoffice.org/index.htm

17. http://325.nostate.net/

18. http://waronsociety.noblogs.org/

19. http://en.contrainfo.espiv.net/

20. For an example see Activist Security v2.7, published June 2008 by www.ActivistSecurity.org. The NAELFPO website maintains an entire page on security (http://www.elfpressoffice.org/security.html) wherein they provide links to nearly 50 separate guides to issues of security including encryption,

forensic, criminal investigation techniques and electronic surveillance.

21. For an example, see *Ozymandias Sabotage Handbook,* available at http://www.reachoutpub.com/osh/via the NAELFPO "resource" page.

22. For example see *Arson-Around with Auntie ALF: Your Guide to Putting Heat on Animal Abusers Everywhere* or *Setting Fires With Electrical Timers: An Earth Liberation Front Guide.* These guides are available on numerous websites and file sharing services.

23. See for example (Auntie ALF, Uncle ELF and the Anti-Copyright gang 2003, 1–20; Fireant Collective 2001, 1–37; Frontline Information Service n.d., 1998, 8–13; Someone n.d., 1–21).

24. See for example the guides discussed (109th Congress 2005, 44, 75–76; Anti-Defamation League 2005, 10; Immergut et al. 2007, 134). The two most widely cited arson guides produced by the ELF and ALF respectively are *Setting Fires With Electrical Timers: An Earth Liberation Front Guide* and *Arson-Around with Auntie ALF: Your Guide to Putting Heat on Animal Abusers Everywhere.*

25. It is interesting to note that the referenced ELF and ALF-produced incendiary guides are nearly entirely devoid of ideological or philosophical discussion or even the mention of animal rights. In his discussion of leaderless resistance in the ELF, author Paul Joosse (2007) writes that, "by not explicitly stating ideological precepts, the manual lends itself to use by anyone, regardless of the person's ideological orientation" (2007, 361).

26. Between 1992–1996 numerous attacks were carried out that shared tactical and thematic traits with ELF actions. The attacks were carried out in England, Holland, Australia, Germany and New Zealand. (Molland 2006, 52–53).

27. The arson occurred on December 19, 2000 in Long Island, New York and was claimed via a communiqué sent to the ELF Press Offices.

28. In at least two ELF communiqués the Zapatista movement was referenced as a source of inspiration. The first, issued in 1997 under the title, "Beltane, 1997" (Best and Nocella, 408-9) and the second, issued on 28 June 1998, and (available at http://www.elfpressoffice.org/comm062898.swf)

29. *Bite Back Magazine* is published irregularly since 2001 and available at: http://www.directaction.info/

30. *No Compromise* is published biannually since 1989. According to the *No Compromise Magazine* website, the publication is "the militant, direct action publication of grassroots animal liberationists and their supporters," with the aim of "unifying grassroots animal liberationists by providing a forum where activists can exchange information, share strategy, discuss important issues within the movement, network with each other in an open and respectful environment and strengthen the grassroots." Website available at: http://www.

nocompromise.org/ with a full archive made available at http://thetalonconspiracy.com/category/periodicals/nocomp/

31. The complete title is *Green Anarchy: an anti-civilization journal of theory & action*. The magazine is published bi-annually since 1999. The *Green Anarchy* website is available at: http://greenanarchy.org/

32. The complete title is *Fifth Estate: an anti-authoritarian magazine of ideas & action*. The magazine is published quarterly since 1965. The *Fifth Estate* website is available at: http://www.fifthestate.org/

33. *Species Traitor* is published irregularly since 2000 and has no website at present.

34. The English language prisoner support groups which specifically track ELF-affiliated prisoners include the North American Earth Liberation Prisoners Support Network (http://www.ecoprisoners.org), the Anarchist Black Cross Federation (http://www.abcf.net) and the currently offline Earth Liberation Prisoners Support Network (http://www.spiritoffreedom.org.uk).

35. In 2003, as part of a Master's thesis, Craig Rosebraugh wrote *The Logic of Political Violence: Lessons in Reform and Revolution* and later, in 2004 he wrote *Burning Rage of a Dying Planet: Speaking for the Earth Liberation Front*. In 2006 Leslie James Pickering wrote *Earth Liberation Front 1997–2002* and has also written articles in the newly formed, pro-ELF magazine *Resistance*.

Critical Thinking

1. How does the organizational structure of ELF benefit the movement?

2. Why is "leaderless resistance" effective?

3. Why do the media treat Eco-terrorism different than Islamic terrorism?

Internet References

Domestic Eco-Terrorism Has Deep Pockets. And Many Enablers.
http://www.forbes.com/sites/henrymiller/2013/07/10/domestic-eco-terrorism-has-deep-pockets-and-many-enablers

The Threat of Eco-Terrorism
http://www.fbi.gov/news/testimony/the-threat-of-eco-terrorism

Whatever Happened to 'Eco-Terrorism'?
http://www.psmag.com/nature-and-technology/whatever-happened-to-eco-terrorism

MICHAEL LOADENTHAL is a doctoral candidate and adjunct professor who finds himself stranded between Cincinnati and Washington, DC, multi-tasking as a father, conspirator and writer. Over the past 15 years he has organized amongst a variety of global direct action movements and at present is conducting top secret research for The Revolution.

Article   Prepared by: Thomas J. Badey, *Randolph-Macon College*

The Year in Hate and Extremism 2014

MARK POTOK

Learning Outcomes

After reading this article, you will be able to:

- Identify the different types of hate groups in the United States.
- Analyze current trends of extremist groups in the United States.
- Discuss connections between politics and extremism.

After four years of spectacular growth driven by the 2008 election of President Obama and the nearly simultaneous collapse of the economy, the radical right in America saw its first significant decrease in 2013. The shrinking numbers of hate groups and, especially, antigovernment "Patriot" groups appear to be the result of a host of factors, ranging from the co-opting of their issues by mainstream politicians, to an improving economy, to law enforcement crackdowns.

The year started out with a national discussion of gun control in the wake of a deadly Connecticut school massacre and a promise that action would come soon on comprehensive immigration reform, two issues that energized the right and seemed to promise an intensification of radical rage. But those issues faded away with little real action, leaving a deflated radical right to wallow unhappily in "losses" including the advance of same-sex marriage and national health care reform, the failure of various nightmarish predictions to materialize, and Obama's re-election.

Those factors, along with the collapse or near-collapse of several major groups for a variety of reasons, seem to have taken some of the wind out of the sails of the radical right, leaving the movement both weaker and somewhat smaller. But that has not dampened the violence and terrorism coming out

of the movement, as a number of cases last year, including a Klansman's alleged attempt to build an X-ray weapon to mass murder Muslims, reflected. And while the number of groups has diminished, they are still at historically high levels, far higher even than the very high number that was seen at the peak of the militia movement in the 1990s.

The number of hate groups last year dropped for the second year in a row, down 7% from 1,007 in 2012 to 939, after reaching a 2011 high of 1,018, according to the latest count by the Southern Poverty Law Center (SPLC). But the more significant drop came among the Patriot groups, which fell 19% from 1,360 groups in 2012 to 1,096 in 2013. That drop followed an unprecedented rise in Patriot groups, which climbed from a mere 149 in 2008 to the all-time high seen in 2012.

Enormous antipathy toward Obama clearly drove the surge in radical groups, not to mention boosting the Tea Party groups that took off in 2009 and various far-right politicians, that may now have ended. Their anger was not directed only at Obama, but at the demographic change he represented—the Census Bureau has predicted that whites will lose their white majority in the United States by 2043. But the president's 2012 re-election, which was unexpected by much of the political right, seemed to have the opposite effect, sapping the energy of many of those who had assumed that Americans would finally rise in righteous fury against him.

In other words, the same groups that were galvanized by Obama's first election and swelled dramatically as a result, were demoralized by his re-election, which seemed to signal that their battle was lost despite enormous effort.

The Changing Landscape

In addition, the radical right seems increasingly conscious that it is losing its battles on many other fronts. Well over half of

Americans now support same-sex marriage, a dramatic rise since 1996, when just 27% did so. Large sections of the GOP are trying to figure out how to appeal to the rapidly growing pool of minority voters, even if they are stymied by others within their party. Global warming and rising oceans seem like an indisputable reality to ever more Americans. Legalization of recreational marijuana in two states reflects an increasingly liberal trend. Even with its troubled rollout, national health care reform is likely here to stay.

The right wing of the Republican Party suffered, too, especially in the wake of the ill-fated 16-day government shutdown led by Sen. Ted Cruz (R-Texas) and backed by the Tea Parties as a way of defunding Obamacare last October. In the shutdown's aftermath, a *Washington Post*/ABC News poll showed that 77% of respondents disapproved of the GOP's actions, and

63%, the highest level in the history of the poll, had an unfavorable view of the party. Just a quarter approved of the Tea Parties, the lowest level since the question was first asked in 2010.

Kurt Schlicthter, a conservative lawyer writing on Townhall.com last year, seemed to capture the demoralized mood when he urged others on the right to learn to live with gay marriage.

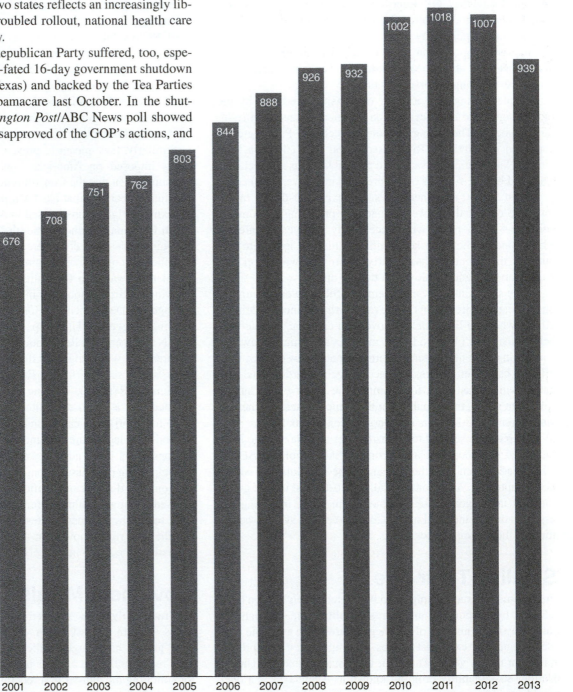

Figure 1 Hate Groups 1998–2013

"The gay marriage fight is over. It is here to stay," he wrote. "Whether the fight ends with a Constitution-twisting Supreme Court ruling or after years or decades as the states adopt it one by one, it's a done deal."

Democracy Corps, a liberal think tank whose principals include James Carville, sounded similar in an analysis last fall entitled "Inside the GOP: Report on focus groups with Evangelical, Tea Party, and moderate Republicans." "[T]he base thinks they are losing politically and losing control of the country—and their starting reaction is 'worried,' 'discouraged,' 'scared,' and 'concerned' about the direction of the country—and a little powerless to change course," it said.

Complementing that, a litany of disasters predicted by the radical right, and often echoed on the more mainstream right, failed to occur. The "gun grab" long expected by Patriot groups and even the National Rifle Association didn't happen. The United Nations didn't invade, and martial law was not declared. The gold bubble—prices of the precious metal were pushed up to almost $2,000 an ounce last summer by fear-driven investors who expected and were apparently preparing for a major collapse—has popped, with prices early this year at around $1,225 and predicted to keep falling. Although many are still hurting, the economy has clearly improved, with stocks in record territory and employment ticking up.

At the same time, law enforcement officials were leaning in on criminal manifestations of the radical right. Since September 2011—when the FBI labeled "sovereign citizens," people who believe they don't have to follow most tax and criminal laws, as comprising a "domestic terrorist movement"—law enforcement officials have been aggressively acting against participants' illegal activities. Last year, for example, the leader of the largest sovereign group, the Republic for the United States of America, was sentenced to 18 years in federal prison for tax fraud.

That pressure seemed to intensify after neo-Nazi Wade Page murdered six people at a Wisconsin Sikh temple in August 2012, leading, among other things, to the dissolution of all 17 U.S. chapters of Volksfront, a leading neo-Nazi skinhead group founded in Oregon. A series of cases in 2013, including the assassination of the head of the Colorado prison system, added force to the apparent crackdown.

Stealing Their Fire

Finally, many issues championed by the radical right have been adopted by purportedly mainstream politicians, in much the same way that a number of state legislatures stole away the core ideas of nativist extremist groups, leading to their rapid diminution in recent years. The idea, for instance, that the United Nations sustainability program known as Agenda 21 is a one-world government conspiracy originated in radical groups like the John Birch Society. But in January 2012 the Republican National Committee adopted a resolution describing it as a "destructive and insidious" scheme that will impose "socialist/communist redistribution of wealth" on America. In fact, the plan, which was signed by President George H.W. Bush in 1992, is completely voluntary and can force no one to do anything.

But that hasn't stopped national and local politicians around the country from joining in the hysteria over Agenda 21. Since the RNC resolution, Alabama has passed a law meant to outlaw any effects of the plan in that state. Similar needless laws have been approved by one chamber of the state legislatures in Arizona, Missouri and Oklahoma. Kansas, New Hampshire and Tennessee have all passed state resolutions condemning the plan. And major political fights over it have broken out in at least half a dozen other states and countless local communities.

Similarly, laws meant to prevent Islamic Shariah law from being imposed on American courts—a totally unnecessary measure, given that the Constitution does not allow for such an eventuality, but one that has been pushed by Islamophobes on the extreme right—have passed in Arizona, Kansas, Louisiana, North Carolina, Oklahoma, South Dakota and Tennessee, and are being considered elsewhere.

Other far-out fears originating on the extreme right also have found their way into the political mainstream. The idea that the Muslim Brotherhood has infiltrated the Department of Justice and the Department of Homeland Security, among others, is being plugged by U.S. Rep. Michele Bachmann (R-Minn.). Last November, U.S. Rep. Louie Gohmert (R-Texas) suggested the president was using the Affordable Care Act as cover to set up a "secret security force." Earlier in 2013, U.S. Rep. Steve Stockman (R-Texas), echoing many Patriot groups, falsely claimed that a proposed United Nations arms treaty "set the stage for [gun] confiscation on a global scale."

And state legislatures around the country have either passed or considered laws, generally related to gun control but also encompassing other issues, that purport to "nullify" federal legislation. The doctrine of nullification, of course, was originally devised as an antebellum defense of slavery and then brought back to life by Southern states resisting school desegregation and the civil rights movement. It has been repeatedly found by the nation's courts to be entirely unconstitutional.

Movement Malaise

The radical right has suffered from its own internal dynamics as well. In the last dozen years, the nation's leading neo-Nazi groups have largely fallen apart. The World Church of the Creator collapsed after its leader was sent to federal prison for soliciting the murder of a federal judge. The Aryan Nations imploded after a lawsuit brought by the SPLC and the 2004 death of its leader. The National Alliance, long the nation's most important hate group, has seen its membership fall from 1,400 people to fewer than 100 since its founder's 2002 death. The implosion has been driven by its new leader's ineptitude and the SPLC's exposure of a series of embarrassing secrets about the group and its leaders.

In the last couple of years, other important groups have also seen more than their share of troubles. The shutdown of Volksfront's U.S. chapters was followed last year by the apparent collapse of its overseas organization. The Council of Conservative Citizens, long the core of the nonviolent white nationalist movement, lost 14 chapters in 2013 and is only sporadically publishing its newsletter. The American Third Position, the nation's largest racist political party, took a new name in a bid to shore itself up but still lost almost half its chapters in 2013.

Also last year, the number of groups espousing Christian Identity, a kind of neo-Nazi reading of the Bible that has been important to both Klan and neo-Nazi groups, declined by about a third. The League of the South, a racist neo-secessionist group, lost several chapters as it struggled to remain relevant. Marginalized anti-LGBT groups increasingly turned to pushing the criminalization of homosexuality abroad as a response to their loss of battle after battle in the United States.

Three of the more quixotic enterprises on the radical right also appeared to be in trouble last year. An attempt to build an armed Patriot city called III Citadel in northern Idaho to ok a serious hit after one of its chief promoters was revealed as a convicted con man. A nearby effort to restart Aryan Nations collapsed after the *Intelligence Report* showed the man who bought land for it was disobeying certain local laws. A stealth plan to turn Leith, N.D., into an all-white enclave—made public by the Southern Poverty Law Center and the *Bismarck Tribune*—also caved in, with its organizer jailed on terrorizing charges after allegedly threatening residents.

None of this is to suggest that the radical right in America does not remain highly dangerous. The weakening of groups often has the effect of fostering, rather than retarding, followers' decisions to finally act out violently. Despite the decline, there are still enormous numbers of radical groups operating— more than 2,000 of them, including hate and Patriot organizations. The single most important factor that has driven the growth of the radical right over the last five years, the ongoing demographic change to a non-white majority over the course of the next three decades, is still a source of enormous angst and rage for many. And the fact that the Tea Parties and the far right of the Republican Party have lost some of their public support does not mean that millions of Americans do not still sympathize. A shocking poll by Fairleigh Dickinson University's PublicMind last spring showed that 29% of Americans think that armed rebellion may soon be necessary.

More detailed reports on radical-right sectors follow.

Anti-LGBT Groups

Anti-LGBT groups suffered a year of devastating losses in 2013 as the legalization of same-sex marriage and other developments cheered pro-LGBT groups immensely. By year's end, a total of 18 states had legalized marriage equality or had a court rule that gay marriage could not be outlawed. (At press time, Utah, one of the 18, was considering an appeal that could halt legalization there.)

And that wasn't all. Minnesota voters rejected a ballot measure that would have codified an anti-gay marriage law in the state constitution. In June, the U.S. Supreme Court struck down the central provision of the Defense of Marriage Act, which prevented same-sex couples from being recognized by states as "spouses" for purposes of federal benefits. Another federal appeals court ruled that California's Proposition 8, which would have made only marriage between a man and a woman legal in California, was not constitutional, confirming a lower court decision.

Although the number of anti-gay hate groups rose slightly over the previous year, the losses suffered by such groups clearly sent many of them abroad as they sought to prevent gay advances wherever they still could. Bryan Fischer of the American Family Association tweeted support for Uganda's draconian anti-gay law. Brian Brown of the National Organization for Marriage spoke against marriage equality in both France and Russia. The latter country, which last year passed a highly controversial law against pro-gay "propaganda," also hosted Paul Cameron, a discredited anti-gay writer who heads the Family Research Institute and spoke to the Russian parliament. Peter LaBarbera of Americans for Truth About Homosexuality went to Jamaica to speak in support of that country's hard-line anti-gay laws.

Black Separatist Groups

The longtime leader of the New Black Panther Party, the white- and Jew-bashing lawyer Malik Zulu Shabazz, relinquished his post last fall in order to focus on his legal career with Black Lawyers for Justice, a group he founded in 1996.

Replacing Shabazz, who will continue on as a "spiritual guide" to the group, was his former chief of staff, Hashim Nzinga. Nzinga, who like Shabazz is known for his anti-Semitism and anti-white racism, pleaded guilty in 2012 to writing a bad check for $3,000, a felony. Last year, he was arrested for selling a gun at a Georgia pawn shop and held in jail for four months. But prosecutors eventually dismissed the charge, saying that Nzinga had not been informed that, as a convicted felon, he was not allowed to possess a gun. Earlier, in March 2013, Nzinga announced the party was offering a $10,000 bounty for the "citizen's arrest" of George Zimmerman, the man who killed unarmed teenager Trayvon Martin but was acquitted in his death.

Christian Identity Groups

Christian Identity, a racist reading of the Bible that describes non-white people as lacking souls and Jews as the biological descendants of Satan, has since World War II provided the theological glue for many U.S. hate groups. But it is a complex theology and, while it recently had an estimated 50,000 adherents, seems to have been losing followers in recent years, especially among young people.

That trend appeared to continue last year as the number of groups that are primarily about Identity dropped from 54 to just 37, mainly because the Chillicothe, Ohio-based Crusaders for Yahweh shut down all 30 of its chapters. A new Identity group, Identity Nation, did appear in 2013 with 10 chapters, but that was not enough to offset the overall decline. That group, based in Franklin, Ind., at first teamed up with a remnant of the Aryan Nations headed by Morris Gullet, but then broke away and began working with another faction of Aryan Nations that is associated with a biker group called Sadistic Souls MC. The Franklin group has begun calling itself a "Christian Identity Brotherhood" and says it has done away with military ranks.

Ku Klux Klan Groups

Although the number of Klan groups held steady at 163 chapters, or klaverns, last year saw what may be the beginning of a trend: Klan groups moving off the Internet in an apparent bid to regain the secrecy that marked their heyday. The United White Knights of the Ku Klux Klan, based in Texas with 30 klaverns, was the first example of that, although others are moving in the same direction.

Most recently, the Fraternal White Knights of the Ku Klux Klan, a group with 10 klaverns based in Tennessee, announced that it had "gone underground so we can be more productive in our struggle. The only way you will be able to contact us from now on is through the old way, word of mouth. . . . We are everywhere."

Klan groups made the news in several ways last year.

In Memphis, Tenn., when one Klan group, the Loyal White Knights of the Ku Klux Klan, organized a March rally against the City Council's decision to change the Confederate-themed names of three high schools, another—the United Klans of America (UKA), based in Alabama—said it opposed the rally and even attempted to work with a local black street gang against racism. Later in the year, in another bizarre moment, a Montana UKA leader met with a local NAACP chapter.

And in upstate New York, Glendon Crawford, a member of the United Northern and Southern Knights of the Ku Klux Klan, was arrested and charged with working to construct an X-ray weapon that he allegedly intended for use on crowds of Muslims. He called it "Hiroshima on a light switch." Crawford was arrested after trying to get financing from two Jewish agencies and another Klan group.

Neo-Nazi Groups

The decline of the National Alliance, once America's most important and best-organized hate group, continued last year. At one point, its leader, Erich Gliebe, said he was ending the system of dues-paying members and instead asking people to simply support the organization financially. Although Gliebe portrayed the change as one that would make the group stronger, it seemed clear that he was trying to hold on to a bequest of some $160,000 from a deceased Canadian member.

The man's bequest is being challenged in court by his sister and several human rights groups in Canada. An affidavit by the challengers listed the criminal acts of a large number of Alliance members, which could cause Gliebe to lose the case—and the bequest. It appeared likely that Gliebe hoped that by ending memberships he would have a better shot at winning the Canadian case.

Racist Skinhead Groups

Since 1994, Volksfront has been one of the country's most important groups of neo-Nazi skinheads. Formed in prison by founder Randal Krager, the group had 17 chapters by 2012 as well as an extensive overseas network of chapters.

In the aftermath of Wade Page's 2012 mass murder at a Sikh temple in Oak Creek, Wis., however, an apparent law enforcement crackdown seemed to push Krager into the decision later that year to shut down all U.S. operations, even though the group had amassed a number of properties and other assets. He also was clearly tired of the struggle with militant anti-racists, who had forced him to leave Portland, Ore., where Volksfront was founded, and wanted to raise his children in peace.

Then, late last year, the *Intelligence Report* published a major investigative story on Volksfront's overseas operations, which encompassed the United Kingdom, Australia, Germany, Slovakia, Portugal and Spain. In response, the units shut down their websites and seemed to disappear from public activism. Some sources have suggested that the units may be active underground, but that is not clear.

Another racist skinhead group, Die Auserwählten (German for "The Chosen Few"), rose and fell with stunning rapidity last year. Formed last May in Pleasanton, Neb., the group, also known as Crew 41, seemed to fall apart a few months later when its leader, Jonathan "Monster" Schmidt, was arrested after allegedly pulling a man from a vehicle and fracturing his skull. Around the same time, the group's South Carolina representative, Jeremy Moody, was arrested with his wife for their alleged murder of a local man who was a registered sex offender and his wife. After that, the group, which contains a number of men with criminal histories, went quiet, although its website remained up, albeit with little activity, at press time.

White Nationalist Groups

The Council of Conservative Citizens, a St. Louis, Mo.-based group that is the direct descendant of the White Citizens Councils that fought against desegregation in the 1950s and 1960s, saw its chapters fall from 38 in 2012 to 24 in 2013, an indication that it is losing steam as founder Gordon Lee Baum ages. The group, which says in its mission statement that it opposes "all efforts to mix the races of mankind," is now only sporadically publishing its once-important *Citizens Informer* newsletter, and its website is less active than in recent years.

The South Africa Project, a racist group based in Mandeville, La., that seeks to draw attention to the imagined genocide of white people in that country, also plummeted, falling from a robust 13 chapters in 2012 to just two last year.

The Pioneer Fund, a group founded in 1937 that has been giving large grants to racist "scientists" for years to study matters related to race and intelligence, was reorganized last year after the death of its head, Jean-Philippe Rushton. A large portion of its remaining assets went to Rushton's son, Stephen, who appears to not be involved in the academic racist movement and who shut down the Michigan-based Charles Darwin Research Institute started by his father in 1989.

The American Third Position is a group that was started in 2009 and has been led for most of its existence by William D. Johnson, who in 1985 began promoting a constitutional amendment that would deport all Americans with "an ascertainable trace of Negro blood." In the years since its founding, it has managed to accumulate some of the nation's best-known white nationalists on its board, and in 2012 it made a major effort to run candidates in various races around the country (none won).

In early 2013, the group changed its name to the American Freedom Party, supposedly because it had done so well in the 2012 elections and wanted to capitalize on that success by picking a more appealing name. But the reality is that the party did terribly in the election, was repeatedly revealed as blatantly racist at its core, and saw its chapter count fall from 17 in 2012 to just nine in 2013.

Critical Thinking

1. What factors led to the increase of hate groups in the United States?
2. What external factors have led to the collapse or near-collapse of several major groups?
3. What internal factors have led to the decline of radical right groups in the United States?

Internet References

ADL: Extremism in America
http://archive.adl.org/learn/ext_us

Growing Threat of Extreme Right-Wing Violence
http://www.cnn.com/2013/04/04/opinion/bergen-right-wing-violence

Terror from the Right
http://www.splcenter.org/get-informed/publications/terror-from-the-right

The Terrorism and Extremist Violence in the United States (TEVUS) Database
http://www.start.umd.edu/research-projects/terrorism-and-extremist-violence-united-states-tevus-database

Article   Prepared by: Thomas J. Badey, *Randolph-Macon College*

2015 Sees Dramatic Spike in Islamic Extremism Arrests

ANTI-DEFAMATION LEAGUE

Learning Outcomes

After reading this article, you will be able to:

- Identify reasons for the increase in arrests of Islamic extremists in the U.S.

- Explain how the use of social media has impacted terrorist recruitment.

- Discuss key trends evident in the demographics of the perpetrators.

Forty-five individuals living in the U.S. have been linked to terrorism motivated by Islamic extremist ideology in 2015 thus far. This surpasses the total of each of the past two years: 26 individuals living in the U.S. were linked to such terrorism in all of 2014 and 22 in 2013.

These numbers include individuals arrested and charged as well as individuals who died abroad allegedly fighting with terrorist organizations and individuals who have traveled or attempted to travel to join terrorist organizations abroad but who have not been arrested or charged at this time. They do not, however, include the many individuals believed to have traveled abroad to join terrorist groups who have not yet been identified by name. In March 2015, FBI Director James Comey stated that approximately 180 Americans have traveled to join the conflict in Syria and Iraq, an unknown number of whom may have joined terrorist organizations.

The number of U.S. residents linked to terrorism per year has varied considerably in the years since 2001, with an approximate average of 28 U.S. residents linked to terrorism annually between 2002 and 2014. The year with the greatest number thus far was 2009, when 58 U.S. residents were charged with terror offenses or otherwise named as having fought or died fighting with terrorist organizations abroad. At least one-third of those individuals were linked to Al Shabaab, the Al Qaeda affiliate in Somalia, which had been actively recruiting Americans.

The overwhelming majority of the cases in 2015 have involved use of the Internet to access terrorist propaganda or to communicate with other extremists or co-conspirators, a testament to the role of social media and internet propaganda in the radicalization process.

Even more than in 2009, this year's increase is related to a particular foreign terrorist organization. All but two of the Americans linked to terrorism in 2015 acted in support of the Islamic State of Iraq and Syria (ISIS)—and one of the other two apparently supported ISIS even though he is accused of having fought with Jabhat al Nusra, Al Qaeda in Syria.

Indeed, 60 of the 71 U.S. residents linked to terrorism motivated by Islamic extremist ideologies since 2014 have supported ISIS—representing about 84.5% of the total number. This support is related at least in part to the group's sophisticated use of social media communication and recruitment, as well as the high volume of coverage surrounding its activity and the ongoing presence of conflict in Syria and Iraq.

If the average of eight individuals per month continues, the number of people living in the U.S. linked to terrorism motivated by Islamic extremism in 2015 can be expected to exceed the 2009 number. Such progression is likely: Reports as of March 2015 have indicated that there are open investigations into potential ISIS supporters in all 50 states. Moreover, as noted, many additional, unidentified Americans are believed to be fighting with the group abroad.

An analysis of those individuals who have been arrested in 2015 may yield greater understanding of the demographics and risk factors of Americans who seek to propagate extremism at home and abroad.

Material Support Cases

Thirty-one of the individuals linked to terrorism in 2015 were charged with providing material support to terrorism. Of them, 20 had joined or attempted to join terrorist groups abroad. Seventeen had joined or attempted to join ISIS, one had joined Jabhat al Nusra (Al Qaeda in Syria), although he had allegedly also considered joining ISIS, and one was a longstanding member of Al Qaeda who was arrested and charged in 2015. Four of the 30 were attempting to aid other Americans in joining ISIS, and 8 were attempting to fund ISIS.

Three additional individuals were not charged with material support but allegedly also planned to join ISIS and another was not charged wtih material support but allegedly worked and possibly fought with Jabhat al Nusra.

Individuals engaged in material support in 2015 generally did not work alone. However, the size of their conspiracies varied.

The largest plot involved at least 9 individuals from Minneapolis, MN. Six of the individuals were arrested in April 2015 and one in February 2015. One individual was arrested in 2014 and one, who is believed to be fighting with ISIS in Syria and actively recruiting Americans, was charged in absentia in 2014.

In February 2015, six individuals were arrested in New York, Illinois, and Missouri, for working together to fund ISIS.

Between February and June of 2015, five individuals were arrested in New York for a plot to enable two of them to travel to join ISIS.

The majority of the other cases involved one or two individuals, often in contact with an undercover agent they believed was a co-conspirator.

Domestic Plots

Seventeen of the individuals linked to terrorism in 2015 also planned or discussed the possibility of a domestic plot, with 10 plots discussed in total. Six of those seventeen individuals also allegedly planned to travel to join ISIS. (Five of those six were also charged with material support; one was not charged with terror charges.) Nine of the plots in 2015 were intended to support ISIS and one was intended to support either ISIS or Jabhat al Nusra, Al Qaeda in Syria. They include:

- **Christopher Lee Cornell** of Ohio was arrested in January for his alleged plot to attack the U.S. Capitol after failing to connect with ISIS members abroad.
- **Abdirahman Sheikh Mohamud** of Ohio was arrested in February and charged in April with joining Jabhat al Nusra. He allegedly returned to the U.S. with the intention of perpetrating an attack against a military base in Texas. Court documents indicate that Mohamud supported both ISIS and Jabhat al Nusra, although he had fought with Jabhat al Nusra.

- **Abdurasul Juraboev** and **Akhror Saidakhmetov** of New York were arrested in February and charged with material support for terror. Court documents state they were attempting to join ISIS and discussing the possibility of a domestic attack.
- An **unnamed** minor from South Carolina was arrested in February and accused of formulating a plot to attack a North Carolina military base and then travel abroad to join ISIS.
- **Hasan** and **Jonas Edmonds** of Illinois were arrested in March and charged with attempting to join ISIS and plotting an attack against a military base.
- **Noelle Velentzas** and **Asia Siddiqui** of New York were arrested in April for allegedly purchasing bomb-making equipment with plans for an attack.
- **John T. Booker** and **Alexander Blair** of Kansas were arrested in April for allegedly attempting to undertake a suicide attack at the Ft. Riley military base.
- **Miguel Moran Diaz** of Florida was arrested in April on charges that he was a felon in posession of a firearm. Reports indicated that he planned to target Miami residents.
- **Elton Simpson** and **Nadir Soofi** of Arizona were shot and killed when they attempted to undertake a shooting at a Garland, Texas community center.
- **Usaama Rahim** of Massachusetts was killed when he drew a knife after being approached for questioning by law enforcement officers. He had allegedly plotted with **David Wright** of Massachusetts and **Nicholas Rovinski** of Rhode Island to behead Pamela Geller (head of the anti-Muslim organization Stop Islamicization of America) on behalf of ISIS; the plot later shifted to attempting to behead a police officer.

There was only one reported domestic plot in 2014, although there were also three instances of criminal acts motivated at least in part by online terrorist propaganda that year. The spike in plots in 2015 may be partially attributed to the increase in terrorist propaganda, particularly from ISIS, calling on followers to commit a domestic attack.

Threat to the Military

As many as five of the 2015 plots targeted the U.S. military. According to law enforcement, Jonas Edmonds was targeting the National Guard base where Hasan Edmonds had trained, using Hasan's uniform and knowledge; John Booker was targeting the Ft. Riley base in Kansas; Noelle Velentzas and Asia Siddiqui discussed targeting military, government or law enforcement; Abdirahman Sheikh Mohamud wanted to kill soldiers at a military base in Texas; and the unnamed South Carolina minor had planned to undertake a shooting at a North Carolina military base.

Military installations and personnel in the U.S. have long been targets for Islamic extremist plots, although the last year that they were targeted with this magnitude was in 2011, when there were four plots directed against military institutions.

Some examples of plots against military institutions since 2011 include:

- **Mufid Elfgeeh** was arrested in 2014 for recruiting others to join ISIS and attempting to kill U.S. soldiers. Court documents indicate that he had purchased firearms with the intention of shooting members of the U.S. military who had returned from Iraq.
- Erwin Antonio Rios was arrested in 2013 and charged with possession of a stolen firearm. He is believed to have been planning to murder U.S. military personnel at Ft. Bragg.
- **Amine El Khalifi** was arrested in 2012 for a plot to bomb the U.S. Capitol building. Court documents indicate he had also considered military targets.
- **Jose Pimentel** was arrested in 2011 for a plot targeting military personnel returning from abroad.
- **Rezwan Matin Ferdaus** was arrested in 2011 for planning to fly explosives-packed model airplanes into the Pentagon in order to "disable their (the American) military center."
- **Naser Jason Abdo** was charged in July 2011 with planning to bomb a restaurant frequented by Ft. Hood personnel and then to target the survivors with firearms.
- **Joseph Anthony Davis** and **Frederick Domingue, Jr.** were arrested in 2011 for a plot to attack a Military Entrance Processing Site in Seattle, Washington.

Two domestic plots against military institutions prior to 2011, the 2009 Ft. Hood shooting and the 2009 shooting at the Little Rock, Arkansas army recruiting center, resulted in casualties.

In addition, two of the individuals arrested in 2015 had themselves been members of the military:

- As noted above, **Hasan Edmonds,** a member of the U.S. National Guard, attempted to join ISIS and assisted his cousin, **Jonas Edmonds,** in formulating a plot against the base where Hasan trained.
- **Tairod Pugh** a former U.S. Air Force mechanic, attempted to travel to join ISIS.

Another individual, Bilal Abood, had served as a translator for the U.S. military in Iraq.

A fourth individual, John T. Booker attempted to join the military in order to commit an attack from within, according to court documents.

In 2014, there were no known veterans arrested but court documents indicate that Colorado resident Shannon Maureen Conley joined a military high school program, the U.S. Army Explorers. Like John Booker, she allegedly signed up with hopes of gaining training and experience that she could use on behalf of terrorists. Conley was arrested for attempting to join ISIS.

Some examples of other veterans arrested on terrorism charges motivated by Islamic extremism include:

- **Matthew Aaron Llaneza** arrested in 2013 on charges that he had planned to bomb a Bank of America building, had been discharged from the marines.
- **Sohiel Omar Kabir** arrested in 2012 for attempting to join the Taliban or Al Qaeda, had served in the Air Force.
- **Craig Baxam** arrested in 2012 for attempting to join Al Shabaab, had served in the army.
- **Naser Jason Abdo** arrested in 2011 for plotting an attack against Ft. Hood, had served in the army.
- **Abu Khalid Abdul-Latif** arrested in 2011 on charges that he had planned to attack a Military Processing Site, had served in the Navy.

Additional examples from 2011 and earlier can be found in the ADL's report on Islamic extremism and the U.S. military.

Notably, many of the former servicemen who plotted attacks also did so against military institutions—possibly in part because they had access to and knowledge of those locations.

ISIS has issued propaganda regarding U.S. soldiers and veterans, claiming they served in Iraq on a futile mission, highlighting casualties, and noting the difficulties veterans face upon returning to civilian life. A video released April 14, 2015, for example, featured images of dead and wounded soldiers with the captions, "mutilated soldiers are coming back to your homeland close to desperation. Eyes are being lost, bodies without legs, we want your blood. . . ." However, there is no information to indicate that such propaganda has influenced veterans and the existence of past arrests of veterans provides even less evidence for such causality.

Age

The individuals linked to terrorism in 2015 range in age from 16 to 47. The average age is 27.2, and the median age is 26. Individuals linked to terrorism in 2014 ranged in age from 15 to 44, with an average age of 24 and a median age of 21. Since 2010, the average age of U.S. citizens and residents linked to terrorism has been 28.6, with a median age of 26.

These numbers partially validate the understanding that individuals are most likely to engage in terrorist activity in their 20s, but also demonstrate that there is no one age demographic that can be associated with violent extremism.

The numbers also point to the large percentage of youths engaging in extremist activity. In total, thirteen of the individuals in 2015—just over 30%—were 21 years old or younger.

Two of the individuals linked to terrorism in 2015 are minors, aged 16 and 17. Five minors were detained while allegedly attempting to travel to join ISIS in 2014 but charges have not been issued in those cases.

Women

Five of the individuals linked to terrorism motivated by Islamic extremism in 2015 were women, resulting in a total of 14 women linked to Islamic extremism since the start of 2014. Women engaging with terrorist groups is not a new phenomenon, but these numbers represent a significant increase, which may result in part from direct recruitment of women by ISIS. ADL documented 12 U.S. women in total charged with terror offenses motivated by Islamic extremist ideology in the 11 years between 2002 and 2013.

Only two of the women arrested since 2014—co-conspirators Asia Siddiqui and Noelle Velentzas—were alleged to have engaged in a domestic plot. Four of the women were allegedly attempting to send money to foreign terrorist organizations—two in a larger conspiracy to send money to ISIS, and two in a larger conspiracy to send money to Al Shabaab. The remaining eight women reportedly traveled or attempted to travel to join ISIS. According to reports, those eight included three minors from Colorado who attempted to travel together; one minor from Chicago who attempted to travel together with her brothers; three adults, two from Colorado and one from Philadelphia, who attempted to travel individually; and one adult from Alabama who reportedly traveled individually and is currently in ISIS-controlled territory.

Families

Of the 69 U.S. residents linked to terrorism motivated by Islamic extremism since 2014, 14 individuals were arrested together with family members. Arrests of siblings, cousins, and other related individuals on terrorism charges have been similarly common worldwide. The presence of this phenomenon demonstrates an additional element of the important role that personal relationships and trust can have in the radicalization process.

Perhaps most iconic in recent years is the case of Boston Marathon bombers Dzhokhar and Tamerlan Tsarnaev. Indeed, the basis for Dzhokhar's defense rested on the argument that he would not have committed the attack were it not for his brother's influence.

Radicalization and recruitment today is focused in online spaces that enable terrorists to reach, recruit and motivate would-be extremists more quickly and effectively than ever before, eliminating the need for in-person, face-to-face interactions. That does not mean, however, that such interactions no longer exist. To the contrary, they are only magnified by online

reinforcement. While many individuals appear to be radicalized primarily via online means, others continue to join extremist groups—and may be statistically more likely to support or undertake extremist action—because of the influence of peers or relatives.

Examples of the U.S. residents linked to terrorism together with family members since 2014 include:

- **David Wright,** a 25-year-old U.S. citizen from Massachusetts, was arrested on June 2, 2015, following the death of his uncle, 26-year-old U.S. citizen **Usaama Rahim,** in a confrontation with law enforcement. Wright and Rahim had conspired along with one other individual to behead police officers.

- **Mohamed Abdihamad Farah,** a 21-year-old apparent U.S. citizen and **Adnan Abdihamid Farah,** a 19-year-old apparent U.S. citizen, both from Minnesota, were arrested on April 19, 2015 along with four other individuals for attempting to travel to join ISIS. Mohamed was arrested in California, where he had gone in an attempt to cross the border into Mexico where he could fly undetected more easily, while Adnan was arrested while still in Minneapolis, Minnesota. According to court documents, the two attempted to travel separately to avoid risk of detection.

- **Guled Ali Omar,** a 20-year-old apparent U.S. citizen from Minnesota was arrested and charged in the same case as the Farah brothers. Omar's older brother, **Ahmed Ali Omar,** is believed to have joined Al Shabaab in 2007. Guled also allegedly attempted to join Al Shabaab in 2012, prior to his 2014 and 2015 attempts to join ISIS. *(Because the siblings were not arrested together, Guled is not included in the figure for individuals arrested with family members).*

- **Abdirahman Sheikh Mohamud,** a 24-year-old U.S. citizen, was arrested in February 2015 and charged with having joined Jabhat al Nusra, Al Qaeda in Syria, and then returning to the U.S. to commit a domestic attack. Mohamud's brother, Abditafah Aden (Aden), is believed to have joined Jabhat al Nusra in August 2013. Court documents indicated that Mohamud communicated with Aden before joining Jabhat al Nusra himself. In September 2013, court documents indicate, Mohamud told Aden he was "proud" of him and that he wanted to "join you in the high ranks as a Mujahid (fighter)." Mohamud also allegedly discussed travel plans and other logistical information with Aden before joining him in Syria. The relationship was particularly crucial because Jabhat al Nusra often requires inside references for fighters before it allows them to join the organization.

- **Ramiz Zijad Hodzic,** a 40-year-old U.S. resident residing in Missouri, was arrested together with his wife, **Sedina Unkic Hodzic,** a 35-year-old U.S. resident residing in Missouri, and four other individuals in February 2015. The group is accused of sending money to aid ISIS. Court documents indicate that the group used online tools to coordinate their activity and at least some members accessed terrorist propaganda online. However, they do not seem to have become radicalized primarily as a result of online sources.

- **Hasan Edmonds,** a 22-year-old U.S. citizen from Illinois and his cousin **Jonas Edmonds,** a 29-year-old U.S. citizen from Illinois, were arrested in March. The two were trying to travel abroad to join ISIS together with Jonas's wife and children. The cousins seemed to prioritize having the entire family join ISIS. Court documents indicate that when Jonas was not able to obtain a passport, he and Hasan began to formulate a plan to attack a military facility and planned for Jonas to "send his family and then seek *shahada* (martyrdom) here in the heart of the *kuffar* (apostate) state."

- **Mohammed Hamzah Khan,** a 19-year-old U.S. citizen from Illinois, was detained at the airport with his 17-year-old sister and 16-year-old brother in October 2014 while allegedly attempting to board a flight abroad to join ISIS. Khan and his siblings all penned similar letters to their parents asking the parents not to call the police, explaining their reasons for traveling, and expressing hope that the parents would join them in ISIS territory.

- Two sisters from Colorado, aged 15 and 17, were detained together with a friend while traveling in an attempt to join ISIS. The Sheriff's Report that documents their case indicates that, when questioned about why they had traveled, "they said, 'Family,' and would not elaborate on any other details about their trip."

Some of the sentiments expressed about ensuring that entire families can join ISIS together may be linked to ISIS propaganda promoting a vision of a religious utopia. As noted, in addition to multiple images of children playing and training in ISIS territory, the group also releases propaganda geared directly to women, characterizing them as essential building-blocks of a new society.

However, family members engaging in terrorism together is by no means a new phenomenon. Other incidents of U.S. residents linked to terrorism together with family members include Hor and Amera Akl, an Ohio couple arrested in 2010 for supporting Hezbollah; Paul and Nadia Rockwood, an Alaska couple arrested in 2010 for compiling a hit list of individuals; and Eljvir, Shain and Dritan Duka, brothers from New Jersey arrested in 2007 for being part of a group conspiring to attack Ft. Dix.

Religion and Ethnicity

At least ten of the individuals arrested in 2015, or just over one fifth, were converts to Islam. That percentage is comparable to the percentage in 2014.

The individuals are also ethnically diverse, proving yet again that there is no set ethnic profile for engagement with Islamic extremism. At least 16 of those arrested in 2015 are Caucasian (and non-Arab), including six Bosnian and five Uzbek natives and at least five individuals who had converted to Islam.

At least seven of the individuals arrested are Somali-American. Between 2007 and 2011, there was growing concern regarding the numbers of Somali-Americans traveling to join Al Shabaab. Such travel has now shifted in favor of travel to ISIS, with American members of Al Shabaab even encouraging their contacts back home to travel to Syria, rather than Somalia.

Criminal Background

At least six of the individuals linked to terrorism in 2015 had a prior criminal record: Jonas Edmonds had been convicted of a felony for robbing a McDonald's restaurant, Joshua Ray Van Haftan was a convicted sex offender, Miguel Moran Diaz had been convicted of cocaine trafficking, Elton Simpson had been convicted of lying to federal agents about his plans to join Al Shabaab, Nadir Soofi had been convicted of minor offenses including unlawful posession of drugs, and Leon Nathan Davis III had been convicted of drug trafficking.

Approximately 10% of the individuals arrested on terror charges motivated by Islamic extremism since 2002 had a previous criminal record.

Geographic Distribution

The arrests in 2015 have taken place in 14 states, including 7 individuals arrested in California (2 of whom were Minnesota residents), 6 individuals arrested in New York, 5 in Minnesota, 4 in Illinois, 3 in Missouri, and 2 each in Ohio, Kansas and Florida. Other states represented are Wisconsin, Florida, Virginia, New Jersey, South Carolina, Texas, Georgia, Massachusetts, Rhode Island, and Pennsylvania. Four of the individuals linked to terrorism this year were associated with Texas, including Elton Simpson and Nadir Soofi, who were from Arizona and were killed while attempting to perpetrate an attack in Texas, Muhanad Mahmoud Al Farekh, who was arrested in Pakistan but whose U.S. residence was in Texas, and Asher Abed Khan, a Houston-area man arrested in Texas for attempting to join ISIS.

Since 2002, individuals have been linked to terror charges related to Islamic extremism from at least 31 states and the District of Columbia. Certain states stand out as having had particularly large numbers of arrests. There have been at least 36 individuals arrested from Minnesota, 31 from New York and from California, and 24 from Illinois.

Appendix
A full list of individuals arrested in 2015 follows:

- January 14, 2015: **Christopher Lee Cornell,** a 20-year-old U.S. citizen from Ohio, was arrested and charged with attempting to attack the U.S. Capitol building.
- February 2015: **Unnamed** 16-year-old minor from South Carolina was arrested for a plot to undertake a shooting at a North Carolina military institution and then travel to join ISIS. He was charged as a minor in possession of a pistol and sentenced in March 2015 to five years in juvenile detention, followed by counseling.
- February 2015: **Hamza Ahmed,** a 19-year-old U.S. citizen from Minnesota, was arrested for attempting to travel to join ISIS and charged with lying in a federal investigation. In May 2015 he was also charged with student loan fraud, which he allegedly used to fund his travel plans.
- February 2, 2015: **Abdirahman Sheikh Mohamud,** a 23-year-old U.S. citizen from Ohio, was arrested and charged with joining Jabhat al Nusra. Court documents indicate that Muhamud returned to the U.S. with the intention of committing a domestic attack.
- February 6, 2015: **Ramiz Zijad Hodzic,** a 40-year-old U.S. resident residing in Missouri, **Sedina Unkic Hodzic,** 35-year-old U.S. resident residing in Missouri, **Armin Harcevic,** 37-year-old U.S. permanent resident residing in Missouri, **Nihad Rosic,** 26-year-old naturalized U.S. citizen residing in New York, **Mediha Medy Salkicevic,** 34-year-old naturalized U.S. citizen residing in Illinois, and **Jasminka Ramic,** 42-year-old U.S. permanent resident residing in Illinois, were arrested and charged with sending funds to ISIS. All 6 are Bosnian natives.
- February 24, 2015: **Abdurasul Juraboev** and **Khror Saidakhmetov,** 24-year-old U.S. residents from New York, were arrested and charged with attempting to join ISIS. Court documents indicate that they had discussed the possibility of a domestic plot.
- February 24, 2015: **Abror Habibov,** a 30-year-old U.S. resident from New York, was arrested in Florida for allegedly aiding Juraboev and Saidakhmetov.
- February 27, 2015: **Ali Shukri Amin,** a 17-year-old U.S. citizen from Virginia was arrested for aiding another individual in joining ISIS. He had also provided online instruction on how to use bitcoin, a virtual currency, to mask provision of funds to ISIS.
- March 18, 2015: **Tairod Nathan Webster Pugh,** a 47-year-old U.S. citizen from New Jersey, was arrested and charged with attempting to join ISIS.
- March 26, 2015: **Hasan Edmonds,** a 22-year-old U.S. citizen from Illinois and **Jonas Edmonds,** a 29-year-old U.S. citizen from Illinois, were arrested and charged with attempting to join ISIS. Court documents indicate the two were also formulating a plot against an Illinois military facility.
- April 2, 2015: **Asia Siddiqui,** a 31-year-old U.S. citizen from Brooklyn, New York and **Noelle Velentzas,** a 28-year-old U.S. citizen from New York, were arrested and charged with plotting to undertake a domestic bomb plot.
- April 2, 2015: **Muhanad Mahmoud Al Farekh,** a 29-year-old U.S. citizen from Texas, was arrested in Pakistan for allegedly having joined Al Qaeda. Al Farekh was charged in January 2015.
- April 3, 2015: **Keonna Thomas,** a 30-year-old U.S. citizen from Pennsylvania, was arrested and charged with attempting to join ISIS.
- April 4, 2015: **Miguel Moran Diaz,** a 46-year-old U.S. citizen from Florida, was arrested and charged with being a felon in possession of firearms. He allegedly planned to shoot people on behalf of ISIS.
- April 7, 2015: **Dilkhayot Kasimov,** a 26-year-old U.S. resident from New York, was arrested for allegedly aiding Juraboev and Saidakhmetov.
- April 9, 2015: **Joshua Ray Van Haftan,** a 34-year-old U.S. citizen from Illinois, was arrested and charged with attempting to join ISIS.
- April 10, 2015: **John T. Booker, Jr.,** a 20-year-old U.S. citizen from Kansas was arrested and charged with attempting to undertake a suicide attack at Ft. Riley military base.
- April 10, 2015: **Alexander Blair,** a 28-year-old U.S. citizen from Kansas, was arrested for allegedly having knowledge of and possibly aiding Booker in his attack.
- April 19, 2015: **Zacharia Yusuf Abdurahman,** a 19-year-old apparent U.S. citizen, **Adnan Farah,** a 19-year-old apparent U.S. citizen, **Hanad Mustafe Musse,** a 19-year-old apparent U.S. citizen, and **Guled Ali Omar,** a 20-year-old apparent U.S. citizen, were arrested in Minneapolis and **Abdirahman Yasin Daud,** a 21-year-old apparent U.S. citizen, and **Mohamed Abdihamid Farah,** a 21-year-old apparent U.S. citizen, were arrested in San Diego for attempting to join ISIS. All are Minnesota residents.

- April 23, 2015: **Mohamad Saeed Kodaimati,** a 24-year-old U.S. citizen from California, was arrested for making false statements involving international terrorism. Kodaimati had allegedly served on a Shari'a (Islamic jurisprudence) court affiliated with Jabhat al Nusra and fought with Jabhat al Nusra.
- May 3, 2015: **Elton Simpson,** a 30-year-old U.S. citizen from Arizona and **Nadir Soofi,** a 34-year-old U.S. citizen from Arizona, were killed while attempting to undertake a shooting at a Texas community center.
- May 14, 2015: **Bilal Abood,** a 27-year-old U.S. citizen from Texas, was arrested for lying to a federal agent. He is believed to have attempted to travel to join ISIS.
- May 21, 2015: **Muhanad Badawi** and **Nader Elhuzayel,** both 24-year-old apparent U.S. citizens from California, were arrested for attempting to travel to join ISIS.
- May 26, 2015: **Asher Abed Khan,** a 20-year-old U.S. citizen from Texas, was arrested for attempting to travel to join ISIS.
- May 27, 2015: **Leon Nathan Davis III,** a 37-year-old U.S. citizen from Georgia, was charged with material support to terror for allegedly attempting to travel to join ISIS. Davis had been arrested in 2014 for violation of his parole when he attempted to board an airplane, and had been charged in February 2015 with illegal posession of weapons by a felon.
- June 2, 2015: **Usaama Rahim,** a 26-year-old U.S. citizen from Massachusetts, was killed when he drew a knife after being approached by law enforcement officials. Rahim had allegedly plotted with **David Wright,** a 25-year-old U.S. citizen from Massachusetts arrested later that day on a charge of conspiracy,

to behead Pamela Geller, head of the anti-Muslim organization Stop Islamicization of America. The two later shifted their plans to allegedly attempt to behead police officers.
- June 10, 2015: **Reza Niknejad,** an 18-year-old U.S. citizen from Virginia, was charged in absentia for allegedly joining ISIS. Niknejad had allegedly been encouraged to travel by Ali Shukri Amin.
- June 11, 2015: **Akmal Zakirov,** a 29-year-old U.S. resident from New York, was arrested for allegedly aiding Juraboev and Saidakhmetov.
- June 12, 2015: **Nicholas Rovinski,** a 24-year-old U.S. citizen from Rhode Island, was arrested and charged with providing material support to terror. Rovinski had allegedly conspired with Rahim and Wright to behead police officers and had discussed traveling to join ISIS.

Critical Thinking

1. Why are terrorists successful in recruiting Americans?
2. How does the use of the Internet influence terrorism in the United States?
3. What can be done to counter terrorist recruitment?

Internet References

FBI official: ISIS is recruiting U.S. teens
http://www.cnn.com/2015/02/03/politics/fbi-isis-counterterrorism-michael-steinbach

ISIS excels at recruiting American teens: Here are four reasons why (+video)
http://www.csmonitor.com/USA/USA-Update/2014/1022/ISIS-excels-at-recruiting-American-teens-Here-are-four-reasons-why-video

Threat of Homegrown Islamist Terrorism
http://www.cfr.org/terrorism/threat-homegrown-islamist-terrorism/p11509

Unit 6

UNIT

Prepared by: Thomas J. Badey, *Randolph-Macon College*

Terrorism and the Media

The media plays an important role in contemporary international terrorism. Terrorists use the media to transmit their message, to intimidate larger populations, and to recruit new members. Since the hijackings at Dawson's field in Jordan in 1970 and the Munich Olympic massacre in 1972, international terrorists have exploited the media and have managed to gain access to a global audience. The media provides terrorists with an inexpensive means of publicizing their cause and a forum to attract potential supporters. In the age of independent fund raising, terrorists have become increasingly dependent on accessible media coverage. As media coverage has become more sophisticated, terrorist organizations have become increasingly conscious of their interactions with the press. Managing public relations, drafting press releases, and arranging interviews have become important functions, often delegated to individuals or groups in the semi-legal periphery of the organization.

The impact of the increasingly symbiotic relationship between terrorists and media has been two-fold. On the one hand, the media has provided terrorists with real-time coverage and immediate 24-hour access to a global public. As long as the explosion is big enough and the devastation horrific enough and there are cameras close by, media coverage of the incident is guaranteed. Holding true to the old axiom "if it bleeds, it leads," the media seems only too willing to provide terrorists with free, unlimited, and at times indiscriminate coverage of their actions.

On the other hand, the media also provides terrorists with a means of ventilation, potentially reducing the number of violent incidents. This outlet subtly influences terrorists to function within certain, albeit extended, boundaries of social norms, as grave violations of these norms may elicit unintended or unwanted public backlash and a loss of support. In light of these contradictory tendencies, the debate about media censorship or self-censorship continues.

The Internet and new media have provided terrorists with instant, unfiltered access to a new audience. Terrorists are becoming increasingly less dependent on traditional media. As the "YouTube" and "Twitter" generation engages in political discourse, terrorists' use of the new media will continue to expand. Simultaneously, a new battle between terrorists and governments for control of the message has begun. Both attempt to use and manipulate the media in new ways.

The articles in this unit explore the relationship between terrorism and the media. First, O'Donnell and Gray provide an overview of the evolution of the relationship between terrorism and the media. They argue that because of its impact on contemporary terrorism, the media can be an important tool in the counterterrorism arsenal. Next, Ken Menkhaus examines how al-Shabaab has used new social media technology to wage, and sometimes win, a global media battle. He believes that social media have hurt al-Shabaab as much as they have helped it. In the third article in this section, Jeffery Goldberg nostalgically remembers a "time when Islamist Extremists wanted to persuade reporters, not kill them." Goldberg suggests that the job of reporters has become more dangerous because extremists no longer need journalists. Their role has been replaced by modern social media such as YouTube and Twitter. In the final selection of this section Peter Hart points to inconsistencies in the reporting by the mainstream media. He argues that media coverage of the Boston bombings highlights the fact that there is no consistent definition of terrorism in the media. He asserts that, for some commentators, how the story was reported seemed to depend more on the suspects' nationality and religion than the facts.

Article   Prepared by: Thomas J. Badey, *Randolph-Macon College*

Media and State Sponsored Terrorism

BRETT O'DONNELL AND DAVID H. GRAY

Learning Outcomes

After reading this article, you will be able to:

- Describe how the media helped the PLO to gain international attention.

- Identify three state sponsors that have used the media to provide misinformation.

- Discuss the ways the media can be used in counter-terrorism.

> "The speed of communications is wondrous to behold. It is also true that speed can multiply the distribution of information that we know to be untrue." Edward R. Murrow

Terrorism expert and political advisor to Presidents, government agencies, and international organizations on the behavior of terrorists Brian M. Jenkins, once stated that "terrorism is a theatre" (Hoffman 2006). No statement in regards to terrorism is truer than this. This statement exemplifies contemporary terrorism in that everything [terrorists] do is done to draw as much attention, on the world stage, to their cause as possible.

In its early stages terrorism was focused on a specific political target with the intention of causing as little collateral damage as possible where the goal was specifically to only kill the target and no one else. The 1972 Olympic attacks by the Palestinian Liberation Organization (PLO) on the Israeli Olympic team changed the future of terrorism. The attacks on the Israeli team drew in worldwide attention and changed how terrorism would be enacted for the next four decades, and most likely will continue to influence terrorism for years to come until it evolves again. It became a realization of terrorist groups everywhere that the media and modern information and technology could be used to draw the world's attention to these devastating acts. The media was used to draw the attention of not just the citizens of the world to their cause but also to get the governments of the world to pay attention to them as well.

Along with this realization by terrorist organization, state sponsors also came to the realization that they could use the media for their own benefit. By providing the people misinformation they could misplace blame on the west for their problems. At the same time they also had to keep their people from realizing the truth and in many cases the states employed only state run media networks and blacked out information from the outside world, especially by blocking out many internet websites and preventing admittance to foreign journalists.

State sponsors of terrorism restricted the most basic of freedoms, the freedom of information. States such as Iran, North Korea, and Libya restricted information to restrain their populations' ability to learn and see what was beyond their borders. It was done to encourage support of the political leaders' agendas, and to misinform the people. The state sponsors made it seem that the terrorist organizations they supported were saviors and heroes, revolutionaries fighting for the people and that the West and Israel were monsters, decadents, hedonists without morals or souls, and the lands they lived in were ruled by tyrants, Hollywood, and money.

Daniel Byman suggested that "cutting the deadly connection between states and terrorist groups is difficult at best and impossible at worst," but there are opportunities for policymakers to take steps to do so. In order to combat state sponsored terrorism the international community can "engage the state sponsor, use massive military force to change a regime, use punitive or coercive uses of military force, threaten military force, economic sanctions, backing insurgency or terrorist groups of one's own, and diplomatic isolation" (Byman 2005).

However, with recent events it is being realized that perhaps the media is not only a symbiotic partner to terrorism in that they both have something to gain and can continue to prosper and survive through exploiting each other, but it is a tool to end terrorism. It is being recognized by the populations of these state sponsors and by the West that the media can be used to educate the people and to inform them that there are better alternatives. States that sponsor terrorism for long periods of time have a history of being poor and suffering from severely broken infrastructures. The people suffering under these awful socioeconomic conditions are finally saying they have had enough. From Morocco to Iran revolts are occurring as the people through the information of the media are realizing they can win, that they can create change.

A Brief History of Terrorism

Before going further it is important to understand the creation of contemporary terrorism in further detail and how the media helped create it. Terrorism arguably, most probably existed in some form since the first organized state existed with a political party, an official leader, and an individual that did not approve of how things were being handled. After all even Julius Caesar was assassinated by his own peers and "friends" that wanted a change and he was a ruler thousands of years before the concept of terrorism became an accepted universal term without a definition.

Terrorism in its earliest stages gained modern acceptance and emerged during the French Revolution. . . . [I]n contrast to its contemporary usage, at the time terrorism had a decidedly positive connotation" (Hoffman 2006). This positive connotation would come as a surprise to many of today's readers as terrorism is quite literally a bad word in the modern English language. The French Revolutionaries that were coined as terrorists were heroes of the people; they became champions of change that sought out to destroy an oppressive ruling class that left them without the basic necessities of food and home. That is not to say that some of their tactics weren't without brutality.

In time terrorism would be adopted by many other parties throughout the world and it would be used as a responsible tool. The Nardonaya Volya of Russia, who were known for targeting specific leaders of the opposition party, would go to great lengths to avoid injuring innocents, even if it cost them the mission and their very lives. But in time terrorism would become distorted and bastardized and used by parties like the Irish Clan na Gael, the IRB, the Nazis, the Italian Fascists, and the Russians under Stalin where hurting innocents and causing destruction were no longer off limits and the accomplishment of the mission was all that mattered. Achieve your goals no matter the cost. It is however, important to remember that what the Nazis and even Stalin did was genocide not terrorism, which is no less evil but just as horrible—only on a much larger scale.

Contemporary terrorism would emerge with the creation of the Palestinian Liberation Organization and the realization by this party that terrorism was more successful not only if you ignored avoiding innocent casualties and avoided property destruction but if you actually sought out to cause them on as large a scale as possible. The PLO is significantly important for two reasons, 1) it was the first of its kind to embrace tactics that involved getting media attention and 2) according to Bruce Hoffman who is arguably the leading terrorism expert in the world, the PLO was the first international terrorist organization (Hoffman 2006).

The PLO would first make its media statements by hijacking planes. This was not an uncommon tactic used by terrorist organizations at the time but instead of just hijacking the planes and making demands they would hijack the plane and kill the passengers to make "a major media event" (Hoffman 2006). These tactics would pale in comparison when they took terrorism to a whole new level in 1972 at the Olympics in Germany.

At the 1972 Olympic event the PLO terrorist cell Black September would take the Israeli team hostage and eventually kill 11 Israeli athletes and coaches as well as one German Police Officer. This massacre drew unprecedented media attention to the actions of the terrorists and PLO cause. "The undivided attention of some four thousand print and radio journalists and two thousand television reporters and crew already in place to cover the Olympiad was suddenly refocused on Palestine and the Palestinian cause. An estimated 900 million people in a hundred different countries saw the crises unfold on their television screens" (Hoffman 2006).

This created a new feeling in terrorists the world over that by drawing media attention to their causes they could gain recognition, and legitimacy. It gave terrorists their greatest tool in whatever "war" they found themselves involved in. By gaining this much attention from the media the terrorist organizations found themselves able to gain support, resources, and in many cases actual legitimacy. The PLO in time would gain political legitimacy-the PLO "a nonstate actor, established formal diplomatic relations with more countries (86) than the actual established nation-state of Israel (72) [and amassed an] annual income of $600 million, of which some $500 million were from investments" (Hoffman 2006).

The PLO was the first international terrorist organization to gain political legitimacy only to be followed by organizations like Hezbollah, however its legitimacy would not last as they could not handle political responsibility and its leadership was found struggling with the challenge.

Terrorism and the Media

Margaret Thatcher once said that "publicity is the oxygen of terrorism." Terrorist organizations embrace the media for without it they lack a significant tool and what has arguably become their most effective weapon. "Terrorists must have publicity in some form if they are to gain attention, inspire fear and respect, and secure favorable understanding of their cause, if not their act" (Soriano 2008). From the perspective of the terrorist, media coverage is the measurement of success for a campaign. "According to Brigitte Nacos, one of the scholars that has most studied this issue, terrorists commit violent acts looking for three universal objectives: to get attention; to gain recognition; and to obtain a certain degree of respect and legitimacy. These objectives are attainable for those individuals who are capable of receiving the most media coverage" (Soriano 2008).

In recent events it would appear that terrorists carefully select their targets in knowing where the most media coverage will be accessible or in which events that would draw the most attention. The attacks on New York City on 11 September 2001 by al-Qaeda made media coverage highly accessible in that the media was readily available and the residents and significant number of tourists visiting would be able to give firsthand accounts and acquire footage of photographs and videos for the media to show the world. Similar to this is the attack on the school in Beslan, Russia in which Chechen rebels killed a large number of school children. This attack although remote was unfortunately well planned because they knew that no media outlet would ignore such a horrific attack on children.

Terrorists and the media have an interesting relationship. French Sociologist Michael Wieviorka performed a study that separated terrorists and their relationships to the media into four levels: "Complete Indifference, where terrorists complete their act of terror with no regard to media coverage; Relative Indifference, in which terrorists complete their act of terror with an understanding that media could assist their cause, but are still uninterested in media coverage; A Media-Oriented strategy, in which terrorist are aware of and utilize the media to further their message; and Complete Breakaway, in which the media is seen as the enemy and the terrorists will respond to the media in the same way they respond to any enemy" (Soriano 2008). It could be argued that contemporary terrorism would show that terrorists are on a mixture of the last three levels and that complete indifference is hardly recognized. One would be hard pressed to find a terrorist organization that does not desire media attention in some form. They are almost all interested in drawing some attention to their cause although keeping the media alive is obviously not a priority. There are many media outlets out there and if a few get eliminated in the process it will only serve to increase the attention to the incident. Whether or not this is productive to the cause is a different argument all together.

In some instances it is debated that the media are the principal authors of the stereotyped and clearly negative vision that society has of terrorist organizations' participants and activities. By this perception the press is considered to be "mere extensions of the enemy" (Soriano 2008). Terrorists can fall into several categories ranging from needing the media, to avoiding it, to hating it. "A series of recent terrorist acts indicates the emergence of trends that impact on the relationship between the media, the terrorist, and government. These include: (1) a trend toward anonymity in terrorism; (2) a trend towards more violent terrorist incidents; and (3) a trend towards attacks on media personnel and institutions" (Perl 1997).

Anonymous terrorism occurs when no one claims responsibility and no demands are made. When the media reports on such instances it is argued that they are amplifying a terrorist's agenda. "Reportage is inevitable; especially if it includes unbridled speculation, false threats or hoaxes, coverage can advance terrorists' agendas, such as spreading panic, hurting tourism, and provoking strong government reactions leading to unpopular measures, including restrictions on individual liberties" (Perl 1997).

Terrorism has also recently taken a turn for the worse in that the incidents are becoming increasingly more violent. This can be attributed either to the advancement of technology or to a more violent terrorist. "The Department of State's Patterns of Global Terrorism: 1996 notes that while worldwide instances of terrorist acts have dropped sharply in the last decade, the death toll from the individual act is rising and the trend continues toward more ruthless attacks on mass civilian targets and the use of more powerful bombs. The threat of terrorist use of materials of mass destruction is an issue of growing concern. . ."

And finally there has been an upsurge in attacks on journalists and media personnel, more so than ever before. "Recent attacks occurred in Algeria, Mexico, Russia, Chechnya, and London, but there have been cases as well in Washington, D.C.

at the National Press Building and at the United Nations in New York. One private watchdog group estimates that forty-five journalists were killed in 1995 as a consequence of their work" (Perl 1997).

Failure to Define Terrorism

Throughout contemporary history dealing with modern terrorism has faced one major obstacle and that is the inability of the world community to come up with a sufficient definition for terrorism. This is no surprise as even government departments within the United States cannot agree on one definition as they each focus on their own mission statement. Defining terrorism eventually turns into an argument of semantics as the modern terrorist will "never acknowledge that he is a terrorist and moreover will go to great lengths to evade and obscure any such inference or connection" (Hoffman 2006). Terrorism is often looked at very subjectively. Terrorism depends largely "on whether one sympathizes with or opposes the person/group/cause concerned. If one identifies with the victim of the violence, for example, then the act is terrorism. If, however, one identifies with the perpetrator, the violent act is regarded in a more sympathetic, if not positive light, and it is not terrorism" (Hoffman 2006).

This inability to create a definition unfortunately transfers over to the media. The western media indiscriminately mixes terms such as revolutionary, guerilla, criminal and terrorist. They do this for maximum effect as the media, in most cases, especially in relation to the United States seeks to create the biggest impact and eerily similar to terrorists seek to get the biggest audience.

This is a significant issue as it makes the west look like they are deliberately trying to be discriminatory against all Muslim organizations, those that are rightly terrorists and those without any association. However, the media in the Arab world is often viewed as being sympathetic towards terrorist organizations again obscuring definitions to make them look like the people's revolutionaries bringing forth a Robin Hood type of quandary.

Terrorist Media

Although terrorism has existed far longer than mass media terrorism has always been about making a statement to the public. Technology has made reaching audiences far easier than ever before with satellite radio and television, and especially with the assistance of the internet. "It seems fair to say that there exists a mutually beneficial relationship between the terrorist and the media of today" (Soriano 2008). Terrorists use the media to spread misinformation and the media uses the terrorists for ratings. According to retired Indian Air Marshal and Air Vice Chief of Staff Bhushan Gokhale, when speaking at the 17th anniversary of the Pune Working Journalists Union, he stated "terrorists are using the media as a tool to spread misinformation and terror, terrorists are using the media as a weapon. For them, a casualty rate of 100-150 is not a big deal. The fact that so many people will be glued to their television screens would ensure that their message of terror is spread" (Goenka

2009). India has now made the homeland security integrate the media as part of its national policy.

Terrorist organizations have found interesting ways of using the media for their own ends. There are two prominent organizations that can be looked at that have very different relationships to terrorist groups. One is declared a terrorist organization by the US Department of State, the Mujahideen e-Khalq (MEK) and the other is an independent television outlet that is denying that it has ties to terrorism, Al-Jazeera.

The Mujahideen e-Khalq (MEK) is an Iranian opposition group working from exile spreading their own information into Iran to help overthrow the current administration. The MEK reaches into Iran using its own satellite television channel and claims a network of activists inside the Islamic Republic. Although designated a terrorist organization some would argue that MEK could be helpful to the United States by driving out President Ahmadinejad. "The MEK represents a viable alternative to the clerical regime in Tehran by halting the nuclear weapons program, introducing economic and political reform, and contributing to regional and global stability. In short, despite its terrorist designation, some argue the MEK can serve as a tool to increase US pressure on Iran to effect positive developments regarding the issues in dispute" (Bahgat 2004).

And then on the other end is Al-Jazeera. Al-Jazeera currently is a media source that claims it is independently run, unlike most media outlets in the Middle East which are state controlled, and has no ties to terrorist organizations. But it has been argued that Al-Jazeera is tied to Osama bin Laden and al-Qaeda, after all Osama is a self-proclaimed viewer of Al-Jazeera.

Al-Jazeera is an Arabic satellite television station created by the monarchy in Qatar in order to provide a more independent Arab point of view. They run on a more Western platform and bring in experts and reporters from both the West and the Arab world. However, the argument that emerges that Al-Jazeera has ties to terrorism is their willingness to allow bin Laden the opportunity to express his opinion through their network, as well as to release videos and written statements through them.

After September 11th the station became a spokesperson for bin Laden and the Taliban. "Though the station presented both the Western and the Taliban sides of the conflict, by giving both sides an equal footing, bin Laden finally had a television media outlet in which he had control over the message being sent to the public" (Soriano 2008). Al-Jazeera argues that they never let bin Laden have control over the message being sent to the public instead insisting that they show both sides of the conflict. With the wars with Afghanistan and Iraq, Al-Jazeera attempted to focus on the victims of the American offensive. By showing both sides, especially al-Qaeda's point of view, the station has become extremely popular. The war and the connection to the terrorist organization of al-Qaeda and the Taliban has been hugely beneficial for the media station. "Though there is discrepancy around the loyalty that Al-Jazeera has for Al Qaeda, and whether or not they act as direct mouthpiece for Osama bin Laden, showing his videos sans editing or not, it is clear there is more sympathy in Al-Jazeera's programming to the Iraqi militants, Palestine and the Muslim world" (Soriano 2008). The Muslim world has a variety of other media outlets

but none as prominent as MEK and Al-Jazeera. Both significantly tied to terrorism yet they each have exceedingly different roles to play.

However, al-Qaeda believes that the West is using media as a tool of war by lying about the motivations behind both the jihad movement and the motivation of Western governments. This is argued in four points "1) the Western media diverts the attention of the Muslim population by focusing on issues that are small or of little importance considering the bigger picture, 2) the media exaggerate the military strength of the west, 3) the media distorts the Arab image and motivation to that of madmen, 4) and the media promotes Western aggression against Islam thus creating a scenario in which American military violence against al-Qaeda is widely accepted" (Soriano 2008). It is obvious that the media is used as a tool of war by both sides. Both believe the other is making them out to be madmen. The war on terrorism is shifting away from a political war to a cultural war which has been the underlying issue all along. With new methods of gaining accurate information and the ability to see or read both sides through the internet people are coming to the realization that not everything they hear is the truth.

Media Control

The media can make great changes in the world of the oppressed peoples but it is not without its issues. The media like any organization needs to be monitored for truth and held responsible for the complications it can create. Some would even go so far as to argue in the past that the media made mass killings by terrorists more likely than less. When the media drew the attention that the terrorist organizations so desperately craved they only spread the desire for a bigger more horrific incident. "Without gain there would be less incentive for the horrific behavior" (Neuwirth 2006).

When all the media agrees on a specific incident a majority of the population would naturally believe they are being told the truth, and why wouldn't they. The media is supposed to be the people's source of accurate reliable information. However, they can turn certain stories into propaganda, intentionally or not. A prime example of the media following their own agenda was when the New York Times printed an article with a picture of an Israeli Policeman and a Palestinian on the Temple Mount, "The photo suggests a Palestinian so badly beaten that blood was running down his face. When in reality the picture was of an Israeli policeman that was protecting the beaten Jewish victim from Arabs (Neuwirth 2006). The New York Times was forced to retract the story by outraged protestors but they did so only reluctantly and with much contestation. The result of this dilemma was the creation of a media watchdog organization. The New York Times is such a prestigious and reliable source of media it brings into question any media organization.

This also brings about the need for the government and media collaboration to monitor stories and keep control. Not only is it to keep the print honest, but it is also to protect the state's population from media releasing information that provides incentives for terrorists or perhaps even provides them with information about a specific target or when to act next.

The Congressional Research Service Intelligence Brief offers some suggestions on how the media and the government can work together. These include: (1) financing joint media/government training exercises; (2) establishing a government terrorism information response center; (3) promoting use of media pools for hostage-centered terrorist events; (4) establishing and promoting voluntary press coverage guidelines; and (5) monitoring terrorism against the media (Perl 1997). These voluntary guidelines can help monitor the media and keep false stories from emerging. However the government has to play a balancing act in that they do not over step their bounds. "The media and the government have common interests in seeing that the media are not manipulated into promoting the cause of terrorism or its methods. On the other hand, neither the media nor policymakers want to see terrorism, or counter terrorism, eroding constitutional freedoms including that of the press" (Perl 1997).

These voluntary guidelines if balanced properly are not just helpful here in the United States but they can also have a significant impact on all states that belong to the United Nations. If all states are granted the basic freedom of information and the press then perhaps these revolutions would appear anywhere the people are oppressed. The guidelines could also help promote free media sources that are not limited or controlled by governments or supported by terrorists. The individuals are doing their part against their oppressors: it is time the democratically free nations do their part to assist them. The United Nations makes claims they are doing all they can by forcing sanctions on the states where these revolutions are occurring, they are freezing assets, and they are holding meetings. Take it a step further and demand the freedom of information.

The Internet

Technology, especially the internet, has made the spread of information far more accessible than ever before. Terrorists use the internet to spread their message, and to recruit. The internet is not only safe and immediate, but allows al-Qaeda and other terrorist groups to speak directly to their audience with an untainted message.

However, the internet has also allowed the populations of states that are often dictatorships, oppressive, and sponsors of terrorists to see the truth and to learn more about the outside world. They learn how things could be, and that the west is not as "evil" as they are made out to be. The people of oppressed nations would like to have a more solidly built infrastructure, education, jobs, and the freedom to make decisions for themselves.

Thanks to the lack of filters on the internet which "acts as a direct media with no filter for language, message or imagery used, television is being pushed to show visuals which they would have shied away from in the past new communication technologies are pushing the boundaries of what television audiences are used to viewing" (Soriano 2008). Along with this and the ability of people to publicly blog opinions, and for two way communications to be established by people in separate parts of the world culture is spreading and blending causing people to see through the misinformation they were shown.

This has led to dissent starting to rise in oppressed areas where media blackouts only partially existed. In the Middle East there has been significant cultural blending due to the internet and the ability of the populations to watch shows from the West and the ability to learn on their own that perhaps their oppressive leaders are the real problem. In 2006 a 56 year old doctor and human rights activist from Gaza named Mona El-Farra used her blog as a window to the world. She states she uses her blog as a way to create a bridge to the outside world. Due to sanctions by Egypt and Israel the people of Gaza have a difficult time traveling. Mona El-Farra said her blog not only "gives Gazans a chance to connect with the rest of the world, their blogs give those outside the region an inside view of Gaza" (Davies 2004). El-Farra's blog has thousands of readers from all over the world and helps encourage a sharing of culture and information.

However, in states like North Korea (and in some cases China) that continue to have total media and internet black outs a shift in the population's view of the leadership has not appeared and protest attempts always seem to fall flat.

Socioeconomic Conditions and a Lack of Information

Experts of terrorism have been arguing consistently for many years as to what causes a person to turn to terrorism. Many would assume that it would be the uneducated and the poor who unwittingly make up the ranks of the terrorist organizations. However, this is not the case as Alan Krueger and Jitka Maleckova through extensive research have found that it is in fact the educated and more economically well off that are more likely to participate in extremism and terrorism than those that are under educated and poor (Krueger 2003). This is significant information because a state with poor socioeconomic conditions may not breed new terrorists but it does allow for an oppressive government that sponsors outside terrorist organizations. When the poverty stricken masses finally become informed and have had enough of their leadership then they can make a change not only better for themselves but by doing so they unintentionally put an end to a state sponsor.

Those that are poverty stricken often have more interest in how to get another meal than participating in a political or militant movement. When applying this logic to Hezbollah they found that an increase in poverty actually led to a "10% reduction in participation and those that have secondary school or higher education have an 8% increase in participation" (Krueger 2003). Extremists involved in the Israeli underground consisted of "disproportionately well-educated and highly paid [individuals including] teachers, writers, university students, geographers, engineers, entrepreneurs, a combat pilot, a chemist and a computer programmer" (Krueger 2003).

"The data seem to suggest that a lack of civil liberties is associated with a higher participation in terrorism and that low income has no direct connection" (Krueger 2003). The finding that "terrorists are more likely to spring from countries that lack civil rights, is further support for the view that terrorism is a political, not economic, phenomenon" (Krueger 2003).

Those that actually have the wealth to become educated often go through schooling controlled by supporters of one terrorist organization or another, creating new extremists. The poor continue to stay poor and disillusioned with no ability to make change, while the educated and well off become misinformed and desire to make change in the wrong way.

The psychological impact of socioeconomics is important to the development of terrorism; however it is the lack of civil liberties that are more important when it comes to the state sponsorship of such groups. Those states that restrict the information of the people, the rights of individuals, the ability to further better their lives, and feed them with misinformation is how the state sponsors keep their people in check. As people become better educated in such societies they learn that they are wrongly informed and they are slowly starting to realize it is their state that causes the problem and no one else.

Revolution 2.0

State sponsors rely on misinformation, lack of information, and oppression to keep the people in check. With a freedom of media and information with the help of modern technology the oppressors are seeing revolutions occur. With revolution and the overthrow of old state sponsors terrorists may be losing their support systems. "Today's global media is the most effective weapon around for both governments and terrorists the maxim still holds that 'war is ultimately coercive [while] terrorism is impressive'; in other words, terrorism compensates for its relative lack of coercive force by relying on 'collective alarmism' to create the forceful reaction of the state it needs to rally people to its cause" (Yahya 2010).

However, with the revolution of the internet, cell phones, and the social network the Middle East is alive with revolution. The American social network is changing the region and spreading the seeds of discontent among the youth. Instead of turning into religious zealots that follow tradition the youth want to be independent, cultured, and most of all they want to work. Unemployment in the region hovers around 30% (Davies 2004). The youth have had the motivation to make change for some time and now they have the tools. On Thursday 24th February 2011 Catriona Davies of CNN reported that a few days after the fall of Egypt's President a young woman of 24 years named Nawara Belal was driving in Cairo when she was verbally abused by an army officer. She got out of the car opened his door and slapped him across the face. She stated "I realized he wouldn't do anything about it, and it gave me the power to do what I wanted to do to every harasser in my past. I would never have been able to do that before the revolution." Many women in Egypt reportedly feel there has been a change in the culture. The country has come a long way, the media is supporting them, but they still have a long way to go.

Governments can use the media in an effort to arouse world opinion against the country or group using terrorist tactics. Public diplomacy and the media can also be used to mobilize public opinion in other countries to pressure governments to take, or reject, action against terrorism (Perl 1997). If the media is a pillar of democracy then perhaps with this new round of revolutions in the Middle East the media, so embraced by the youth, can become a pillar that creates democracy there. Only time can tell if the Muslim Brotherhood or democratic leadership will be put in places like Libya, Egypt, and Bahrain.

When speaking of the protestors in Egypt German Chancellor Angela Markel stated "In their eyes you can see what power freedom can have, by stepping down, President Mubarak had rendered a last service to the people of Egypt" (Davies 2004). In Libya reporters for MSNBC stated that the protestors were friendly and that they "believed the media helped overthrow the governments of Egypt and Tunisia" (MSNBC 2011). Hopefully soon Gadhafi will realize his cause is lost and step down allowing the people of Libya a chance to make a new future for themselves after decades of oppression.

To further show the influence the media has had on recent events in the world the revolutions of the Middle East have started to spread to China. According to Jo Ling Kent at CNN attempts at pro-democracy rallies fell flat last week [but] protestors are making a second attempt. The initial attempts were made for 20th February 2011 but either out of lack of information or fear of government reprisal a protest was never held. The Chinese protestors are attempting to use Facebook, Twitter and YouTube, all of which are banned in mainland China. Perhaps a second attempt will be more successful as cell phones are just as prominent in China as they are in many other parts of the world, and those may not be as protected by the state as the internet is. Years ago protests were regional affairs; today with the media and technology they truly are global.

The media changed with the PLO and altered the face of terrorism for the rest of the contemporary age. It is possible that with changes in technology, media may be changing terrorism for a second time, but this time for the better. With revolutions occurring in most major states that sponsor terrorism, the terrorist groups are losing their support systems, their resources, and their sanctuary. Perhaps if the United Nations and the West can help encourage the freedom of information contemporary terrorism can be combated with its own best weapon.

References

Arango, Tim. "World Falls for American Media, Even as It Sours on America." New York Times 30 NOV 2008. Web. 26 Feb 2011. www.nytimes.com/2008/12/01/business/media/01soft.html?_r=2.

Bahgat, Gawdat. "Oil, Terrorism and Weapons of Mass Destruction: The Libyan Diplomatic Coup," The Journal of Social, Political and Economic Studies, vol. 29, no. 4 (Winter 2004).

Byman, Daniel. Deadly Connections: States that Sponsor Terrorism, Cambridge University Press, 2005.

Davies, Catriona. "Gaza bloggers build bridges to outside world." CNN World 04 Feb 2011. Web. 26 Feb 2011. www.cnn.com/2011/WORLD/meast/02/04/gaza.bloggers/index.html.

Goenka, Viveck. "'Terrorists use media as a tool'." Indian Express 18 DEC 2009. Web. 26 Feb 2011.www.indianexpress.com/news/terrorists-use-media-as-a-tool/555588/.

Hoffman, Bruce. Inside Terrorism. New York: Columbia University Press, Second edition, 2006.

Jo Ling Kent. "Organizers call for 2nd round of demonstrations across China." CNN World 27 Feb 2011. Web. 27 Feb 2011. www.cnn.com/2011/WORLD/meast/02/04/gaza.bloggers/index.html.

Krueger Alan B. and Jitka Maleckova, "Education, Poverty and Terrorism: Is there a Causal Connection?", Journal of Economic Perspectives, Volume 17, Number 4 (Fall 2003).

Mamdani, Mahmood. Good Muslim, Bad Muslim: A Political Perspective on Culture and Terrorism American Anthropologist New Series, vol. 104, no. 3 (Sep., 2002), pp. 766-775

Soriano, Manuel R. Torres. Terrorism and the Mass Media after Al Qaeda: A Change of Course? Athena Intelligence Journal vol. 3, no 1, (2008), pp. 1-20.

MSNBC Staff. "Libya protesters to try to capture Qadhafi." MSNBC 24 FEB 2011. Web. 26 Feb 2011. www.msnbc.msn.com/id/41731365/ns/world_news-mideastn_africa/.

Neuwirth, Rachel. "How the Media Enable Terrorism." American Thinker 02 Aug 2006. Web. 26 Feb 2011. www.americanthinker.com/2006/08/how_the_media_enable_terrorism.html.

Perl, Raphael F. "TERRORISM, THE MEDIA, AND THE GOVERNMENT." CRS ISSUE BRIEF 22 OCT 1997. Web. 26 Feb 2011. www.fas.org/irp/crs/crs-terror.htm.

Rampton, Sheldon. "The Media: Terrorist Tool?" PR WATCH 13 FEB 2003. Web. 26 Feb 2011. www.prwatch.org/node/1734.

Tessler, Mark and Michael D. H. Robbins. "What Leads Some Ordinary Arab Men and Women to Approve of Terrorist Acts against the United States?" The Journal of Conflict Resolution vol. 51, no. 2 (Apr., 2007), pp. 305-328

Yahya, Birt. "Terrorism, Politics and Media Controversy." Musings on the Britannic Crescent 25 NOV 2010. Web. 26 Feb 2011. www.yahyabirt.com/

Critical Thinking

1. What effect did the 1972 Olympics have on terrorist attacks with regards to the media?
2. How do terrorist organizations benefit from the media?
3. How, according to al-Qaeda, is the West "using the media as a tool of war?"

Create Central

www.mhhe.com/createcentral

Internet References

Arab Media: Tools of the Government, Tools of the people
www.cfr.org/democracy-and-human-rights/usip-arab-media-tools-government-tools-people/p8798

10 Most Censored Countries
www.cpj.org/reports/2012/05/10-most-censored-countries.php

Terrorism and the Media
www.drtomoconnor.com/3400/3400lect07.htm

Article

Prepared by: Thomas J. Badey, *Randolph-Macon College*

Al-Shabaab and Social Media: A Double-Edged Sword

KEN MENKHAUS

Learning Outcomes

After reading this article, you will be able to:

- Describe the evolution of the use of social media by al-Shabaab.

- Assess the impact of use of social media by terrorist organizations.

- Discuss the positive and negative impact of the use of technology on terrorist organizations.

"Savvy" is one of the more popular adjectives employed by the media and security analysts alike to describe al-Shabaab, a jihadi group in Somalia.[1] This descriptor is not a reference to the organization's military strategies, its handling of internal schisms, its management of the 2011 Somali famine, its relations with foreign jihadists, or its standing with the Somali people. In fact, all of these issues have been disastrously mishandled by al-Shabaab's leadership.[2] The group's savvy has instead manifested in its use of new social media technology to wage, and sometimes win, a global media battle.

Al-Shabaab, which enjoyed a mercurial ascent from obscurity to notoriety between 2007 and 2008, has distinguished itself as one of the most sophisticated—and, in more recent times, conflicted—jihadi users of communication technology. In its early years, it effectively used Internet chat rooms, websites, and YouTube videos to recruit and fundraise internationally. Its real-time tweets during the group's terrorist attack on Nairobi's Westgate Mall in September 2013 became almost as big a media story as the attack itself. Yet in the past two years, the group has also aggressively sought to ban or control use of communication technology inside Somalia, considering it as much a threat as a tool.[3]

From a policy standpoint, al-Shabaab's proficiency with social media is seen as a tool that might allow the group to better coordinate, fundraise, recruit, and demoralize its enemies. From a theoretical standpoint, al-Shabaab's relationship with communication technology appears to lend support to those constructivist theories that seek to explain why Islamic extremist groups devote so much energy to social media. In 2006 Marc Lynch argued that al-Qaeda took a "constructivist turn" after 2001, focusing less on organizational strength and holding of territory and more on winning the battle to "frame the narrative" as a war of civilizations between Islam and the West—and amplifying that message through new media technology.[4] The observation that al-Qaeda has over time become less of an organization and more of a "virtual jihad" principally devoted to its role as catalyst of transformational new norms, identity, discourses, and worldviews in the *umma*—Islamic community—is grist for constructivists' mills.[5] It appears to reaffirm the primacy of the war of ideas, identity, and beliefs in shaping the behavior of state and non-state actors, exactly as constructivists would predict.

Can the same be said of al-Shabaab's preoccupation with cyberspace? Does it deploy the Internet and Twitter mainly for fundraising and recruitment to advance its war aims, as a realist would expect? Is it instead more committed to a wider, al-Qaeda-inspired, constructivist project to advance a radical Islamist counternarrative that transcends the battle for terrain in Somalia? Or could al-Shabaab's devotion to a Twitter and Internet-driven media strategy be more venal—a desperate attempt to stay alive in the global echo chamber of the Internet, the only arena where it can still enjoy sympathy, relevance, and an occasional rhetorical victory?[6] Could all three of these explanations hold water at different points of time since 2006?

This article explores the trajectory of al-Shabaab's use of new technologies since the group first emerged in 2006, assesses the impact of these technologies on the group and its objectives, and queries conventional wisdom on al-Shabaab's use of social media. It concludes that communication technology in particular has been a double-edged sword for al-Shabaab, rendering it vulnerable to lethal security risks and exposing its deep internal schisms even as the technology amplifies the group's messaging globally. It questions whether the group's use of technology has in fact been as savvy as many commentators have claimed, or just basic competence in its use of video, Internet, Twitter, and a thesaurus that millions of tech-proficient teenagers worldwide can match. It also questions whether one can even attribute savvy to an entire jihadi group when its employment of some new social media may only reflect the contribution of a handful of educated armchair jihadists from the Somali diaspora. It considers whether al-Shabaab has the ideological gravitas and the reputation to engage in an al-Qaeda-inspired campaign to reshape norms and worldviews, and whether Twitter can be a tool for "shaping a narrative" in no more than 140 characters.

Context: New Communication Technologies and the Somali Setting

Al-Shabaab's emergence in the unique setting of Somalia has shaped both the group's tactics and its use of technology. For over two decades, Somalia has been a collapsed state with no functional central government, allowing private businesses to operate in a dangerous but entirely unregulated environment. For example, in the mid-1990s Somalia was the site of Africa's first and most efficient cellphone companies as well as the continent's biggest and most efficient global remittance *(hawala)* companies.[7] Somalis continue to exploit new communication technologies at a fast rate, most recently with the rapid expansion of mobile money transfer technology. Thus, Somalia has been a surprisingly conducive setting for the rapid adoption of new technologies.

Somalia's large diaspora—estimated at over one million people—also contributes to the country's unique context. The diaspora is a critical source of remittances to the homeland, sending an estimated $1.5 billion per year.[8] Somalia's heavy reliance on remittances has meant that the development of a strong telecommunication infrastructure across the country was a matter of economic survival.

The explosion of the Somali diaspora in the early 1990s coincided with the rapid growth of the Internet, which the diaspora quickly adopted. The diaspora's close and active links to the homeland and the news-hungry "information culture" in Somali society proliferated dozens of diaspora-run news websites, many of which advanced parochial clan perspectives.[9] Only 1.2 percent of the Somali population uses the Internet, so websites are mainly by and for the diaspora.[10] However, web-based news is picked up and spread through other means of communication in Somalia, including radio and more recently, satellite TV.[11]

The protracted crisis in Somalia and negative coverage of the country in Western media also produced a generation of Somalis in the diaspora who felt besieged and humiliated. They expressed nostalgia for a lost era of Somali national unity and became predisposed to embrace alternative narratives that emphasized Somalia as a victim of external aggression and conspiracies. Some variations of this line of thinking gravitated toward a more assertive Islamist (or Islamo-nationalist) identity than had been common in past Somali political discourse. Somali news websites and blogs became, and remain, a hotbed for the construction of a revisionist explanation of the protracted Somali crisis. Some aspects of this reframing exercise have merit, while other aspects are little more than therapeutic narrative. News stories on these websites are selected and highlighted in ways that reinforce the story of external oppression and Somali victimhood. This diaspora-driven narrative has coalesced into a fairly coherent belief system that enjoys widespread currency among many, though not all, Somali intellectuals and opinion-shapers. Al-Shabaab's public relations unit—the "HSM Press Office"—has thus been able to tap into an existing grievance narrative, repackage it in more radically Islamist garb, and promote it to an audience that had already bought into much of the storyline prior to al-Shabaab's ascent.[12]

Al-Shabaab, which began as a small group of Somali ex-*mujahideen* in a Sharia court militia in Mogadishu between the years 2002 and 2005, quickly rose to prominence as the main source of armed resistance against a two-year Ethiopian military occupation of southern Somalia in 2007–2008.[13] The organization came into existence in a society that was already very nimble at adopting new technologies. In the Somali context, al-Shabaab was, with few exceptions, not a leader in the use of new technology; rather, it merely took advantage of existing local capacity and innovation. Al-Shabaab has put that new technology to use in a number of different capacities—fundraising in the diaspora, movement of funds, recruitment, communicating with supporters and operatives, control of populations, espionage, public relations, and threats.

Al-Shabaab and the Internet

Al-Shabaab made effective use of the Internet when the group emerged as the main source of armed resistance to the Ethiopian military occupation of southern Somalia in 2007–2008. Its use of the Internet focuses on external audiences—primarily the Somali diaspora and Muslims around the world, and occasionally al-Shabaab's enemies, when it attempts to demoralize, mock, or warn them. Messaging is therefore done mainly in English and Arabic, though recently it has added Swahili content. Its media wing, al-Kataib Media Foundation, is responsible for producing videos destined for the Internet. Most of the content management for websites sympathetic to al-Shabaab is done abroad by members of the Somali diaspora.

During its early and most militarily active years (2002–7008), the group sought to use the Internet to convey a powerful narrative with the immediate purpose of mobilizing funds and recruitment abroad. It also successfully harnessed the Internet to "brand" al-Shabaab as a globally recognizable movement. Al-Shabaab quickly became an icon of armed Islamic resistance with considerable appeal to a wide cross-section of Muslims, so much so that the group name and identity successfully franchised into neighboring Kenya and Tanzania.[14]

A big part of al-Shabaab's attractiveness in 2007–2008 was its powerful narrative, which won a sympathetic hearing from a wide audience. That narrative portrayed their jihad as a legitimate act of self-defense by a Muslim people militarily occupied by imperialistic Christian Ethiopian invaders, who were backed by the "great enemy of the Muslim people," the United States. At the time, it was difficult to go wrong with this messaging, which appealed both to Islamic sensibilities and to Somali nationalism. It was also difficult for Somalis to openly oppose the messaging—that risked their perception as un-Islamic and sympathetic with the enemy Ethiopia. For al-Shabaab, the messaging had the added benefit of focusing the ideas on what the group opposed, rather than what it supported.

Al-Shabaab's Internet-based media campaign has focused on several themes, some of which have had greater resonance than others. One of its recurring themes—the quest to build a global Caliphate—is embraced by a few members of its top leadership but has not resonated with most Somalis at home or in the diaspora. A recent attempt—a 2013 video "Woolwich Attack: It's an Eye for an Eye"—is one of its most technically sophisticated productions to date and revisits the call to create an Islamic Caliphate.[15] But the vast majority of Somalis who heed the call to join the struggle do so out of a combination of various Islamo-nationalist motives that privilege Somali, not global, issues.

Al-Shabaab's most effective approach has been its clever exploitation of the Somali diaspora's sense of alienation, identity crisis, and lack of purpose. To this end it has invoked Islamic concepts of both jihad and *hijrah* (religious migration).[16] It has challenged Somalis abroad to "get up off their couch" in the infidel's land, find meaning in their life by liberating their homeland from the infidel oppressor, and if necessary, "die like a lion."[17] One suicide bomber's testimonial spoke directly to both the imperative of *hijrah* and the glory of jihad, while tapping into the themes of honor and humiliation that resonate strongly in Somali culture: "I advise you to migrate to Somalia and wage war against your enemies. Death in honor is better than life in humiliation . . . To the Somalis living abroad, are you happy in your comfort while your religion, your people are being attacked and humiliated?"[18] In another video, a British-Somali jihadi makes the call for *hijrah* explicit, calling for all Muslims who are "living in the land of disbelief, the lands of oppression, to make *hijrah* to the land of glory, to the land of *izzat* (honor), to the land of jihad."[19]

Adventure has also been a surprisingly powerful and effective message conveyed through the Internet. Romanticized images of jihadi fighters in the bush, with inspirational Islamic chants in the background, have had—at least in the years 2007–2008—a powerful pull among some Somali diaspora youth. Al-Shabaab has made good use of the first wave of diaspora recruits, featuring them in video testimonies that call on friends to join them. The recruits emphasize the glory and excitement of jihad (one oddly describing it as "the real Disneyland") and boast about their positions of leadership, prowess with guns, and their kills of infidels.[20] Collectively, this messaging has attracted a combination of the devout, the nationalistic, and the adventure-seekers, not all of whom possess a very strong understanding of Islam, jihad, Somalia, or al-Shabaab.

Al-Shabaab has made use of the Internet in a variety of different ways. YouTube video postings were an early and very successful tool. Though most of its videos are removed for violating YouTube policies, they are reposted on sympathetic websites.[21] The group has struggled to post recent videos on jihadi websites, as Western governments have actively sought to block them, but al-Shabaaab has ultimately succeeded in getting them out by posting them on multiple websites.[22] Its videos have been uneven in quality but have improved over time. Some have been direct recruitment and fundraising pitches, typically involving clips of diaspora fighters wielding weapons and calling on others to join; testimonials by martyrs before a suicide attack; and glorified scenes of jihadi training and ambushes. One of the earliest instances of al-Shabaab video recruiting via YouTube was a series of short films featuring a non-Somali American, Omar Hammami "Al-Amriki," who self-radicalized in the United States, joined al-Shabaab, and rose up the ranks of the group despite his inexperience.[23] Al-Shabaab saw in him a propaganda goldmine, an articulate white American Muslim who turned against the infidel United States to wage jihad.[24] The videos included grainy, hand-held shots of Hammami giving instructions to Somali jihadists prior to an ambush on an Ethiopian convoy, explaining the jihad to viewers, calling on Muslims to join, and singing jihadi rap songs. The latter attracted the most attention.[25] Though the lyrics of his songs were, by any standard, sophomoric and the actual singing cringe-worthy, al-Shabaab seemed convinced that this was a public relations coup. Alarmed counterterrorism experts devoted time to worrying if the unlistenable jihadi rap would attract more recruits to Somalia.

By 2009 both the quality and messaging of al-Shabaab video productions became more professionalized, with direct support from al-Qaeda's al-Sabab Media foundation. In the December 2008 release "No Peace without Islam," al-Shabaab—then at the height of its power and popularity—put together a triumphant narrative integrating both local and global grievances. It depicted a vast global conspiracy (American/Zionist/United Nations/humanitarian/Ethiopian) against Islam in Somalia while at the same time voicing Somali nationalist outrage over the presence of infidel, Crusader occupying forces on "our soil."[26] The video was derivative of al-Qaeda messaging, but the integration of the al-Qaeda plotline with the armed struggle to liberate Somalia was very effective. Al Kataib mastered the use of high-quality video clips from global news sites and delivered a powerful narrative that focused on conspiracy, liberation, the *murtad* or apostate Somali government, and the weakness of the United States. Emblematic of the triumphalism of al-Shabaab during that period was the narrator's broad smile as he taunted the United States over the 1993 Black Hawk Down disaster in Mogadishu, specifically over how the more "manly" Somali youth dragged the dead bodies of American soldiers on the streets of the city and how the American soldiers "cried like women" for protection before they died.

More recent al-Kataib video productions have tended to be slicker and framed as quasi-news documentaries. In some instances, a "reporter" presents a story of an Al-Shabaab victory that begins in an objective tone before sliding into a pro-Al-Shabaab narrative designed both to win over supporters and demoralize the enemy.[27] In other videos, al-Kataib cuts to the chase, presenting battlefield victories and gory footage of dead soldiers from the African Union Mission in Somalia (AMISOM).[28] This has been a powerful tool for discrediting AMISOM when it denies casualties, but to date has not produced the desired backlash in troop-contributing countries like Uganda and Burundi.[29]

Al-Shabaab has also carefully selected sympathetic local and foreign journalists for short documentaries or for sit-down interviews with its spokesperson.[30] These presumably independent media stories run the risk of losing control of the messaging, but they also allow al-Shabaab to broadcast a message to a vast audience via an established news organization. On their part, sympathetic journalists and producers who are given access to al-Shabaab inject just enough mild criticism of the group to throw off an unsuspecting consumer of the news, but then proceed with a story that is in line with the messaging

al-Shabaab wants to get across.[31] Whether this is a matter of concordance of views, a quid pro quo for continued access, or another arrangement is difficult to know.

Until 2009 al-Shabaab ran its own official website, carrying news, video clips, religious guidance, edicts, and issuance of threats.[32] Since the site's closure, it has relied on a network of pro-al-Qaeda and other sympathetic websites to carry its press releases and videos.[33] They present themselves as neutral news sites, mostly carrying stories and blog items from other news outlets, but upon closer inspection, they select stories and op-eds that advance a narrative that reinforces al-Shabaab's worldview.[34] They serve as a reminder that although al-Shabaab may be in a state of crisis as an organization, the narrative it has captured, refined, and advanced continues to resonate with a portion of the Somali community at home and abroad.

Especially in its early years, before the threat of counterterrorism surveillance grew significantly, al-Shabaab made particularly good use of chatrooms. Investigations of diaspora recruitment into al-Shabaab revealed that the group regularly brought its military commanders into chatrooms where they reported and fielded questions on battles waged and the state of the jihad, as well as diaspora fighters communicating with sympathizers, potential recruits, and the merely curious "jihobbyists."[35] Facebook has also at times been an important social media tool for al-Shabaab. It continues to issue new releases and threats in this manner, though its main utility is a means by which individual jihadists from the diaspora communicate with and debate friends from back home.[36]

Al-Shabaab's usage of new technologies has changed with the shifting fortunes of the group since 2006. Initially al-Shabaab focused on practical use of technologies in direct support of the insurgency, especially fundraising and recruitment. Recruitment efforts abroad were successful by any measure in the years 2007–2008. Hundreds of members of the Somali diaspora in Europe and North America joined the group (with others staying back in their adopted countries and playing a support role), and several hundred foreign *mujahideen* (i.e., those not of Somali ethnic descent) also found their way to Somalia. Recruitment abroad declined after 2008 (except from East Africa) in part because of increasingly negative perceptions of the group. Al-Shabaab's aggressive call for recruits was coupled with calls for financial support, which yielded substantial fundraising in the diaspora in the years 2007–2008.[37] Financial contributions from the disapora began to dry up starting in 2009 as a result of a loss of diaspora enthusiasm for al-Shabaab. The designation of al-Shabaab as a terrorist organization by the United States and several other Western countries in 2008 also contributed to the loss of funding, as it created grave legal risks for would-be fundraisers.

Starting in 2009, as it suffered losses and setbacks, the group expanded its focus to include a waging of a war of ideas and promotion of counter-narratives against its enemies in Somalia and Kenya. This trend accelerated with the bloody 2013 purge within the group, in which hard-line leader Ahmed Godane led a campaign that killed most of his internal rivals. This gutted al-Shabaab's leader- ship and led to the consolidation of power of an "extremist fringe. . . imbued with a 'takfiri ethos' that legitimizes the killing of other Muslims, and a commitment to the cause of international jihad and the restoration of an Islamic caliphate."[38]

The 2013 video "Woolwich Attack: It's an Eye for an Eye" is especially instructive as a case of al-Shabaab's attempt to go global with its messaging. Al-Shabaab seized on the deadly street attack of U.K. soldier Lee Rigby by two British Muslim converts of Nigerian descent to take up the call of the late Anwar al-Awlaki and his *Inspire* magazine and ask Muslims in the West to wage jihad at home. "Use whatever you can get your hands on" to kill infidels, implores the video.[39]

This attempt to succeed al-Awlaki as the mobilizer of "lone wolf" jihadis in the West marks a new aspiration horizon on the part of the HSM Press Office.[40] On that count, it has failed—the video has not, to date, inspired a single lone wolf terrorist attack by a Somali or anyone living in the West. Furthermore, this failure also suggests that al-Shabaab may be giving up on aspirations to become a mass mobilization movement in Somalia, which had been entirely within its reach in 2007–2008. Its messaging abroad now seems designed to incite a very small number of hardened radicals to take random violent action in the West or East Africa rather than to persuade large numbers of Somalis and other Muslims to embrace its cause. Its domestic actions also mirror this apparent policy shift—the group has become increasingly indifferent to winning the hearts and minds of the masses, preferring to groom a small number of suicide bombers to wreak maximum havoc. This shift is one of the many factors that led to deep internal schisms in the group in the years 2010–2013.

The shift in messaging toward a call for global jihad and restoration of a global caliphate also raises the question of whether al-Shabaab actually possesses the Islamic credentials and theological gravitas to assume the mantra of an Anwar al-Awlaki or an Ayman Zawahiri. One of the group's most searing critics was al-Qaeda member Fazul Abdullah Mohamed, who was associated with al-Shabaab as a security advisor until his death in 2011.[41] In a personal diary he posted on a jihadi website, Fazul was quite dismissive of al-Shabaab leaders for their lack of grounding in Islamic teachings and principles and their ignorance of the correct conduct of jihad, as well as other matters.[42]

Fazul had a point. Al-Shabaab has a number of strengths, but leadership with strong grounding in al-Qaeda's teachings is not one of them. The group emerged in 2006 as a militia and was composed first and foremost of mujahideen, not mullahs. Most of Somalia's collection of authoritative Islamic scholars are outside, not within, the al-Shabaab fold. The group's unopposed leader since the bloody purge and consolidation of power in 2013, Ahmed Godane, is a *takfiri* jihadi committed to the fight for a global caliphate. However, he presents himself in an "uncharismatic and reclusive" manner, manages to alienate and then kill even his closest allies, and marginalizes al-Shabaab's religious scholars.[43]

Ironically, the al-Shabaab figure who best articulated a persuasive, wellinformed, global jihadi narrative was one of the members whom al-Shabaab killed in the bloody internal purge of 2013, Omar Hammami. When not indulging in jihadi rap, Hammami's instructional videos conveyed withering critiques of moderate Muslims, the powerful obligation Muslims must have to the umma, and the call to migrate and liberate Islamic countries.[44]

The other impediment to al-Shabaab's aspirations to play a role as champion of a global jihadi narrative is reputational. Both al-Shabaab as an organization and Somalia as a nation carry baggage in parts of the Islamic world that make it difficult for a Somali group to play a leading role in a war of Islamic ideas. Racial and other discriminatory attitudes in parts of the Arab world toward Somalis would certainly make it difficult to accept a Somali movement seeking to play a vanguard role in Islamic mobilization and teaching. This is not to say that such a role for a Somali group is not possible, but it would amount to a case of reverse missionary work. To date, Somalia has been the site where Islamic clerics from other parts of the world come to propagate the "correct" teachings of Islam, not the other way around. And, as a jihadi organization, al-Shabaab has a reputation even within al-Qaeda as being too thuggish and, since 2012, as intensely hostile to non-Somali jihadists. This suggests that even if al-Shabaab's propagandists have constructivist ambitions to relocate their jihad to cyberspace, they may face real difficulties gaining traction beyond a narrow demographic. Waging a war of narratives requires not only the right medium and right message, but also the right messenger.

The group's use of social media has carried a major risk of losing control over messaging, as multiple sources within the movement send out their own tweets, Facebook messages, and videos. This has exposed the group to the danger of mixed messages, and has also meant that internal tensions and other "dirty laundry" become aired in public. This exploded in al-Shabaab's face in 2012 when internal disputes and damaging accusations within the group's leadership were played out online. The most embarrassing such episode occurred in March 2012, when Omar Hammami, up to then the poster boy for al-Shabaab propaganda, released an Internet video in which he said his life was in danger due to threats by al-Shabaab.[45] The HSM Press Office initially tweeted a denial: "We assure our Muslim brothers that #AlAmriki is not endangered by the Mujahideen & our brother still enjoys all the privileges of brotherhood."[46] Later, it went on the offensive, claiming in another tweet that Hammami's claims "stem purely from a narcissistic pursuit of fame."[47] Thereafter, Hammami went on the offensive himself, launching a barrage of tweets accusing Ahmed Godane of abuse of civilians, abuse and marginalization of the foreign jihadis, acting like Hitler, and so on. Al-Shabaab and it followers retorted with a withering array of character attacks, which culminated in declaring Hammami an apostate.[48]

The crisis worsened in early 2013, when an al-Shabaab figure (apparently a top foreign fighter) using a nom-de-guerre published an online open letter, "Yes There Are Problems," with extremely grave accusations against Godane. The charges highlighted a deep rift between Godane and the foreign fighters, charging Godane with abuses that included arrest of foreign jihadis without charges, torture in secret prisons, declaration that foreign jihadis who leave Somalia without permission are apostates, and failure to meet or consult with foreign fighters. In a damning indictment of al-Shabaab, the author stated that the purpose of the letter was to "relieve myself in front of God and the nation of all the aggressions and legal violations committed by some of us [. . .and to] warn all lovers of jihad among the foreign jihadis inside or outside the country that the situation is not as it is depicted by the movement."[49]

This embarrassment was followed shortly thereafter by another scathing indictment from within the group—this time from Ahmed Godane's close friend, mentor, and co-founder of al-Shabaab, Ibrahim Haji Jaama al-Afghani. Al-Afghani posted an open letter in Arabic to al-Qaeda's leader Ayman Zawahiri, in the name of al-Shabaab's "silent majority," warning that the movement had lost support from the Somali people and risked failure due to the abusive leadership and decision-making of Godane. It reiterated the charges of abuse of foreign fighters and added a host of additional charges, such as "marginalizing al-Shabaab scholars; inciting young jihadists against scholars and leaders by issuing threats of liquidation; preventing certain scholars from publishing, teaching, or even giving sermons."[50]

Al-Shabaab's internal schisms, which in an earlier era might have been contained, spilled across Twitter and into the public arena for all to see. The damage was incalculable, especially throughout the two external audiences al- Shabaab had spent so much time trying to cultivate—the Somali diaspora and al-Qaeda. The group's reputation was damaged even further by its bloody 2013 internal purge, which garnered extensive coverage on Somali websites and which shocked even the group's sympathizers. The Internet and social media were clearly not al-Shabaab's friends at this point. What became clear is that social media's greatest strength—its intensely, chaotically democratic nature—was the antithesis of what a controlling jihadi leader like Godane desired.

Al-Shabaab and Twitter

Al-Shabaab's use of Twitter since 2011 has attracted more attention than its use of any other social media, in part because of the novelty of the group tweeting in real time about its terrorist attack on Nairobi's Westgate Mall in September 2013. Even before the Westgate attack, one social media expert concluded that "the Somali Islamist militant group al-Shabaab runs by far the most interesting social media feed in the insurgency industry."[51]

Why Twitter? A social media with such limited content would seem to be an exceptionally poor platform for the development of a counternarrative. Yet al-Shabaab has demonstrated that micro-blogging does have some utility. First, what Twitter has given al-Shabaab is a means of delivering instant sound byte messages that give journalists pithy quotes on which to draw and that challenge Western, AMISOM, and Somali government narratives.[52] The re-tweeting of messages by the 15,000 or more followers of @HSMPress was a major amplifier—the START project estimates that a total of 4.5 million al-Shabaab tweets appeared on user timelines before its account was shut down.[53]

Second, under the right circumstances, Twitter actually has more utility in narrative-building than meets the eye. The START project's content analysis of al-Shabaab's tweets determined that the single most important objective of the group—comprising one-third of all its tweets—was projecting a narrative.[54] This would have constituted a truly jumbled narrative if assembled at a rate of 140 characters per message. But START's findings make sense when set against an observation made earlier in this article—that al-Shabaab has never been the creator of a narrative, but rather an inheritor of a Somali grievance narrative that was already well-formulated by the time the group came into existence. Thus, what al-Shabaab has been able to do with Twitter is reinforce an existing narrative with shards of evidence that fit the worldview of its sympathizers, while reshaping it with more radical Islamist messaging. What al-Shabaab was doing effectively with Twitter before its account was shut down was not that different from what politically partisan new channels do with their news ticker—deliver a steady flow of shards of evidence that reinforce the existing belief system of their audience. This is especially important for a jihadi group, for which cognitive dissonance and doubt are more dangerous than a drone.

For all of the significance of al-Shabaab's Twitter war, the group's tweeting has had a short history to date. It began in late 2011 and quickly acquired new followers for its entertaining taunting of the Kenyan military spokesperson, Major Emmanuel Chirchir, who was also using Twitter as part of the Kenyan military public affairs campaign.[55] From that point on, the al-Shabaab Twitter account became a heavily followed stock source of quotes as well as the group's favorite means of communication. However, since the Westgate attack, its use of Twitter has been repeatedly interrupted by rapid closure of its new accounts. As a consequence, Twitter is now a less viable means of communication for the group.

Unfortunately for al-Shabaab, the educated diaspora members responsible for the tweets starting in 2011 became infatuated with their verbal sparring skills and command of English, so much so that the tweets soon came across as more about them than about al-Shabaab. The tweets were painfully pretentious in style and arrogant in tone, and hence off-putting, even when the content had merit. Dropping words like "desultory," "wretched," and "thorny quagmire" seemed designed to prove that at least one al-Shabaab member possessed a Master's degree, or a thesaurus. Some of the stilted language bordered on self-parody, as when @HSMPress responded to a critic with the tweet "what's beyond abhorrence is the collective Western Crusade against Islam of which you seem quite blasé about if not supportive."[56] This pedantic tone remained a problem right up to the closure of the group's Twitter account and blunted the effectiveness of the medium.[57]

Al-Shabaab's real time-tweeting during the Westgate terrorist attack set a precedent, and for that reason garnered significant media attention. Using Twitter, it took responsibility for the attack; justified the attack as revenge for Kenya's armed occupation of southern Somalia and the civilian casualties there; warned Kenya of more attacks unless it withdrew from Somalia; conveyed to its Muslim audience that jihadis in the attack were allowing Muslims to go free, killing only the infidels; and taunted the Kenyan government for its weak response and "incoherent ramblings." Al-Shabaab also tweeted photos from inside the Mall, boasting, with its usual puffed-up language: "Here are 2 of the mujahideen inside the #Westgate Mall, unruffled and strolling around the Mall in such a sangfroid manner." It also indulged in self-congratulations in the third person voice, tweeting "A spectacular AlShabaab attack, with 50 + dead and guaranteed extended media coverage is finalized." And it sought to frame the attack as the start of a great Islamic awakening: "A new era is on the horizon. A new dawn, illuminating the path to #Khaliifa. It's a paradigm shift."[58]

The Westgate attack revealed another unexpected problem for al-Shabaab. The main point of using Twitter was to maintain direct control over messaging. But bogus Twitter accounts purporting to be the official al-Shabaab Twitter complicated the situation, and this grew worse when the group's account was closed. International media took tweets from the imposters and cited them in stories, including false claims that some of the jihadis were Somali diaspora from Minnesota. This caused subsequent embarrassment to those journalists but also exposed the fact that al-Shabaab had now lost control of its messaging. With every new Twitter account closed as soon as it was opened, al-Shabaab had to email journalists to inform them the tweets were not from them.[59] The only silver lining for the group was that its sympathizers in the blogosphere seized on the incident as proof that the Western media never checks its facts and therefore, cannot be trusted.

The most serious loss of control of messaging that al-Shabaab suffered via Twitter was not the bogus accounts, but the extensive use of Twitter by Omar Hammami during his bitter feud with the Godane. If, as the START project contends, one of the principal goals of jihadi groups in communication strategy is to project "group integrity and cohesion," al-Shabaab failed badly on this score. Hammami was an intriguing case of jihadi use of social media not just because of his jihadi rap and his Twitter feud with his al-Shabaab rivals, but also because of his recourse to Twitter to engage in intense exchanges with followers, some of whom he knew to be counterterrorism analysts. He began tweeting in May 2012 and continued until his death at al-Shabaab's hands in September 2013.[60] His use of Twitter in the last year of his life appears to have been less an effort to project a narrative and more a desire for human contact and attention, and to leave a record of his existence before his imminent death.

Al-Shabaab and Cellphones

One of al-Shabaab's enduring technology problems is that all traceable electronic communications are risky if the user is a high-value counter-terrorism target. A growing number of top al-Shabaab commanders have been taken out by U.S. drone strikes or missiles, and observers strongly suspect that traced cellphone and Internet usage have played a role in tracking those individuals. As a result, al-Shabaab leaders now minimize or avoid cellphone usage and Internet-based communication. In a recent interview, an al-Shabaab leader acknowledged that he stays off the Internet on his iPad lest he fall victim to "birds in the sky."[61] Ironically, a group that has earned a reputation for sophistication in use of social media in its global messaging has been forced to resort to low-tech measures for its local internal communications.

Fears concerning smart phone use by local spies, whose goal is to betray the positions of al-Shabaab leaders, led the group to take the extraordinary step in January 2014 of issuing an edict via Facebook that banned mobile and fiber optic Internet access in areas it controls and threatened to treat anyone violating the ban as "the enemy."[62] It followed this up with an attack on an office of the largest telecom provider in south Somalia, Hormuud, prompting it to suspend most of its Internet services across the country.[63] It also launched a sweep of the strategic port town of Brava—one of its last remaining urban strongholds, and likely the target of an AMISOM offensive—to confiscate smart phones, which it outlawed in November 2013.

Even so, Somali cellphone services have been of use to the group in other ways. Al-Shabaab has benefited from the telecommunications sector principally as a target funding—whether from "taxation," extortion, or active support.[64] A UN Monitoring Group report from 2012 estimates that the contributions to al-Shabaab from one telecommunication firm, Hormuud, added up to hundreds of thousands of dollars per year. That same report warned that Hormuud employees actively monitor phone calls on behalf of Al-Shabaab.[65]

Al-Shabaab's ability to tax populations under its control has been undermined with the arrival of mobile money transfer services such as ZAAD, which were introduced in Somalia in 2009.[66] These services allowed Somalis to make cashless local business transactions on their cell phones as well as increasingly receive remittances from abroad. This was a problem for al-Shabaab because transactions became impossible to tax. Consequently, al-Shabaab declared mobile money transfers "un-Islamic" and banned them.[67] At the same time, the UN Security Council in 2012 accused the owner of ZAAD and its parent company Hormuud Telecom of colluding with al-Shabaab to use ZAAD to funnel money for the group undetected.[68]

Conclusion

New communication technologies have hurt al-Shabaab as much as they have helped it. The organization has exploited the Internet and social media to recruit, fundraise, issue threats, monitor enemies, amplify its messaging, and reinforce its narrative. It has used remittance and telecommunications sectors to move money and raise revenues. At the same time, this technology has exposed the militant group to lethal armed counterinsurgency strikes, broadcasted its internal feuds, and rendered it impossible for al-Shabaab's leadership to control its image and message. Consequently, the group has a schizophrenic relationship with new communication technologies, simultaneously using them to communicate globally while seeking to ban or restrict them domestically. Over time, these new technologies have become more of an Achilles heel and less of an asset to al-Shabaab. The unregulated and hyper-democratic nature of the new social media has collided with the leadership's obsession with tight control.

The evidence reviewed here suggests that claims of al-Shabaab's "savvy" use of social media and the Internet are generally but not entirely true. Some of its videos have been powerful and have helped it build a brand that for a time was very popular. Its employment of Twitter to instantly send photos or sound bytes have helped it shape media coverage, and its use of chatrooms and Facebook have given it a very strong recruitment tool. But the group has also been amateurish at times in use of these tools, from the pompous tone of its tweets to the jihadi rap that was more a source of derision than inspiration.

Al-Shabaab's success in harnessing social media to advance a radical narrative was not an act of creation, but of appropriation. Al-Shabaab inherited an existing Somali grievance narrative, which it adapted, repackaged in more radical Islamist garb, and transmitted with social media back to an audience which had already internalized the basic story line. Al-Shabaab used Twitter to reinforce, not build, that narrative with shards of evidence and images that conformed to the belief system of its target audience. Twitter can be a more effective tool for narrative wars than meets the eye, but only if the audience has already accepted the broad contours of a grievance narrative.

Finally, the al-Shabaab case suggests that both realist and constructivist theories are helpful lenses through which to view jihadi use of social media. The explanatory value of the two theories depends in part on the state of play of the jihadi movement itself. Al-Shabaab has always been in the business of projecting a narrative, but in its early years—when it was advancing on the battlefield and holding territory—its main goal in using social media was for tangible assets—funds and recruits, as a realist would anticipate. Al-Shabaab's shift toward a greater focus on advancing a global jihadi narrative occurred at a time when its ability to hold territory, win battles, and maintain organizational coherence was waning. This points to the possibility that jihadi groups like Al-Shabaab tend to embrace the "constructivist" war of ideas via new social media not so much as an expansion of their activities but as a form of strategic retreat. In this sense, they replicate the behavior of leaders of failed states by devoting more energy to projecting a narrative to win recognition and support from an external audience than to earning legitimacy at home.[69] Failing states and failing jihadi movements, it turns out, have more in common than either would care to admit.

Notes

1. See, for instance: "Al-Shabab Showed Gruesome Social Media Savvy During Attack," CBS News, September 24, 2013.
2. For a cataloguing of the group's misfortunes since 2009, see: Christopher Anzalone, "Al-Shabab's Setbacks in Somalia," *CTC Sentinel* 4, no. 10 (October 2011), 22–25; Ken Menkhaus, "Al-Shabab's Capabilities Post-Westgate," *CTC Sentinel* 7, no. 2 (February 2014), 3–8; Roland Marchal, "The Rise of a Jihadi Movement in a Country at War: Harakat al-Shabaab al Mujaheddin in Somalia" (Paris: SciencesPo CNRS, 2011); and

Matt Bryden, *The Re-invention of Al-Shabaab: A Strategy of Choice or Necessity?* (Washington, D.C.: CSIS, February 2014).

3. This ambiguous relationship with new technology was nicely captured in a recent *Al Jazeera* story recounting how a top al-Shabaab official used his iPad in the field even as his group has banned Internet access through mobile devices. See: Hamza Mohamed, "Al-Shabaab's Governor: One Man and His iPad," *Al Jazeera,* February 26, 2014.

4. Marc Lynch, *Al-Qaeda's Constructivist Turn* (Praeger Security International, May 5, 2006).

5. Steve Coll and Susan Glasser, "Terrorists Turn to the Web as Base of Operations," *Washington Post,* August 7, 2005.

6. The group continues to be a major terrorist threat in Somalia and Kenya, but has far less public support than in the period from 2007–2008. It is, as this author and others have argued elsewhere, both weaker and more dangerous in the short term. See: Menkhaus, "Al-Shabab's Capabilities."

7. Joseph Winter, "Telecoms Thriving in Lawless Somalia," *BBC News,* November 19, 2004.

8. Laura Hammond et al., *Cash and Compassion: The Role of the Somali Diaspora in Relief, Development, and Peacebuilding* (Nairobi: UNDP, 2011).

9. BBC World Service Trust, "The Media in Somalia: A Force for Moderation?" Policy Briefing #4 (November 2011): 1.

10. "Internet Users in Africa," Internet World Stats: Usage and Population Statistics, 2012.

11. Radio remains the most important source of news in Somalia, despite the fact that al-Shabaab has shut down some stations and forced others in its areas of influence to broadcast only readings from the Qur'an and al-Shabaab approved news, which has caused a sharp drop in listeners. In 2013, there were over 30 radio stations operating in Somalia. For a full survey of Somali media, see: "Somalia Media and Telecom Landscape Guide," Infoasaid, January 2012.

12. HSM is the acronym for the full name of the group, Harakat al-Shabaab al-Mujahideen.

13. For definitive studies of the early organization of al-Shabaab, before it had even taken on its current name (Al-Shabaab was adopted as a group name sometime in 2006, when it formed the strongest wing of the Islamic Courts Union armed forces), see: *Counter-terrorism in Somalia: Losing Hearts and Minds?* Africa Report no. 95 (Nairobi/Brussels: International Crisis Group, July 11, 2005); *Somalia's Islamists,* Africa report no. 100 (Nairobi/Brussels: International Crisis Group, December 12, 2005); Cedric Barnes and Harun Hassan, "The Rise and Fall of Mogadishu's Islamic Courts" (London: Chatham House Africa Program, March 2007).

14. For coverage of the East African affiliates of Al-Shabaab, see: Bryden, "The Reinvention of Shabaab;" Menkhaus, "Al-Shabab's Capabilities," UN Monitoring Group on Eritrea and Somalia, "Report of the UN Monitoring Group on Eritrea and Somalia pursuant to Security Council Resolution 2060 (2012)," S/AC.29/2013/SEMG/OC.62 (New York: UN,

19 June 2013), 14–17; and *Kenyan Somali Islamist Radicalization,* Africa Briefing no. 85 (Nairobi/Brussels: International Crisis Group, January 25, 2012).

15. For a corrupted version of the video, see: "Al-Kataib Media Productions The Excellent Video Woolwich Attack It's an Eye for an Eye," Internet Archive. For a sympathetic summary of the main themes of the video, see: "Al Shabaab Releases Hour Long Video on Woolwich Attack," Harar24, October 16, 2013.

16. Alexander Meleagrou-Hitchens, Shiraz Mahar, and James Sheehan, "Lights, Camera, Jihad: Al-Shabaab's Western Media Strategy" (London: ICSR, 2012).

17. Andrea Elliott, "A Call to Jihad, Answered in America," *New York Times,* July 11, 2009. See also: "Joining the Fight in Somalia," *New York Times,* October 30, 2011.

18. For quote, see: Meleagrou-Hitchens, Mahar, and Sheehan, "Lights, Camera, Jihad," 7.

19. Ibid., 13.

20. The most recent recruitment video, "The Path to Paradise," featured three "Minnesotan Martyrs." See: "Kenya Mall Terror Attack Group Al-Shabab Still Draws Somalis from US," *CBS News,* September 26, 2013. Most of the first wave of diaspora recruits are now dead or defected.

21. An "Al-Kataib" search on YouTube at the time of this writing produced three media productions. More can be found on third party sites.

22. "Al Shabaab Releases Hour Long Video on Woolrich Attack," Harar24.com, October 16, 2013.

23. For a rich look at Hammami's background and his path to radicalization and Somalia, see: Andrea Elliott, "The Jihadist Next Door," *New York Times Magazine,* January 27, 2010.

24. Hammami, who died at the hands of al-Shabaab rivals during the group's bloody in-fighting in 2013, was born of a Muslim father of Arab descent and a southern white Christian mother.

25. His rap is still available on YouTube. For example, see: "amriki rap," YouTube, May 5, 2009.

26. For access to this video, see: "No Peace Without Islam," Iraq War: Non-English Language Videos, Internet Archive, 2008.

27. START, "Lights, Camera, Jihad," 30.

28. One of its more effective videos on this count is the 2010 release "Mogadishu, The Crusaders Graveyard," which shows extensive scenes of armed combat with AMISOM forces. See: "Mogadishu, The Crusaders Graveyard," Internet Archive, Iraq War: Non-English Language Videos, 2010.

29. Al-Shabaab frequently posts video and photos of dead AMISOM soldiers as part of an effort to project an image of a victorious army, to demoralize its enemy, and in some cases to undercut AMISOM when it denies losses on the battlefield. To view one example, where Al-Shabaab posted images of 60 Burundian soldiers killed in a battle, see: Neil Ungerleider, "How Al-Shabaab Uses the Internet to Recruit Americans," Fast Company Blog, September 23, 2013.

30. "Al-Shabaab woos Coast youth as noose tightens," Harar24. com, April 19, 2014; Jamal Osman, "Exclusive: Inside an Al-Shabaab Training Camp," *Channel 4 News,* December 16, 2013; For a recent *Al Jazeera* interview with Al Shabaab spokesperson Sheikh Ali Dhere, see: "Somalia's Al-Shabab Vows to Make Comeback," *Al Jazeera,* February 24, 2014.

31. Jamal Osman's "Exclusive" portrayal of an Al Shabaab training camp is one recent example.

32. "Home Page," Kataaib.net.

33. For instance, see: "Home Page," al-Qimmah.

34. Harar24.com is one of a number of such news sites.

35. Elliott, "The Call to Jihad."

36. Ibid.

37. The calls for contributions were broadcast via the internet, but the actual collections were done by local supporters, who then sent the cash via remittance companies.

38. Bryden, "The Reinvention of Al-Shabaab," 2.

39. "Al Shabaab Releases Hour Long Video," Harar24.com.

40. Bryden, "The Reinvention of Al-Shabaab."

41. Fazul describes himself in correspondence to Osama bin Laden that he was, in 2006, head of a "secret security portfolio" within the Islamic Courts Union that the political leadership of the courts knew nothing about—the group that would later take on the name Al-Shabaab. See: Nelly Lahoud, "Beware of Imitators: Al Qa'ida through the Lens of its Confidential Secretary" (West Point, NY: Combating Terrorism Center Harmony Program, June 4, 2012), 82, 90–92.

42. The Arabic language original of his diary, "The War Against Islam," is archived at the West Point Combating Terrorism Center website.

43. Crisis Group. "Somalia's Divided Islamists," Africa Briefing # 74 (Nairobi/Brussels: May 19, 2010), 4. This is the best source on ideological differences within Somali Islamists; Hassan Abukar, "The Letters: How Al Qaeda failed in Mali and Somalia," Wardheernews.com, April 13, 2013.

44. START, "Lights, Camera, Jihad," 23–8.

45. Spencer Ackerman, "Rapping Jihadi Now Fears Terrorism Pals will Kill Him," *Wired,* March 19, 2012.

46. Ibid.

47. Ibid.

48. The most elaborate was a 17-page attack. See: Abu Hamza Al-Muhajir, "Turning Away from the Truth Won't Make it Disappear: Demystifying the Abu Mansur Saga," Selected Wisdom.

49. "Open Letter to Al-Shabaab Leader Reveals: 'Yes, There are Problems'" Sabahionline.com, April 30, 2013.

50. Hassan Abukar, "The Letters: How Al Qaeda Failed in Mali and Somalia," Wardheernews.com, April 13, 2013.

51. Will Oremus, "Follow Friday: Terrorists Who Tweet," Slate. com, March 2, 2012.

52. Andoni Berasategui, "VE Virtual Messaging in Somalia: Al-Shabaab Virtual Messaging and Avenues for Counter-Messaging," (Presentation for the ACSS, Addis Ababa, February 25, 2014).

53. START, "Research Brief: Violent Jihadism in Real Time: Al Shabab's Use of Twitter," January 2013.

54. START, "Light, Camera, Jihad," 34.

55. David Smith, "Al-Shabaab in War of Words with Kenyan Army on Twitter," *The Guardian,* December 13, 2011.

56. Quoted in Will Oremus, "Twitter of Terror," Slate.com, December 23, 2011.

57. In one of the last tweets before its account was closed, @HSMPress announced "a paradigm shift."

58. The al-Shabaab Twitter account is closed; these quotes are from stored copies of the tweets.

59. Mukhtar Ibrahim, "Westgate Attack: Al-Shabaab and the Comedy of Errors," *Sahan Journal,* September 26, 2013; See also David Barnett, "Are You Looking at an Official Shabaab Twitter Account?" *Long War Journal,* September 25, 2013.

60. Jim Berger, "Omar and Me," *Foreign Policy,* September 16, 2013.

61. Mohamed, "Al-Shabaab's Governor."

62. Somalia Newsroom, "Unraveling Al-Shabaab's Partial Internet Ban and Other Stunts in Somalia," January 15, 2014.

63. Limited Internet access was still available, but not for mobile phones and iPads. See: Shaf'ii Mohyadiin, "Mobile Phone Internet off in Somalia After al-Shabaab Order," Hiraan.com, February 8, 2014.

64. Al-Shabaab requires all businesses to pay it taxes, a demand backed by threats. Whether the firms pay willingly, view it as extortion, or consider it protection money varies from case to case.

65. UN Security Council, SC/10545, "Security Council Committee on Somalia and Eritrea Adds One Individual to List of Individuals and Entities," February 17, 2012.

66. C. Penicaud and F. McGrath, "Innovative Inclusion: How Telecom ZAAD Brought Mobile Money to Somaliland," Mobile Money for the Unbanked Project, Gates Foundation, July 2013.

67. "Al-Shabaab Bans Mobile Phone Money Transfers in Somalia," *BBC News,* October 18, 2010.

68. UN Security Council, SC/10545, "Security Council Committee on Somalia and Eritrea Adds One Individual to List of Individuals and Entities," February 17, 2012. See also: "Somalia's Telecoms: Cashless Doesn't Mean Broke," *MobileMoneyAfrica.*

69. Preoccupation with the privileges and perks of external recognition by leaders of juridically sovereign failed states is a well-documented dynamic. For instance, see: Pierre Engelbert, *Africa: Unity, Sovereignty, and Sorrow* (Boulder: Lynne Rienner, 2009).

Critical Thinking

1. How has al-Shabaab used social media to its advantage?
2. Why did al-Shabaab declare mobile money transfers "un-Islamic" and ban them?
3. What are the future implications for the use of social media by terrorist organizations?

Internet References

START
http://www.start.umd.edu/news/start-research-brief-al-shabaabs-use-twitter

The Atlantic: When Terrorists Take to Social Media
http://www.theatlantic.com/international/archive/2013/02/when-terrorists-take-to-social-media/273321

Wilson Center: New Terrorism and New Media
http://www.wilsoncenter.org/publication/new-terrorism-and-new-media

---

KEN MENKHAUS is Professor of Political Science at Davidson College and a specialist on the Horn of Africa.

Article   Prepared by: Thomas J. Badey, *Randolph-Macon College*

Before the Beheadings

JEFFREY GOLDBERG

Remembering a time when Islamist extremists wanted to persuade reporters, not kill them.

Learning Outcomes

After reading this article, you will be able to:

- Determine the role of journalists before social media.
- Understand the relationship journalist and terrorist once had.

In the spring of 2000, I lived for a month in a Taliban madrasa, a religious seminary, located on the Grand Trunk Road outside of Peshawar, in Pakistan. The chancellor of the madrasa, a wrinkled, bearded, and often barefoot man named Samiul Haq, was said to be a confidante of Mullah Omar, the Taliban leader. I did not believe, when we first met, that he would agree to my presence in his school. I was open about my intentions: my goal was to write about the religious education of Pashtun boys who would soon be fighting on behalf of the Taliban, and by extension al-Qaeda, in Afghanistan.

It turned out that Haq was keen to have me understand the work of his madrasa. In our first meeting, he even made an attempt at bonding. "The problem is not between us Muslims and Christians," he said. "The only enemy Islam and Christianity have is the Jews. It was the Jews who crucified Christ."

In my travels, Palestinian terrorists generally understood the implication of my last name, as did many members of Hezbollah, the Shia extremist group. But Islamists in Pakistan and Afghanistan seemed less Semitically attuned.

"I'm Jewish," I said.

He paused. "Well," he said, "you are most welcome here."

Not long after my stay at the madrasa, I visited a mosque outside Muzaffarabad, in Kashmir. The mosque was affiliated with Lashkar-e-Taiba, the group that would go on to commit the famous massacre in Mumbai in 2008.

The subject of my religion came up in conversation. The imam was fascinated. He was anti-Semitic, but impersonally so. His abstract detestation of Jews was trumped by a practical curiosity. He phoned a friend who, like him, had never met someone from my tribe. That friend brought another friend. Soon, we were having a colloquy on several subjects—the putative righteousness of Osama bin Laden's cause, the alleged treachery of Bill Clinton—but our focus narrowed to matters of faith. I raised the subject of Muhammad's often complicated, sometimes violent relationship with the Jews of Arabia. These men, like many Muslims, believed that the Jews had behaved perfidiously toward their Prophet, and they endorsed Muhammad's decision to behead some 600 of his Jewish enemies, the males of the vanquished Banu Qurayza tribe.

Back then, it did not seem foolhardy to engage Muslim terrorists on the subject of beheading.

It was not as though they didn't already hate Jews, and Americans. Even in the 1990s, the hatred, particularly in Pakistan, was sometimes palpable. I once went, at night, to a sketchy section of Rawalpindi, to interview a man named Fazlur Rehman Khalil, the leader of a terrorist group then called Harkat ul- Mujahideen. Khalil had co-signed bin Laden's 1998 fatwa calling for the killing of Americans and Jews. He gave me tea, and told me that he would happily use nuclear weapons to eradicate the enemies of Islam. "If we had them, we would use them as necessary. But they're very expensive," he said. The conversation turned to the fatwa. Why Jews?, I asked. "Because you are from Satan," he said. When we were done with the interview, our transaction complete, I left for my hotel.

I had glimpsed a treacherous and secret subculture, and I was happy, because a reporter's deepest need is to see what is on the other side of a closed door. In exchange, I would tell people in the West about Khalil and his beliefs. I was appalled by his message, and I wanted readers to understand the horror of it. But Khalil believed he was doing good works, and he wanted the world to celebrate his philosophy. Back then, the transaction worked for both parties. Today, when I think about the meeting, I shudder.

I spoke recently with a friend, Dexter Filkins, of *The New Yorker,* about the assumptions we used to make. I first met Dexter in the spring of 1998, on the runway of the airport in Kabul, a couple of months after bin Laden issued his fatwa. The order seemed like the grandiose outburst of an impotent fantasist, and Western reporters who traveled in Afghanistan did not take it seriously, at least not as concerned their own safety. "I used to tell people that as a reporter for an American news organization, it was like we were wearing armor," Dexter recalled. "People just didn't go after American reporters."

The attacks of 9/11 weren't the decisive break in the relationship between jihadists and journalists. It was the decision made by a set of extremists in Pakistan to kidnap the *Wall Street Journal* reporter Daniel Pearl in January 2002 that represented a shift in jihadist thought. To his kidnappers, Pearl was not a messenger to the outside world, but a scapegoat to be sacrificed for the sins of his fellow infidels. Murder was becoming their message.

Danny Pearl was the reporter who first gave me telephone numbers for important figures in Pakistani extremist circles. Danny was generous, Danny was careful, but Danny was unlucky. Even after his murder, I convinced myself that this horrible moment was the exception that proved the rule. Non-Jewish reporters, meanwhile, could tell themselves that Danny's death had more to do with his religion than his profession.

"It just seemed to me like a freakish anomaly," Dexter said. "I went to the tribal areas in Pakistan, to Wana, by taxi, after he was killed. It used to be pretty easy. You could go into situations that were very dangerous, and the chances of being hurt were very small."

Today, of course, Western journalists who seek out jihadists are courting death. The beheadings of James Foley and Steven Sotloff by ISIS, the Islamic State terror group, are persuasive arguments for prudence.

Why have some groups rejected the notion of journalistic neutrality? For one thing, the extremists have become more extreme. Look at the fractious relationship between al-Qaeda and ISIS, which is an offshoot of al-Qaeda but which has rejected criticism from Qaeda leaders about its particularly baroque application of violence.

Another, more important, reason relates to the mechanisms of publicity itself. The extremists don't need us anymore. Fourteen years ago, while I was staying at the Taliban madrasa, its administrators were launching a website. I remember being amused by this. I shouldn't have been. There is no need for

a middleman now. Journalists have been replaced by YouTube and Twitter. And when there is no need for us, we become targets.

Three years ago, Dexter and I Both Found Ourselves in Pakistan again, staying in the same anonymous guest-house in Islamabad, which seemed safer than any alternative. Especially after the killing of Osama bin Laden, when so many people in Pakistan were contemplating revenge, the large hotels had become irresistible targets for terrorists. They were also infested with agents of the Inter-Services Intelligence (ISI) directorate, the handmaiden of many of the terrorist groups.

I was reporting on the security of Pakistan's nuclear weapons; Dexter was investigating the murder of a Pakistani journalist who was killed, apparently, by agents of the ISI. Both topics were dangerous territory, and we came under harassment. I was followed; Dexter's phone was tapped. Each time I returned to the guesthouse, I could tell that strangers had been in my room. One day, I got a call from someone who identified himself as a reporter for a major Urdu daily newspaper. "We understand that you're a prominent Zionist, and we want to write about you on the front page," he said.

Such an article would have gotten me killed. The reporter's call represented an invitation from the ISI to leave Pakistan right away. I knocked on Dexter's door. He had been in the country for a month, and he seemed haunted. His room reminded me of Martin Sheen's in the opening scene of *Apocalypse Now.* Time to go, I said. In the taxi to the airport, we discovered that Dexter's visa had expired. We edited his passport with a Sharpie, while standing behind a tree outside the terminal. The ISI did not impede our departure.

Each unhappy place has its own rules. In Iran, Western reporters are often welcome, and sometimes arrested while performing their duties. In Gaza over the summer, Hamas, the Muslim Brother hood's Palestinian branch, was both eager to help reporters inspect the damage done by Israeli air strikes, and rigorous about denying reporters access to the rocket crews launching attacks on Israeli civilians. In Lebanon, Hezbollah maintains a sophisticated media-relations operation designed in part to thwart independent reporting.

I no longer spend much time with Islamist groups. Today, even places that shouldn't be dangerous for journalists are dangerous. Whole stretches of Muslim countries are becoming of-limits. This is a minor facet of a much larger calamity, but it has consequences: the problems of Afghanistan and Pakistan and Syria and Iraq are not going away; our ability to see these problems, however, is becoming progressively more circumscribed.

Once, in Upper Egypt, in Minya, a Salafist cleric was lecturing me on the characteristics of unbelievers. It was a typical rant, and it ended with a justification for sacred violence, to be directed by followers of the one true faith against those who defy God. I must have been tired, or frustrated, because I impulsively asked: "Why haven't you personally killed any unbelievers? What are you waiting for?" Left unspoken was: *Here's my throat.*

He answered simply, "Everything happens according to a plan." In other words: *All in good time.*

Young reporters sometimes come to me for advice about working in the Middle East. In years past, I would tell them that this was an excellent idea: save some money, go learn Arabic, be a newspaper stringer, grab for the big stories, and you'll have an interesting life. Steven Sotloff was one of those who sought my advice. His Middle East career was already under way (he was living in Israel at the time), and I prefer to think that he could not have been dissuaded.

But I'm capable of learning, and my advice now is to go somewhere else.

Critical Thinking

1. How has social media affected the security of journalists?
2. Has the diminishing role of the journalist impacted the type of information we receive?
3. Why didn't terrorists carry out any violence toward journalists before?

Internet References

ALJAZEERA America News
http://america.aljazeera.com/opinions/2015/1/charlie-hebdo-deadmuslimjournalistsfreedomofspeech.html

The Journalism of Terror
https://medium.com/@Storyful/the-journalism-of-terror-how-do-we-bear-witness-when-everybody-is-a-witness-749344c7a45a

NEWSEUM
http://www.newseum.org/2015/02/05/terrorism-and-press-freedom-mothers-journalists-speak-out

Article   Prepared by: Thomas J. Badey, *Randolph-Macon College*

Terror Returns'—Along with Media Fixations

Boston Bombings Revive Fear of "Islamic Rage"

PETER HART

Learning Outcomes

After reading this article, you will be able to:

- Understand the role of the media in attacks such as the Boston bombing.
- Examine the impact of the use of the term "terrorism" on public perceptions.
- Discuss the role of the traditional media in framing the narrative.

It is not surprising that the Boston Marathon bombing was treated as an event of enormous significance. Beyond the dramatic manhunt, the story had obvious political dimensions. The two explosions were labeled terrorist attacks almost from the start, and the tragedy jump-started media rhetoric about the supposed gaps in law enforcement surveillance, the persistence of "Muslim rage" and the return of terrorism within the United States.

"A five-day battle in the war on terror," was how Scott Pelley described the ordeal on **60 Minutes** (4/21/13). "TERROR RETURNS" was the banner headline of **USA Today** (4/16/13) the day after the bombings, with another front-page headline that read, "That Post-9/11 Quiet? It's Over."

Coverage and commentary of this sort underscores the fact that terrorism has no consistent definition in media, and that some acts that could be called terrorism either escape the label or vanish down the memory hole. The snipers in the Washington, D.C., area killed 10 people about a year after the 9/11

attacks. A shooter at a Tennessee Unitarian church killed two people, part of a plan to murder liberals. A man crashed a plane into an IRS building in Austin, Texas, in 2010. Six were massacred at a Wisconsin Sikh temple in August 2012.

But for whatever reason, these attacks—and others like them, many unsuccessful—failed to meet the media's standard for terrorism. (The **New York Times** seemed to understand the problem with this line of thinking; a Web headline, "Bombings End Decade Without Terror in U.S.," was eventually changed to "Bombings End Decade of Strikingly Few Successful Terrorist Attacks in U.S.")

If one accepts the conventional definition of terrorism— violence against civilians intended to send a political message—then it was not clear at the outset that the Boston bombings were terrorist attacks. And for some commentators, the categorization and thus the importance of the story seemed to depend on knowing more about the suspects' nationality and/or religion. "If this is an international terror attack, the repercussions will be severe," warned Fox host Bill O'Reilly (4/16/13). "And if it's homegrown, that will be another stain on American history."

The comment is instructive, reflecting a sentiment that exists beyond O'Reilly: An attack connected to foreign interests would be much more significant than domestic terrorism. Indeed, when the FBI released photos of the suspects—both listed as "white"—MSNBC host Chris Matthews (4/18/13) wondered:

> To be blunt, and not to be [getting] into political profiling or racial profiling, but when you look at a picture that

we're looking at now, are there people that can look at that picture, study it and decide whether a fellow like that is from Yemen or other parts like that? Can they figure it out by looking at a picture?

A vivid example of racializing the bombers could be seen on the cover of the **Week** magazine (5/3/13), which featured a cartoon drawing of the Tsarnaev brothers, identified by police as the perpetrators, darkened to appear something other than the Caucasians that they were (Brofiling, 4/30/13).

While literally transforming the suspects into non-whites was exceptional, the assumption was ubiquitous that their religious background trumped their whiteness, if you will, and guaranteed that their violence would be treated as terrorism. **Guardian** columnist Glenn Greenwald (4/22/13) put it succinctly: "As usual, what terrorism *really* means in American discourse—its operational meaning—is: violence by Muslims against Americans and their allies."

In that vein, the Boston bombings came to be understood as a return of 9/11—not in the scope of the attacks or the cost in innocent lives, but as a reminder of a certain type of danger. "With the death of Osama bin Laden, Islamic rage did not go away. In fact, in some ways it's more dangerous," explained veteran NBC anchor Tom Brokaw on **Meet the Press** (4/21/13). Referring to Dzhokhar Tsarnaev, the brother who survived a shootout with police, he said: "He's a Chechen, but their beef is with Russia, not with us. But he's also a Muslim. And the fact is that that Islamic rage is still out there."

On CBS's **Face the Nation** (4/28/13), host Bob Schieffer explained:

> You know, once Osama bin Laden was killed, we had people around here saying that the war on terrorism is over, the threat is over. I guess we found out in Boston that that's not entirely true. It does seem to be a different kind of terrorism that we're up against right now.

Fox's anchor Bill O'Reilly (4/25/13) declared, "The overwhelming evidence is that these two brothers killed four Americans and hurt more than 200 others in the name of Allah, period."

It's not clear what O'Reilly meant by "overwhelming evidence"; what the surviving Tsarnaev brother reportedly told investigators was that the two were actually motivated by "the American wars in Iraq and Afghanistan" (**Washington Post,** 4/23/13). Speculating about Islam's purported connection to the bombings was obviously much easier than wrestling with the fact that the suspect, like several others linked to terror incidents (**Guardian,** 4/24/13), allegedly claimed to be responding to U.S. warfare.

Brokaw on **Meet the Press** was one of the few prominent pundits to discuss this background:

> We have got to look at the roots of all of this because it exists across the whole subcontinent, and the Islamic world around the world. And I think we also have to examine the use of drones. . . . There are a lot of civilians who are innocently killed in a drone attack in Pakistan, in Afghanistan and in Iraq. And I can tell you, having spent a lot of time over there, young people will come up to me on the streets and say: "We love America. If you harm one hair on the head of my sister, I will fight you forever." And there is this enormous rage against what they see in that part of the world as a presumptuousness of the United States.

Coincidentally, the coverage of the Boston aftermath coincided with a Senate hearing on the U.S. drone program (**Democracy Now!,** 4/25/13), where lawmakers heard from Farea al-Muslimi, a young Yemeni activist who spoke movingly of the effect that a drone strike had on his village: "What the violent militants had previously failed to achieve [in my village], one drone strike accomplished in an instant. There is now an intense anger against America." Those comments were scarcely covered in the corporate media.

More often, the idea that there could be a connection between military violence in Iraq or Afghanistan and attacks on civilians in the United States was rejected, most vociferously by **New York Times** columnist Tom Friedman (4/28/13), who called it a "popular meme among radical Muslim groups." He went on:

> It is amazing to me how we've come to accept this non sequitur and how easily we've allowed radical Muslim groups and their apologists to get away with it. . . . Dzhokhar claims the Tsarnaev brothers were so upset by something America did in a third country that they just had to go to Boylston Street and blow up people who had nothing to do with it (some of whom could have been Muslims), and too often we just nod our heads rather than asking: What kind of sick madness is this?

"What is going on in your community," the **Times** pundit demanded of Muslims, that would permit this sort of violence? This is especially rich coming from the same person who enthusiastically supported the U.S. wars in Afghanistan and Iraq; in the case of the latter, during an interview on "Charlie Rose" (5/30/03), he specifically defended it as vengeance for the 9/11 attacks and a way to strike back against the "terrorist bubble" in the Muslim world:

> What they needed to see was American boys and girls going house to house, from Basra to Baghdad, and

basically saying: "Which part of this sentence don't you understand? You don't think, you know, we care about our open society, you think this bubble fantasy, we're just gonna let it grow? Well, Suck. On. This."

That, Charlie, is what this war is about. We could have hit Saudi Arabia; it was part of that bubble. Could have hit Pakistan. We hit Iraq because we could.

The views of an elite columnist like Friedman overlap considerably with the downmarket right-wing pseudo-populism of Fox's O'Reilly, who was trafficking in ugly Islamophobia (4/23/13):

It's clear the two Boston bombers were jihadists. They believed they have a right to kill children to serve their religion. Who else does that? What other theology in this world justifies murdering innocent people? The answer is? Only radical Islam allows terror murder. That's the truth.

O'Reilly went [on] to complain that "most Muslims on this Earth are good people, but they are not helping to neutralize the jihad. They are not standing up against it in any numbers. And that includes American Muslims; they largely remain silent."

So they're good people who do little to criticize terrorism, according to O'Reilly. According to Gallup polling (8/2/11), Muslim Americans are the religious group least likely to believe that "for an individual person or a small group of persons to target and kill civilians is sometimes justified"; just 11 percent agreed, versus 22 percent of Jewish Americans, 23 percent of nonbelievers, 26 percent of Protestants and 27 percent of Catholics. (Muslims were also much less likely to believe that military attacks on civilians were sometimes justified.)

O'Reilly would also insist, without any evidence, that there was likely more to this plot: "Some left-wing media already touting the lone-wolf theory that the two young terror bombers acted alone; nobody helped them kill four Americans and injure more than 200 others in Boston last week." Of course, that wasn't a left-wing media conspiracy—it was what law enforcement officials were saying from the very early stages of their investigation (**LA Times**, 4/23/13).

But O'Reilly wasn't alone in denying that the Tsarnaevs could have acted alone; two different guests on CNN's "Lead" (4/29/13) declared that there must have been a conspiracy.

Attempts to cause mass slaughter are not extremely rare in the United States—**USA Today** (12/19/12) counted 774 people killed in 156 incidents between 2006 and 2010, or one mass slaying every two weeks—and in most cases most people have no trouble believing that the perpetrators could have acted alone, whether politically motivated or not. But the Boston Marathon bombings were put in the category of "Islamic terrorism"—which somehow meant that the regular rules of evidence no longer apply.

Critical Thinking

1. How does media reporting affect public perception of a terrorist incident?

2. Does the media treat domestic and international terrorism differently?

3. Why are some incidents identified as "terrorism" and others not?

4. Why is the "Islamic rage" narrative so powerful?

Internet References

BBC News
http://www.bbc.com/news/world-us-canada-32197049

Government Technology
http://www.govtech.com/public-safety/Social-Media-Big-Lessons-from-the-Boston-Marathon-Bombing.html

NPR News
http://www.npr.org/2015/04/03/397213144/-the-brothers-examines-motivation-behind-boston-marathon-bombing

Unit 7

UNIT

Prepared by: Thomas J. Badey, *Randolph-Macon College*

Terrorism and Religion

Since the revolution in Iran in 1979, the topic of religion has played an increasingly prominent role in discussions of international terrorism. Fears of a resurgence of fundamentalist Islam have spawned visions of inevitable clashes of civilizations. Even before the events of September 11, 2001, the term religious terrorism had become a staple in the vocabulary of many U.S. policymakers. The emergence of groups like Boko Haram and ISIS have further exacerbated this tendency.

While there is currently no commonly accepted definition of religious terrorism, one should note that in the popular press the term religious terrorism is often used as a euphemism for political violence committed by Muslims. It is naïve to presume that all political violence committed by members of a particular religious group is necessarily religious violence. The relationship between religion and political violence is much more complex.

Experts have noted that many of today's religious terrorists were nationalists yesterday and Marxists the day before. Unlike their historical predecessors like the *Thugs* in India who killed to sacrifice the blood of their victims to the Goddess *Kali,* today's religious terrorists more often see violence as a means of achieving political, economic, and social objectives. Religion is seen as a means, rather than an end in itself. In many cases religious ideologies have taken over where other ideologies have failed.

Ideologies are systems of belief that justify behavior. They serve three primary functions: (1) They polarize and mobilize populations toward common objectives; (2) They create a sense of security by providing a system of norms and values; and (3) They provide the basis for the justification and rationalization of human behavior. Ideologies do not necessarily cause violence. They do, however, provide an effective means of polarizing populations and organizing political dissent.

While the emergence of religious ideologies signals an important shift in international terrorism, the role of religion in international terrorism is often exaggerated or misunderstood. Religion is not the cause of contemporary political violence. It does, however, provide an effective means for organizing political groups. In some parts of the world political extremists have infiltrated the mosques, temples, and churches and have managed to hijack and pervert religious doctrine, superimposing their own views of the world that encourage the use of violence.

The articles in this unit provide an overview of the relationship between religion and terrorism. In the first article in this unit, Heather Gregg attempts to differentiate religiously motivated terrorism from traditional terrorism. She examines the goals of religious terrorism, their leadership and target selection, and offers suggestions for counterterrorism strategies. Next Hüseyin Cinoğlu asserts that religion has been used by terrorist organizations to legitimize violence. He argues that as such, religion serves multiple functions. It has become the cure for alienation, it eliminates the need to appeal to larger audiences and helps to identify and rationalize terrorists' target selection. The third article, by Paul Marshall, serves as a reminder that violent extremism is not unique to one particular religion. Marshall argues that Hindu extremism and violence have been tolerated by the Indian government and largely ignored by the United States.

He believes that the growth of Hindu nationalism poses a real threat to India's pluralistic democracy. Finally, Tyler Huggins examines Christian Extremism in the United States. He argues that while Americans have no problems with labeling other culture's fundamental or violent sub-religions as extremists, they choose to ignore the violent actions and rhetoric of radical Christian groups. He suggests that this has created a double standard of extremism in the United States.

Article

Prepared by: Thomas J. Badey, *Randolph-Macon College*

Defining and Distinguishing Secular and Religious Terrorism

HEATHER S. GREGG

Learning Outcomes

After reading this article, you will be able to:

- Explain the difference between secular and religious terrorism.

- Identify the three goals of religious terrorism.

- Discuss potential counterterrorism responses to religious terrorism.

Introduction

A conventional wisdom has emerged that the current wave of religiously motivated terrorism propagates acts of unrestrained, indiscriminant violence, and that it is irrational, thus offering few, if any, policy options for counterterrorism measures. Jean-Francois Mayer asserts, for example: "When religious beliefs are used for justifying violence, violent actions tend to become endowed with cosmic dimensions, and there is nothing left to restrain them."[1] Similarly, Bruce Hoffman argues: "For the religious terrorist, violence first and foremost is a sacramental act or divine duty executed in direct response to some theological demand or imperative. Terrorism assumes a transcendental dimension, and its perpetrators are thereby unconstrained by the political, moral, or practical constraints that seem to affect other terrorists."[2]

These assertions about religion's role in terrorism stem from two challenges in the literature. First, scholarship on religious terrorism tends to focus on one particular motivation— apocalyptic, millennial, or messianic terrorism, in which groups use violence to hasten the end of times and usher in an anticipated new world. Religious terrorists, however, have other goals, some of which are earthly in their aims; these goals are often categorised as political, not religious.[3] Second, religious terrorism has not been clearly distinguished from its traditional more secular counterpart with a definition of what makes it unique from other forms of terrorism, if it is unique at all.

In order to better understand religiously motivated terrorism, this article will do four things. First it aims to define and differentiate religiously motivated terrorism from traditional terrorism, including leftist groups, right wing groups, and ethnic-separatist terrorists. Second, it will provide a range of goals for religious groups and how terrorism serves these goals. In particular, the article investigates three objectives: fomenting the apocalypse, creating a religious government, and establishing a religiously pure state. Third, within these goals, the article will consider the role of leadership and target selection of religious terrorists for their uniqueness and commonality with traditional terrorism. Finally, the article concludes by offering suggestions for mitigating religiously motivated terrorism.

Defining Traditional and Religious Terrorism

Before distinguishing traditional and religious terrorism from one another, terrorism needs to be defined in its own right. There is little consensus on the definition of terrorism, both within academic and policy circles.[4] Walter Laqueur argues that this lack of consensus is largely due to the fact that there is not one type of terrorism and that terrorism, as a tactic, is constantly changing its means, motives and actors.[5] Drawing primarily from Bruce Hoffman, this article defines the tactic of terrorism as a) the use or threat of violence; b) the targeting of civilians, property, or government; c) the intent of creating fear aimed at altering the status quo; and d) a group activity.[6]

This definition stresses that terrorism, first and foremost, is a tactic. As such, non-state and state actors can employ terrorist tactics. This article, however, will focus specifically on non-state actors. Second, this definition stresses the corporate nature of terrorists and their tactical use of violence with the goal of changing the existing political, social, military, or religious order. To be sure, individuals or "lone wolves" can employ terrorist tactics to achieve similar goals, but this article will concentrate on groups that use terrorism to achieve a stated goal. Finally, this definition is particularly useful for exploring religiously motivated terrorism because it considers goals that may not be strictly political, such as changing the social and religious order of a state or region. As will be described, religious groups that use terrorism have political goals, but they also have social and religious goals that are distinct from political objectives.

Traditional Terrorism: Left, Right and Ethnic-Separatist

Traditional terrorism is typically divided into three subcategories: left, right and ethnic-separatist.[7] Terrorism of the left refers primarily to Anarchist, Marxist and socialist oriented ideologies. This type of terrorism was most active in the 20th century, particularly in Western and Eastern Europe, Latin America and, to a lesser extent, the Middle East. Anarchist groups were most popular in Europe around the turn of the 20th century, particularly in Russia, where movements emerged with the aim of destroying the monarchy and the state.[8] Examples of left-wing Marxist groups include the Argentinian *Montoneros* and ERP, the Italian Red Brigades, the German Red Army Faction (also known as the Baader Meinhof group), and the Palestinian Popular Front for the Liberation of Palestine (PFLP). All of these groups were inspired by Marxist or socialist ideologies.[9] This sub-category of traditional terrorism, although active during the Cold War, has declined since the 1980s.[10] Religious terrorism, by-and-large, has not been associated with this branch of terrorism.[11]

Right-winged terrorism refers to groups with racist, fascist, or nationalistic motives and goals. This type of terrorism was strong between the World Wars and reasserted itself beginning in the 1980s and continues to the present. Early examples include the Ku Klux Klan in the United States, and fascist-inspired movements like the Rumanian Iron Guard of the 1930s.[12] Resurgent right-wing terrorism includes groups like the neo-Nazis in Europe and the United States, and violent anti-immigration groups.[13] Religious terrorism has often been categorized as a new breed of right-winged terrorism.[14] However, as will be argued below, religious terrorism has traits that

look like right-winged racism but also contains elements that do not fit into this category.

Ethnic-separatist terrorism[15] consists of groups that use terrorism to strive for autonomy or independence from a state or military force. Examples of ethnic-separatist terrorists include groups seeking independence from an occupying force, such as the Jewish Irgun in Palestine under the British Mandate, the PLO under Israeli occupation, and the IRA under British occupation.[16] Another example within this subset is groups that seek separation from an existing state such as the ETA in the Basque province of Spain.[17] Academic research also associates religious terrorism with this branch of traditional terrorism.[18] However, it is important to distinguish ethnic-separatist terrorists that contain religious elements but whose primary goals are non-religious from terrorist groups that have religious goals. An example of a religious-ethnic group with non-religious goals is the IRA. Although its constituency is primarily Catholic, the IRA's aim is to expel British forces in the region and reunite Northern Ireland with the Republic, not to create a religious government or state. By contrast, an example of a religious/ethnic group with religious goals is the Palestinian Hamas, which is pushing for the expulsion of Israeli forces from the West Bank and Gaza Strip and the creation of an Islamic state in Palestine.[19] Table 1 summarizes traditional terrorism.

Table 1   Traditional Terrorism

	Definition Goals	**Examples**
Left	• Anarchist—destroy the government	• Argentinian Montoneros/ERP
	• Marxist—foment workers' revolution	• Red Brigades, German/Japanese Red Armies
	• Socialist—economic restructuring	• Palestinian PFLP
		• Colombian ELM
Right	• Racist—racial supremacy	• Ku Klux Klan
	• Fascist—state-sponsored, militant racism/nationalism	• Rumanian Iron Guard
	• Nationalistic	• Neo-Nazis
Ethnic–Separatist	• Dispel foreign occupying force	• Irgun
		• PLO
	• Create ethnically independent state	• IRA
		• Basque ETA

Religiously Motivated Terrorism

Religiously motivated terrorism, although containing elements of all three branches of traditional terrorism, needs to be distinguished analytically from traditional terrorism in order to better understand its workings. However, similar to discussions on terrorism in general, current literature on religiously motivated terrorism lacks consensus on a definition and how it differs from traditional terrorism, if at all. David Tucker even argues that the term "religious terrorism" is not of much use because of confusion over its definition.[20] Mark Juergensmeyer suggests that religiously motivated terrorism came to the foreground in the 1980s and is marked by extreme brutality and seemingly irrational motivations and goals.[21] Bruce Hoffman argues that religion serves to uniquely legitimate and justify violence in religious terrorism but does not explain how religious ideology differs from Marxist or Fascist ideology in inspiring terrorist acts.[22] Walter Laqueur argues that religious terrorism is the "new terrorism of the right" and that it has more to do with nationalism than religion. But this definition fails to explain movements like Aum Shinrikyo, who desire to destroy the world, not assert their nationalist claims, or Al-Qaeda, which has transnational goals.[23]

Religious terrorism scholar David C. Rapoport offers another argument for what differentiates religious from secular terrorism. He posits that the justification and precedents of religious terrorism differ from traditional forms; religious terrorists use sacred texts and historic examples that are not present in secular terrorism. Secular terrorism, in contrast, develops a culture of actions and boundaries that restrains the scope of violent acts.[24] This argument relies on the internal aspects of religion—its scriptures and traditions—without explaining why these internal traits justify and mandate violence by some groups at sometime and not others. In other words, his argument does not include factors external to a religious group and how these factors may bear on explaining the variation of peace and violence within religions.

Finally, Mark Sedgwick suggests that religious terrorism is best understood by considering its immediate and ultimate objectives. He proposes that "while the ultimate aims will be religiously formulated, the immediate objectives will often be found to be almost purely political."[25] Sedgewick's observation is useful for realizing that religious terrorists' goals are not purely religious. However, this article will challenge his dichotomy between short and long term, and non-religious and religious goals, proposing that certain terrorists can have immediate goals that are religious, specifically apocalyptic terrorists, while others can have long-term objectives that are political, such as creating a religious government.

Finally, these debates within the literature and lack of consensus on what makes religiously motivated terrorism unique from traditional terrorism can be clarified by looking not just at the presence of scripture, religious symbols or adherents, but by focusing on uniquely religious goals for which these groups are fighting. In other words, the use of scripture or presence of religious symbols is not enough to distinguish a group and its use of terrorism as uniquely religious. As previously noted, there are examples of groups that use religion as a form of identity or draw from scriptures and symbols to motivate followers, but their goals fall within the confines of traditional terrorism. Furthermore, non-religious factors may cause groups to use terrorism for religiously salient goals. For example, groups may use terrorism with the aim of overthrowing governments that they believe are not upholding the tenets of a particular religion and installing a religious government in its place. The cause of the terrorist act is something outside of the faith, but the goal is uniquely religious.

Therefore, this article proposes that religiously motivated terrorism can be defined as: *the threat or use of force with the purpose of influencing or coercing governments and/or populations towards saliently religious goals*. The discussion below will elaborate on three goals in particular: fomenting the apocalypse, creating a religious government, and religiously cleansing a state or area.

Religious Terrorism's Goals: Apocalypse, Theocracy, and Religious Cleansing

In order to better understand religiously motivated terrorism and distinguish it from its traditional counterpart, it is useful to identify specific examples of uniquely religious goals for which groups may be striving. This article highlights three goals in particular: fomenting the apocalypse, creating a religious government, and religiously cleansing a state. These goals are not exhaustive, but do cover the majority of religiously motivated violence seen today.

Apocalyptic Terrorism

Some groups have apocalyptic goals; their primary aim is to cause cataclysmic destruction to people, property, and the environment with the hope of fomenting the end of time and ushering in religious promises of a new world. This pursuit is uniquely religious and is perhaps the most common stereotype of religiously motivated terrorism. Apocalyptic terrorism exists both within traditional religions and "cults" or New Religious Movements (NRM). For example, Rapoport argues that apocalyptic terrorist groups—what he calls millennialist groups—are inspired by longings for the coming of the messiah, which will coincide with the end of the world.[26] Mayer argues that apocalyptic imagining is a cause of terrorism in cults and NRM but, by itself, does not usually result in violence. Rather, groups that turn to terrorism are responding to a mix of millennialism, real world threats, and internal disputes.[27]

An example of an apocalyptic group within an existing religious tradition is the Gush Emunim in Israel. In 1984 members hatched a plot to blow up the Muslim Dome of the Rock Shrine in Jerusalem, the third most holy site in Islam, in order to spark a nuclear and chemical confrontation between Israel and Muslim countries. The goal was to create "catastrophic messianism," disastrous circumstances that would hasten the coming of the messiah.[28] The most common example of a NRM group that used terrorism with apocalyptic aims is the Japanese cult Aum Shinrikyo, which deployed Sarin gas in a Tokyo subway in 1995. Its overarching goal was instigating World War III and ultimately "destroying the world to save it."[29] The attacks killed 13 and injured more than 700 people.

Of the three religious goals outlined here, apocalyptic terrorism is the most dangerous for two reasons. First, the paradox of 'destroying the world'—causing catastrophic death and destruction—to create a new and better world seems the furthest removed from rational thought and negotiation. This makes counterterrorism measures especially difficult; it appears that there is little the U.S. government, or anyone else, can give these groups to alter their aims.

Second, the goal of destroying the world is particularly ripe for the use of WMD as a means of achieving such ends, which makes apocalyptic groups particularly dangerous. However, it is also important to note that many apocalyptic terrorists have turned their violence inward in order to foment the apocalypse, as opposed to attacking those outside the group. Some examples of inwardly violent groups include the apocalyptic cult The People's Temple, headed by Jim Jones, in which over 900 members committed suicide *en masse* in anticipation of an apocalyptic standoff with the U.S. government. Another example is Heaven's Gate, which believed that suicide would free the members' souls.[30] The standoff between U.S. Federal agents and the Branch Davidians at the Mount Carmel compound in Waco, Texas, also fulfilled apocalyptic expectations of the cult group, and resulted in the death of 76 men, women and children.[31] Mayer notes that examples like these, while apocalyptic and violent, may not fall under the definition of terrorism per se, because their goals do not extend beyond the confines of their immediate group.[32] Nevertheless, they offer important clues about the conditions under which apocalyptic thinking emerges and results in mass violence.

The Creation of a Religious Government

Groups also use terrorism as a means of creating a religious government. This goal is most commonly associated with militant Islamic groups and their desire to establish a government run by *Shari'a* law. For example, the Lebanese Twelver Shia organization Hezbollah has used terrorism against the state of Israel and against its own government with the ultimate goal of creating a religious government in Lebanon, inspired by the theocracy in Iran. Somewhat similarly, the Sunni Palestinian Hamas has used terrorism against Israel with the immediate aim of ending its occupation of the West Bank, Gaza Strip and potentially all of Israel, but with the ultimate aim of creating a religious government in Palestine.[33]

The desire to create a religious government also exists in other traditions. "Reconstruction Theology" is one interpretation of Christian scriptures that calls for the creation of a Christian theocratic government in the United States. Reconstruction Theology has inspired groups such as the Christian Identity Movement, which is linked to the paramilitary training camp the Covenant, the Sword and the Arm of the Lord (CSA). This movement aims to use terrorism as a means of compelling change within the U.S. government. Oklahoma City bomber Timothy McVeigh had ties to both Christian Identity and CSA.[34]

Terrorists vying for the creation of a religious government are often confined within a state's borders, such as the Christian Identity Movement in the United States. These groups, however, can also have transnational ties and goals through sponsorship from likeminded groups outside their borders and from other states. This is true of the Lebanese Hizbollah, which receives financial and material support from the government of Iran, which is also Twelver Shia.[35] Transnational ties are also evident in Kach and its successor organizations, which receives considerable support from likeminded Jews in the United States.[36] Hamas is also reported to receive money from Saudi Arabia, the Gulf States and Iran.[37]

Transnational ties of religious terrorism groups also appear to stem from leaders that have ties to groups in other countries. This is true of Kach/JDL, whose leader, Meir Kahane, was born in the United States and co-founded the JDL there but then immigrated to Israel and formed Kach, which is made up primarily of American-born Jews who have moved to Israel.[38] Hassan Nasrallah, the leader of Hizbollah, has personal ties to Iran and Iraq, especially through his seminary training in both countries.[39]

In addition to the goal of creating a religious government within a state, there are groups vying to create religious regions or super-states. Currently, some groups are working to establish a pan-Islamic entity that will transcend state borders. Perhaps the best example of this type of transnational religious terrorism is Al-Qaeda. Following the end of the Soviet-Afghan War in 1989, Al-Qaeda spread its ideology of jihad through leadership ties and training centers to Muslim countries around the globe. After September 11th, bin Laden called for the restoration of the Caliphate as a necessary objective to unite and protect the worldwide Muslim community.[40] Like-minded groups, such as Al-Qaeda in Iraq, Al-Qaeda in the Islamic Maghreb and Al-Qaeda in the Arabian Peninsula share these goals. Likewise, groups like Jemiyyah Islamia in Southeast Asia have named the creation of a regional Caliphate as one of their stated objectives.[41]

It is worth noting that non-violent pan-Islamic movements exist, which attempt to achieve their ends by means other than terrorism. The most notable example is the Muslim Brotherhood, which exists in over 70 countries, and is strongest in Egypt, Jordan, and Syria. Although initially a movement that used violence and terrorism, the Brotherhood has called for the creation of a pan-Islamic government by the "da'wa", or calling Muslims back to the faith, and through political reform, education and service to Muslims, generally not by means of terrorism and violence.[42] Another organization that eschews violence, Hizb ut-Tahrir, has made the restoration of the Caliphate one of its stated goals.[43] Both of these groups, despite their official claims to non-violence, have been implicated in spreading intolerant ideologies that inspire acts of violence within cells or by individuals acting on their own. For these reasons, both the Muslim Brotherhood and Hizb ut-Tahrir are regarded with caution by countries in which they are active.[44]

The creation of religious governments, through violent or peaceful means, presents important domestic and international security concerns to the United States and the international community. The treatment of religious minorities and secular groups is a problem under governments that embrace and promote a particular interpretation of a religion, and could lead to basic human rights violations and spark internal instability. Regionally, the creation of theocracies could prompt refugees to flee an ideology they do not espouse. Theocracies could also stir up religious fervor in like-minded religious adherents beyond its borders, causing regional instability. The creation of the Islamic Republic of Iran in 1979 is a case-in-point for both domestic and international security concerns sparked by the creation of a religious government. Iran's theocracy has been notoriously intolerant toward religious minorities, particularly the Baha'i, as well as to secular opposition groups. Regionally, Iran has caused instability by spreading religious fervour to countries with Shia populations, especially Iraq, Bahrain, Saudi Arabia, and Lebanon, in addition to an all-out war with Iraq from 1980 to 1988.

Lastly, it is useful to note that groups agitating for the creation of a religious government often disagree among themselves as to the nature and scope of religion's involvement in the state. For example, religious political parties exist in countries ranging from Israel (Jewish) to India (Hindu) to Pakistan (Islamic and Christian) to Sri Lanka (Buddhist), but within each of these countries, there is a wide variance of opinions on how a religious state should work. Sri Lanka presents an interesting example. In 1956, the Sri Lanka Freedom Party (SLFP) ran on a platform that promised to give Buddhism a preferential place in the country, along with other allowances to the Sinhalese majority, which is primarily Buddhist. When the government failed to deliver on these promises, a Buddhist Monk assassinated the prime minster in 1959. Buddhist discontent later led to the creation of a Buddhist revolutionary movement that used terrorism to agitate for a Buddhist theocracy in Sri Lanka.[45] Somewhat similarly, Israeli Prime Minister Yitzak Rabin was assassinated in 1995 by the Israeli Yigal Amir because he believed that Rabin was compromising the true integrity of the Jewish state by negotiating with the Palestinians.[46] Therefore, efforts aimed at creating a religious state are destabilizing because they throw into question what the state should look like and who speaks for the religion.

Terrorism and Religious Cleansing

Religious terrorists also aim to eradicate "infidels"—the unfaithful within their tradition or in other religions—in order to create a religiously pure state.[47] This goal differs from the creation of a religious government in that groups aim to make all the citizens within a state's border or region conform to their interpretation of the faith; it is religious cleansing, which includes battles with other religious groups as well as those within a religion whose interpretation of the faith differs from the group's.

Religious cleansing can be expressed in specific terms, such as the eradication of another group, or in broad terms, such as the cleansing of a culture, ideas or norms that do not conform to the group's worldviews. For example, Jewish settlers associated with the JDL/Kach movement in the West Bank, particularly in Hebron, have named as one of their goals the expulsion of non-Jews from land that they believe is divinely theirs.[48] This is a battle against other religions. In addition, however, the movement is battling Jews who do not conform to their interpretation of the faith along with the Israeli government, which it believes is not upholding the tenets of the faith. Rabbi Meir Kahane, the co-founder of the JDL and the founder of Kach stated in an interview in the 1980s that it is the requirement of Israel, as a Jewish state, to create a government based on the Torah, and that those who do not see this, are not truly Jewish. "A Jewish state means that, at a minimum, there must be a majority of Jews; a Jewish sovereignty with the power to make our own laws . . . My hope as a religious Jew, which is the hope of every sincere and religious Jew, is to have a state governed by the Torah."[49] As previously noted, Kahane and his organisations inspired violent actions aimed at achieving these goals, including assassination, murder, and attempted destruction of religious sites.

Terrorism aimed at religious cleansing appears similar to non-religious terrorism aimed at ethnic cleansing. However,

Table 2   Religious Terrorism

	Definition Goals	Examples
Apocalyptic	• Cataclysmic destruction to people, property, environment • Hasten arrival of a "ew world"	• Aum Shinrikyo • Elements of JDL/Kach • Some strains of Christian Identity
Create Religious Government	• Abolish secular state • Create a state governed by religious law and doctrine • Create trans-state religious government	• Lebanese Hizbollah • Christian Identity • Hamas • Elements of JDL/Kach
Create Religiously Pure State	• Remove groups from other religions • Remove groups within same religion with different interpretations of faith	• Elements of JDL/Kach • LeT • Shiv Sena/RSS

religious cleansing is different for the important reason that religion, not ethnicity, is the salient defining characteristic of both the terrorist group and the target. This means that religious terrorist groups can be multi-ethnic, such as Al-Qaeda, which is made up of Muslims from all over the worldwide community, but not multi-religious; they are all Muslim. Furthermore, terrorism aimed at religious cleansing may also look like religious fratricide, where violence is intra-religious. In these cases, groups use terrorism to rid an area or country of co-religionists that they believe are corrupting or not upholding the true tenets of the faith. In both cases, the salient characteristic between these groups is faith, not differing ethnicities. Table 2 summarises the goals of religious terrorism.

Leadership and Targets of Religious Terrorists

In addition to the goals for which groups are fighting, religious terrorism has additional attributes that distinguish it from its traditional counterparts, including unique sources of leadership and some of its targets. A common perception is that religious groups that use terrorism are led by a cleric, or a similar religious leader, such as an imam, 'alim, rabbi, or swami. However, not all leaders of terrorist groups have such *bona fide* leaders; rather the origin of the religious leader's authority comes from several key sources. For example, religious authority can be self-appointed, such as Shoko Asahara, the spiritual leader and

founder of Aum Shinrikyo.[50] Religious authorities can also be charismatic figures from outside the clergy of a traditional religion, such as Osama bin Laden and Ayman al Zawahiri, the key leaders of Al-Qaeda.[51] Religious authorities within terrorist groups can also be individuals who are trained as religious clerics or scholars. Examples of this type of authority are Sheikh Fadlallah, the spiritual leader of the Lebanese Hizbollah, who was trained as a Shia cleric in Najaf, Iraq, and Qum, Iran, and Meir Kahane of the JDL and Kach, who was trained as a Rabbi in the United States.

These different types of leadership in religiously motivated terrorism may seem puzzling at a glance, but they emphasise that religious power has more than one source and its legitimacy resides with the followers. In the case of bin Laden, his influence was derived from a combination of charisma and admiration for his purported success as a warrior in the Afghan-Soviet war and with various terrorist operations. With others, such as Nasrallah and Kahane, it was religious training. Still, with some it is self-proclaimed divine connections, as with Asahara and Koresh. Nevertheless, despite the source of their religious authority, the presence of a religious leader who is recognised as legitimate and who is given the authority to speak on behalf of the faith by his or her followers is typical to most religious terrorist movements. Religious authority, in other words, rests with a group's followers.

Similarly, religious terrorists have an array of different targets, which reveals important clues about their goals. Broadly speaking, religious terrorists tend to have two types of targets: tactical targets that serve specific, earthly goals and are no different from other forms of terrorism; and symbolic targets.

Tactical targets are means to a bigger, earthly campaign. For example, terrorists seeking to create a religious government target the workings of the state, including attacks on heads of state and government officials. Examples of these types of targets include the Egyptian Gamaat's assassination of Anwar Sadat in 1981 and Yigal Amir's assassination of Yitzak Rabin in 1994.[52] These types of attacks also include targeting a government's infrastructure and sources of power, such as the attack on the Alfred P. Murrah building in Oklahoma in 1995, believed to be inspired in part by the Christian Identity Movement.[53]

Religious terrorists also target the presence of foreign governments within their borders or region, including military forces, such as Israeli soldiers in the West Bank, Gaza Strip, and Golan Heights. Palestinian Islamic militants have targeted Israeli Defense Forces (IDF) as part of their aim of liberating the land from foreign occupiers. Likewise, the Lebanese Hizbollah targeted IDF soldiers occupying southern Lebanon with the aim of their expulsion.[54] Religious terrorists also targeted U.S. forces in Saudi Arabia. Bin Laden named the presence of U.S. troops on Saudi soil, the home of Islam's holiest cities, as threatening and humiliating to Islam. In 1996 and again in1998, he declared that attacks against "Satan's U.S. troops" were necessary for the protection of Muslims and for cleansing infidel forces "out of all the lands of Islam."[55] Another example of these targets is religious terrorist groups who have attacked foreign embassies, including Egyptian Islamic extremists' bombing of the Egyptian embassy in Pakistan in 1995 and Al-Qaeda's 1998 bombings of U.S. embassies in Kenya and Tanzania.

In addition to specific domestic targets, religious terrorists often have targets that extend beyond the borders of the state in which they reside. Religious terrorists have targeted third party states that support domestic regimes. For example, radical Islamic militants in Egypt named the United States as one of its targets for its support of Sadat's and Mubarak's regimes, which they saw as oppressive and un-Islamic.[56] Likewise, Islamic militants in Pakistan have named the United States as a target for its support of the Pakistani regime, which is mainly secular in its outlook and goals.[57]

These tactical targets look no different than secular, Marxist, anarchist or ethnic-separatist terrorists bent on political change or revolution.[58] For example, Anti-U.S. sentiment is strong within the non-religious Colombian FARC terrorist group, particularly for U.S. aid to the current Colombian government.[59] This sentiment could potentially translate into attacks on U.S. civilians and property.[60] Likewise, British troops in Northern Ireland have been the target of republican terrorist groups with the end-goal of expelling these forces and reuniting Northern Ireland with the Republic, which is not a uniquely religious goal.[61] What makes terrorism toward these targets ultimately religious is that they are stepping-stones to greater religious goals—the creation of a religious government.[62]

In addition to tactical targets aimed at changing regimes or compelling the withdrawal of foreign influences, religious groups also use terrorist tactics to attack individuals and groups that they believe are threatening their interpretation of the faith. For example, religious terrorists target citizens and property that represent the religious "other." Examples include attacks on Christian churches in Indonesia in December of 2000, believed to be the work of Islamic terrorists in the region, and more recent attacks on Christians in Pakistan.[63] Other examples include the Indian Hindu militant group Shiv Sena, which aims to promote Maharashtria Hindus in Mumbai and drive Muslims from India. Bal Thackeray, Shiv Sena's founder, called for the creation of Hindu suicide bombers to target Muslims in 2002 and 2008.[64] Religious terrorists can also target other groups' religious sites. Examples include the above-mentioned church bombings, and the plot by Jewish extremists in Israel to blow up the Muslim Dome of the Rock shrine in Jerusalem. These targets tend to be unique to religious terrorists and support the aim of cleansing the land of the religious "other."

These types of attacks also include intra-religious attacks on those believed to be apostates within the faith. An example of this type of targeting is *takfir* violence in Islam, where militant groups draw from religious sources to justify killing Muslims that they believe are not upholding the true practice of the faith. Al-Qaeda in Iraq, for example, has attacked Iraqi Shia, claiming that they are apostates to Islam.[65] These attacks look similar to ethnic-separatist attacks on minorities in regions they believe to be their own, but are unique in that the targets are focused on cleansing an area of perceived religious impurities.

Religious terrorists also have symbolic targets, which mostly operate on an abstract level and tend to be specific to religious goals and objectives. Most notably, religious terrorists can attempt to attack "culture," values and norms that do not conform to the religious ideals of the terrorist group. Examples of this include attacks on movie theaters, discos, bars and other social gathering points. For example, Muslim extremists set fire to a hotel in Turkey in 1993, targeting "leftist writers and intellectuals," killing over 40 people.[66] Warring fundamentalist groups in Algeria violently suppressed *Rai* music in the 1990s for its mix of Western and Mediterranean styles, including attacking and then eventually exiling the singer Khaled.[67] In India, Hindu militants have destroyed numerous paintings of Muslim artist Maqbool Fida Husain, particularly works depicting Hindu deities.[68] In the United States, Christian Identity activists bombed a lesbian bar, targeting what they perceive as symbols of the secular, immoral state.[69]

These targets are abstract because the definition of culture is largely amorphous; it is difficult if not impossible to find the source of culture and remove it fully. Therefore, unlike the state, the source of culture cannot be targeted specifically and abstract targets become the only real choice. Abstract targets, however, require a certain degree of decoding by counterterrorism forces and often the meaning and significance behind certain attacks may be missed.

Finally, apocalyptic groups aim to maximize violence and mass casualties; the goal is chaos with the hope of ushering in a new era, either in this world or the next. Aum Shinrikyo, for example, sought total destruction, which knows no bounds between domestic and international and names no specific targets. For groups such as these, the end-goal, at least on an earthly plane, is mass violence and destruction. The cataclysmic nature of apocalyptic terrorism is an additional reason why this specific type of religious terrorists needs to be considered as a distinct and unique category. Its use of violence to achieve transcendent goals is different from other forms of religious terrorism with more limited goals.[70] Table 3 summarizes religious terrorism's domestic and international targets.

Table 3   Religious Terrorism's Targets

	Specific Targets	Abstract Targets
Domestic	• Workings of the state—assassinate leaders, attacks on infrastructure, undermine authority of state	• Attacks on secular art and other cultural institutions • Attacks on secular intellectuals • Attacks on historic, other religious sites/ artifacts
International	• States that support regimes • Foreign government presence/militaries • International tourists	• "Secular" or "Western" culture • Globalization

Conclusion

This article has argued that religious terrorism has characteristics that make it uniquely different from traditional secular left-wing and right-wing terrorism, specifically in the goals for which religious terrorists are striving. Three salient religious goals were presented: the apocalyptic aim of destroying the world, the creation of a religious government, and the creation of a religiously pure state. Of these three goals, apocalyptic actions aimed at 'destroying the world to save it' are the most threatening because they suggest the use of WMD with mass casualties and damage to property. In addition to goals, religious terrorism is also differentiated by the presence of religious leaders, which do not derive their authority from one source, but rather are given legitimacy by their followers. Finally, religious terrorists tend to have two types of targets, specific and abstract. Specific, tactical targets include the state or adversarial groups; as such, they look similar to targets of left and right wing terrorists. However, religious terrorists also have symbolic targets that represent secular or other religious cultures and values, both within states and internationally, targets that are unique. Apocalyptic terrorists make no distinction between domestic and international, specific and abstract. Instead, they are concerned with the one pursuit of cataclysmic destruction.

These arguments suggest several counterterrorism measures aimed at mitigating or eradicating terrorism performed in the name of religion. All of these courses of action require a basic understanding of the group, its leadership, and the goals for which the group is fighting. Furthermore, none of these types of religiously motivated terrorism can be countered by the use of force alone.

First, apocalyptic terrorism presents unique counterterrorism challenges. Groups that believe that causing mass casualties and chaos will hasten the end of times are operating on a rationale that does not conform to earthly logic. Their acute worldview and goals suggest that they are not open to negotiation or compromise. With this in mind, a strategy of containment combined with targeting leadership is the best path to undermining these groups. Specifically, counterterrorism strategies should first focus on preventing the spread of the group's apocalyptic worldview. An important means to this end is to avoid fulfilling the group's prophecies. If the group is anticipating persecution or a fiery confrontation with the alleged 'forces of evil', a state's excessive use of force could make this dream come true. Rather than targeting the group, a better counterterrorism approach would be to understand the role that leadership plays in generating the apocalyptic worldview and, if the group is driven by one or a few key leaders, target those individuals. Research and empirical examples suggest that apocalyptic groups are highly leadership driven, especially in New Religious Movements; therefore targeting the leaders may cause the group to fall apart.[71] The goal with this approach is to change the group's worldview by taking out its propagator or, at a minimum, render the group unable to carry out its apocalyptic dreams.

Groups that use terrorism with the goal of creating a religious government have several counterterrorism options. As previously described, groups vying for the creation of a theocracy often disagree on how the state should look and who should speak for the faith. These fissures offer important opportunities for creating in-fighting within and amongst groups and weakening the overall movement. In particular, if governments can help foster a culture of debate and create public opportunities for airing groups' plans for creating a religious government, these disagreements could build. The overall goal with this strategy is to cause the movement to implode. Using force against these groups and their leaders may be counterproductive, especially if the groups have a base of support, active or passive, and the population is not supportive of the state. In these cases, force would most likely validate the group's criticisms of the state and could possibly turn popular support in the group's favour.

Groups that use terrorism bent on religiously cleansing an area within a state are best countered by treating these groups as criminals and by using law enforcement to monitor and punish their actions. This approach serves two important counterterrorism functions. First, treating these groups and their acts as criminal and illegitimate undermines their ideology and authority. Second, using law enforcement, as opposed to greater, more kinetic approaches, minimises national and international exposure of the group and makes them appear like any other criminal group, as opposed to a world-changing religious movement. In other words, deploying greater force against these groups could send a message that they are a big threat and raise awareness of their cause and seeming success. The goal, rather, is to minimise the group's publicity and de-legitimate their actions. The challenge with this approach is that states may not have the law enforcement capacity to monitor, arrest, and prevent these groups from taking action. Anti-Christian terrorism in Nigeria is a case-in-point.

Within these three types of religious terrorism, paying attention to leadership is critical. As argued, religious groups that use terrorism have leaders that are recognised as legitimate by their followers, but do not necessarily possess *bona fide qualities* such as religious education or clerical training. A useful path for undermining these religious leaders is through other religious leaders that also have legitimacy. For example, beginning in 2002, key leadership of the Egyptian Gamaat have written treaties and spoken out against Al-Qaeda's leadership and interpretations of Islam, especially Jihad.[72] One of the leaders of Egyptian Islamic Jihad, Dr. Fadl, followed suit in 2008 with his own denunciation of Al-Qaeda's ideology.[73] These debates suggest that scriptures, beliefs and tenets are open to debate and that no single leader can corner the market on truth.

Finally, it is important for counterterrorism forces to pay attention to what religious terrorists attack, because these targets offer important clues for the groups' goals, which in turn affect the type of countermeasures employed. Groups that are focused on state targets are more likely to be vying for political control, whereas targeting other groups within the faith or other religions suggest a goal of religious cleansing. Mass casualties and damage that seem indiscriminate, illogical and excessive suggest apocalyptic aims.

Just as there is more than one type of religious terrorism, there is more than one countermeasure to undermine a group's goals. Better understanding of such groups, their leadership and goals, will allow for a more nuanced approach and, hopefully, lead to greater success in undermining their message and their use of terrorism in the name of religion.

Notes

1. Jean-Francois Mayer, "Cults, Violence and Religious Terrorism," *Studies in Conflict and Terrorism,* Vol. 24 (2001), pp. 361–376. Quote taken from p. 369.

2. Bruce Hoffman, "Holy Terror: The Implications of Terrorism Motivated by a Religious Imperative," *Studies in Conflict and Terrorism,* Vol. 18, No. 4 (1995), pp. 271–284. Quote taken from p. 272.

3. Mark Sedgwick, "Al-Qaeda and the Nature of Religious Terrorism," *Terrorism and Political Violence,* Vol. 15, No. 4 (2004), pp. 795–814.

4. Laqueur claims that the term "has been used in so many different senses as to become almost meaningless, covering almost any, and not necessarily political, act of violence." See: Walter Laqueur, *The Age of Terrorism* (Boston: Little, Brown and Company, 1987), p. 11. Bruce Hoffman includes a large-n summary of 109 definitions of terrorism and the frequency of certain words used to describe the phenomenon. In addition, Hoffman notes that the U.S. government has a number of definitions of terrorism. For example, the State Department, the FBI and the Department of Defense all have different definitions of terrorism that demonstrates the disagreement on what defines the act. See: Bruce Hoffman, *Inside Terrorism* (New York: Columbia University Press, 1998), pp. 37–39.

5. Walter Laqueur, *The New Terrorism: Fanaticism and the Arms of Mass Destruction* (New York: Oxford University Press, 2000), p. 6.

6. Bruce Hoffman defines terrorism as "the deliberate creation and exploitation of fear through violence or the threat of violence in the pursuit of political change." Hoffman further lists five criteria that define terrorism: political aims and motives; violence or threat of violence; generation of fear beyond the initial act of violence; conducted by an organisation with a chain of command; and a non-state group. See: Hoffman, *Inside Terrorism,* p. 43.

7. David C. Rapoport calls this last category "anti–colonial terrorism," which he identifies as the third of four waves of terrorism. However, ethnic-separatist covers anti-colonial as well as other movements that aim to create autonomous regions, independence, or self-determination but are not under colonial rule, such as Basque Spain or the Kurds in Turkey. See: David C. Rapoport, "The Four Waves of Modern Terrorism," in Audry Kurth-Cronin and James M. Ludes (eds.), *Attacking Terrorism: Elements of a Grand Strategy,* Washington, DC, Georgetown University Press, 2004, pp. 46–73.

8. Rapoport, "The Four Waves of Modern Terrorism;" Hoffman, *Inside Terrorism,* pp. 17–18; and Laqueur, *Age of Terrorism,* p. 15. For a discussion on social and personal motivations of these different types of terrorism, see: Martha Crenshaw, "The Causes of Terrorism" *Comparative Politics,* Vol.13, No. 4 (July 1981), pp. 379–399.

9. For a further discussion on these groups, see: Rapoport, "The Four Waves of Modern Terrorism," Laqueur, *The New Terrorism,* pp. 24–32; and Hoffman, *Inside Terrorism,* pp. 80–84. See also: Marco Rimanelli, "Italian terrorism and society, 1940s–1980s: Roots, ideologies, evolution, and international connections," *Studies in Conflict and Terrorism,* Vol. 12, No. 4, (1989), pp. 249–296.

10. Laqueur, *The New Terrorism,* p. 80; Rapoport, "The Four Waves of Modern Terrorism." See also Alison Jamieson. "Identity and Morality in the Italian Red Brigades," *Terrorism and Political Violence,* Vol. 2, No. 4 (Dec 2007), pp. 508–520.

11. It is interesting to note that Orsini argues that Marxist-based terrorists, including particularly the Italian Red Brigades, had eschatological goals that made it not unlike a religion

and, therefore, their acts could be understood as religiously motivated terrorism. See: Alessandro Orsini, *Anatomy of the Red Brigades: The Religious Mindset of Modern Terrorists* (Ithaca: Cornell University Press, 2011).

12. Laqueur, *Age of Terrorism*, p. 14; and Laqueur, *The New Terrorism*, p. 22, respectively.

13. For a further discussion on right-wing terrorism, see: Laqueur, *The New Terrorism*, chapter 5: "Terrorism and the Far Right," pp. 105–126.

14. Bruce Hoffman, *Recent Trends and Future Prospects of Terrorism in the United States* (Santa Monica: RAND Corporation, 1988); Laqueur, *The New Terrorism*, p. 31.

15. Laqueur's term. He also calls this sub-category "nationalist extremist" and "nationalism and separatism terrorism," *The New Terrorism*, p. 127; and *The Age of Terrorism*, chapter 6, respectively. Hoffman calls this sub-category "Ethno-Nationalist Separatist Terrorism," *Inside Terrorism*, p. 85.

16. For more details on the IRA, see: Mark Juergensmeyer, *Terror in the Mind of God: The Global Rise of Religious Violence* (Berkeley: University of California Press, 2003), pp. 36–43. For a discussion on the Irgun, see: Hoffman, *Inside Terrorism*, pp. 48–56. For more details on the PLO, see: Hoffman, *Inside Terrorism*, pp. 69–75.

17. For further details on these groups, see: Laqueur, *The New Terrorism*, pp. 32–36.

18. Laqueur, *The New Terrorism*, p. 148.

19. Shaul Mishal and Avraham Sela, *The Palestinian Hamas: Vision, Violence and Coexistence* (New York: Columbia University Press, 2000).

20. David Tucker, "What Is New About the New Terrorism and How Dangerous Is It?" *Terrorism and Political Violence*, Vol. 13, No. 3 (2001), pp. 1–14, especially p. 8.

21. Mark Juergensmeyer, "Understanding the New Terrorism," *Current History*, Vol. 99, No. 636 (2000), pp. 158–163. See also, Mark Juergensmeyer, *Terror in the Mind of God*.

22. Hoffman, *Inside Terrorism*, p. 88.

23. Laqueur, *The New Terrorism*, pp. 127, 148.

24. David C. Rapoport, "Sacred Terror: A Contemporary Example from Islam," in Walter Reich (ed.), *Origins of Terrorism: Psychologies, Ideologies, Theologies, States of Mind* (Baltimore: Johns Hopkins University Press, 1990), pp. 103–130.

25. Sedgewick, p. 795.

26. David C. Rapoport, "Why Does Religious Messianism Produce Terror?" in Paul Wilkinson and Alasdair M. Stewart (eds.), *Contemporary Research on Terrorism* (Aberdeen: Aberdeen University Press, 1987).

27. Mayer, pp. 361–376.

28. Juergensmeyer, quoting a term from Ehud Sprinzak, *Terror in the Mind of God*, p. 54; Hoffman, *Inside Terrorism*, pp. 100–105; and Hoffman, "Holy Terror," p. 278.

29. For more details on Aum Shinrikyo, see: Juergensmeyer, chapter 6: "Armageddon in a Tokyo Subway," *Terror in the Mind of God*, pp. 102–111; Hoffman, *Inside Terrorism*, pp. 121–127; and Ian Reader, *A Poisonous Cocktail? Aum Shinrikyo's Path to Violence* (Copenhagen: NIAS Books, 1996). See also: Robert Jay Lifton, *Destroying the World to Save It: Aum Shinrikyo, Apocalyptic Violence and the New Global Terrorism* (New York: Henry Holt and Co., 1999); Angus M. Muir, "Terrorism and Weapons of Mass Destruction: The Case of Aum Shinrikyo," *Studies in Conflict and Terrorism*, Vol. 22, No. 1 (1991), pp. 79–91; David E. Kaplan and Andrew Marshall, *The Cult at the End of the World: The Incredible Story of Aum* (London: Hutchinson, 1996); D. W. Brackett, *Holy Terror: Armageddon in Tokyo* (New York: Weatherhill, 1996); Gavin Cameron, "*Multi-track Microproliferation: Lessons from Aum Shinrikyo and Al Qaida*," *Studies in Conflict and Terrorism*, Vol. 22, No. 4, (1999), pp. 277–309; William Rosenau, "Aum Shinrikyo's Biological Weapons Program: Why Did it Fail?," *Studies in Conflict and Terrorism*," Vol. 24, No. 4, (2001), pp. 289–301; Ian Reader, "Spectres and Shadows: Aum Shinrikyo and the Road to Megiddo," *Terrorism and Political Violence*, Vol. 14, No.1, (2002), pp. 145–186.

30. Laqueur includes these cults in his list of millennialist terrorists, noting that not all millennialists are violent. However he does not offer an explanation for why some of these groups turn violent and others do not. More work needs to be done on apocalyptic groups to understand why some turn their destruction inward, and why some turn their destruction outward to the world around them. See: Lacqueur, *The New Terrorism*, pp. 83–88. For more on apocalyptic and violent cults, see: Lorne L. Dawson, *Comprehending Cults: The Sociology of New Religious Movements* (Oxford: Oxford University Press, 1998); Philip Jenkins, *Mystics and Messiahs: Cults and New Religions in American History* (New York: Oxford University Press, 2000); Lorne L. Dawson, "The Study of New Religious Movements and the Radicalization of Home Grown Terrorists: Opening a Dialogue," *Terrorism and Political Violence*, Vol. 22, No. 1 (2009), pp. 1–21.

31. Dick J. Reavis, *The Ashes of Waco: An Investigation* (New York: Simon and Schuster, 1995), p. 13; Michael Barkun, "Appropriated Martyrs: The Branch Davidians and the Radical Right," *Terrorism and Political Violence*, Vol. 19, No. 1 (2007), pp. 117–124; and Jayne Seminare Docherty, *Learning Lessons from Waco: When the Parties Bring Their Gods to the Negotiating Table*, (Syracuse: Syracuse University Press, 2001).

32. Mayer, pp. 362–363.

33. Islam is divided between two major branches, the Sunni (the majority) and the Shia. There are further subdivisions within each of these branches, including the Twelver and Ismaili Shias. For more details on the Hizbollah, see: Magnus Ranstorp, *Hizb'allah in Lebanon: The Politics of the Western Hostage Crisis* (London: St. Martin's Press, 1997); for Hamas, see Mishal and Sela.

34. For more details, see Juergensmeyer, pp. 27–35, *Terror in the Mind of God*. See also Bruce Hoffman, *Recent Trends and Future Prospects of Terrorism in the United States* (Santa

Monica, RAND, 1988), chapter four: "The Increase in Terrorist Activity of Other Groups: Right-Wing Terrorism," pp. 25–41.

35. Ranstorp, p. 36; and Hilal Khashan, "The New World Order and the Tempo of Militant Islam," *British Journal of Middle Eastern Studies,* Vol. 24, No. 1 (1997), pp. 5–24, especially p. 15.

36. Kach and other Kahane-inspired groups were designated "foreign terrorists" by the U.S. State Department in 1997, making U.S. domestic fund-raising for the groups illegal. However, these groups continue to raise money, especially for the Kahane Memorial Fund, which supports the cleansing of Arabs from what is believed to be Israeli land. See: Steven Erlanger, "US Labels 30 Groups as Terrorists: Omits IRA," *New York Times,* October 9, 1997; and Dean E. Murphy, "Terror Label No Hindrance to Anti-Arab Jewish Group," *New York Times,* December 19, 2000, respectively.

37. Two further hypotheses on Iranian and Saudi funding of these groups deserve mention. First, Khashan argues that Iranian funding was more an attempt of Iran to assert itself in regional politics, and in particular to counter U.S. containment, than to spread the revolution abroad. This explains why Iran funded Shias and Sunnis alike. See: Khashan, pp. 15–16. Gilles Kepel argues that Iran and Saudi Arabia have been embroiled in a form of religious spiraling, trying to counter each other's influence by both funding the same radical Islamic groups, preventing one or the other's ideology from taking hold. See: Gilles Kepel, *Jihad: The Trail of Political Islam,* translated by Anthony F. Roberts, (Cambridge: Harvard University Press, 2002), pp. 5–6. This latter hypothesis is also argued by Guilain Denoeux, "The Forgotten Swamp: Navigating Political Islam," *Middle East Policy,* Vol. 9, No. 2 (June 2002), pp. 56–81.

38. Juergensmeyer, *Terror in the Mind of God,* pp. 53–54.

39. Ranstorp, pp. 27–30.

40. *Messages to the World: The Statements of Osama Bin Laden,* (ed.) Bruce Lawrence (New York: Verso Press, 2005), p. 121.

41. Elana Pavlova, "From a Counter Society to a Counter-State Movement: Jemaah Islamiyah According to PUPJI," *Studies in Conflict and Terrorism,* Vol. 30, No. 9 (2007), pp. 777–800, especially, p. 783.

42. It is important to note that the Brotherhood engaged in violent and terrorist activities in the early years of the movement in Egypt, including the assassination of a judge and an assassination attempt on President Nasser. The movement also acknowledges that violent movements, such as Hamas, Egyptian Islamic Jihad, and the Islamic Group, have emerged from within the ranks of the Brotherhood. See Sana Abed-Kotob, "The Accommodationists Speak: Goals and Strategies of the Muslim Brotherhood in Egypt," *International Journal of Middle East Studies,* Vol. 27 (1995), pp. 321–339; and Yvonne Y. Haddad, "Sayyid Qutb: Ideologue of Islamic Revival," in John E. Esposito (ed.), *Voices of Resurgent Islam* (Oxford: Oxford University Press, 1983), pp. 67–99.

43. Timothy R. Furnish, "The Man Who Would Be Mahdi," *Middle East Quarterly,* Vol. 9, No. 2 (2002), pp. 53–59.

44. Regarding the Muslim Brotherhood, see: Daniel L. Byman and Tamara Cofman Wittes, "Muslim Brotherhood Radicalizes," *The Brookings Institution,* January 23, 2014, http://www. brookings.edu/research/papers/2014/01/muslim-brotherhood-radicalizes-byman-wittes, downloaded on February 1, 2014. Hizb-ut-Tahrir has been banned throughout Central Asia over concerns that it is inciting violence and instability in this region, see: "Radical Islam in Central Asia: Responding to Hizb-ut-Tahrir, *International Crisis Group,* Asia Report No. 58, June 30, 2013, http://www.crisisgroup.org/en/regions/asia/central-asia/058-radical-islam-in-central-asia-responding-to-hizb-ut-tahrir.aspx, as of February 1,2014.

45. David Little, *Sri Lanka: The Invention of Enmity* (Washington, DC: US Institute of Peace, 1994); Stanley Tambiah, *Buddhism Betrayed? Religion, Politics and Violence in Sri Lanka* (Chicago: University of Chicago Press, 1992).

46. Juergensmeyer, *Terror in the Mind of God,* pp. 46–48; and Hoffman, *Inside Terrorism,* pp. 104–105.

47. Hoffman, "Holy Terror," p. 275.

48. Juergensmeyer, *Terror in the Mind of God,* p. 55.

49. Raphael Mergui and Philippe Simonnot, *Israel's Ayatollah: Meir Kahane and the Far Right in Israel* (Worchester: Saqi Books, 1987), pp. 29–37. Quote taken from pp. 30–31.

50. Reader, pp. 18–23; Hoffman, *Inside Terrorism,* pp. 120–123; Juergensmeyer, *Terror in the Mind of God,* pp. 107, 114–116.

51. Bin Laden holds a degree in business administration, but has no formal clerical training. However, it is worth noting that Islamic Studies is compulsory in Saudi Arabian Universities. See: "A Biography of Osama Bin Laden," *Frontline,* www.pbs.org, downloaded on 6/27/02.

52. For a detailed account of Sadat's assassination, see: Gilles Kepel, *The Pharaoh and the Prophet,* translated by Jon Rothschild, (London: Al Saqi Books, 1985). For details on Rabin's assassination, see: Juergensmeyer, *Terror in the Mind of God,* pp. 46–48; and Hoffman, *Inside Terrorism,* pp. 104–105.

53. Hoffman, *Inside Terrorism,* pp. 105–130.

54. Ranstorp, pp. 53–55. IDF forces withdrew from the "security zone" in southern Lebanon in May of 2000, but have remained in the disputed Shebba Farms area.

55. "World Islamic Front Statement," February 23, 1998, www.fas .org, downloaded on 6/27/02. The1996 statement by Osama Bin Laden, quoted by Kepel, *Jihad,* p. 13.

56. John L. Esposito, *The Islamic Threat: Myth or Reality* (Oxford: Oxford University Press, 1992), pp. 93–97.

57. This is one of the believed goals of the April 2002 attack on a Protestant church in Pakistan, see: Paul Watson, "Bomber Died in Church Blast, Pakistini Authorities Conclude," *Los Angeles Times,* March 30, 2002.

58. Sedgwick refers to these acts of terrorism within religious groups as immediate, and "almost purely political," p. 795.

59. See, for example, Rafael Pardo, "Columbia's Two Front War," *Foreign Affairs* (July/August 2000), pp. 64–70.

60. The FARC has been named as the only non-Islamic terrorist group with both capabilities and motivation to target the United States, see: "Coding Terrorist Groups, *Project Air Force Counter Terrorism Threat Team* (Santa Monica: RAND, May, 2002 briefing).

61. Juergensmeyer, *Terror in the Mind of God,* pp. 36–43.

62. This observation mirrors Mark Sedgewick's argument. See: Sedgewick, pp. 789–814.

63. "Indonesian Leader Condemns Church Bombings that Killed 15," *New York Times,* December 26, 2000; and Alissa J. Robin, "Church Killings Deal New Blow to Pakistan Chief," *Los Angeles Times,* October 29, 2001, respectively.

64. BBC News, "Bal Thackeray: Hindu Leader and Shiv Sena Founder, Dies," *BBC News,* November 17, 2012, http://www.bbc.co.uk/news/world-asia-india-20376653, downloaded 1/8/13.

65. Mohammed M. Hafez, *Suicide Bombers in Iraq: The Strategy and Ideology of Martyrdom* (Washington, DC: US Institute of Peace, 2007), p. 70.

66. "News Summary," *New York Times,* July 3, 1993.

67. Jon Pareles, "Lively Exports From Algeria and Egypt," *New York Times,* February 12, 2002.

68. Somini Sengupta, "A Muslim Artist and Hindu Images: It's a Volatile Mix," *New York Times,* June 16, 1998.

69. Hoffman, *Inside Terrorism,* p. 30.

70. Tucker, p. 4.

71. Empirical examples include Aum Shinrikyo, Branch Davidians, and The People's Temple. See: Robert S. Robins and Jerrold M. Post, Chapter 5: "From the Individual to the Collective Apocalypse," *Political Paranoia: The Psychopolitics of Hatred* (New Haven: Yale University Press, 1997), pp. 113–140.

72. Heather S. Gregg, "Fighting Cosmic Warriors: Lessons Learned from the First Seven Years in the Global War on Terror,"

Studies in Conflict and Terrorism, Vol. 32 (2009), pp. 188–208, especially p. 204.

73. Lawrence Right, "The Rebellion Within: An Al-Qaeda Mastermind Questions Terrorism," *New Yorker,* June 2, 2008.

Critical Thinking

1. What is the difference between secular and religious terrorism?

2. Are the three main goals sought by religious terrorism attainable?

3. How can states best respond to religious terrorism?

Internet References

Contrasting Secular and Religious Terrorism
www.meforum.org/1826/contrasting-secular-and-religious-terrorism

MONTREP
http://www.miis.edu/academics/researchcenters/terrorism/about/Terrorism_Definition

FBI
http://www.fbi.gov/about-us/investigate/terrorism/terrorism-definition

Palestine-Israel Journal
http://www.pij.org/details.php?id=80

HEATHER S. GREGG is an Associate Professor at the Naval Post-graduate School's Department of Defense Analysis, where she works primarily with Special Operations Forces. Prior to joining NPS, she was an associate political scientist at the RAND Corporation. She is the author of the 'The Path to Salvation: From the Crusades to Jihad' (Potomac 2014) and is co-editor of 'The Three Circles of War: Understanding the Dynamics of Conflict in Iraq' (Potomac 2010).

Article   Prepared by: Thomas J. Badey, *Randolph-Macon College*

Sociological Understanding of the Relationship between Terrorism and Religion

HÜSEYIN CINOĞLU

Learning Outcomes

After reading this article, you will be able to:

- Describe how religion is used to legitimize violence.

- Explain the difference between the functionalist and the conflict theory approach.

- Discuss how religion frees terrorists from having to appeal to a larger constituency.

Introduction

Sociology is one of the rare disciplines that offer effective analytical and theoretical tools to investigate, analyze and interpret events in individuals' social life. It not only offers vast venues to its students to better grasp the realities around them, but at the same time sociology presents alternative windows for them to observe them. Usually each of those windows enables one to focus on particular aspects of the social phenomenon at hand. This characteristic of sociology should not be taken as its weakness at all. As a matter of fact it is that characteristic of sociology that makes it a powerful tool, because after healthy application of its theoretical perspectives one can easily see social realities in their purest form.

As a matter of fact, one of the major goals of this article is to explore ways to apply pure sociology to terrorism, especially to the type claiming to act either on behalf of or to protect religion (Islam). There is a current trend in the literature to define this type of terrorist groups as "terrorist organizations exploiting (the teachings of) religion". Throughout the article this definition will be utilized.

In this article the author conducts an extensive literature review to investigate how social sciences in general and sociology in particular see terrorism exploiting religion. A special reference has been given to classical sociological perspectives to better understand the interrelatedness among individuals, social structures, religion, and terrorism.

Significance of Study: Importance of Theoretical Applications

Theories are necessary components for us to systematically observe, interpret, give meanings and/or revisit, reinterpret and scientifically understand the events that are happening in our lives. Unfortunately, especially after September 11, 2001 incidents, terrorism became an inseparable part of people's lives all over the world. It is the researcher's personal opinion that when struggling to better understand why some people could ever commit such acts indiscriminately, scholars and practitioners need to go beyond commonsense, personal beliefs and biases, and should turn to theoretical/scientific ways to understand terrorism. It is especially imperative for practitioners to comply with this rule since they also have the responsibility of changing the policies to offer better living standards to the people whom they are supposed to serve. Therefore, this paper is dedicated to explore terrorism exploiting religion from a more theoretical perspective.

Theory and Terrorism

According to Akers (2000, pg. 1) theories are about and related to real life situations, such as our behavioral preferences on a matter and our experiences with other individuals and institutions. Akers (2000) also divides theories into two general categories. As to the first group, he specifically talks about the theories that explain or deal with the making and/or enforcing of criminal law. Apparently, the ones that are placed in this group tend to deal with the deterrence strategies, and also the process of forming legal measures against criminals. To him (Akers, 2000), the other group of theories tend to assume more theoretical and abstract perspectives on crime, which he calls (2000, pg. 4) "theories of criminal and deviant behaviors". In this part he compiles the theories elaborating on why some people commit crimes while others in similar social, economic, political and environmental situations do not. And as Ronald

Beiner (1997) points out "The point of theory isn't to think safe thoughts, but dangerous thoughts". To that end, terrorism has become something that people in modern times increasingly encounter either directly by being victimized or indirectly by being exposed to its aftershocks through the media.

Having known the impossibility of creating the best and ultimate theory for terrorism, reinterpreting or reshaping the existing ones became a venture for many scholars. Actually, it is because of that we have a trend in criminology and sociology to create new theories or redesign contemporary ones to deal with terrorism. We clearly see this trend in political theories to understand crime, in some theories related to religion, in globalization theories, some sociological and criminological theories and also theories trying to explain the occurrence of any types of crime from an economical perspective.

So far, the nature of the relationship between terrorism and sociology was scrutinized. However, the relationship between sociology and religious terrorism is still vague or needs some improvements. This part of the paper will elaborate on the relationship between religion and sociology, and the part following that will specifically be dedicated to religious terrorism and its sociological interpretation.

Major Sociological Perspectives and Religion

No religion or at least no major religions favor or encourage armed struggle and violence as the first and final resort. On the other hand, this does not necessarily mean that religions in essence are opposed to the using of violence at all. The nature of the relationship between the two has already been scrutinized by sociology.

A) Functionalism and Religion

According to functionalism, religion is a social institution with specific and crucial tasks in the survival of the society. Most functionalists do not question religion as to why people created or have it, but they tend to focus more on the functions of the religion. According to them, religion is pivotal in the preservation of status quo and preventing rapid social changes and movements. As was mentioned before, rapid changes come as a shock to society, and like other living organisms, it may not survive afterwards. Therefore, religion functions in a way to ensure, support, and encourage evolution over revolutions (Durkheim, 1933).

B) Conflict Theory and Religion

Unlike functionalists, with their variations, conflict theory followers tend to see religion as a tool that was not only utilized by the powerful in their efforts of exploiting workers, but also religion is created by them. These thinkers assert that, owners of the means of production (members of bourgeoisie class) created religion as a mechanism to keep workers (proletariat) under constant supervision and control. As compensations for the sufferings of this world, religion offers or promises wealth and happiness in the hereafter. That's why Marx (1844) identifies religion as the "opiate of the masses". To him, religion gives a false happiness and a notion of comfort which deflects workers' attention from their real condition (being exploited by the rich) to an uncertain future promise of happiness.

C) Symbolic Interactionism and Terrorism

On the other hand, symbolic interactionist theory mostly endeavors to develop an analytic understanding of religion with a relatively more micro level perspective than the first two theories (functionalist and conflict theories). The literature suggested that creation of social networks is fundamental in the creation of meaning systems by the individual. Those meaning systems are essential parts of individuals' identity, and his or her place in the group or in the society. In short, religion becomes a symbol and a meaning system that is possessed by a group, which is also imposed on newcomers. After adopting the meaning system of that particular group, and choosing that group as the symbolic network, that group takes on the role of the reference group for that individual. On the other hand, maintaining the membership becomes dependent upon future obedience to the norms of the group and cherishing their values (Wimberley, 1998).

As could be seen from the above explanations, each sociological tradition has different views on religion. They do have weaknesses and strengths over others. For example, functionalists are very effective in identifying and analyzing the functions of religions in maintaining a healthy society and in supporting evolution; while on the other hand, they might easily be characterized as ineffective in seeing the religion's role in generating conflict in the society. And conflict theory might be competent in identifying the conflict directly or indirectly generated by religion; while on the other hand, they might not draw our attention to some of its major latent and manifest functions. Those functions are essential in maintaining the order and equilibrium. Symbolic Interactionism mostly deals with individual level attributes of religion, and its power of reshaping the self through the symbolic networks that it offers to individuals. The main concern of this perspective is not to explain and reveal the functions of religion in maintaining the equilibrium or as the generator of conflict, but they place considerable amounts of importance over its role in the self identity formation through symbolic meanings, values and networks. In sum, these three perspectives separately provide the reader with diverse and rich perspectives that are very helpful in the analyses of the religion as a phenomenon. However, conciliation and combination of the three and presenting a single sociological examination about the relationship is still a hefty and unlikely task.

Religion and Terrorism

The relationship between religion and terrorism became more evident with the attacks of September 11, 2001. Although it may be seen as a new phenomenon, in reality religious terrorism is centuries old. However, the intensity of the attacks and increase in the numbers of religiously motivated terrorist groups is a new development. Rapoport (1984) states that the relationship between religion and terrorism is three tiered. Until the nineteenth century, religion was almost like the only motivational force that terrorists used to draw inspirations from. From the nineteenth century to the 1960s, the majority of the terrorist groups were secular in nature. In other words, they were not using religion as their justifying and legitimating source. The majority of them had ethnic, nationalistic, political, separatist, etc. agendas. And from the 1960s to our day, the world witnessed, and is still witnessing in a sense, the reemergence of strong ties between religion and terrorism.

Hoffman (1998) gives a detailed analysis of the nature of the relationship between them. To him, sociological analysis of the existing relationship between religion and terrorism needs to center on four basic factors.

A) Religion as Key Legitimating Force for Violence

Due to its creation of "us vs. them" (infidels, dogs, mud people, etc), religious imperatives have the potential to lead more violent actions. Religion offers its followers a unique value system with the power to legitimize and justify the approved acts. Terrorist groups' interpretation of these value systems dramatically differ from the mainstream. Most of the time, even at the risk of being expelled as outcasts, they choose to deviate from the fundamental teachings of their religions. This is especially the case for Islamic terrorist groups. One of Islam's uniquenesses comes from its involvement with almost every aspect of human life. Islam as a monotheistic religion has a predetermined view on human life. According to Islam, the life (human or animal) is sacred, and taking of one innocent human life is equal to killing of the whole humankind. Therefore, the Islam that the groups refer to needs to be different than the Islam the mainstream refers to.

Additionally, the nature of the acts of terrorism requires determined and dedicated individuals who are willing to commit the types of acts that the group wants. Those individuals will need a very strong reinforcement in order to continue acting towards the group's goals. Religion comes in handy as an external, independent, powerful, respected, and unquestionable source for energy. The terrorist groups use/abuse the power of Islam through their differing interpretations in a way to promote violence as the only means to achieve religious ends which, under normal circumstances, are to be achieved through legitimate means.

That is why new recruits undergo intense training sessions where they are also exposed to new interpretations of religious values, norms, goals, means, etc. This is very evident in Turkish Hizbullah, as was mentioned in their propaganda book (Bagasi, 2004), new recruits are indoctrinated and rescued from the insufficient/mislead and passive interpretations of Islam during those training sessions. The group does not limit education only to new recruits. Turkish Hizbullah is known for its emphasis on continuing education through the pamphlets, books, and other training materials that the group prepared.

B) Religion as the Cure to Alienation

Due to their dramatically different radical perspectives of the world, the members of terrorist groups inevitably feel a strong sense of alienation. According to Durkheim (1897), alienation is the sense of powerlessness, isolation, normlessness, and feeling a gradual estrangement from the mainstream. In this state, alienated individuals relatively feel as if they do not need the whole society to sustain their existence. Therefore, they may choose not to conform to the norms, and might prefer to rebel. For terrorists, the major source for alienation comes from the very belief system that they possess and the action system as well. Most terrorist groups' members, either to solidify their membership or to become a full-fledged member, are required or even forced to participate in terrorist acts. Cinoğlu (2008) sees this stage as the probable ultimate turning point for individuals, and also he identifies it as the major source for alienation.

However, terrorist groups' perspective of alienation is somewhat different than the one mentioned above. According to them, their deeds and ideology are not the source of alienation, on the contrary, they are the cure for alienation. These groups tend to believe that alienation is functional since it wakes up people from the daily routines and channels them towards alternative ways to deal with their lives. Using alternative ways for explanations, individuals will have the chance to observe the exploitative nature of society over them, and they will also be able identify that it is that exploitative characteristic of the society that creates alienation. Therefore, terrorist groups become the cure, rather than being the cause of alienation. This becomes evident when we consider their goals, the majority of which center around changing or protesting the status quo (Koseli, 2006).

The hands of religious terrorist groups are stronger here. Because, they believe they have a divine institution (no human influence, comes directly from God) that supports their arguments (Seligman & Katz, 1996). As a matter of fact, no religion in the world sees violence as the first resort in their quest to deal with others, even invaders. Islam has strict rules about the use of armed measures even in wars. For instance all children, non-combatant civilians, plants, animals cannot be seen as legitimate targets under any circumstances (Aktan, 2004). However, Islamic terrorist groups tend to have their own versions of interpretation of religious texts, and through long indoctrination processes, their members believe that those interpretations are the true ones, and the previous ones were blended in by enemies of Islam. Actually, that is one of the reasons why they do not hesitate to target and kill fellow Muslims or even respected Muslim religious leaders, since they see those people as helpers of infidels (others, out-group).

In short, newer interpretations of religion by terrorist groups are seen as sources for cure to alienation not only for the members, but also for all the people who feel alienated from the society.

C) Religion Sets Free the Group from the Need to Appeal to Larger Constituents

Organizations use those constituents to gain new members who are vital in the group's survival and transferring the cause, values, and norms to future generations. In other words, for terrorist organizations, they serve as the pool from which new recruits are drawn, therefore the numbers of sympathizers (candidates who are sympathetic to the group's activities and its perspective) are fundamentally important. In short, for their survival and to be able to maintain their vitality, groups need their own constituents to appeal (Hoffman, 1998). The majority of terrorist groups are no exception to that. However, the religiously motivated terrorist groups deviate from that, widely due to their inner dynamics and general agenda. Most Islamic terrorist organizations believe that trying to only please people and seek their approval are very close to the acts of blasphemy and a major disrespect to God's might. To them, it is God whose sanction is needed to be sought. In their version of Islam, God specifies the goals for not only organized members such as their fellow group members, but also for every Muslim. So it is the job of every Muslim to fulfill those tasks. Therefore, their main duty is not to appeal to those bystanders, but to have them realize that God's will was hidden from them for centuries and make them actively involved in their struggle.

The statements above make Islamic terrorist groups relatively free of the feeling to appeal to larger constituents, since it is God who will protect their movements, not the people. This is not the case for secular terrorist groups. Most of them believe that their survival is radically dependent upon the flow of new members. This sole fact forces them to create a separate group of people in the society. As will be explained below, other than the "us and them", they also believe that there are others in the society, who are in between or outside of the prior two categories. Secular terrorist organizations see others as potential groups from which they could draw new recruits. That's why appealing to others becomes one of the most essential parts of their activities.

D) Religion as Helper in Target Selection

One of the unexpected consequences of religious involvement in terrorism is that it saves the organizations from spending energy/time to distinguish groups or people among larger crowds as their legitimate targets. Therefore, every group regardless of their religion (they might be fellow Muslims as well) becomes a legitimate target due to the justifying reasons mentioned above.

One of the major differences between secular terrorist groups and religious terrorist groups comes from their classification of the society (Pape, 2003). According to secular terrorist groups, society is comprised of three distinct groups: us, them, and others. Us represents the in-group members, while them represents the total opposite or the group that conflicts with in-group members. Others are the people who do not want to be a part of the conflict, and choose not to support any one of the sides, and choose not to align themselves with any one of the groups. The majority of the secular terrorist groups do not see others as threats and do not target them unless it is strategically imperative to their cause.

However, religiously motivated terrorist groups, especially Islamic terrorist groups do not have three-layered approach to the society. They tend to believe that the society is made up of two groups of people: us and them. And they do not believe it as "us and them", however, "us vs. them" approach would explain their view of society more illustratively. They tend to believe that there is a cosmic war going on for centuries and everybody is a part of it, will be a part of it in the future, or could be considered a part of it. Their interpretation of religion (Islam for Islamic terrorist groups), would allow them to make that distinction and will also provide legitimization and justification for the deeds that will be committed, and also will provide a cure for alienation.

That would not be unfair to present this as one of the major reasons for higher numbers of fatality and indiscriminate targeting practices of religious terrorism. For instance, to Turkish Hizbullah, the meaning of killing someone is reduced down to a justified means to achieve God's will which was long overdue. According to Bagasi (2004), even if the armed struggle is still the last resort, when it is employed, innocent ones who are killed are considered as casualties of Jihad (holy war) and they automatically are considered as martyrs, while on the other hand, the ones that are not innocent (enemies of God, members of Hizbusseytan [party of Satan]) are the ones who received and will also continue to receive God's fair punishment in the hereafter. Therefore, in the end, terrorist acts are not hurting people because it enables innocents to go to heaven. In other words, Turkish Hizbullah is actually not to be blamed for killing indiscriminately, because if the victims are innocent, they might lose their chances of living the remainders of their lives, but when compared to an eternal life in heaven, this loss becomes a very insignificant sacrifice that majority is supposed to make willingly (Bagasi, 2004). And by punishing the members of Hizbusseytan, they also get to be the hand of God in this world, which pretty much makes them Hizbullah (party of God, individuals who are on the path of God). They see themselves as the awakened subjects of God since they know what God truly wants, and in what manner.

Conclusion

First, sociology acknowledges the importance of religion on individuals' daily social life. Its impact becomes more evident especially when an individual faces a phenomenon that he or she cannot explain but strives to understand, or suffers from something that he or she cannot stop. At that juncture, religion becomes one of the most powerful agents that could offer meaningful arguments or suggest patience for an unearthly reward for the current sufferings. Unfortunately it is that very potential of religion that makes it the energy and motivational source for some terror groups. Terrorist groups also need individuals who are committed to serve and foster the group that they are a part of, even at the expense of themselves. Those direly needed committed individuals come with a price, and offerings of religion become practical and cost-effective charges to pay. However, as stated above, no major religion suggests violence as a first resort. This constitutes the major challenge for terrorist groups. Those organizations find ways to revisit, reread and reinterpret the teachings and create themselves sanctuaries within religion (Islam).

Second, this article also evaluated the historical trend in terrorism where we witness a surge in the number of religiously motivated terrorist groups, especially Islamic ones. Religiously motivated terrorist organizations tend to differ dramatically from the more secular groups in many major ways. Target selection practices, the sources for motivational and justification factors, and the perspectives on the society as a whole constitute the most significant differences. Those differences are sufficient to explain the increase in the number of fatalities when actually the number of incidents is in decline throughout the world.

Third, according to the literature review, it became evident that sociology has many arguments and comments to make about terrorism exploiting religion. However, it also became clear that many analyses on terrorism noticeably lack theoretical background. Therefore, this area might be considered fertile for scholars and experts with sociology background.

References

Akers, R. (2000). *Criminological Theories: Introduction, Evaluation, and Application.* Los Angeles: Roxbury.

Aktan, H. (2004). An Islamic perspective: Terror and suicide attacks. In Ergun Capan (Ed.), *Acts of terror and suicide attacks in the light of the Qur'an and the Sunna.* (pp. 27–40). New Jersey, USA: Light Publication.

Bagasi, I. (2004). Kendi Dilinden Hizbullah ve Mücadele Tarihinden Önemli Kesitler. Turkey: Unknown Publisher.

Cinoğlu, H. (1998). *An Analysis of Established Terrorist Identitiy in Political and Military Wings of Turkish Hizbullah.* Unpublished dissertation. University of North Texas, Texas, USA. (Chair David. A. Williamson)

Durkheim E. (1897). *Suicide.* The Free Press reprint in 1997.

Durkheim, E. (1933). *The Division of Labor in Society.* (Translated by George Simpson). New York: The Free Press.

Hoffman, B. (1998). *Inside terrorism.* New York: Columbia University Press.

Koseli, M. (2006). *Poverty, inequality and terrorism in Turkey.* Unpublished Doctoral Dissertation. Virginia Commonwealth University. Richmond, Virginia, USA.

Marx, K. (1844). *A Contribution to the Critique of Hegel's Philosophy of Right.* Germany: Deutsch-Französische Jahrbücher.

Pape, R. A., (2003). The strategic logic of suicide terrorism. *The American Political Science Review, 97,* 343–361.

Rapoport, D. C. (1984). Fear and trembling: Terrorism in three religious traditions. *The American Political Science Review,* 78(3): 658–677.

Ronald Beiner (1997). *Philosophy in a Time of Lost Spirit: Essays on Contemporary Theory.* Canada: University of Toronto Press.

Seligman, C. & Katz, A. N. (1996). The dynamics of value systems. In C. Seligman, J. M. Olson & M. P. Zanna (Eds.), *The psychology of values: The Ontario symposium* (vol. 8). Hillsdale, NJ: Erlbaum.

Wimberley, R. C. (1998). *Encyclopedia of religion and society.* In William H. Swatos, Jr (Ed.), *Commitment.* Lanham, MD: AltaMira Press.

Critical Thinking

1. How has religion been used as a cure for social alienation?
2. What impact does religion have on target selection?
3. How are religious ideologies different from other ideologies used by terrorist?

Create Central

www.mhhe.com/createcentral

Internet References

Does Religion Cause Terrorism? It's Complicated
www.huffingtonpost.com/2011/08/31/religion-terrorism_n_944143.html
"www.cfr.org/weapons-of-mass-destruction/preventing-catastrophic-nuclear-terrorism/p10067"

Contrasting Secular and Religious Terrorism
www.meforum.org/1826/contrasting-secular-and-religious-terrorism

Terrorists Often Manipulate a Religion's Base to Push Their Ways
www.theledger.com/article/20121217/EDIT02/121219339

DR. HÜSEYIN CINOĞLU is a lecturer at the Turkish National Police Academy, International Center for Terrorism and Transnational Crime (UTSAM), hcinoglu@pa.edu.tr

Article   Prepared by: Thomas J. Badey, *Randolph-Macon College*

Hinduism and Terror

PAUL MARSHALL

Learning Outcomes

After reading this article, you will be able to:

- Identify the goals of Hindu Extremists.
- Explain the problems that extremism can create in Asia.
- Discuss the mistreatment and abuse of minorities in India.

Since September 11, 2001, the world's attention has properly been focused on the violence of Islamic extremism, but there are also major violent trends in Hindu extremism that have largely been ignored in the United States. In India, this violence is supported by Hindu extremists and their allies in the Indian government, which is currently led by the Bharatiya Janata Party.

One reason for our lack of attention here is that India is not a religiously reactionary state like Saudi Arabia or Iran, and in fact faces its own threats from Islamist militants in Indian-controlled Kashmir, as well as Islamist terrorist attacks throughout the country, most notably the dramatic storming of the Indian parliament in 2001 and the deadly bombing in Bombay that killed fifty-two people in August 2003. India is a strong ally in the war on terrorism and continues to have strong democratic traditions and institutions. It has developed friendlier relations with America and Israel; Ariel Sharon made a state visit in September. The Indian government has also loosened the previously heavily regulated economy to produce one of the highest growth rates in the world, and the Bombay stock market rose 50 percent in 2003. Yet despite these strengths, there is much sectarian hatred in India and it is expressed in frequent, sometimes programmatic, violence.

In the past decade, extremist Hindus have increased their attacks on Christians, until there are now several hundred per year. But this did not make news in the U.S. until a foreigner was attacked. In 1999, Graham Staines, an Australian missionary who had worked with leprosy patients for three decades, was burned alive in Orissa along with his two young sons. The brutal violence visited on Muslims in Gujarat in February 2002 also brought the dangers of Hindu extremism to world attention. Between one and two thousand Muslims were massacred after Muslims reportedly set fire to a train carrying Hindu nationalists, killing several dozen people.

These attacks were not inchoate mob violence, triggered by real or rumored insult; rather, they involved careful planning by organized Hindu extremists with an explicit program and a developed religious-nationalist ideology. Like the ideology of al-Qaeda and other radical Islamists, this ideology began to take shape in the 1920s as a response to European colonialism. It rejected the usually secular outlook of other independence movements; in place of secularism, it synthesized a reactionary form of religion with elements of European millenarian political thought, especially fascism.

Until the nineteenth century, the word "Hindu" had no specific religious meaning and simply referred to the people who lived east of the Indus River, whatever their beliefs. (The Indian Supreme Court itself has held that "no precise meaning can be ascribed to the terms 'Hindu' and 'Hinduism.'") It was only when the census introduced by the British colonial authorities in 1871 included Hindu as a religious designation that many Indians began to think of themselves and their country as Hindu.

Twentieth-century agitation against the British led to the rise not only of the secular and socialist Congress movement but also of the rival Hindu nationalist movement collectively known as the Sangh Parivar ("family of organizations"). The Parivar proclaims an ideology of "Hindutva," aimed at ensuring the predominance of Hinduism in Indian society, politics, and culture, which it promotes through tactics that include violence and terror. Its agenda includes subjugating or driving out Muslims and Christians, who total some 17 percent of the population. It castigates them as foreign faiths, imposed by foreign conquerors—even though Christians trace their origins in India to the Apostle Thomas in the first century and Islam came to India in the seventh and eighth centuries.

The Sangh Parivar's central organization is the Rashtriya Swayamsevak Sangh (RSS), founded by Keshav Hedgewar in 1925. Hedgewar was influenced by V. D. Savarkar, who believed that Hindus were the descendants of the ancient Aryans and properly formed a nation with a unified geography, race, and culture. Savarkar's 1923 book *Hindutva—Who is a Hindu?* declared that those who did not consider India as both fatherland and holy land were not true Indians—and that the love of Indian Christians and Muslims for India was "divided" because each group had its own holy land in the Middle East.

M. S. Golwalkar, the RSS's sarsangchalak (supreme director) from 1940 to 1973, sharpened these themes. In 1938, commenting on the Nuremberg racial laws, he declared: "Germany has also shown how well-nigh impossible it is for races and cultures, having differences going to the root, to be assimilated into one united whole, a good lesson for us . . . to learn and profit by." In an address to RSS members the same year, he also asserted: "If we Hindus grow stronger, in time Muslim friends . . . will have to play the part of German Jews." He insisted that "the non-Hindu . . . must either adopt the Hindu culture and language, must learn to respect and revere Hindu religion . . . Or [they] may stay in the country wholly subordinated to the Hindu nation, claiming nothing, deserving no privileges." On March 25, 1939, the Hindu nationalist Mahasabha Party, an RSS ally, likewise proclaimed: "Germany's solemn idea of the revival of the Aryan culture, the glorification of the swastika, her patronage of Vedic learning, and the ardent championship of Indo-Germanic civilization are welcomed by the religious and sensible Hindus of India with a jubilant hope."

This racism and religious and cultural chauvinism brought the Sangh Parivar into conflict with other strands of Hinduism, especially those taught by Mahatma Gandhi. Golwalkar castigated Gandhi as being soft on Muslims, while Gandhi in turn called the RSS "a communal body with a totalitarian outlook." Hindu nationalists blamed Gandhi for the partition of the subcontinent into India and Pakistan in 1947 and accused him of dismembering Mother India. The conflict did not stop at words: Gandhi's assassin was Nathuram Godse, a former RSS member and Savarkar associate.

The RSS is now a major paramilitary organization with millions of members. Its educational wing, the Vidya Bharati, has some twenty thousand educational institutes, with one hundred thousand teachers and two million students. The Vidya Bharati schools distribute booklets containing a map of India that encompasses not only Pakistan and Bangladesh but also the entire region of Bhutan, Nepal, Tibet, and parts of Myanmar, all under the heading "Punya Bhoomi Bharat," the "Indian Holy Land." The RSS also has separate organizations for tribal peoples, intellectuals, teachers, slum dwellers, leprosy patients, cooperatives, consumers, newspapers, industrialists, Sikhs, ex-servicemen, overseas Indians, and an organization for religion and proselytization, as well as trade unions, student and economic organizations, and a women's chapter.

Other Sangh Parivar organizations include the Bajrang Dal and the Vishnu Hindu Parishad (VHP-World Hindu Council), which engage in propaganda, virulent hate campaigns, and sometimes violence against religious minorities. The VHP was formed in 1964 to unite Hindu groups and serve as the RSS's bridge to sympathetic religious leaders. It has sought to radicalize Hindus by claiming that Hindus are under threat from an "exploding" Muslim population and a spate of Christian conversions, and it organized the 1992 nationwide demonstrations that culminated in the destruction of the Ayodhya mosque by Hindu mobs.

In January 2003, the head of the RSS described the Jesuits in India as the "pope's soldiers" and alleged that they had taken an oath to use "violence and barbaric means to decimate all those who don't follow the Roman Catholic religion." Sangh Parivar groups have also been pressing for a ban on religious conversions from Hinduism, which they allege are being done by "force, fraud, and inducement." They accuse Christian missionaries (who comprise about one half of one percent of the Christians in India) of converting people by offering them money, medical help, and education. Because of this widespread Hindu extremist propaganda, it now appears that a majority of Hindus support a ban on Hindus changing their religion.

The Bharatiya Janata Party (BJP), which has since 1998 formed the national government of India at the head of a coalition of centrist parties, is tied to the RSS, VHP, and Bajrang Dal, and functions as the Sangh Parivar's political wing. Prime Minister Atal Behari Vajpayee publicly praises the RSS, attends its functions, and has feted the organization's leadership at his residence. Other senior BJP officials, such as Home Affairs Minister L. K. Advani, are RSS associates. At the national level the BJP advances the ideology of Hindutva through propaganda, the manipulation of cultural institutions, undercutting laws that protect religious minorities, and minimizing or excusing Hindu extremist violence. At the state level its functionaries have abetted and even participated in such violence.

The BJP appoints school officials who alter textbooks and curricula to emphasize Hinduism; they also require that Hindu texts be taught in all schools. Moreover, it has appointed Sangh Parivar adherents to key positions in autonomous bodies such as the Prasar Bharati, which controls the official media, the National Film Development Corporation, the Indian Council of Historical Research, and the National Book Trust.

BJP lawmakers have also attempted to restrict minority religious groups' international contacts and to reduce their rights to build places of worship. It works to pass anti-conversion laws and to alter the personal laws that govern marriages, adoptions, and inheritance. It practices legal discrimination against Dalits ("untouchables") who are Christian and Muslim, but not against those who are Hindu. With BJP support, laws have recently been adopted in Tamil Nadu and Gujarat states that restrict the ability of Hindus to change their religion, and proposals for national restrictions have been made. Pope John Paul II described these developments in June 2003 as "unjust" and said they prohibited "free exercise of the natural right to religious freedom."

The current legal status of religious conversion in India is ambiguous. In a 1977 judgment, the Supreme Court ruled that "converting" people was not a fundamental right, that conversions could potentially impinge on freedom of conscience, and that, if conversions disrupt community life, they could amount to "disturbing public order." The states of Gujarat, Madhya Pradesh, Orissa, Tamil Nadu, and Arunachal Pradesh have a legal ban on "forced conversion." Officials of the National Commission for Minorities, a government body with the mandate to protect minorities, believe that such laws are unconstitutional; and despite many investigations into allegations, no "forced conversions" have ever been documented or proven.

While restrictions on conversion—or, more precisely, restrictions on the legal recognition that someone has in fact converted—affect all Indians, they are particularly onerous for Dalits. Because of their desperate status in Indian society, many lower-caste Hindus have considered converting in order to escape their religiously defined plight (most Christians in India are from Dalit background). In 1956, B. R. Ambedkar, a Dalit leader, declared that he had converted to Buddhism to escape Hinduism. Perhaps as many as one hundred thousand Dalits have followed his example. In 1981, about a thousand Dalits converted to Islam in Tamil Nadu. In August 2002, 250 Dalit youth from the same area converted to Christianity. Apart from their directly religious significance, such conversions erode the dominance of traditional Hinduism's higher castes, especially the Brahmins, and undercut the power of landowners, generally higher-caste, over their laborers, who are frequently lower-caste. The attempts to forbid religious conversion are also attempts to keep the underclass in its place.

The BJP policies on Hindutva and conversion coincide with increasingly violent attacks by Hindu militants on religious minorities. Attacks on Christians, especially in the states of Gujarat, Madhya Pradesh, and Orissa, have surged in recent years. India's Home Ministry (internal security) and its National Commission for Minorities officially list over a hundred religiously motivated attacks against Christians per year, but the real number is certainly higher, as Indian journalists estimate that only some ten percent of incidents are ever reported. These attacks include murders of missionaries and priests, sexual assault on nuns, ransacking of churches, convents, and other Christian institutions, desecration of cemeteries, and Bible burnings.

The other major target of Hindu extremists is the Muslim community, which is haunted by the fear of recurrent communal riots that have taken the lives of thousands of Muslims and Hindus since Indian independence. During the outbreak of violence in Gujarat in February 2002, many of the victims were burned alive or dismembered while police and BJP state government authorities either stood by or joined in. The mobs had with them lists of homes and businesses owned by Muslims, lists that they could have acquired only from government sources.

After the massacre, state BJP officials also impeded the investigation. In the high-profile "Best Bakery Case," a judge dismissed charges against twenty-one defendants on trial for setting fire to a Muslim-owned bakery and killing and injuring its owners because the main witness, a nineteen-year-old girl, stated that she could not identify any of the attackers. She later told the press that "she testified falsely after local Hindu politicians repeatedly threatened her family . . . and after concluding that prosecutors, who made no effort to meet with her before the trial, were not serious about gaining convictions." On September 12, 2003, the Chief Justice of India's Supreme Court expressed his disgust with the situation by declaring publicly that he has "no faith left in the prosecution and the Gujarat government."

Following the violence, Gujarat's Chief Minister, Narendra Modi, a BJP member, called upon his supporters to "teach a lesson" to those who "believe in multiplying the population," referring to Muslims. Other Sangh Parivar officials were even more explicitly threatening. VHP International President Ashok Singhal described the Gujarat carnage as a "successful experiment" and warned that it would be repeated all over India. After the December 2002 BJP election victory in Gujarat, VHP General Secretary Pravin Togadia declared, "All Hindutva opponents will get the death sentence, and we will leave this to the people to carry out. The process of forming a Hindu rule in the country has begun with Gujarat, and VHP will take the Gujarat experiment to every nook and corner of the country."

To maintain the political coalition that enables it to rule at the national level, the BJP downplays its specifically religious goals and portrays itself as a moderate party. But it also allies with the Sangh Parivar to appeal to its base. In its 2004 recommendations, the U.S. Commission on International Religious Freedom proposed that India be included on the State Department's official shortlist of the worst religious persecutors for its "egregious, systematic, and ongoing" violations of religious rights.

Since it is the world's largest democracy, good relations with India are important to the U.S. It is also a growing trading partner, a possible geopolitical counterweight to China, and a strong U.S. ally in the war on terrorism. But the growth of often-violent Hindu nationalism threatens India's tolerant traditions and pluralistic democracy. If religious extremism continues to grow, it will, as we have learned elsewhere, drag India's democracy, economy, and foreign policy down with it. In the face of such a threat, we cannot afford to be silent.

Critical Thinking

1. Why has the U.S. media ignored Hindu extremism in India?
2. Who are the primary targets of Hindu violence?
3. Why does the Indian government ignore this threat?
4. Is India's vison of pluralistic democracy a myth?

Internet References

Hudson Institute
http://www.hudson.org/research/4575-hinduism-and-terror
The Guardian
http://www.theguardian.com/commentisfree/2014/sep/08/al-qaida-india-hindu-extremists
The National
http://www.thenational.ae/news/world/south-asia/hindu-terror-what-does-it-mean

PAUL MARSHALL Senior Fellow, Center for Religious Freedom

Article   Prepared by: Thomas J. Badey, *Randolph-Macon College*

Christian Extremists and Homegrown Terrorism

TYLER HUGGINS

Learning Outcomes

After reading this article, you will be able to:

- Identify similarities between extremists from different religions.
- Summarize the history of Christian extremism in the United States.
- Discuss the role Christianity plays in American culture.

*I*n 1986, Dr. George Tiller's abortion clinic was firebombed. In 1993, Shelly Shannon, member of the Army of God, shot Dr. Tiller in both arms outside his clinic. During her prosecution, she stated there was nothing immoral about her attempt to exterminate Tiller. On her attributed wing of the Army of God website it reads this quote from Genesis: "Whoso sheddeth man's blood, by man shall his blood be shed: for in the image of God made he man." Dr. Tiller lived for 16 more years until Scott Roeder summarily executed him at point blank range as the doctor ushered at a local church. Roeder's roommate said that he and Roeder considered themselves members of the Army of God.

Before the rabbit hole is sampled, analyzed and conclusively wrapped up, perhaps it's best to offer an acceptable definition of Extremism. For the benefit of this exploration, Extremism is best connoted as the actions or ideologies of individuals or groups who take a political idea to its limits, regardless of unfortunate repercussions, and show intolerance toward all views other than their own. An Extremist is the person who advocates the use of force or violence and embodies the connotation pre-depicted.

Here are the questions that must be asked: What is a Christian Extremist? What is the history of Christian Extremism in America? Why does the military care about Christian Extremism? Why did they subsequently stop caring and what does this mean about the double standard of Christian Extremism?

John George and Laird Wilcox's book *American Extremist* uses 22 identifiers for recognizing extremist enclaves, which is mercifully collapsed into a list of six key characteristics here: Unresponsive sweeping generalizations; dualism worldview; assumption of moral superiority; doomsday thinking; emphasis on emotional responses; and advocacy of double standards.

Unsurprisingly, this list prompts unsettling self-diagnoses. It's not uncommon practice to pass off opponents and critics as evil or allow emotions to trump reason. Heck, that's politicking 101. Rest easy, occasional lapses into emotionally driven tirades doesn't qualify as extremism (although it could be argued that everyone is partially extreme about something: the greatness of Lionel Messi, poppy seed bagels and so on). The difference between enraged bellowing and Extremism is best delineated in this quote about Extremism from, surprisingly, the Department of Defense: "As a caution, we are all fallible human beings, and some of us may resort to these behaviors from time to time without bad intentions. With extremists, these lapses are not occasional; rather, they are habitual and a strongly established part of an extremist's character." Think McCarthyism.

Disclaimer: Before reading the following analysis, be aware that the ensuing practice is performed without any consideration to faith. As a result, the analysis may read harsh, especially to practicing Christians. With the variable of faith in play, some of these actions are more reasonable to undertake or condone.

When slid under George and Wilcox's microscope, the Christian Right appears securely within the confines of American Extremism. This isn't coincidental; the two researchers included the Christian Right intentionally as a case study. Here's why: dualism, a popular identifier of Extremists, is easily recognized within Christian Right ideology. The dualist worldview of black/white or good/evil fits quite well into the god/satan; hell/heaven; and angel/demon dichotomy that reigns in scripture and frequents the binary logic of Christians (there's good, evil and no in between) often invoked by the Christian Right.

Dualists frequently mistake similar for same (this person shares my religious beliefs therefore must share my political/moral/economic sentiments) and stumble into logical fallacies when asked to back assertions while ignoring contradictory information (fossil records and carbon dating). As a practicing member of Christianity, the threat of dualism is subverted by the continuum of one's own path with Christ of faith. When a religious pocket transitions into dualism, Extremism reigns. Think Westboro.

Extremists tend to have a penchant for lawlessness; the Christian Right is no different. God's law supersedes the law of man, and when man's law ignores or flaunts god's law (marriage equality, pro-choice) the Christian Right is indignant and riled. This sense of superiority gives birth to victimhood, the idea that the code of ethics adhered to by the Christian Right is under assault, or persecuted. Such indignation tends to lead to dooms-day thinking (beware the wrath of God for such lawlessness) and violent acts performed in the name of God (bombing of abortion clinics). Extremism, unlike someone's extreme love for poppy seed bagels, borders and sometimes spills into violence.

Propaganda plays an integral role in Extremism and more radical ideologies. The use of propaganda (heavily metaphorical and symbolic imagery that tells people how to think) thrives on Facebook, especially on Christian Right pages. The cross; hands in prayer; lambs; links between military and religion, all tend to inform people how to think instead of providing the means for viewers to think clearly. To the credit of the Christian Right, the social network excels in telling people how to think and preventing people from thinking for themselves (it's how they generate revenue). And so the Christian Right's usage isn't outside the norm. There is a bigger issue at play, however. Propaganda isn't education—it's manipulation on a mass scale.

Let's pause for the history of Christian Extremism in America.

Christian Extremism isn't an unknown practice. For years, Christian Extremists (some mentally stable, others unstable) have bombed abortion clinics, assaulted pro-choice doctors and attacked homosexuals on morally just grounds. Christian Extremists have grown radical enough for terrorism scholar Aref M. Al-Khattar to categorize several Christian groups as far right-wing terrorists.

There are many such Christian Right militant groups in America, but the most known and most active are as follows: Westboro Baptist Church, Ku Klux Klan, The Covenant, The Sword and The Arm of the Lord (CSA), Defensive Action

(aka Army of God), and the Freemen Community. The Klan and Westboro's abhorrent acts are well documented, but the other groups aren't as infamous. The CSA was a prominent far-right paramilitary Christian group until they were raided and arrested by the FBI in 1985. Army of God was behind many of the attacks on abortion clinics, wielding force and violence to enforce their anti-abortion and anti-homosexuality causes. The Freemen hail from Montana, and were notorious for attempting to use counterfeit checks to stock their armory and fund their activities. In 1995, the Freemen found themselves in the same FBI quagmire as the CSA, and after many days of negotiations surrendered and were promptly arrested.

And now we return to identifying the characteristics of an Extremist.

Double standards rest snugly next to the dualist mindset. If someone adheres to the us/them and/or good/evil paradigm, it follows that what applies to them doesn't necessarily apply to us and vice versa.

The Christian Right's use of the double standard shapes public perception of more violent rhetoric and actions as out-landish, but not necessarily extreme. Christianity dominates American culture, allowing the more polemic enclaves to operate under the guise of conservatism and moral rigidity. From the perch of American Christian culture, linking these Christian enclaves (the Christian Right) with their Islamic or Jewish equivalents is unfathomable, even though each represents a hyper-conservative take on their religious structure.

What results is a double standard: the Christian Right's conservative morals (within the context of American culture) differ from other religions' conservatism and morality (within the context of Zionism; or the Quran; or the administrations of Joseph Smith). Recently, (and oddly) this double standard was undermined by the most unlikely organization: The Department of Defense.

In mid-2013 a contentious report surfaced within the DoD labeling the Christian Right as Extremist and categorizing their members under the same umbrella term as jihadists and known terrorist cells. The inflammatory Extremist label came from a report commissioned by the Department of Defense and performed by the Southern Poverty Law Center.

The report hardly summarizes the military's philosophies toward Christianity. Forty-nine percent of all Department of Defense members rally under the Christian flag, with slightly over 17 percent of the DoD identifying as evangelical Christians (conversely, nearly 63 percent of military chaplains are evangelicals). Despite the public outcries regarding Obama's anti-Christian crusade, military ranks are swollen with Christian membership. To criticize Christianity denies the military nearly *half* of its recruits. And the military is in no shape to drop its recruiting numbers.

Regardless of the DoD's position on the Christian Identity (perhaps the military heads are the Christian Right behind closed doors, but there isn't much evidence to support that theory), the Extremist label didn't sit well with the Christian Right. In light of the statistic that "fifty-six percent of domestic terrorist attacks and plots in the U.S. since 1995 have been perpetrated by right-wing extremists," according to [the] Think Progress study, the extremist label doesn't seem far-fetched.

In November, Secretary of the Army John McHugh stated that the Christian Right "were not extremist according to Army regulations." His statement was released during adversity from conservative organizations and appeared to settle the matter. Tactfully, the military shifted the derision of conservative media toward the Southern Poverty Law Center.

The duplicitous actions of the DoD plays right into the double standard of the Christian Right. Unable to tolerate the same standards as applied to other religious extremists (the DoD report used George and Wilcox's identifiers), the Right claimed persecution by the DoD and the Obama administration. And so, under duress the military stood down. Which, ironically, reconfirmed the double standard identifier of Christian Extremism.

If Americans don't take issue with labeling other culture's fundamental or violent sub-religions as extremists or terrorists, then we can't ignore the violent actions and rhetoric of our own religions. That is, unless we wish to remain within the double standard of Extremism.

Critical Thinking

1. What is a Christian Extremist?
2. How are Christian extremists different from Islamic extremist?
3. What role does propaganda play in society's perception of Christian extremists?
4. Is there a double standard when it comes to Christian extremism?

Internet References

Geopolitical Monitor: Terrorism and Fundamentalism Are Not Exclusive to Islam
http://www.geopoliticalmonitor.com/terrorism-and-fundamentalism-are-not-exclusive-to-islam

Raw Story
http://www.rawstory.com/rs/2015/01/americas-10-worst-terror-attacks-by-christian-fundamentalist-and-far-right-extremists

Think Progress
http://thinkprogress.org/justice/2014/12/04/3599271/austin-shooter-christian-extremism

USA Today
http://www.usatoday.com/story/news/nation/2015/01/17/number-of-homegrown-terrorists-is-rising/21940159

TYLER HUGGINS is a contributing writer at *Highbrow Magazine.*

Unit 8

UNIT

Prepared by: Thomas J. Badey, *Randolph-Macon College*

Women and Terrorism

The role of women in international terrorism is complex. Women are often portrayed purely as victims of political violence. The fact that women have played a critical role in the evolution of contemporary international terrorism and that they continue to play critical roles in many terrorist organizations is often ignored.

In the 1970s, women like Ulrike Meinhof and Gudrun Ensslin of the German Baader-Meinhof Gang, Mara Cagol of the Red Brigades in Italy, Fusako Shigenobu of the Japanese Red Army, and Leila Khaled of the Palestine Liberation Organization held key roles in their organizations and significantly influenced the development of modern terrorism. While often less visible than their male counterparts, women are once again actively involved in international terrorism. Women like American Lori Berenson, a former anthropology student at MIT, who became involved with the Tupac Amaru Revolutionary Movement (MRTA) and Shinaz Amuri (AKA Wafa Idris), a 28-year-old volunteer medic who became a Palestinian heroine after she killed herself in a suicide bombing, are the role models for a new generation of women.

The role that women play in contemporary international terrorism varies widely from region to region. Culture rather than ideology appears to play a critical role. As both perpetrators and victims of violence, the role of women in terrorism is not easily understood.

This section attempts to explore the various facets of women's involvement in international terrorism. In the first article entitled "The Badass Women Fighting the Islamic State," Mohammed A. Salih describes the role of women in the Kurdistan Worker's Party (PKK) fight against the Islamic State in northern Iraq through the eyes of Avesta, a 24-year-old female squad commander. She is just one of roughly half of the organization's leaders that are women. Next, Margaret Gonzalez-Perez describes the evolution of radical Islamic ideology and its deviation from traditional Islamic thought. She argues that strategic and tactical considerations are more important than ideology when it comes to the use of female suicide bombers. In the third selection, Soeren Kern examines the various roles of British female jihadists in Islamic State (ISIS). According to Kern, Great Britain is now the leading European source of female jihadists in Syria and Iraq. Finally, Jacob Zenn and Elizabeth Pearson examine "Women, Gender and the Evolving Tactics of Boko Haram." They argue that 2013 marked a significant change in Boko Haram's targeting and use of women. This has led to gender-based changes in Boko Haram's tactics and its use of women which have resulted in increasing gender-based violence against Christians.

Article   Prepared by: Thomas J. Badey, Randolph-Macon College

Meet the Badass Women Fighting the Islamic State

Guerrillas from Turkey's Kurdistan Workers' Party are on the front lines in northern Iraq. Many of the organization's leaders, including 24-year-old Avesta, are women.

MOHAMMED A. SALIH

Learning Outcomes

After reading this article, you will be able to:

- Explain some of the roles women play in the Kurdistan Worker's Party (PKK).

- Discuss the challenges the Kurdistan Worker's Party faces in the fight against the ISIS.

- Describe the "triumphs" the Kurdistan Worker's Party feels it has had against the Islamic State.

Makhmour, Iraq—Avesta enters the cramped room in a teachers' residence turned temporary military base, ready for a meeting with her fellow fighters. The six commandos rise to shake her hand. She greets each individually. "Hello, *heval*," she says, calling them by the Kurdish word for comrade. Then she lays down her Russian sniper rifle, and tea and coffee are served.

The Islamic State's fearsome fighters are just around 10 miles away, but the Kurdish snipers, some still teenagers, are mostly relaxed. They debate the merits of drinking coffee versus tea, discuss the situation in the camp, and joke with each other. "You are very photogenic," one of the fighters tells Avesta cheerfully as she poses for a photo. She smiles shyly as others burst into laughter.

Avesta is only 24, but she looks much older, with piercing gray eyes. Her long face is wrinkled and roughened; her hands are calloused. Her sniper rifle is at her side at all times; when it isn't hanging from her back, it's resting within arm's reach—a constant companion to her uncertain life as a Kurdish guerrilla.

Avesta, whose nom de guerre is the same as the holy book of Zoroastrianism, a religion that Kurds consider as their original creed, commands a group of 13 fighters, eight of them female, from the Kurdistan Workers' Party (PKK)—a rebel group that has fought the Turkish state for three decades in pursuit of Kurdish rights. They wear olive and gray uniforms of baggy pants and a vest, with a wide cloth belt around their waists.

Avesta's squad arrived in Makhmour, a dusty town in Iraqi Kurdistan, by bus on August 6 from a PKK base in the Qandil Mountains, a range that spans the Iraqi, Turkish, and Iranian borders. They are among the hundreds of Kurdish volunteers from around the region who have descended on Iraqi Kurdistan to fend off the vicious jihadists of the Islamic State.

Following a four-day battle that ended on August 10, the Kurdish guerrillas retook control of their main target, a camp populated until early August by more than 10,000 Kurdish refugees from Turkey, many of whom are believed to be PKK supporters.

During the battle, Avesta used her sniper rifle to shoot at Islamic State fighters, providing cover for her comrades as they advanced toward the jihadists' front lines. "They were not as capable fighters as their propaganda claimed," she said. "They mostly fought from afar with heavy weaponry like mortars and artillery."

Avesta is no stranger to heavy combat. The PKK has fought for three decades against the Turkish military, NATO's second-largest. Avesta fought in major PKK battles against Turkey in

2012, 2008, and 2005. The PKK fighters are up for the challenge of the jihadists, she says. "The Islamic State fought rigorously. But it was not as severe as our previous fights with the Turkish army," she said. "The Turks have warplanes and air power."

Seeing the atrocities committed by the jihadists against Kurds in Sinjar and other areas, Avesta says she and others in her unit volunteered to be among the first group of PKK guerrillas sent to Makhmour. Her unit takes its orders from the PKK command in the Qandil Mountains. But on the ground in Makhmour, the unit also has some "limited" coordination with Iraqi Kurdish Peshmerga troops, Avesta says.

Like many who joined the PKK's ranks, she was radicalized at a young age. The trigger came when she saw her brother's mutilated body. He was a PKK fighter, too, and died in a clash with Turkish security forces in 2005. Shortly afterward, she left her hometown, Van, in Turkey's southeast and headed to the mountains to take up arms. She was 15.

Avesta attended an intense boot camp where she was immersed in the party's revolutionary leftist ideology and view of women's role in society, and trained to use weapons. In the mountains, PKK fighters live in isolation in bare-bones camps. The organization's rules prohibit romantic relationships, and the fighters have little access to their families.

It was as a young woman in the rugged mountains of southeast Turkey and northern Iraq that Avesta says she discovered herself. "It was in the mountains that I found out women can be also powerful," said Avesta. The ranks of the PKK, a Marxist organization, are filled with women, a rarity in the conservative cultures of the Muslim world. About half of the organization's leaders are women. And the Kurdish guerrilla group stands in especially stark contrast to the radical fundamentalism of the Islamic State, which confines women's role to mostly domestic tasks such as raising children, cooking, cleaning, and pleasing their husbands.

"It gives us strength and motivation when a woman like Avesta is our commander," says Kendal, a 19-year-old male fighter in Avesta's unit. "She gave us orders during the fighting and instructed us on tactics."

The PKK and its Syrian affiliate, the YPG, played a crucial role in securing an escape route from Mount Sinjar, in Iraq's western Nineveh province, all the way to Syria. Thousands of members of the Yazidi religious minority trapped on the mountain by the Islamic State fled to safety and returned to Iraqi Kurdistan through Syrian Kurdish territory. PKK fighters have also been deployed to Kirkuk, in northern Iraq, to boost Peshmerga lines.

But even if the presence of Avesta and her comrades in Iraq has helped beat back the Islamic State, other challenges lie ahead. For one, there are tensions with the Iraqi Kurds. Relations between the two groups have long been strained. The PKK and Iraqi Kurdish forces have fought each other on numerous occasions, from the late 1980s to the early 2000s. While Avesta said that the PKK liberated the refugee camp and played a major role in capturing the town of Makhmour from the Islamic State, Iraqi Kurdish officials insist that Iraqi Kurdish Peshmerga carried out the bulk of the fighting.

The PKK's participation in the fight against the Islamic State has not yet stirred a strong reaction in neighboring Turkey. But given that Turkey considers the PKK a hostile organization and at the same time enjoys close political and economic ties with Iraqi Kurds, Ankara might not react favorably if the PKK decides to establish a long-term presence in Iraqi Kurdistan. A prolonged PKK presence in Iraqi Kurdistan—especially if the Islamic State is defeated in northern Iraq—could undermine the authority of the Kurdish government on its territory and give rise to tensions among Turkey, Iraqi Kurds, and the PKK.

The PKK presence could also raise red flags for the West, a critical ally to the Kurds, as the war against the Islamic State moves forward. The PKK is designated a terrorist group by the United States and a host of European countries.

Avesta shrugs off such designations. "We have been called terrorists for years," she said while walking through the camp, returning from a quick tour of inspecting a guard post to make sure it is fortified in case the Islamic State attacks. "But we say to those countries: Come and see this war and then judge for yourselves . . . . The [Islamic State] beheads civilians . . . . We have rescued civilians."

With Islamic State jihadists pushed out of the Kurdish areas around Makhmour, the guerrillas at the refugee camp have no plans yet to go back to their bases in the Qandil Mountains. For the time being, they are busy training some of the few hundred camp residents who have returned on how to protect themselves.

Experience has taught these fighters to take no chances. They have used their time since driving out the Islamic State to set up fortifications in and around the camp and at nearby Mount Qarachukh.

The PKK fighters take turns manning the checkpoints and fortifications. After her meeting with her comrades ends, she picks up her sniper rifle and bids them farewell. She and a male comrade get into a dusty car and head off to stand guard at the checkpoint at the camp's entrance. From there, she can see the hazy horizon south of Makhmour, where the Islamic State still maintains a foothold.

UPDATE Sept. 13, 2:20pm: *Avesta was killed on Sept. 12. According to a spokesperson for the PKK guerillas in northern Iraq, she was leading a unit in a joint PKK-Peshmerga operation to re-take a village near Makhmour when a bullet fired by an Islamic State militant struck her in the neck. She was put in a Peshmerga Humvee headed for the hospital in Makhmour that* *was struck by an improvised explosive device. She died soon after, on the way to Erbil, the capital of Iraqi Kurdistan, for further treatment.*

Critical Thinking

1. How does Avesta feel the Kurdistan Worker's Party has empowered her?

2. What challenges does the Kurdistan Worker's Party face in its fight against ISIS?

3. How does Avesta rationalize the activities of the PKK?

Internet References

Inside the Kurdistan Workers Party (PKK)
http://www.cfr.org/turkey/inside-kurdistan-workers-party-pkk/p14576

The Roles of Women in Terrorism, Conflict, and Violent Extremism
http://www.globalcenter.org/wp-content/uploads/2013/04/NCF_RB_LS_policybrief_1320.pdf

Turkey Decides to Hit Kurdish Rebels Instead of ISIS
http://time.com/3507187/turkey-kurdish-rebels-pkk-isis-kobrani

Women Fighting ISIS Share Stories from the Battlefield
http://www.huffingtonpost.com/2014/10/20/women-fighting-isis_n_6016812.html

Article   Prepared by: Thomas J. Badey, *Randolph-Macon College*

Britain's Female Jihadists

Soeren Kern

Learning Outcomes

After reading this article, you will be able to:

- Explain the role British female jihadists have played in the Islamic State.

- Discuss the British female jihadists' use of social media networks as a recruitment tool.

- Describe some of the motivations women have to join the Islamic State.

"My son and I love life with the beheaders."—British jihadist Sally Jones.

Mujahidah Bint Usama published pictures of herself on Twitter holding a severed head while wearing a white doctor's jacket; alongside it, the message: "Dream job, a terrorist doc."

British female jihadists are now in charge of guarding as many as 3,000 non-Muslim Iraqi women and girls held captive as sex slaves.

"The British women are some of the most zealous in imposing the IS laws in the region. I believe that's why at least four of them have been chosen to join the women police force."—British terrorism analyst Melanie Smith.

Great Britain is now the leading European source of female jihadists in Syria and Iraq.

As many as 60 Muslim women between the ages of 18 and 24 are believed to have left Britain to join the jihadist group Islamic State [IS] during the past twelve months alone, according to British terrorism analysts.

Dozens more have inquired about joining IS since the beheading of American journalist James Foley in Syria in August 2014 set off a frenzy of enthusiasm within jihadist circles.

Many of the women seem to be motivated by the hope of finding a jihadist husband, analysts say, apparently because they covet the cultural and religious "prestige" conferred upon Muslim widows whose husbands have died as "martyrs" for Allah.

Until recently, most of the British women affiliated with IS have been restricted to performing domestic chores such as cleaning and cooking. Lately, however, some women have become restive and have demanded a greater role in the IS enterprise.

Several British women are now engaged in IS recruiting efforts, using social media platforms such as Facebook and Twitter to encourage a new wave of British jihadists to travel to Syria and Iraq.

A half-dozen other women have been incorporated into a female-only militia called the Al-Khansaa brigade, based in the Syrian city of Raqqa, where the IS has set up its headquarters.

Al-Khansaa—named after a seventh-century female Arab poet who was a contemporary of the Muslim Prophet Mohammed—was established in February 2014 with the purpose of exposing male enemy jihadists who try to disguise themselves by wearing women's clothing in order to avoid detection and detention at IS checkpoints.

The brigade was also established to detain civilian women in Raqqa who do not follow the Islamic State's strict interpretation of Islamic Sharia law, including the requirement that all women be fully covered in public and that they be accompanied by a male chaperone.

In an interview with the blog "Syria Deeply," Abu Ahmad, an IS official in Raqqa, explained the rationale behind Al-Khansaa. He said:

"We have established the brigade to raise awareness of our religion among women, and to punish women who do not abide by the law. There are only women in this brigade, and we have given them their own facilities to prevent the mixture of men and women."

British terrorism analyst Melanie Smith told the *Daily Telegraph* that Al-Khansaa is a Sharia law police brigade whose social media accounts are run by British women and written in English.

"The British women are some of the most zealous in imposing the IS laws in the region," Smith said. "I believe that's why at least four of them have been chosen to join the women police force."

The Al-Khansaa brigade has now expanded its remit to operating brothels for the use of IS fighters. The result is that British female jihadists are now in charge of guarding as many as 3,000 non-Muslim Iraqi women and girls who are being held captive as sex slaves, according to British media.

"It is the British women who have risen to the top of the Islamic State's Sharia police and now they are in charge of this operation," another analyst told the *Daily Mirror.* "It is as bizarre as it is perverse."

A key figure in the Al-Khansaa brigade is said to be Aqsa Mahmood, a 20-year-old woman from Glasgow, Scotland who left for Syria in November 2013. Mahmood attended private schools and had wanted to become a doctor, but she dropped out of university without warning and vanished overnight in order to become a jihadist and marry an IS fighter.

Using the jihadist name of Umm Layth (Arabic for "Mother of the Lion") on Twitter (account now suspended), Mahmood has encouraged other British Muslim women to leave their families behind in order to join the jihad in Syria. She wrote:

"Biggest tip to sisters: don't take detours, take the quickest route, don't play around with your Hijrah [religious pilgrimage] by staying longer than 1 day for safety and get in touch with your contacts as soon as you reach your destination."

Mahmood, who says she is dedicated to the "pursuit of Allah's pleasure," added: "Once you arrive in the land of jihad, [IS] is your family."

In two tweets Mahmood described the kinship she felt with fellow Muslims in the Islamic State. Before referring to the place as "paradise," she concluded:

"Wallahi [I swear] I will never be able to do justice with words as to how this place makes me feel or what Ansaar of Shaam [helpers of Syria] have done for me and Allah only knows how much I love and appreciate these people for His sake. . ."

In another post, Mahmood called on Muslims to imitate those who murdered British soldier Lee Rigby outside the Woolwich Barracks in London in May 2013. "Follow the examples of your brothers from Woolwich, Texas and Boston," she wrote, referring also to the shooting in Fort Hood, Texas in November 2009 and the Boston Marathon bombings in April 2013.

Mahmood also called on Muslims to conduct jihad operations on British streets. In a recent tweet, she counselled: "If you cannot make it to the battlefield, then bring the battlefield to yourself."

She also wrote about martyrdom: "Allahu Akbar, there's no way to describe the feeling of sitting with the Akhawat [sisters] waiting on news of whose Husband has attained Shahadah [martyrdom]."

British media have published photographs of a burqa-clad Mahmood holding a shotgun, and of a child holding an AK-47 machine gun.

Mahmood's parents have said they cannot understand why their daughter ran away from home to become a jihadist:

"Our daughter was brought up with love and affection in a happy home, attended Craigholme private school, went to university and was always taught to show respect for mankind and was well integrated into this society. She may believe that the jihadists of ISIS are her new family but they are not and are simply using her.

"If our daughter, who had all the chances and freedom in life, could become a bedroom radical, then it is possible for this to happen to any family."

Another British jihadist linked to the Al-Khansaa brigade, a 21-year-old medical student who goes by the name Mujahidah Bint Usama, published pictures of herself on Twitter holding a severed head while wearing a white doctor's jacket. The gruesome image appears alongside the message "Dream job, a terrorist doc," followed by images of smiley faces and love hearts.

Usama's Twitter account has now been suspended, but in her description of herself she wrote: "Running away from jihad will not save you from death. You can die as a coward or you can die as a martyr."

Yet another British jihadist, a 22-year-old convert to Islam named Khadijah Dare, has vowed to become the first female jihadist to execute a British or American captive.

Writing under the Twitter name Muhajirah fi Sham (Arabic for "immigrant in Syria"), Dare asked for links to video footage of the beheading of James Foley. In a slang-filled tweet she wrote:

"Any links 4 da execution of da journalist plz. Allahu Akbar. UK must b shaking up ha ha. I wna b da 1st UK woman 2 kill a UK or US terorrist!(sic)".

In another tweet, Dare wrote:

"All da people back in Dar ul kufr [land of disbelievers] what are you waiting for . . . hurry up and join da caravan to where the laws of Allah is implemented."

"No one from Lewisham [a borough in southeast London] has come here apart from an 18-year-old sister shame on all those people who afford fancy meals and clothes and do not make hijra [Mohamed's flight from Mecca to Medina in 622]. Shame on you."

Dare was born in London and converted to Islam at age 18, when she began worshipping at the Lewisham Islamic Center, a mosque linked to the radical cleric Abu Hamza and the two killers of Lee Rigby.

Dare moved to Syria in 2012 to marry a Swedish jihadist named Abu Bakr. The marriage was arranged through his mother on Facebook and she did not meet him until the day of their wedding. Dare recently published pictures of her son holding an AK-47 rifle.

In a Channel 4 documentary that aired in July 2013, Dare, who at that time went by the name Maryam, said:

"I couldn't find anyone in the UK who was willing to sacrifice their life in this world for the life in the hereafter . . . I prayed, and Allah ruled that I came here to marry Abu Bakr."

She also called on other British Muslims to join the jihad:

"You need to wake up and stop being scared of death. . .we know that there's heaven and hell. At the end of the day, Allah's going to question you. Instead of sitting down and focusing on your families or your study, you just need to wake up . . . ."

On August 31, the *Daily Mirror* reported that Dare's jihadist rants have turned her into a "celebrity jihadi" who has become an "immense threat" due to her popularity. The newspaper reported that British security services have now made finding her a "top priority" over fears that radical Muslims are answering her calls to leave the UK to join IS in the Middle East.

In a four-minute video entitled, "Answering the Call—Foreign Fighters (Mujahedeen) in Syria," a burka-clad Dare appears firing an AK-47 rifle and pleading with fellow Brits to fight by her side in Syria. Speaking in a London accent, she said:

"These are your brothers and sisters as well and they need your help. So instead of sitting down and focusing on your families or focusing on your studies, you need to stop being selfish because time is ticking."

Not all British female jihadists are in their teens and twenties. A 45-year-old British convert to Islam named Sally Jones recently issued threats via Twitter to behead Christians. Jones, who changed her name to Umm Hussain al-Britani, wrote: "You Christians all need beheading with a nice blunt knife and stuck on the railings at Raqqa. Come here I'll do it for you!"

Police say Jones, who also goes by the name Sakinah Hussain, travelled to Syria in late 2013 after converting to Islam and developing an online romance with a 20-year-old British jihadist from Birmingham named Junaid Hussain.

Hussain, who uses the alias Abu Hussain al-Britani, was jailed in 2012 for running a computer hacking group known as Team Poison. He escaped to Syria in 2013 while on bail, and has been posting extremist messages on social media pledging to conquer the world and kill infidels.

Police fear Hussain is masterminding a plan to teach jihadists how to empty the bank accounts of rich and famous Britons to fund terror attacks.

According to British media, Jones, originally from Kent in southeast England, was once an aspiring musician with an all-girl punk rock band but ended up spending a lifetime on social welfare benefits. She is now raising her 10-year-old son from a previous marriage as a Muslim under the Islamic State.

In an interview with *The Sunday Times*, Jones reflected on her new circumstances: "My son and I love life with the beheaders."

Critical Thinking

1. What role have social media networks played in recruitment in terrorist organizations?

2. What types of roles do women have within organizations like the Islamic State?

3. Is there a specific profile female recruits of the Islamic State fit?

Internet References

ICCT: European Female Jihadists in Syria: Exploring an Under-Researched Topic

http://www.icct.nl/download/file/ICCT-Bakker-de-Leede-European-Female-Jihadists-In-Syria-Exploring-An-Under-Researched-Topic-April2015(1).pdf

ISIS 'Manifesto' Spells Out Role for Women

http://www.theatlantic.com/education/archive/2015/03/isis-manifesto-spells-out-role-for-women/387049

Women as Victims and Victimizers

http://iipdigital.usembassy.gov/st/english/publication/2008/05/2008052217 2353srenod0.6383936.html#axzz3XUzka5Po

SOEREN KERN is a Senior Fellow at the New York-based Gatestone Institute. He is also Senior Fellow for European Politics at the Madrid-based Grupo de Estudios Estratégicos/Strategic Studies Group.

Article   Prepared by: Thomas J. Badey, *Randolph-Macon College*

Women, Gender and the Evolving Tactics of Boko Haram

JACOB ZENN AND ELIZABETH PEARSON

Learning Outcomes

After reading this article, you will be able to:

- Explain Boko Haram's evolved use of Gender Based Violence.

- Evaluate why Boko Haram views the utilization of women as an effective tactic.

- Describe how Boko Haram views gender in its ideology.

Introduction

The Islamist terrorist group known as Boko Haram, but whose formal name in Arabic is *Jamā'a Ahl al-sunnah li-da'wa wa al-jihād* (Sunni Group for Preaching and Jihad), has been active in Nigeria since 2002, when it was founded by Muhammed Yusuf (Tonwe & Eke 2013: 234). Translated from Hausa, 'Boko Haram' means 'Western Education is Sinful', and this reflects the group's two main aims: the opposition of what it considers to be the secular westernisation of Nigeria, especially co-educational learning and democratic elections; and the creation of an Islamic state in Nigeria, or at least in the country's majority Muslim northern states (Ibid: 235).

The Nigerian government has violently opposed Boko Haram, and in July 2009 successfully, but only temporarily, quashed an uprising by the group across north-eastern Nigeria (Adesoji 2010: 98). The uprising led to the deaths of 800 Boko Haram members, including Yusuf. The extra-judicial killing of Yusuf was recorded on cell phones and the footage became widely accessible on the Internet, which only increased his "martyrdom" status in the eyes of his followers (IRIN News, 18 July 2011). One year later, in July 2010, Boko Haram's new leader, Yusuf's former second-in-command, Abubakar Shekau emerged from hiding and announced in a statement released to journalists that "jihad has begun"(Zenn 2013).

Since July 2010 Nigeria has experienced both a resurgence in Boko Haram militancy and an evolution to more sophisticated attacks and jihadist ideology, modelled on al-Qaeda (Pham 2012: 3-6). More than 3,500 people have been killed in the conflict since 2010, and after more than four years of Shekau's leadership, the violence shows no signs of abating (Agbiboa 2014: 41). Shekau has called out to other jihadist groups, including Al-Qaeda leaders, such as Ayman al-Zawahri and the late Abu Musa'ab al-Zarqawi, as well as Al-Qaeda in the Islamic Maghreb (AQIM) and Al-Shabaab. Boko Haram's international links are however not as developed as those of its splinter group of mostly AQIM-trained militants, Ansaru, which has closer operational ties to the global Al-Qaeda network (Long War Journal, 13 November 2013).

The increasingly international character of Boko Haram has become a focus of analysis ever since Boko Haram's suicide car bombing attack on the UN Headquarters in Abuja in August 2011. This article, however, addresses a less-researched aspect of Boko Haram's activities: gender-based violence (GBV) and Boko Haram's instrumentalization of women in its operations, culture and ideology (Barkindo et al. 2013: 4).

GBV in Context

GBV is defined by the UN as '*physical, sexual or mental harm or suffering to women, including threats of such acts, coercion or arbitrary deprivation of liberty, whether occurring in public or in private life*' (World Health Organization). The term, however, also applies to violence specifically targeted against men and boys (UNFPA 2012: 3). 'Gender' is understood as socially constructed norms and roles both limiting, and permitting, the actions and expectations of men and women (Butler 1999: 6; Mu'Azu & Uzoechi 2010: 122).

Within Nigeria, GBV transcends region, religion and ethnicity, with physical and sexual abuse affecting as many as 35.1%

of Igbo women and 34.3% of Hausa-Fulani women (Oladepo et al. 2011). Nigerian cultural traditions have included female genital mutilation, forced marriage and widowhood practices, including hairshaving and restriction to the home (Ifemeje 2012: 138). Nigerian law is also infused with discriminatory practices against women, including an implied legal backing to the assault of a wife in Section 55 of the penal code, and, in Section 6 of the criminal code, a lack of legal recognition for rape within marriage (Ibid.: 143).[1] GBV also affects men in Nigeria and sexual violence has been a tactic of government forces against men in detention in order to humiliate and disempower them (Peel 2004: 65).

This analysis will specifically focus however on Boko Haram and gender, arguing that there is evidence that gender is now an increasingly significant component of Boko Haram's tactics, messaging, and violence.

The first section explores Boko Haram's recent campaign of gender-based abductions in its escalating conflict with the security forces. The second section explores tactics, and provides evidence of Boko Haram's shift to include women in its operations and the extensive targeting of Christian women. The final section considers the rationale for instrumentalizing women within the framework of Boko Haram's ideology and culture.

Instrumentality: Women As Pawns

2013 marked a significant evolution in Boko Haram's tactics. Boko Haram carried out a series of kidnappings, in which one of the main features was the instrumental use of women, in response to corresponding tactics by the Nigerian government. Kidnapping is a recent development for the group and the first suggestions of this tactic emerged in Boko Haram statements in January 2012. It was then that the group's leader, Abubakar Shekau, issued a video message threatening to kidnap the wives of government officials in response to the government imprisoning the wives of Boko Haram members (Associated Press, 27 January 2012).

However, Boko Haram's first actual kidnapping operation was carried out one year later in February 2013, with the abduction of a seven-member French family in northern Cameroon, then brought back to Nigeria (The Guardian, 19 April 2013). The family group included four children (Ibid.). Between February 2013 and May 2013, the kidnapping strategy was brought directly to Nigerian soil, with the abductions of more than a dozen government officials and their families in Boko Haram's main base of Borno State. In May 2013, Boko Haram carried out a mass assault on a police barracks in Bama, Borno State in which militants captured 12 Christian women and children (Agence France-Presse, 13 May 2013). This was

a prolonged attack, and the abductions followed a fierce battle with security forces in which more than 100 people were killed. On May 7, 2013, Shekau claimed the kidnappings of these 12 women and children in Boko Haram's name. In another video message, he then promised to make these hostages his 'servants' if certain conditions, such as the release of Boko Haram members and their wives from prison, were not met (Agence France-Presse, video, 13 May 2013).

Shekau's statement related to the Nigerian government's arrest in 2012 of the wives and children of several Boko Haram leaders, for which the Bama kidnappings were a response. More than 100 women and children had been detained, among them Shekau's own wives. Also arrested were the wife and children of the commander for Kano, Suleiman Muhammed; the pregnant wife of the commander for Sokoto, Kabiru Sokoto, who gave birth while in prison; and the wife of the suicide-bomber who attacked the 'This Day' media house in Abuja in April 2012 (Barkindo et al. 2013: 22). These arrests were not unusual in themselves. The targeting of suspects' family and friends is a common policing practice in Nigeria, according to Nigerian security experts (Interview with Beegeagle, 2013). The significance was the deliberate deployment of such practices to strike at the heart of Boko Haram through Boko Haram's female family members, which in turn has had a significant impact on Boko Haram's strategy.

This capture of Boko Haram militants' family members was cited as a grievance in almost all Shekau's video statements in 2012 and 2013. In his first statement after the mass detentions, Shekau explicitly accused the government of "kidnapping" women (YouTube, 11 January 2012). Subsequent video messages reiterated this theme, with complaints of a sustained government strategy of arrests of Boko Haram family members. When in mid-September 2012 the government detained a further ten women associated with Boko Haram, Shekau responded with his fifth video message. In this video, which was made public on September 30, 2012, Shekau threatened revenge on wives of government officials. He also speculated on the possible sexual abuse of the Boko Haram family members by security forces, when he said '. . . *they have continued capturing our women. . . . In fact, they are even having sex with one of them. Allah, Allah, see us and what we are going through*' (YouTube, 30 September 2012). He made clear the intention to target 'enemy' women in return, '*Since you are now holding our women, (laughs) just wait and see what will happen to your own women . . . to your own wives according to Sharia law*' (Ibid). These events demonstrate an established cycle of government detentions of women related to Boko Haram, and the group's retaliatory abduction of Christian women.

All these women were targeted for instrumental purposes, as none of those captured on either side had any direct involvement in the conflict. The women abducted by Boko Haram at Bama, for example, were visiting relatives working at the police station (Al-Jazeera, 26 May 2013). After they were released several weeks later in exchange for the release of the wives of Boko Haram members, the women were interviewed by Al-Jazeera. They said that the Boko Haram members told them explicitly that their abduction was a response to the government's detention of their own wives and children. They had been in 'the wrong place at the wrong time' (Ibid.).

Correspondingly, there is no evidence that the female relatives of Boko Haram members who were arrested by the government had any direct involvement in the group's activities. While Boko Haram has in the past paid young boys to carry out operations, such as arson attacks and intelligence gathering, there is no indication that women have been carrying out such activities (Punch News, 30 November 2013). Nor, according to a leading Nigerian security expert, is it probable that female relatives of Boko Haram operatives would be informed if their husband were an active Boko Haram member (Anonymous, Interviewed by Jacob Zenn, May 2013). In one case in 2012, for example, a pregnant Cameroonian woman and child were found in a Kano flat that also served as a Boko Haram hide-out. She appeared entirely ignorant that her husband was suspected of planning an attack on a church that killed at least twenty people (PM News Nigeria, 1 May 2012).

Evolving Conflict, Evolving Tactics

The cycle of gender-based abduction and detention and increased violence in Nigeria is evolving, and has expanded since Nigerian President Goodluck Jonathan announced a State of Emergency in Borno, Yobe and Adamawa States in May 2013 (CNN, 14 May 2013). Since 2013, the Civilian Joint Task Force (JTF) has joined security forces in employing new methods against Boko Haram, such as the mass arrest of male suspects in the early hours of the morning, the disappearance of suspects, and the use of young teenage men, fluent in the local Kanuri language and culture to operate checkpoints (Human Rights Watch News, 29 November 2013). Male supporters of Boko Haram have therefore become uniquely vulnerable to detention and abuse, particularly by the Civilian JTF, which is essentially staffed by volunteers.

Since then, a series of unusual arrests in Maiduguri, Borno state, suggests an immediate and gendered responsive shift in Boko Haram tactics. In June 2013, an AK-47, a pistol and improvised explosive devices (IEDs) were found in the garments of two 'shivering' veiled women in Maiduguri (Vanguard News, 30 June 2013). Two months later, two women hiding rifles in their clothing were among five suspected Boko Haram militants who were arrested by the security forces (The Guardian Nigeria, August 2013). Also in August 2013, a woman was detained alongside a 35-year old male Boko Haram suspect (Vanguard News, 17 August 2013). Additionally, male Boko Haram members have reportedly disguised themselves as women in veils in order to evade arrest. In one case, in July 2013, three men dressed as veiled women were killed, and around twenty others arrested, in an attempted attack on a police station (Daily Trust, 6 July 2013).

This mirrors a pattern seen in the adaptive responses of other terrorist organisations in times of unique pressure on men (Cunningham 2003: 172; Ortbals & Poloni-Staudinger 2013: 44). In Iraq, for example, women were similarly deployed to smuggle arms and execute suicide bombings, during a clamp-down on Al-Qaeda in the mid-2000s (Sjoberg & Gentry 2011: 15; Bloom 2011: 210). A direct order from the leader of al-Qaeda in Iraq, Abu Mus'ab al-Zarqawi, this capitalised on women's superior ability to evade security checks, cache weapons in clothing, and attract less suspicion as suicide bombers (Ibid.: 210-4). His intention was also to shame men into action (Ibid.), although there is as yet no indication of this aim within Boko Haram.

The tactical use of women due to the lesser suspicion they arouse has also been evident in Islamist violence in Pakistan and Indonesia; and within the conflict in Israel and Palestine (Ibid: 177). Historically, it is a pattern seen in liberation campaigns such as the Algerian resistance against the French, in which women were initially ordered to smuggle weapons; later, recognising the vital role they could play, female supporters of the resistance became willing volunteers for such tasks (Minne & Clarke 2007: 344), (Horne 2002:124).

Targeting and Abusing Christian Women

The State of Emergency has manifested in other Boko Haram activities involving women, with a reported increase in GBV against Christian women in northern areas of Nigeria, and increasing levels of sexual violence including rape, torture and also murder. A recent study for Nigeria's Political Violence Research Network suggests that more than 45% of those killed by Boko Haram are Christian women and children (Barkindo et al. 2013: 17-22). This, too, appears to be connected to the increased government pressure on Boko Haram in strongholds in northeastern Nigeria, with insurgents abducting Christian women as they flee the security forces. The Christian Association of Nigeria has been reporting the abduction of Christian teenagers since July 2013 (Agenzia Fides, 23 July 2013). Researchers speaking to women in the northeastern regions have uncovered a picture of violence and intimidation, with women increasingly targeted with kidnap, forced marriage and compulsory conversion to Islam (Barkindo et al. 2013:17–29).

Some of this GBV appears tactical. In one widely reported case from November 2013, a Christian teenager told how she was abducted by Boko Haram from a rural region of Gwoza, Borno State, and forced to cook and clean for the group. This 19-year old girl, Hajja, was held for three months, during which time she was also forced to convert to Islam, set to be married to one of the group, and pressured to carry out operational tasks for the fourteen-strong team of men who took her. Hajja was made to lure government soldiers into positions where they could be targeted, and to watch as their throats were slit by Boko Haram members after they were captured—killings in which the Muslim wife of the Boko Haram cell leader reportedly participated (The Blaze, 19 November 2013). A Gwoza official estimates more than a dozen other Christian women remain in captivity in similar circumstances (Reuters, 17 November 2013), and young girls are particularly targeted (Wall St Journal, 14 January 2014).

Such practices are reminiscent of the behaviour of rebel movements in conflict zones in other parts of Sub-Saharan Africa, in tactically exploiting women. Civil conflicts in Mozambique, Sierra Leone and Rwanda have all witnessed GBV in the abduction, sexual violence and forced marriage and conscription of enemy women into insurgent groups (Mazurana & McKay 2003: 11–17; Turshen 2001: 5; Coulter et al 2008: 9–12). In Uganda, soldiers with Joseph Kony's Lord's Resistance Army (LRA) were routinely engaged in the sale and 'transfer' of women (Amnesty International 1997: 17; Turshen 2000: 811–2). In these cases women were targeted both for their assets, and as 'assets' in themselves. Their value was reproductive, and productive, providing skills such as cooking and cleaning, necessary to a wartime labour force (Turshen 2001: 1). Unlike earlier civil African conflicts such as those in Eritrea or Mozambique, in which women's rights were part of the insurgent ideology, these later conflicts have predominantly only objectified and exploited women (Coulter et al 2008: 9–17).

If the abduction of women by Boko Haram is tactical, other violence against Christian women appears primarily punitive. In Maiduguri, in August 2013, a Christian student reported an attack by Boko Haram on her university accommodation: the men were murdered, the women segregated into Muslim and non-Muslims, and the Christian women systematically raped (Barkindo et al. 2013: 23). Such attacks on Christian women by Boko Haram can be regarded as an extension of other institutionalised and long-term discriminatory practices against them in northern regions (Onapajo & Uzodike 2012: 32). Women have faced broad discriminatory practices in both the professional and domestic spheres. They have been targeted in acid-attacks for 'un-Islamic' practices, such as a failure to wear the hijab, or for taking a job (Turaki 2010). Women are also often accused of 'dishonouring Islam'. In 2006, riots ensued in which more than 50 Christians were killed, mostly women and children, after a Christian female teacher confiscated a Qur'an from a student in Bauchi (Alao 2009: 40). This generic culture of discrimination against Christians has enabled the escalation in recent violence.

Gender in Boko Haram's Ideology and Culture

There have been no explicit calls in Boko Haram's ideology for this level of violence against Christian women, or women in general (Barkindo et al. 2013: 5). However, Boko Haram's command to Jihad often features exhortations to terrorise Christian communities or, in its words, a "War on Christians", and the victimisation of women is a tactic within this strategy (Punch News, 11 July 2012; Coulter et al. 2008: 13).

Shariah law is also a factor. Boko Haram's emphasis on the forced imposition of Shariah facilitates GBV through rigidly gendered ideological structures (Onuoha 2010: 57). The rise of Boko Haram coincided with the adoption of Shariah in 12 northern states, and was to some extent a by-product of this (Akanji 2009: 55-60). The version of Shariah law supported by Shekau and Boko Haram promotes narrow gender roles for men and women, enforcing strict rules on women's dress and sexual conduct and instituting other discriminatory and abusive practices against women. These range from the enforced segregation of schoolchildren, to the public flogging of women for fornication (BBC, 7 January 2003). Gendered norms have been adopted by Boko Haram's leaders, who have listed among the values to be opposed, '..the rights and privileges of Women, the idea of homosexualism, lesbianism.. rape of infants.. blue films, prostitution..' and beauty pageants, all associated with Western ideals (Zenn 2013b; World Stage, 18 March 2012).

Boko Haram's ideology casts men in hyper-masculine combat roles, their duty to violently oppose the west. By contrast, '..unarmed men, youths, women, cripple and even under age..' are exempt from battle and constitute illegitimate targets (Sahara Reporters, 22 January 2012). Muslim women—in contrast to Christian women—have customarily been spared, even where Boko Haram has targeted Muslim men, as in an attack on a college in Yobe in September 2013. All male students were killed, but female students were not (International Business Times, 29 September 2013). This binary understanding of gender norms permits GBV to serve as a display of power (Solangon & Patel 2012: 425). Abuses of Christian women both serve to mark their difference from Muslim women, and strike at Christian men, by demonstrating their inability to protect 'their' women.

This combative ideological masculinity appears to have specific resonance with a section of disenfranchised Nigerian men.

It was predominantly such men who gathered to watch Boko Haram's founder, Muhammed Yusuf, when he spoke in television interviews, or simply led Friday prayers. Yusuf's appeal was to a population dominated by unemployed, poor males (Onuoha 2010: 57–8). These men were angry and frustrated over the perceived corruption of the Nigerian government, on which Yusuf lectured, and mass unemployment (IRIN News, 18 July 2011).

Globalisation can be regarded as a factor in such violence and feelings of grievance, with the fracturing of men's traditional identities impacting on their willingness to turn to extremist groups (Connell 2005: 73; Maalouf 1996: 90–93). In the face of social change, the reform of traditional gendered practices and the gradual adoption of 'Western' values, gender-based violence and binary gender norms can perform as a source of self-worth (Barker & Ricardo 2005: v; Kimmel 2003: 603–620). These norms are not a necessary characteristic of Islamist groups. Nigeria's earlier Islamist movement Yan Izala, established in 1978, in fact promoted an emancipatory programme of rights for women, when compared with some other Salafist movements (Loimeier 2012: 141).

The impact of grievances, globalisation and poverty on Nigerian violence suggests that ideology is one of a number of possible factors in GBV committed by Boko Haram members and supporters. Indeed, Alao proposes that Nigerian radicalisation predominantly concerns matters of ethnicity, commercial rivalries and power (Alao 2009: 22). Agbiboa also cites local disputes, poverty, corruption and long-term injustices committed without police action as drivers for religious and ethnic violence (Agbiboa 2014: 50).

Criminal motives may also play a role. In Maiduguri, six Christian women were abducted and repeatedly raped by insurgents who claimed this as sexual 'jizya', a tax paid by Christians under Islamic law. However, the surname of one of the women distinguished the group as ethnic Berom, who are perceived by Boko Haram as "immigrants" to northern Islamic lands. The rape therefore effectively served as a punishment, and a threat to leave (Barkindo et al. 2013: 23). In other sexual attacks against women, the victims' perception has been that the assaults were driven by an essentially 'criminal' element of the group (Ibid. p. 29). Indeed, ideology is unlikely to drive all Boko Haram members, as some are undoubtedly coerced into joining the group (AOV & NWGOV 2013: 43). The level of control of Boko Haram leadership over the activities of such elements is questionable, and has as yet not been pronounced upon by Shekau.

Conclusion

This article focused on Boko Haram, with the aim of shedding light on a neglected but developing aspect of the group's operations: gender-based changes in Boko Haram's tactics and its instrumental use of women, resulting in increasing GBV targeted at Christians. It outlined the instrumental use of women by both Boko Haram and Nigerian security forces in a cycle of abductions and detentions dating from 2012. Three conclusions can be drawn from these retaliatory actions.

Firstly, as implied by Shekau's video messages, abductions of women have since 2012 come to constitute a semi-official Boko Haram tactic, in response to similar tactics by government. Secondly, it seems clear that the recent violence and ensuing state of emergency is causing Boko Haram to evolve tactically, engaging women in support roles in the group, disguising men as women to avoid arrest, and abducting Christian women. Thirdly, women are being targeted by both sides in Nigeria's conflict, for purely instrumental reasons. They do not yet appear to be actively and willingly participating in violence to a significant extent.

The article also briefly explored the complex factors in the evolution of Boko Haram's tactics. Shariah law, at the heart of Boko Haram, and with a strict control and restriction of women's liberty is implicated in GBV, but other factors emerge. Local grievances and frustrations drive men towards Boko Haram, and a sense of security in its gender norms; perhaps also to GBV. Women victims themselves suggest criminality is a factor in GBV, with women stripped of assets, or raped as an end in itself. Additionally, GBV by Boko Haram is contextualised by an institutionalisation of broader discriminatory practices within Nigeria, but also by the similar sexual targeting of women in other civil conflicts in sub-Saharan Africa, where women are constructed as assets, and exploited as such, and by similar tactical developments in other terrorist groups when under extreme pressure.

It is also important to note that, although this piece focused on Boko Haram, the group does not have a monopoly on violence against women in Nigeria. Government troops have also been accused of looting, theft, murder and rape (IRIN News, 18 July 2011). It is hard to envisage an end to Boko Haram's violence, while government forces employ violence with impunity. Nor while discriminatory practices remain to some extent endemic. This is not to discount the activities of the many proactive Nigerian women; Nigerian women's groups have indeed been a powerful voice in protesting violence (Patch 2008: 40).

This analysis is still limited by the lack of research carried out with women supporters of Boko Haram. More research is needed with women in Boko Haram strongholds to ascertain their views. However, the strict gender norms of Boko Haram suggest that if women do carry out operations for the group, this is unlikely to constitute more than an emergency measure, and will not affect women's status organisationally. This is consistent with current trends in other terrorist groups (Global Observatory, 21 August 2013).

It is hoped that this piece has made clear that gender norms do figure in the Nigerian conflict, and within Boko Haram's culture, activities and ideology specifically. This article aims to provide an introduction to the importance of a further exploration of gender within the group, as a path to understanding, and ultimately preventing, Nigeria's ongoing and escalating violence.

Notes

1. The criminal code was enacted in 1945, the penal code in 1960.

Bibliography

Action on Armed Violence, and the Working Group on Armed Violence (2013), *The Violent Road, An Overview of Armed Violence in Nigeria* via http://aoav.org.uk/2013/the-violent-road-nigeria-north-east/

Adesoji, Abimbola (2010), 'The Boko Haram Uprising and Islamic Revivalism in Nigeria', *Africa Spectrum,* Vol. 45 No. 2, pp. 95–108.

Agbiboa, Daniel E. (2014), 'Peace at Daggers Drawn? Boko Haram and the State of Emergency in Nigeria', *Studies in Conflict & Terrorism,* Vol.37, No. 1, pp. 41–67.

Agence France-Presse, 13 May 2013, 'New Boko Haram video claims attacks, shows hostages', via http://mg.co.za/article/2013-05-13-new-boko-haram-video-claims-attack-shows-hostages accessed 9/1/2014

Agence France-Presse, Video, 13 May 2013, 'Nigeria Islamist video claims attacks, shows hostages', via http://www.youtube.com/watch?v=n6qZM36oq8E

Agenzia Fides, 23 July 2013, 'Boko Haram: Christian girls kidnapped and Islamized, schools targeted', via http://www.fides.org/en/news/34019-AFRICA_NIGERIA_Boko_Haram_Christian_girls_kidnapped_and_Islamized_schools_targeted#.UuOvF7TLdLN accessed 24/1/2014.

Al-Jazeera News, 26 May 2013, 'Freed Nigerian Hostages Tell of Ordeal' via http://www.youtube.com/watch?v=36Vlok6GrKQ

Akanji, Olajide O (2009), 'The politics of combating domestic terrorism in Nigeria', in Wafula Okumu and Anneli Botha (eds), *Domestic terrorism in Africa: defining, addressing and understanding its impact on human security,* (Pretoria: Institute for Security Studies).

Alao, Abiodun (2009), 'Islamic radicalization and violence in Nigeria: A country report', *Security and Development,* via http://www.securityanddevelopment.org/pdf/ESRC%20Nigeria%20Overview.pdf

Amnesty International Report (1997), *Uganda: "Breaking God's Commands": the Destruction of Childhood by the Lord's Resistance Army,* (New York: Amnesty International).

Amnesty International Report (2012), *Nigeria: Trapped in the Cycle of Violence,* (London: Amnesty International).

Associated Press, 27 January 2012, 'Nigeria sect leader threatens new attacks' via http://www.utsandiego.com/news/2012/jan/27/nigeria-sect-leader-threatens-new-attacks/all/?print accessed 10/1/2014.

Barker, Gary and Ricardo, Christine (2005), 'Young Men and the Construction of Masculinity in Sub-Saharan Africa: Implications for HIV/AIDS, Conflict, and Violence', *Social Development Papers: Conflict, Development and Reconstruction,* (The World Bank) Paper No. 26.

Barkindo, Atta, Gudaku, Benjamin Tyavkase, Wesley, Caroline Katgurum (2013), 'Boko Haram and Gender Based Violence Against Christian Women and Children in North-Eastern Nigeria Since 1999', *NPVRN Working Paper* No. 1, (Amsterdam: Open Doors International).

BBC News, 7 January 2003, 'Analysis: Nigeria's Sharia split' via http://news.bbc.co.uk/1/hi/world/africa/2632939.stm

Bloom, Mia (2011), *Bombshell, The Many Faces of Women Terrorists,* (C. Hurst and Co.: London).

Butler, Judith (1999), *Gender Trouble: Feminism and the Subversion of Identity,* (Routledge Classics: London).

CNN, 14 May 2013, 'Nigerian President declares emergency in 3 states during "rebellion"' via http://edition.cnn.com/2013/05/14/world/africa/nigeria-violence/ accessed 13/1/2014.

Connell, Robert W. (2005), 'Globalisation, Imperialism and Masculinities', in Kimmel, Michael, Hearn, Jeff and Connell, Robert W. (Eds.) *A Handbook of Studies on Men and Masculinities,* (Sage).

Coulter, Chris, Persson, Mariam and Utas, Mats (2008), *Young Female Fighters in African Wars, Conflict and Its Consequences,* (Nordiska Afrikainstitutet : Stockholm).

Cunningham, Karla J. (2003), 'Cross-Regional Trends in Female Terrorism', *Studies in Conflict & Terrorism,* Vol. 26, No. 3, pp. 171–195.

Daily Trust, 6 July 2013, 'Nigeria: women as Boko Haram's new face' via http://allafrica.com/stories/201307081607.html accessed 12/1/2014.

Danjibo, D. N. (2009), 'Islamic Fundamentalism and Sectarian Violence: The "Maitatsine" and "Boko Haram" Crises in Northern Nigeria. Peace and Conflict Studies Programme', *Institute of African Studies,* (University of Ibadan) via http://www.ifra-nigeria.org/IMG/pdf/N-_D-_DANJIBO_-_Islamic_Fundamentalism_and_Sectarian_Violence_The_Maitatsine_and_Boko_Haram_Crises_in_Northern_Nigeria.pdf.

Fawole, O.I., Ajuwon, A.J, Osungbade, K.O. & Fawega, C.O. (2002), 'Prevalence and nature of violence to young female hawkers in motor parks in South Western Nigeria', *Health Education Research,* 102:230–238.

Global Observatory, 21 August 2013, 'Women Terrorists Today Follow Men's Ideologies: Interview with Mia Bloom' via http://www.theglobalobservatory.org/interviews/563-women-terrorists-today-follow-mensideologies-interview-with-mia-bloom.html

The Guardian, 19 April 2013, 'French family seized in Cameroon by suspected Boko Haram Islamists freed' via http://www.theguardian.com/world/2013/apr/19/french-family-kidnapped-cameroon-freed accessed 9/1/2014.

The Guardian Nigeria, August 2013, 'JTF, vigilance group capture five suspected terrorists' via http://www. theguardianmobile. com/readNewsItem1.php?nid=16303 accessed 12/1/2014.

Horne, Alistair (2002 reprint) [1977 original], *A Savage War of Peace: Algeria 1954-1962,* (London: Pan Macmillan).

Human Rights Watch News, 29 November 2013, 'Boko Haram abducts women, recruits children' via http://www.hrw.org/news/2013/11/29/nigeria-boko-haram-abducts-women-recruits-children accessed 13/1/2014.

Ifemeje, Sylvia Chika,(2008), 'A critique of gender discriminatory practices in Igbo customary marriages', *Journal of Women and Minority Rights,* Vol. 1, No. 1, pp. 57–61.

Ifemeje, Sylvia Chika (2012), 'Gender-Based Domestic Violence in Nigeria: A Socio-Legal Perspective', *Indian Journal of Gender Studies,* Vol. 19, No. 1, pp. 137–148.

Igbellina-Igbokwe, Nkiru, (2013), 'Contextualizing Gender Based Violence Within Patriarchy in Nigeria', *Pan-African Voices for Freedom and Justice* (Pambazuka News), Issue 632, via http://www.pambazuka.org/en/ category/features/87597

IRIN News, 18 July 2011, 'Analysis: Understanding Nigeria's Boko Haram radicals' via http://www.irinnews.org/report/93250/analysis-understanding-nigeria-s-boko-haram-radicals

International Business Times, 29 September 2013, 'Boko Haram slaughter 50 students in Nigeria college dorm' via http://www.ibtimes.com/boko-haram-militants-slaughter-50-students-nigeria-collegedorm- 1412504

Johnmary, Ani Kelechi (2012), 'Violent Traditional Gender Practices and Implications for Nation Building Process in Nigeria', *Public Policy and Administration Research,* Vol. 2, No. 5, pp. 44–56.

Kimmel, Michael S. (2003), Globalization and its Mal(e)Contents : The Gendered Moral and Political Economy of Terrorism, *International Sociology,* Vol. 18, pp. 603–620.

Loimeier, Roman (2012), 'Boko Haram : The Development of a Militant Religious Movement in Nigeria', *Africa Spectrum,* Vol. 47, Nos. 2-3, pp. 137–155.

Long War Journal, 13 November 2013, 'US adds Boko Haram, Ansaru to list of foreign terrorist groups' via http://www.longwarjournal.org/archives/2013/11/us_adds_boko_haram_t_1.php#ixzz2rVxy4jHh

Maalouf, Amin (1996), *In the Name of Identity: Violence and the Need to Belong,* (Penguin: London).

Mazurana, Dyan and McKay, Susan (2003), *Girls in Fighting Forces in Northern Uganda, Sierra Leone, and Mozambique, Policy and Program Recommendations,* (International Centre for Human Rights and Democratic Development and University of Wyoming and the University of Montana).

Minne, Daniele, Djamila, Amrane & Clarke, Alistair (translation) (2007), 'Women at War', Interventions: *International Journal of Postcolonial Studies,* Vol. 9, No. 3, pp. 340–349.

Mu'azu M. T. and Uzoechi B. C. (2010), 'Gender Issues in Curriculum Implementation at the Basic Education Level in Nigeria', *Nigerian Journal of Curriculum Studies,* Vol. 17. No. 3, p. 122.

Okpaga1, Adagba, Chijioke, Ugwu Sam, Okechukwu, Eme Innocent (2012), 'Activities of Boko Haram and Insecurity Question in Nigeria', *Arabian Journal of Business and Management Review,* Vol. 1, No. 9.

Oladepo, Yusuf OB, and Arulogun OS (2011), 'Factors Influencing Gender Based Violence Among Men and Women in Selected States in Nigeria', *African Journal of Reproductive Health* December 15(4):78–86.

Onapajo, Hakeem & Uzodike, Ufo Okeke (2012), 'Boko Haram terrorism in Nigeria', *African Security Review,* Vol. 21, No. 3, pp. 24–39.

Onuoha, Freedom C (2010), 'The Islamist challenge: Nigeria's Boko Haram crisis explained', *African Security Review,* Vol. 19, No. 2, pp. 54–67.

Ortbals, Candice D. and Poloni-Staudinger, Lori (2013), *Terrorism and Violent Conflict: Women's Agency, Leadership and Responses,* (Springer: New York).

Patch, Jonathan (2008), 'Women and Non-violent Forms of Activism in the Niger Delta Oil Resource Conflict', *Undercurrent,* Vol. 5, No. 3 p. 39.

Peel, Michael (2004), 'Men as Perpetrators and Victims', in *Rape as a Method of Torture,* ed. Michael Peel. (London: Medical Foundation for the Care of Victims of Torture) pp. 61–70.

Pham, J. Peter (2012), 'Boko Haram's Evolving Threat', *Africa Security Brief,* Vol. 20, pp. 1–8 (African Center of Strategic Studies), via www.ndu.edu/press/lib/pdf/Africa-Security-Brief/ASB-20.pdf accessed 10/1/2014.

Pew Research (2009), 'Mapping the Global Muslim Population: A report on the size and distribution of the World Muslim Population', accessed via http://www.pewforum.org/newassets/images/reports/ Muslimpopulation/Muslimpopulation.pdf accessed 22/3/2013.

PM News Nigeria, 1 May 2012, 'Cameroonian among women captured during Kano JTF raid' via http://pmnewsnigeria. com/2012/05/01/cameroonian-among-women-captured-during-kano-jtf-raid/ accessed 10/1/2014.

Punch News, 11 July 2012, 'We're behind plateau mass killings—Boko Haram' via http://www.punchng.com/news/were-behind-plateau-mass-killings-boko-haram-%E2%80%A2-says-christians-should-accept-islam-ifthey-want-peace/

Punch News, 30 November 2013, 'Boko Haram paid us only N5000 each, to burn schools' via http://www.punchng.com/news/b-haram-recruits-children-for-attacks-hrw/

Reuters, 17 November 2013, 'Insight: Boko Haram, taking to hills, seize slave "brides"' via http://www.reuters.com/article/2013/11/17/us-nigeria-security-islamists-insight-idUSBRE9AG04120131117 accessed 24/1/2014.

Sahara Reporters, 22 January 2012, 'Boko Haram: why we struck in Kano' via http://saharareporters.com/news-page/boko-haram-why-we-struck-kano

Schweitzer, Yoram (2006), 'Dying for Equality?', *Memorandum* 84 (Tel Aviv: Jaffee Center for Strategic Studies), p. 8.

Sjoberg, Laura and Gentry, Caron (2011), 'Introduction', in Sjoberg, Laura and Gentry, Caron E. (eds.) *Women, Gender and Terrorism* (University of Georgia Press: Georgia).

Smelser, Neil J. (2007), *The Faces of Terrorism: Social and Psychological Dimensions,* (Princeton: Princeton University Press).

Solangon, S., & Patel, Preeti (2012), 'Sexual violence against men in countries affected by armed conflict', *Conflict, Security & Development,* Vol. 12, No. (4), pp. 417–442.

The Blaze, 19 November 2013, 'Nigerian Terrorists Reportedly Abducting Christian Women, Forcing them to Convert and Then Marry Islamic Militants' via http://www.theblaze.com/stories/2013/11/19/nigerianterrorists- reportedly-abducting-christian-women-forcing-them-to-convert-and-then-marry-islamicmilitants/ accessed 24/1/2014.

Tonwe, Daniel A. and Eke, Surulola J. (2013), 'State fragility and violent uprisings in Nigeria', *African Security Review,* Vol. 22, No. 4, pp. 232–243.

Turaki, Yusufu (2010), *Tainted Legacy: Islam, Colonialism and Slavery in Northern Nigeri*a, (McLean,VA).

Turshen, Meredeth (2000), 'The Political Economy of Violence against Women During Armed Conflict in Uganda', *Social Research,* Vol. 67, No. 3, pp. 803–824.

Turshen, Meredeth (2001), 'The Political Economy of Rape: An Analysis of Systematic Rape and Sexual Abuse of Women During Armed Conflict in Africa', in C. Moser and F. Clarke eds. *Victors, Perpetrators or Actors: Gender, Armed Conflict and Political Violence,* pp. 55–68 (Zed Books: London).

United Nations Population Fund (2012), *Addressing Gender-based Violence,* via www.unfpa.org/. . ./documents/. . ./final%20 sexual%20violence%20CSW%. . .

Vanguard News, 30 June 2013, 'Vigilante arrests two women with assault rifle, IEDs in Maiduguri', via http://www.vanguardngr.com/2013/06/vigilante-arrests-2-women-with-assault-weapons-ied-in-maiduguri/ accessed 12/1/2014.

Vanguard News, 17 August 2013, 'JTR, Vigilante Arrest Female Boko Haram Suspects' via http://www.vanguardngr.com/2013/08/jtf-vigilante-arrest-female-boko-haram-suspects/ accessed 26/1/2014.

Vanguard News, 28 October 2013, Nigeria, *Borno cautions 'Civilian JTF' against abuse of power,* 28 October 2013 via http://www.vanguardngr.com/2013/10/borno-cautions-civilian-jtf-abuse-power/

Wall Street Journal, 14 January 2014, *Nigeria rebels drag children into battle,* via http://online.wsj.com/news/articles/SB100014240527023047731045792692697781352679364 accessed 15/1/2014.

Wendt, Alexander (1987), 'The Agent-Structure Problem in International Relations Theory', *International Organization,* Vol. 41, No. 3, pp. 335–370.

World Health Organization, 'Health topics, Violence Against Women' via http://www.who.int/topics/gender_ based_violence/en/

World Stage, 18 March 2012, 'Boko Haram Menace, Why is the World not Listening to this Man' via http://www.worldstagegroup.com/worldstagenew/index.php?active=news&newscid=4200&catid=23

YouTube, 11 January 2012, 'Message to Jonathan from Abubaker Shekau' (translation) via http://www.youtube.com/watch?v=eNg73vN86K8

YouTube, 30 September 2012, 'A Message to the World' via http://www.youtube.com/watch?v=txUJCOKTIuk&sns=em

Zenn, Jacob (2013), Boko Haram's Recruitment Strategies, *Combating Terrorism Center,* via http://www.ctc.usma.edu/posts/boko-harams-international-connections

Zenn, Jacob (2013b), 'Boko Haram Recruitment Strategies', *John Campbell Blog,* (Council on Foreign Relations) via http://blogs.cfr.org/campbell/2013/04/16/boko-haram-recruitment-strategies/

Critical Thinking

1. Has the utilization of women as a tactic proved effective for Boko Haram?

2. How have women been used as a tactic both by Boko Haram and the groups fighting it?

3. What roles have women played within Boko Haram?

Internet References

Amnesty International: Nigeria: Abducted women and girls forced to join Boko Haram attacks
https://www.amnesty.org/en/articles/news/2015/04/nigeria-abducted-women-and-girls-forced-to-join-boko-haram-attacks/

Boko Haram
http://www.nctc.gov/site/groups/boko_haram.html

Nigeria: Boko Haram Abducts Women, Recruits Children
http://www.hrw.org/news/2013/11/29/nigeria-boko-haram-abducts-women-recruits-children

---

JACOB ZENN is an analyst of African and Eurasian Affairs for The Jamestown Foundation in Washington DC and a legal adviser on international law of freedom of association. He authored "Northern Nigeria's Boko Haram: The Prize in Al-Qaeda's Africa's Strategy" in 2012 and currently consults on countering violent extremism in West Africa and Central Asia.

ELIZABETH PEARSON has recently completed an MA in International Conflict Studies in the War Studies Department at King's College London, where she was a Simon O'Dwyer Russell Prize-winner 2012–2013. Her research interests are radicalisation, gender and terrorism. Elizabeth also has more than fifteen years experience as a radio producer, reporter and feature-maker, and works freelance, mainly for BBC Radio Four.

Unit 9

UNIT

Prepared by: Thomas J. Badey, *Randolph-Macon College*

Government Response

Government responses to terrorism are varied, multifaceted, and complex. Decisions about domestic and foreign policy priorities, government spending, and the use and nature of military intervention are shaped by threat perceptions. While U.S. counterterrorism spending has increased significantly since 9/11, choices about how this money is to be used have become more difficult as various constituencies lobby to have their voices heard.

As policymakers struggle to allay public concerns, choices between spending for security today and preparing for the threats of the future have become more difficult. The tragedy of September 11 and the subsequent anthrax attacks have fueled fears about catastrophic terrorism. This makes choices about public policy priorities even more difficult. Given limited resources, should governments focus their efforts on existing crises and the most likely threats, or should they focus their resources on countless potential vulnerabilities and catastrophic threats, which many experts agree may be possible but not likely? Ideally, governments should do both. Realistically, even in a resource-rich environment, governments have to make difficult choices.

Decisions about when or how to use military force are equally complex. Should governments adopt preemptive or defensive postures? Should governments focus their resources on state-sponsors of terrorism, or should they focus their efforts on capturing or killing the leaders of existing terrorist groups? Does the long-term deployment of a military force to a foreign country increase or reduce the threat of terrorism? Should nonproliferation be a priority in the war on terrorism?

Finally, it is important to note that the U.S. commitment to the war on terrorism has not only had an impact on long-term U.S. foreign policy objectives but also the foreign policies of others. There is an opportunity cost to foreign policy decisions. By prioritizing a particular set of objectives, governments inevitably sacrifice others. This impacts not only U.S. policies but also the policies of other states. By making terrorism a policy priority, the U.S. influences and shapes the policies of others, as states may act in support of U.S. policy or take advantage of the vacuums created by such policies.

How governments view terrorism plays a critical role in their response. This unit highlights some of the methods governments use to respond to the threat of terrorism. In the first article, "Countering Terrorism in Democracies: Fighting fire with fire?" Aurelie Garbay argues that some governments respond to terrorism by resorting to measures that breach constitutional and international constraints. Focusing on the United States and Spain, she asserts that the use of torture by the State can be used by terrorists to justify their attacks and lend credence to their claims that they are fighting against a violent and oppressive regime. She concludes that fighting fire with fire is the worst possible response to terrorism. Next, Afeikhena Jerome asserts that there are important "Lessons from Colombia for Curtailing the Boko Haram Insurgency in Nigeria." Jerome suggests that despite how different the two countries may seem to be on the surface, Nigeria has much to learn from Colombia in dealing with the Boko Haram insurgency. Next, Scott N. McKay and David A. Webb compare counterterrorism in Indonesia and the Philippines. They argue that the United States can learn from counterterrorism support in Indonesia and the Philippines, and that these lessons should be applied to its future counterterrorism assistance efforts. Lastly, Brian M. Perkins looks at Pakistan's response to domestic terrorism after the Peshawar school attack. In December 2014, the Pakistani government implemented a 20-point National Action Plan (NAP). Perkins posits that the NAP, combined with civil society's increased willingness to stand up to militants could significantly reduce violence.

Article   Prepared by: Thomas J. Badey, *Randolph-Macon College*

Countering Terrorism in Democracies: Fighting Fire with Fire?

Aurélie Garbay

Learning Outcomes

After reading this article, you will be able to:

- Identify how states comply with the Rule of Law.

- Identify the potential consequences of the use of torture

- Discuss the inherent tension between a states right to security and individual rights and freedoms.

The recent attacks perpetrated in Paris were an immense shock for democratic States. No matter the preventive measures set up—intelligence gathering mechanisms, discreet surveillance measures, or dispersion of inmates—Saïd and Chérif Kouachi and Ahmed Coulibaly reminded Democracies that they must protect themselves, their citizens and their values, from the terrorist threat. However, one of the main perils for democratic systems remains in their answer to terrorism. Indeed, facing an unpredicted act of exceptional physical and symbolic violence, States may be tempted to fight fire with fire[1] by maximizing their repressive action, but also by setting up measures in breach with their constitutional and/or international constraints. It was the case of the United States after the 9/11 attacks: the adoption of the Patriot Act led to massive restrictions of fundamental rights and freedoms, together with drifts and abuses such as illegal detentions and the use of torture on suspected terrorists. It was also the case of the Spanish response to terrorism: both during Franco's dictatorship and under the current democratic regime, the use of incommunicado detention—a secret detention regime—led the European Court of Human Rights (ECtHR) to condemn the Kingdom of Spain six times[2] for its lack of effective investigations regarding torture allegations during custody. Considering the recent decisions by the ECtHR and its acceptance to hear new

complaints, and the problems continuously highlighted by the Council of Europe Committee for the Prevention of Torture, attention will be mainly focused in these developments on the Spanish case.

The example of the use of torture in Democracies, and the impunity often granted to State agents perpetrating such acts, provides a clear but alarming illustration of possible drifts in reaction to terrorist attacks. It also leads to a reflexion in order to understand why Democracies must fight against terrorism, and more generally against criminality, using instruments complying with the Rule of Law.

Torture as an Infringement of the Rule of Law

To be considered as complying with the Rule of Law, a State must respect the constraints it committed itself to[3], should they come from its constitution or the ratification of international conventions—e.g. the European Convention on Human Rights (ECHR). Thus, fundamental rights and freedoms enshrined in these norms should be ensured and not be affected by measures adopted by the State. However, when fighting against a criminal phenomenon, democratic States must address the issue of conciliating opposed objectives: the right to security on one side, individual rights and freedoms, on the other side. To this end, restrictions of rights and freedoms are admitted under specific circumstances. For instance, and according to the ECtHR case law, the preservation of public order justifies the dissolution of a political party calling to violence or praising terrorism.

However, several democratic systems committed themselves to never admit restrictions to specific rights and freedoms. It is notably the case, in the framework of the ECHR, for the absolute prohibition of torture, enshrined in article 3 of the Convention.

Consequently, any attempt to this right is in breach with the Rule of Law, and challenges the democratic essence of this State.

The Spanish system provides a clear illustration of this issue. Indeed, Spain ratified the ECHR, and its constitution—under article 15—forbids the use of torture. Nonetheless, Spain set up a highly repressive apparatus in order to fight against terrorism, that challenges the absolute interdiction of torture. It is notably the case of the incommunicado detention: for five days and without any video recording, the suspected terrorist is forbidden to have contacts with people other that the State security agents, a forensic doctor appointed by State authorities—and so is the forensic doctor in charge of a counter-expertise[4]—and a lawyer, also appointed by State authorities and only after the suspect's first official statement—without any time restrictions.[5] Such conditions, for sure collide with prescriptions regarding rights to medical and legal assistance, and create a situation of isolated confinement, which makes it possible de facto for State agents to torture suspects, despite the constitutional and conventional framework prohibiting the use of torture.

Torture as a Systemic Failure

The democratic essence of the State is all the more at stake that the use of torture by State agents is not only the result of legal "gaps", but also linked to its acceptance by the system itself. Indeed, weaknesses in the legislation may be counterbalanced by the action of the judiciary. In case of torture allegations, effective official investigations in order to establish the truth, but also appropriate sanctions when the use of torture has been proven are a clear and strong signal to State agents that any violation will not be accepted, and will be punished.

However, the paradox of the fight against terrorism by Democracies relies on the fact that democratic systems may accept deviant means in order to ensure their survival. The Reason of State—understood as an imperative on behalf of which State authorities accept infringements of the Rule of Law as serving the public interest[6]—would thus justify a certain degree of tolerance for torturers. In this scenario, Courts, when they do not acquit the State agents, sanction the use of torture with lenient penalties that do not have any dissuasive effect. Eventually, the Executive may pardon convicted torturers, which not only undermines the symbolic value of the fault by granting them a form of impunity regarding what should be absolutely prohibited, but also comforts torturers in the validity of their methods. Consequently, systemic failures lead to the fall of the system as a Democracy.

The lack of investigations, related to the procedural aspect of article 3 of the Convention, was a key argument in the six complaints heard by the ECtHR on torture allegations in custody, and led Spain to be considered as having violated the ECHR provisions.[7] Regarding the Executive attitude towards torture,

the Kepa Urra Guridi case[8] shows that, although judges sentenced to prison civil guards for torture, less than a year after the last appeal, the Ministry of Justice initiated proceedings which ended in pardons granted by the King for the State agents.[9]

Fighting Fire with Fire as the Worst Response to Terrorism

Despite their constitutional and international constraints, Democracies may be tempted by torture. However, torture appears to be ineffective[10] as, under water boarding, "walling", and other "enhanced interrogation techniques", suspects are likely to admit any crime they have not committed in order to stop the sufferings. This was one of the main conclusions of the CIA's report on its detention and interrogation programme.[11]

In addition, fighting fire with fire would have disastrous effects both on those who target Democracies, and on Democracies' citizens. Regarding terrorists, the use of illegal means would echo their claim that the Institutions they fight against are violent and oppressive, and, hence, the use of torture by the State could be used to justify their attacks. Regarding Democracies' citizens, the use of torture would break the "social contract": infringements of the Rule of Law, accepted if not organised by the system, would create among society a fear of being tortured and would annihilate citizens' trust in their State and its bodies. In the end, the terrorist project, "the deliberate use of violence and threat of violence to evoke a state of fear (or terror)"[12] in order to "threaten peace (…) and democratic institutions and their functioning and to undermine aspects of the Rule of Law"[13] of Democracies, could be considered as achieved.

A few days after the attacks at the railway station of Atocha, Javier Solana called "to fight for the Rule of Law, within the Rule of Law".[14] It is, indeed, the responsibility of Democracies to respond to terrorism with instruments complying with the Rule of Law, but also to face and address their own failures. Democratic States must hence remind that only if these conditions are met should their democratic essence remain.

Notes

1. Schwimmer W., Preface to the "Guidelines of Human rights and the fight against terrorism" adopted by the Committee of Ministers of the Council of Europe on 11 July 2002 at the 804th meeting of the Ministers' Deputies.

2. Related to Basque terrorism, see: San Argimiro Isasa v. Spain, case n° 2507/07, 28th September 2010; Beristain Ukar v. Spain, case n° 40351/05, 8th March 2011; Otamendi Egigurren v. Spain, case no 47303/08, 16th October 2012; Etxebarria Caballero v. Spain, case n° 7406/12, 7th October 2014; Ataun Rojo v. Spain, case n° 3344/13, 7th October 2014. Related to a

Catalan movement, see, Martinez Sala and others v. Spain, case n° 58438/00, 2nd November 2004.

3. Delmas-Marty M., Libertés et sûreté dans un monde dangereux, Seuil, 2010, p. 30.

4. Ley de enjuiciamiento criminal, article 510-4.

5. Ley de Enjuiciamiento Criminal, articles 520 and 527 combined.

6. Senellart M., Machiavélisme et raison d'Etat, PUF, 1989, p. 5.

7. See, for instance, Martinez Sala and others v. Spain, §159; Ataun Rojo v. Spain, §34 and followings.

8. United Nations Committee Against Torture, Kepa Urra Guridi v. Spain, Communication n° 212/2002, U.N. Doc. CAT/C/34/D/212/2002 (2005).

9. Interestingly, while the appeal was pending before the Supreme Court, one of the civil guards continued to work as French-Spanish anti-terrorism coordinator and was following a programme, with the authorization of the Interior Ministry in order to be promoted.

10. For a psychological approach, see for instance the works and reports by psychologists of the Centre Primo Levi dedicated to the care of victims of torture and political violence.

11. Report released in December 2014.

12. Crelinsten R.D., "Terrorism as political communication: the relationship between the controller and the controlled", in Wilkinson P., & Stewart A.M., (ed.), *Contemporary research on Terrorism,* Aberdeen University Press, 1987, p. 6.

13. European Parliament, Resolution on combating terrorism in the European Union, OJ C055, 24/02/1997, p. 27.

14. Solana J., "Three ways for Europe to prevail against the terrorists", in *Financial Times,* 25th March 2004

Critical Thinking

1. Why do some democratic states resort to the use of torture?
2. Do infringements of the Rule of Law serve the public interest?
3. Are enhanced interrogation techniques an effective way of gaining intelligence?
4. What dangers come from fighting fire with fire?

Internet References

Fighting terrorism at EU level, an overview of Commission's actions, measures and initiatives
http://europa.eu/rapid/press-release_MEMO-15-3140_en.htm

Senate Select Committee on Intelligence
http://www.intelligence.senate.gov/study2014/sscistudy1.pdf

What is the Rule of Law
http://worldjusticeproject.org/what-rule-law

AURÉLIE GARBAY is a Ph.D. Candidate and teaching assistant in Public Law at the University of Pau and Pays de I'Adour (France). Her research focuses on the alterations of the democratic framework faced by Democracies fighting against terrorism, and more precisely in the light of the fight against Basque terrorism.

Article   Prepared by: Thomas J. Badey, *Randolph-Macon College*

Lessons from Colombia for Curtailing the Boko Haram Insurgency in Nigeria

AFEIKHENA JEROME

Learning Outcomes

After reading this article, you will be able to:

- Provide a brief summary of the evolution of Boko Haram.

- Explain how the Nigerian government has responded to Boko Haram.

- Identify possible actions the Nigerian government can take to reduce the threat.

- Discuss similarities between insurgencies in Colombia and Nigeria.

Nigeria is a highly complex and ethnically diverse country, with over 400 ethnic groups. This diversity is played out in the way the country is bifurcated along the lines of religion, language, culture, ethnicity and regional identity. The population of about 178.5 million people in 2014 is made up of Christians and Muslims in equal measures of about 50 percent each, but including many who embrace traditional religions as well.

The country has continued to experience serious and violent ethno-communal conflicts since independence in 1960, including the bloody and deadly thirty month fratricidal Civil War (also known as the Nigerian-Biafran war, 1967–70) when the eastern region of Biafra declared its secession and which claimed more than one million lives. The most prominent of these conflicts recently pitched Muslims against Christians in a dangerous convergence of religion, ethnicity and politics. The first and most dramatic eruption in a series of recent religious disturbances was the Maitatsine uprising in Kano in December 1980, in which about 4,177 died.

While the exact number of conflicts in Nigeria is unknown, because of a lack of reliable statistical data, it is estimated that about 40 percent of all conflicts have taken place since the country's return to civilian rule in 1999.[1] The increasing wave of violent conflicts across Nigeria under the current democratic regime is no doubt partly a direct consequence of the activities of ethno-communal groups seeking self-determination in their "homelands," and of their surrogate ethnic militias that have assumed prominence since the last quarter of 2000. Their grievances have typically found expression in bitter political complaints, sectarian crises stoked by political elites and incendiary media rhetoric, and violent insurgencies.

The latest among these violent and decimating sectarian grievances is the Boko Haram insurgency. Boko Haram, a violent but diffuse Islamist sect, has grown increasingly active and deadly in its attacks against state and civilian targets in recent years. It feeds on a narrative of historically deep-rooted resentment against, and vengeance for state abuses in order to recruit members and sympathizers. With increasing regularity since 2009, the sect has attacked Nigeria's police and military, rival clerics, politicians, schools, religious buildings, public institutions, and civilians. The brutal insurgent activities of Boko Haram have included the bombing of the national police headquarters in June 2011; a suicide attack on a United Nations building in Abuja in August 2011; the destruction of the Air Force Base in Maiduguri in December 2013; and innumerable other repeated attacks that have killed dozens of students, burnt and devastated villages, and destroyed infrastructure. Their grievances against the police are particularly deep-seated as many of their followers are locked up in police cells, and their late leader, Mohammad Yusuf, was killed in police custody in 2009.

Boko Haram's April 2014 abduction of 276 schoolgirls from Chibok has attracted extensive international attention, thanks to the on-going global mobilization in this regard by the *#BringBackOurGirls* social media campaign.

An ocean away, Colombia has come a long way in its half-century fight against insurgency, drug trafficking, kidnapping, and murder. The country entered the 21st century on the brink of becoming a failed state. By 2000, the Government of Colombia no longer had a monopoly on the exercise of authority in a considerable area of Colombian territory, where guerrillas and drug traffickers ruled instead. After decades of bloody conflict, Colombia has begun in recent years to make unprecedented strides in its war against insurgency. The strength of the major insurgency group, the 50-year-old Revolutionary Armed Forces of Colombia (FARC), once considered the best-funded insurgency in the world, is at its most vulnerable state in decades. The numerical strength of FARC declined between 2002 and 2010 from 16,000 fighters to 8,000, and 967 municipalities representing 88 percent of the country registered no terrorist attacks from FARC or other insurgent groups in 2013. Kidnappings have dropped by more than 90 percent since 2002, and the country has been able to rein in narcotics trafficking to some extent. There are other successes too: in October 2012, the authorities began peace talks with FARC, which, if eventually successful, will put an end to one of the world's longest conflicts; trade and the GDP are up; Medellín, the nation's second-largest city, is lauded as the "most innovative city in the world;" and Colombia is popping up on tourist "top 10" lists everywhere. The country also even made the final round at the 2014 Soccer World Cup.

This study investigates the useful lessons from Colombia's experience in dealing with insurgency, especially with FARC, for Nigeria's on-going strategy to curtail the Boko Haram insurgency, based on field study conducted in the summer of 2014.

The Evolution of Boko Haram

The beginnings of the insurgent activities of Boko Haram—often translated as "Western education is forbidden" or, using its Arabic name *Jama'atu Ahlis Sunnah Lidda'awati walJihad* (People Committed to the Propagation of the Prophet's Teachings and Jihad)—in Nigeria date back to the early 2000s. It emerged as a small, radical Sunni Islamic sect in the 1990s that worshipped at the al-Haji Muhammadu Ndimi Mosque in Maiduguri, capital of Borno State. The group advocated a strict interpretation and implementation of Islamic law for Nigeria. Its leader, Mohammed Yusuf, was a charismatic and popular Qur'anic scholar who not only proselytized widely throughout northern Nigeria but also assisted in the implementation of Sharia (Islamic law) in several northern states in the early 2000s. The failure to achieve the expected full implementation of Sharia in northern Nigeria helps explain some of the deep-rooted resentment and anger of a considerable number of Muslim youths at what they perceived as the government's

"deception" and "insincerity." This resentment fueled their call for an authentic Islamist revolution.[2]

While the sect's leadership did not initially engage in violence, its followers were involved in periodic skirmishes with police during its formative years.[3] At that time, the group's activities were limited in scope and were contained within several highly impoverished states in the predominately Muslim North.

In 2003, Yusuf fled to Saudi Arabia, ostensibly to study, but in reality to escape arrest after the police had declared him wanted following incessant attacks and the burning down of some police stations by a more radical splinter group of about 200 members led by Abubakar Shekau and Aminu Tashen-Ilimi. This group had split from the mainstream movement in 2012 and settled in neighbouring Yobe State. Then Borno state deputy governor, Adamu Dibal, reportedly met Yusuf while on Hajj and used contacts with the security agencies to obtain permission for him to return to Maiduguri.

Yusuf rose to much greater prominence when he reportedly formed an alliance with Ali Modu Sheriff, a politician and wealthy businessman who became Governor of Borno State. Yusuf allegedly promised to deploy his influence and religious authority to provide political support for Sheriff if, upon becoming Governor, Sheriff would implement Sharia.

In fulfilment of this agreement, the state government allegedly provided funds to Yusuf through Buji Foi, a disciple of Yusuf whom Sheriff made religious affairs commissioner when he became Governor in 2003. Yusuf used the money to organize an informal microcredit scheme that gave his disciples capital to set up businesses. They in turn gave part of their profits as alms to the group, which began amassing arms, mostly Kalashnikovs from neighbouring Chad.

Cracks appeared in the purported Yusuf-Sheriff alliance, however, after the latter reneged on his promise to implement Sharia fully in the state. Yusuf began to direct sermons against Sheriff and his government, ultimately branding him an apostate. In 2007, Buji Foi resigned as religious affairs commissioner in protest.

The year 2009 marked a turning point in Boko Haram's transformation. In July 2009 at least 700 people were killed during an attempt by Nigerian security forces to suppress the group. In the aftermath of the attempt, their leader, Mohammed Yusuf, was killed in police custody. The group subsequently appeared to dissipate, but re-emerged a year later under new leadership. It orchestrated a large prison break in September 2010 that freed hundreds, including many of its members. Some Boko Haram militants may have fled to insurgent training camps in the Sahel in 2009–2010. The group has built ties with transnational extremist groups in the region, which have reportedly provided Boko Haram with insurgency training and increasingly sophisticated weaponry. Since 2011 Boko Haram attacks have featured improvised explosive devices (IEDs), car bombs, and, periodically, suicide attacks, but fighters also continue to inflict a heavy toll using small arms and arson.

Boko Haram is not a monolithic organization.[4] It has several splinter groups, some of which have formed alliances with foreign Islamist groups, such as al-Qaeda in the Islamic Maghreb (AQIM) and al-Shabaab in Somalia, which have helped in bringing about the radicalization of its leadership. The number of Boko Haram fighters is estimated in the hundreds to low thousands and its organizational structure is often described as diffuse, and increasingly so since the death of Yusuf.

Boko Haram's attacks have increased substantially in frequency, reach, and lethality since 2010, occurring almost daily in parts of northeast Nigeria, and periodically beyond. Their attacks were directed initially and primarily against state and federal targets, such as police stations, but they have also targeted civilians in schools, churches, mosques, markets, bars, and villages. Cell phone towers and media outlets have also been attacked, for both tactical and ideological reasons. The group has assassinated local political leaders and moderate Muslim clerics. Its deadliest attacks include a coordinated series of bombings in Kano, northern Nigeria's largest city that killed more than 180 people in January 2012; an attack on the village of Benisheikh in September 2013 that killed more than 160 civilians; and an assault on another northeastern village, Gamboru, that may have killed more than 300 people in early May 2014.

Since July 2014 the Boko Haram insurgency has entered a dangerous new phase in which the insurgents are beginning to operate like a conventional army. In Borno, Adamawa, and Yobe states the insurgents are now aggressively challenging the Nigerian military through direct confrontation in open and sustained battle. They are reported to be using armored vehicles, including tanks and heavy weapons, some stolen from the demoralized Nigerian army.

Boko Haram has erected flags over the towns it has invaded, forcing any remaining residents to follow its strict version of sharia or be killed in what appears to be an imitation of the caliphate proclaimed in parts of Iraq and Syria by the Islamic State.

More than 5,000 people are estimated to have been killed in Boko Haram-related violence since 2009, including at least 2,000 in the first half of 2014, making Boko Haram one of the deadliest terrorist groups in the world. Borno State has largely borne the brunt: it accounts for 3,136 deaths between 2006 and 2013, followed by Yobe and Adamawa respectively. United Nations and Nigerian officials report that more than six million Nigerians have been affected by the conflict between Boko Haram and Nigerian state authorities. By another account, more than 650,000 people had fled the conflict zone by August 2014, an increase of 200,000 since May 2014. Nigeria's

heavy-handed response to Boko Haram's insurgent and terrorist operations has also taken a toll on civilians.

Responses to the Insurgency: Military

The Nigerian Armed Forces has 130,000 active frontline personnel and 32,000 reserve personnel, ranking it 47th in the world in terms of conventional potential strength.[5] It is reputed to be well-versed in counterinsurgency due to its wealth of experience in operating in insurgency environments such as Liberia, Sierra Leone and the recent operations in Mali, as well as successive participation in both the United Nations (UN) and African Union (AU) led peacekeeping operations across the world. Since the Congo crisis in 1960, Nigeria has contributed both military and police personnel to more than 40 peacekeeping operations worldwide. By June 2013, about 5,000 officers and men of the Nigerian Armed Forces were serving in nine UN Peacekeeping missions within and outside Africa.

Nigeria's major response to the insurgency since 2010 has been the deployment of its Joint Task Force (JTF), consisting of the Army, Air Force, Navy, State Security Services, and Police under unified command structures. It encourages increased intelligence-sharing, force coordination and unity of direction, which are considered essential for any counterinsurgency operation, although this has been limited. The Nigerian parliament passed anti-terrorism legislation, originally introduced in 2011, in 2013. The law was designed, in part, to facilitate greater counterterrorism coordination, but interagency cooperation and information sharing remains limited by Nigeria's federal structure, which has caused confusion between chief state security officers and federally-controlled security forces.

Nigerian JTF counterinsurgency operations in the northeast have been "generally repressive," relying heavily on military-led operations to kill and capture "scores" of Boko Haram insurgents since the movement was first brutally crushed in 2009.[6] While this use of force has clearly enabled the JTF to pressure Boko Haram strongholds in Borno, Yobe and Adamawa and reduce the scope of its activity, it has also produced large-scale extrajudicial killings, mass arrests and intimidation of civilians, who are treated as insurgent sympathizers.

The JTF, augmented by "civilian vigilantes," has been implicated in extrajudicial killings of militants and civilians, which may have galvanized support for the insurgents. Such excesses have further alienated both the population and international observers.

Several factors have constrained the Nigerian security force response, most notably security sector corruption and mismanagement. The $470 million Public Security Communications

System (PSCS) project, initiated by the late President Umaru Yar'Adua's administration and handled by the Chinese contractor ZTE Corporation for the installation of CCTV cameras in Abuja to detect or prevent aime, was poorly executed and has been abandoned. Nigerian troops are also not adequately resourced or equipped to counter the insurgency. A lack of investment in training, failure to maintain equipment and dwindling coopera- tion with Western forces has damaged Nigeria's armed services. Unlike Nigerian peacekeepers in the 1990s, who were effective in curbing ethnic bloodshed in Sierra Leone and Liberia, those in Mali in 2013 lacked the equipment and training needed to be of much help against al-Qaeda-linked forces. A recent report by Chatham House points out that soldiers in the northeast are suf- fering from malfunctioning equipment, low morale, desertions, and mutinies. Despite a large increase in government spending on the army from a security budget totaling almost $5.8 billion, little of it has found its way to the front lines. Four hundred- eighty Nigerian soldiers were alleged to have fled to Camer- oon in August 2014, when they were confronted with superior weapons in the hands of Boko Haram insurgents. In June 2014, ten generals and five other senior security staff were reportedly court martialed for arming and providing intelligence to the group, with 12 of them sentenced to death in September 2014.

Civilians/Local Peoples

In response to escalated attacks, "Civilian JTFs," or *Yan Gora* ("those who hold the cane") comprising local militia, have also been formed by local communities in the areas affected by and under siege of the insurgency. Since June 2013, they have sup- ported operations in Maiduguri and also serve as a source of intelli- gence and a proxy force to avoid direct confrontation with the sect.

Armed with machetes, axes, bows and arrows, clubs, swords and daggers, these "Civilian JTFs" (CJTF) usually invade the homes of known and suspected Boko Haram members, hacking them to death or manhandling and then handing them over to the military.

With their assistance, the security situation around Maiduguri has improved significantly. Their success in helping to drive many insurgents out of Maiduguri and largely stopping Boko Haram killings and bombings in the city is said to be at the cost of a proliferation of human rights violations.

Political, Socio-Economic, and Diplomatic Response

Since 2012, Nigeria has tried to address the Boko Haram chal- lenge on multiple fronts, though these efforts have so far met with little success. The first effort was an increase in the defense budget from N396.5 billion ($2.56 billion) in 2012 to N968.127

billion ($5.69 billion) in 2014. The justification for much of this increase was to combat Boko Haram. In September 2014, the National Assembly approved a $1bn external loan for the Federal Government to upgrade the equipment, training and logistics of the Armed Forces and security services in order to enable them to confront the insurgents more forcefully. Other measures include strengthening anti-terrorism legislation, boosting the capacities of the military and other security agencies, exploring dialogue with the insurgents, declaring a state of emergency in the North- east and launching military offensives against the group.

Political negotiations with Boko Haram have largely been unsuccessful despite rapprochement overtures towards the Government in 2011 and 2012. A major factor has been the group's unreasonable demands, including, for example, calls for the Islamization of Nigeria and President Goodluck Jona- than's conversion to Islam.

The consensus among analysts is that the Government must attack the root causes of disaffection that push unemployed youths towards radicalization by Boko Haram, such as poverty and unemployment. A similar approach was taken in the Niger Delta with the Niger Delta Amnesty Program that was used to douse the insurgency in that region.

Recent presentations from the National Security Adviser, Sambo Dasuki, suggest that a shift may be taking place towards recognizing this, with the unveiling of a "soft approach" in the form of the March 2014 "Countering Violent Extremism" pro- gram that outlined plans for capacity-building and economic development in the northeast, as well as for developing part- nerships with faith groups and local stakeholders in a bid to co-opt these groups in a de-radicalization campaign. Not much has been heard in terms of its implementation.

International Response

The June 2014 Paris Conference deepened international support for Nigeria's counterinsurgency campaign through an agreement by regional powers such as Cameroon, Chad, Niger, and Benin to share intelligence with Nigeria. The United States, United Kingdom, France, and Israel, having already provided counter- terrorism, counterinsurgency, logistical and capacity-building assistance in recent years, have increased support as part of the effort to find the Chibok girls. It remains unclear to what extent Nigerian officials are cooperating with foreign advisers and experts. The government has been criticized in domestic and international press reports for what has been widely per- ceived as a slow response to the abduction of the schoolgirls in April 2014, and to offers of international assistance in support of the investigation and possible rescue efforts. Nigeria's record of human rights abuses, combined with suspicions of malicious Western intentions, has limited the scope of future Western counterinsurgency support beyond the Chibok search operation.

Colombia: A History of Violence

The deep divisions in Colombian politics that were to shape the country's modern history and development emerged shortly after independence from Spain in 1810, precipitating a battle between the two dominant political parties, the Conservatives (Partido Conservador Colombiano, or PCC) and the Liberals (Partido Liberal Colombiano, or PL).

This intense rivalry between the conservatives and the liberals continued throughout the 19th and early 20th centuries and came to a head in "La Violencia" (1948–1958), sparked by the assassination of a presidential hopeful, Jorge Eliecer Gaitan, a period during which an estimated 250,000 people lost their lives. This marked the beginning of the current violent internal armed conflict that has lasted for more than half a century.

Following bipartisan support of a bloodless military coup in 1953 and the signing of a power sharing agreement in 1957, the National Front system emerged. Liberals and conservatives agreed to alternate the presidency and apportion government positions.[7] The agreement excluded other political parties and was elite-controlled, catalyzing a new phase of violence where the state perpetrated massive atrocities against peasant farmers. The country then entered into a long period of intense crime and mayhem, characterized by drug lords controlling large swaths of the state, and kidnapping and assassination on a scale unprecedented anywhere else in the world.

In the mid-1960s there was a blossoming of insurgencies with the emergence of multiple armed guerilla groups, most notably the Fuerzas Armadas Revolucionarias de Colombia (Revolutionary Armed Forces of Colombia, or FARC), and to a lesser degree, the National Liberation Army (ELN). This was a reaction to factors such as the exclusion of political movements outside of the National Front, the marginalization of the rural poor, the influence of communist and socialist ideologies, and the ineffectiveness of the judicial system. These groups took control of significant areas of the country and ultimately fused with much of the narco-trafficking community in widespread drug related violence that undermined the legitimacy of state power, while pursuing their original vision of political revolution.

These problems mutated in various ways, but persisted for three decades such that by 1999 Colombia was a country in deep trouble and on the precipice of being a failed state—its murder, kidnapping, and extortion rates were among the highest in the world and travel and tourism were unsafe. The resultant insecurity had pushed the Colombian economy into recession, and unemployment was moving above 15 percent. The "brain drain" and capital flight that followed took a heavy toll on the country's stability. On the military side, whole battalions of the Colombian army were being decimated in open combat. The military was demoralized and, despite some very talented leadership, headed

in the wrong direction. Meanwhile, illegal right-wing armed groups were committing massacres and assassinations with the same intensity as FARC had done, and very powerful international trafficking organizations, such as the Medellin and Cali Cartels, penetrated and corrupted many government institutions and contributed to the overall climate of lawlessness.

Since then, however, the situation has dramatically improved. The major turning point in Colombia was "Plan Colombia" that began during the presidency of Bill Clinton but was sustained and built upon by President George W. Bush, followed by the election of President Álvaro Uribe in 2002.

Uribe also brought a level of focus to the conflict that had never been previously seen, using his personality and energy to infuse a more intense and committed effort into the security forces as well. He also expanded the size of the armed forces and tightened their links with local communities, which contributed to the building of intelligence about the enemy to make attacks more precise and effective. By the end of his tenure in 2010, war-related civilian death rates were down by half. Colombia was beginning to enjoy an economic renaissance made possible by greater foreign investment and the return of many businessmen and other economic leaders who had fled the country.

Uribe's defense minister, Juan Manuel Santos, became Colombia's president in 2010. He continued many of his predecessor's policies, but sought to change the narrative at a political level. He began to emphasize possible peace talks with the FARC and a post-conflict vision for the country in general. This apparent softening of the political leadership's approach to the war brought criticism from Uribe, but did not lead to a diminution of the military effort by the Colombian Armed Forces under the leadership of defense minister Juan Carlos Iflnzon, who continued to take the fight to the enemy. Precise, intelligence-based attacks against high-value targets, implemented largely by skilled commandos, have continued to be the hallmarks of the recent approach.

However the job is not yet done. Colombia is still violent, and there is no peace deal yet with either the FARC or ELN. Large parts of the country remain vipers' nests of criminality and drug trafficking. Nonetheless, Colombia has several lessons for Nigeria in the management of insurgency.

Lessons from the Colombian Experience for Nigeria
Strong, Effective Leadership Is Essential to Success In Asymmetric Conflict

The tipping point between muddling through and moving toward victory in Colombia was the election of leaders who translated bold vision into action since the beginning of Uribe's administration in 2002. There is little doubt that much of the progress in Colombia is the direct product of exceptional leadership from 2002 to 2013. The philosophy of having a clear, grand strategy, then holding people accountable down to the lowest level, has had a major impact in the current positive situation in Colombia.

Fixing the Army

Colombia has been able to transform its army from an ineffective, garrison-bound band into an aggressive force that has crippled the FARC and ELN. Reform of Colombia's army began during Andrés Pastrana's term as president (1998–2002) and accelerated during President Álvaro Uribe's tenure (2002–2010). In 1998, at the urging of U.S. officials, Pastrana replaced the top three leaders in the army with new generals who were trained at U.S. military schools and who had extensive combat experience at the battalion and brigade levels. This new trio then replaced subordinate commanders who lacked aggressiveness in the field.

Colombia also reorganized its army into a mobile and highly skilled professional component, and a conscript component formed for local security. The professional component of the army established numerous air-mobile, ranger, mountain warfare, counter-drug, and Special Forces battalions. These units improved the army's overall effectiveness by specializing in specific tasks. To overcome Colombia's mountainous and forested terrain, the army also invested heavily in equipment such that the Colombian army currently operates the world's third-largest fleet of UH-60 Blackhawk assault helicopters.

The military, under its reform-minded leadership, is also adapting to new changes such as respect for human rights. It has consistently emerged in Colombian polls as one of the most respected institutions in the country.

Abandon the Conventional Military-Centric Approach

There are no purely military solutions to pulling a nation or region out of the death spiral of violent extremism. As the Colombian experience demonstrates, there is a need to abandon the conventional military-centric approach as the one and only option for insurgency and other asymmetric conflicts. While not ignoring the importance of using military force, stability, political-economic-social development, rule of law, popular well-being, and sustainable peace all depend on effective and legitimate control of the national territory. Thus, a military-centric approach must be balanced with a population-centric approach for maximum effect and legitimacy.

Wage War on Corruption as a Priority

In Colombia, frustration with inequality and corruption created the spark that set off larger anti-government movements such as the FARC. To be legitimate in the eyes of the people, governance has to be even-handed, relatively transparent, oriented toward human rights, and free of corruption.

Over the past few years, the apprehension, prosecution, and conviction of military members for human rights abuses and reporting "false guerrillas" in order to cover up extrajudicial killings also showed the public that officials would be held accountable.

Financing Counter-Insurgency

Colombia has no doubt shown the way forward with regard to the financing of counterinsurgencies. It successfully put the burden of expanding the state presence of security operations across the territory on the shoulders of the wealthiest members of society. This was accomplished by using special powers granted to the government during an emergency situation to establish a wealth tax (Impuesto al Patrimonio), popularly known as the War Tax. The first of such taxes was collected on a one-off basis in 2002 and yielded five percent of government revenue or one percent of GDP. A total of 420,000 taxpayers contributed in that year, of which 120,000 were high-income individuals.[8] Started in 2004, the War Tax was extended through 2011, however payments will continue through 2014 in the form of a surtax on the tax due in 2011.

The proceeds were entirely earmarked for security and managed by an Ethics and Transparency Commission, including 12 members from the private sector. It is estimated that the tax raked in over $800 million a year, allowing Colombia to modernize its military.

Conclusion

The Boko Haram insurgency has no doubt become Nigeria's albatross. Unless it is skillfully managed, it may become an indeterminate war and a threat to Nigeria's fragile democracy. Disparate as the two countries may seem to be on the surface, Nigeria has much to learn from Colombia in dealing with the Boko Haram insurgency. In a globalized world, surely lessons on governance and peace-building should find no barriers.

Notes

1. Salawu, B. "Ethno-Religious Conflicts in Nigeria: Causal Analysis and Proposals for New Management Strategies", European Journal of Social Sciences—Volume 13, Number 3 (2010) pp. 345–353.

2. International Crisis Group, "Curbing Violence in Nigeria (II): The Boko Haram Insurgency". Africa Report N°216, 3 April 2014.

3. Blanchard, L. P., 'Nigeria's Boko Haram: frequently asked questions', Congressional Research Service, June 2014. http://fas.org.

4. Pérouse de Montclos, A. "Nigeria's Interminable Insurgency? Addressing the Boko Haram Crisis". Chatham House, 02 September 2014.

5. A total of 106 countries were evaluated. For more details, see Global Firepower, available at http://www.globalfirepower.com/country-military-strength-detail.asp?country_id=nigeria, accessed 13th September 2014.

6. See Alam Waterman, "Unravel the scourge of this evil:" Nigeria's counterinsurgency operations against Boko Haram, Discussion Paper, Consultancy Africa Intelligence, August 2014 for an excellent account of Nigeria's response to Boko Haram.

7. Metelits, C. *Inside Insurgency: Violence, Civilians, and Revolutionary Group Behaviour.* (New York University Press, New York), 2000.

8. Flores-Macias, G.A. "Financing Security through Elite Taxation: The Case of Colombia's 'Democratic Security Taxes'." Working Paper No. 3. Brighton: International Center for Tax and Development (ICTD), 2012.

Critical Thinking

1. How has the Nigerian government responded to the insurgency?
2. What are the similarities between the insurgencies in Colombia and Nigeria?
3. What can Nigeria learn from Colombia in dealing with the Boko Haram insurgency?
4. What are the most important elements of an effective counterinsurgency?

Internet References

Boko Haram
http://www.cfr.org/nigeria/boko-haram/p25739

Neighbors of Nigeria Take on Boko Haram
http://www.nytimes.com/2015/03/10/world/africa/neighbors-of-nigeria-take-on-boko-haram.html

What is Boko Haram?
http://www.trackingterrorism.org/group/boko-haram

AFEIKHENA JEROME is Coordinator, State Peer Review Mechanism, Nigeria Governors Forum.

Jerome Afeikhena, "Lessons From Colombia For Curtailing The Boko Haram Insurgency In Nigeria," *Prism*, vol. 5, no. 2, 2015.

Article   Prepared by: Thomas J. Badey, *Randolph-Macon College*

Comparing Counterterrorism in Indonesia and the Philippines

Scott N. McKay and David A. Webb

Learning Outcomes

After reading this article, you will be able to:

- Identify three types of terrorist groups that exist in Southeast Asia.

- Explain the difference between the Indonesian and Pilipino approach to counterterrorism.

- Discuss the factors that the United States needs to consider when offering counterterrorism support.

Terrorism in Southeast Asia predates the American post-9/11 war on terrorism. But since 2001, terrorist groups in Indonesia and the Philippines have emerged as significant security challenges within these states, as well as indirect threats to U.S. national security. The United States has made substantial direct and indirect contributions to the counterterrorism (CT) efforts within these states, with varying returns on investment.

Despite differing responses to terrorism, Indonesia and the Philippines are both commonly viewed as CT success stories, as terrorist groups have been degraded and links to al-Qa'ida have been weakened. But while terrorist operations in Indonesia have declined in the post-9/11 era, attacks have increased in the Philippines. Last month, an operation targeting international terrorists on the southern island of Mindanao resulted in the death of 43 Philippine national police commandos.[1]

Between 2002 and 2013, the U.S. provided $262 million in security assistance funding to Indonesia, and $441 million in security assistance to the Philippines.[2] The U.S. has also provided direct military-to-military support in the Philippines, advising and training Philippine CT forces over the last decade.

Due to differences in culture, institutions, capabilities, and U.S. assistance, the Indonesian and Philippine governments have implemented distinctive CT strategies. Indonesia has relied on national police to degrade terrorist networks, while the military has been the primary CT force in the Philippines.

This article evaluates CT efforts in Indonesia and the Philippines in order to compare and contrast host-nation approaches and corresponding U.S. support. This article also highlights American best practices, which may be transferrable to U.S. support for CT in other parts of the world.

Our research has led to two significant conclusions. First, based on several quantitative measures of effectiveness, the law enforcement-based Indonesian CT approach has been more effective than the military-based CT approach of the Philippines, although the multi-faceted nature of terrorism within the Philippines arguably makes the task of CT in the Philippines more difficult. And second, the U.S. can be most effective when providing tailored CT support, based on the nature of the terrorist threat and host nation culture and national capabilities.

Terrorism in Southeast Asia

Prior to 9/11, Southeast Asian states viewed terrorism as low-level, localized threats, with little impact on their national security interests. The United States, meanwhile, was largely preoccupied with Middle Eastern terrorist groups.[3] But following 9/11, as linkages between al-Qa'ida and Southeast Asia emerged, the United States started to pay more attention to terrorism in the region—specifically in Indonesia and the Philippines.[4] The Bali bombings on October 12, 2002, however, were a wake up call for Southeast Asia. Ambassador Alfonso T. Yuchengco, the Philippine permanent representative to the United Nations (U.N.), said that "10/12" was to Indonesia and

Southeast Asia what 9/11 was to the United States and the West, "awakening Southeast Asia to the threat of Islamist terrorism."[5]

Three types of terrorist groups exist in Southeast Asia: global, regional, and national.[6] Southeast Asian terrorist groups are interconnected, however, often sharing leaders, members, tactics, and objectives. Global terrorist groups such as al-Qa'ida have recruited and trained operatives throughout the region, and have maintained connections to Southeast Asian terrorist groups since the anti-Soviet jihad in Afghanistan. Regional terrorist groups, such as the Indonesian-based Jemaah Islamiyah (JI), seek to create an Islamic state throughout Southeast Asia. And nationalist groups such as the Abu Sayyaf Group (ASG) in the Philippines seek an Islamic separatist state in the southern islands of Mindanao. Al-Qa'ida's persistent presence in Southeast Asia and its connection to regional and nationalist terrorist groups in Indonesia and the Philippines have prompted the U.S. to proactively support Indonesian and Philippine CT efforts over the last decade.[7]

Terrorism and CT in Indonesia

Jemaah Islamiyah—aligned with al-Qa'ida and overlapping in leadership and membership since the 1990s[8]—gained international attention through the Bali nightclub bombings in 2002, which were the most deadly terrorist attacks in the world since 9/11.[9] Among the approximately 500 casualties were Americans, Australians, Canadians, Europeans, Japanese, and Indonesians.[10]

JI followed the Bali bombings with annual high profile bombing attacks in Indonesia over the next three years, to include the bombing of the J.W. Marriott Hotel in Jakarta on August 5, 2004, which killed 11 and wounded 150; the bombing of the Australian embassy in Jakarta on September 9, 2004, which killed 11 and wounded 160; and another Bali bombing on October 1, 2005 which killed 20 and injured 129.[11]

In the aftermath of the 10/12 attacks, the Indonesian government accepted American and international assistance to combat terrorism, and initiated a thorough reform of the Indonesian national security apparatus.[12] Key aspects of Indonesia's CT evolution since 2002 include legal reform to enable the prosecution of terrorists, improved domestic CT forces, and the deradicalization of convicted terrorists.

The U.S. has provided hundreds of millions of dollars in security funding to support CT in Indonesia, but little direct support in the form of military training and advising. The Australian government—motivated by the Bali bombings, Jakarta embassy bombing, and persistent terrorist threats throughout the region—has provided trainers and advisors to Indonesian CT forces. American funds and Australian direct support enabled the creation of the Indonesian national CT force, known as Detachment 88, in 2003. Detachment 88 is responsible for investigations, intelligence, and hostage rescue, in addition to traditional CT operations, and has distinguished itself as an elite CT force. It has had success in targeting and dismantling terrorist organizations throughout Indonesia.[13]

The evolution of the CT apparatus in Indonesia has yielded tangible results, including the detention and prosecution of a significant percentage of JI leadership, and a successful start to a deradicalization program and legal reforms. However, governmental corruption, prison over-crowding, and a recent wave of ISIS propaganda will lead to future terrorism challenges, despite the short-term successes against JI. Continued progress is required to maintain the success that Indonesian CT forces have achieved in the past decade.

Terrorism and CT in the Philippines

January's tragic clash between members of the Philippine National Police Special Action Force (SAF) and members of the Islamic separatist group known as the Bangsamoro Islamic Freedom Fighters (BIFF) highlights several notable security trends in the Philippines. The 12-hour firefight ensued during a raid to capture Zulkifli bin Hir, a Malaysian-born operational leader and bomb maker within Jemaah Islamiyah, who had reportedly been in the Philippines since 2003 training ASG bomb makers. This incident highlights the long-standing connections between Southeast Asian terrorist groups, the continuing instability in the southern Philippines, and the new and increasing role of the Philippine National Police in the CT mission that had been dominated by the Philippine military until 2010.

The Philippines is confronted with the most diverse set of internal security challenges in Southeast Asia.[14] The Philippine communist insurgency, known as the New People's Army (NPA), has existed since 1968,[15] and is—in the eyes of the Philippine government—the most significant internal security threat, because of the NPA's dispersed disposition and ability to influence the Philippine capital region on the island of Luzon.[16] But in recent years, the most newsworthy security challenge within the Philippines has emerged in the southern island region of Mindanao, where Muslim separatist groups have sought autonomy for centuries.

The Moro Islamic Liberation Front (MILF) has transitioned from separatist terrorist group to political party, as the peace process has achieved fragile autonomy for the MILF. But radical factions such as ASG and BIFF seek a completely independent Islamic state under Sharia law. ASG has proven to be the most nihilistic terrorist group in the Philippines, conducting a bombing at the Davao International airport on March 5, 2003, which killed 21 and injured 148; and conducting a bombing on a Philippine super-ferry on February 27, 2004, which killed 116 and injured 300, the worst terrorist attack in Asia since the 2002 Bali bombings.[17]

In contrast to Indonesia, the Philippine government had been in conflict with terrorist groups for decades before the start of the so-called global war on terrorism. The Armed Forces of the Philippines (AFP) has the structure, the aptitude, and support of both the government and the populace to pursue the terrorist groups. Philippine law enforcement forces, however, lack capacity and public support, based on a history of ineptitude and corruption.[18]

CT in the Philippines, therefore, has been traditionally a military responsibility, and while the military CT forces can effectively clear terrorist safe havens, weak local governments and law enforcement units are incapable, and often unwilling, to hold and build in isolated areas such as Mindanao.[19] Since 2010, the Philippine government has made an effort to pass the domestic CT mission from the military to the national police, but the transition has been slow and beleaguered by distrust and competition between the two organizations.[20]

American CT support has arrived in the form of hundreds of millions of dollars of security funding, as well as the continual deployment of U.S. troops to the Philippines to train and advise the Philippine CT forces. Due to the links between Abu Sayyaf Group and al-Qa'ida, ASG has been the primary focus of Operation Enduring Freedom-Philippines (OEF-P) for the United States. Through OEF-P, American advisors have enabled the Philippine security forces to contain and severely disrupt ASG to the point where the group no longer poses a significant threat to the Philippine capital region in Luzon. But despite the commitment of the Philippine government and the support of the United States, ASG and other Islamic separatists groups remain persistent security challenges within the Philippines.

Effectiveness of CT Responses

Two quantitative measures can help explain the CT effectiveness of these two states from 2002–2013. The first is an assessment of the trends in terrorist attacks according to the Study of Terrorism and Responses to Terrorism (START) Global Terrorism Database (GTD).[21] The data clearly indicates that terrorist attacks have declined in Indonesia while increasing in the Philippines.

From 2002–2007 the relative number of attacks for the two countries are similar, with the Philippines experiencing slightly more attacks throughout this period, which is understandable due to the diversity of Philippine terrorist groups. In 2002, Indonesia suffered 43 terrorist attacks compared to 48 attacks in the Philippines. In 2007, terrorist incidents in the Philippines spiked upward to 65 attacks, while attacks in Indonesia fell to only two attacks.

Attacks increased in both countries over the next six years, but overall, attacks in the Philippines increased 13-fold between 2002 and 2013 (from 48 attacks to 652) and fell by 26 percent in Indonesia during the same time period (from 43 attacks in 2002 to 32 in 2013). Although one could argue that the uptick in the Philippine attacks is due to the relative strength of the various terrorist groups that operate there, another plausible argument is that Indonesian CT has been more effective than Philippine CT.

The second quantitative measure of effectiveness is an analytic tool that measures national responses to terrorist activity. This tool was first featured in a 2014 article that evaluated the relative effectiveness of CT operations in Indonesia, the Philippines, and Thailand.[22] The model determined the average time between CT operation and a subsequent terrorist attack to be eleven days in Indonesia, as compared to eight days in the Philippines. Thus, a CT intervention such as an arrest, indictment, or imprisonment had a larger magnitude of effectiveness in Indonesia.[23] Although there are several factors that could explain the lag in a terrorist group's ability to operationally respond in these cases, this model provides a second quantitative indication that Indonesian CT efforts may have been more effective than Philippine CT efforts.

American Lessons Learned

There are several lessons to be learned from American CT support in Indonesia and the Philippines. These conclusions, though germane to the terrorism threats and responses within these specific states, may also be applicable to other international situations where the United States must assist a host-nation with CT efforts.

1. When planning a CT strategy, the United States must consider the unique history, culture, and capabilities of the host nation. These factors, combined with effectiveness of the host-nation's military, law enforcement, judicial system, and local governance, must be understood to properly tailor CT strategy. The Indonesian law enforcement-based CT approach has been more effective than the military-based Philippine CT approach, but Philippine culture and national capabilities would not have supported an Indonesian-style CT program in the Philippines in 2002. So the United States was wise to tailor support through the Philippine military, while concurrently working with Indonesian law enforcement for CT purposes. Properly tailored American CT support will best contribute to the effectiveness of the collective CT strategy.

2. Local governance, to include effective legislative and judicial systems are prerequisite ingredients if the

host-nation military is to be the leading CT force. The Philippine military-led CT model had effective results against the terrorist groups, but weak local governments and law enforcement were not prepared to follow up on the security gains achieved by the military. If an initial military-based CT response is required, then the host nation should employ a dual-track approach to develop the capacity of the host-nation's civil institutions. Transitioning the CT mission from the military to the police requires national support, and the military must be willing to share intelligence and tactics, techniques, and procedures with law enforcement. Friction remains between Philippine military and law enforcement, due to many years of military-led CT in the Philippines.

3. Technical and tactical training to support CT functions such as investigation, intelligence, and targeting are more helpful than blindly-sent financial aid. For example, in Indonesia, the investigative and forensic training provided to Detachment 88 greatly enhanced its targeting effectiveness in recent years, and the training of a cyber investigation team led to a new means of gathering intelligence and prosecution of terrorists that otherwise would have been unavailable.[24] Cyber team training and integrated targeting methods for Indonesian CT practitioners provided more of an impact than purchased equipment alone.

4. The U.S. should seek to capitalize on the capabilities, expertise, and positive reputation of allies in the host-nation's region to assist in CT efforts. In Indonesia, Australia took an active role in providing aid and training to Indonesian CT forces, complementing the financial aid from the United States. Australia provided specialized law enforcement training for Detachment 88 as well as funding for its training facilities.[25] Additionally, Australia still provides forensic assistance to support Indonesian CT operations, enabling Detachment 88 to successfully prosecute the insurgents that are captured. Australian involvement was also more palatable to the Indonesian population than American involvement. In Indonesia, direct American support would have likely been negatively perceived, while direct support from Australia was not seen as threatening to the Muslim majority. In future situations, the United States should encourage direct support from allies who have similar interests within the host-nation, but might be perceived in a more positive light than Americans.

5. A form of de-radicalization or reintegration should be considered as a part of the legal and judicial reforms within the host-nation. Both Indonesia and the Philippines incorporated de-radicalization programs with varying degrees of success. The host-nation will have to develop such a program based on its cultural norms and national goals, but the United States can assist in this process by providing funding and infrastructure. De-radicalization is essential to reintegrate captured terrorists into the host-nation society.

Conclusion

The United States has made significant direct and indirect contributions to CT efforts in Indonesia and the Philippines, with varying returns on investment. The United States seems to have received a better return on CT investment in Indonesia as terrorist attacks have declined since 9/11, while attacks have increased dramatically in the Philippines during the same time period. It is difficult, however, to determine whether these trends should be attributed to Indonesian CT efforts, or the efficacy and resilience of Philippine terrorist groups (or a combination of both). The United States can learn many lessons, however, from its CT support in Indonesia and the Philippines, and these lessons should be applied to future CT assistance efforts.

The views expressed here are those of the authors and do not reflect the official policy or position of the Department of the Army, the Department of Defense, or the U.S. Government.

Notes

1. Arlene Samson-Espiritu and Tim Hume, "43 Philippine police killed by Muslim rebels while hunting bomb makers" CNN, January 27, 2015.

2. Aid data was compiled from the U.S. State Department FY Congressional Budget Justification for Foreign Operations. FY data was taken from the FY +2 request for 2002–2013. INCLE, FMF, IMET, and NADR funds were included in these figures.

3. Rommel Banlaoi, *Counter Terrorism Measure in Southeast Asia: How Effective Are They?* (Philippines: Yuchengco Center, 2009), pp. 23–24.

4. Banlaoi, p. 24.

5. Alfonso Yuchengco, "Islamist Terrorism in Southeast Asia," *Issues and Insights,* no. 1-03 (Honolulu: Pacific Forum CSIS, January, 2003), p. 1.

6. Banlaoi, p. 23.

7. Bruce Vaughn, "Terrorism in Southeast Asia," *Congressional Research Service Report for Congress,* February 7, 2005, pp. 4–5.

8. Vaughn, pp. 6–7.

9. Ibid., p. 11.

10. Ibid.

11. Banlaoi, p. 20.

12. Peter Chalk, "The Evolving Terrorist Threat to Southeast Asia: A Net Assessment," Rand National Defense Research Institute (United States: 2005), p. 152.

13. Ibid., p. 154.

14. Ibid., p. 33.

15. Chalk, p. 36.

16. Virginia Bacay-Watson, interview August 2014, at the Asia Pacific Center for Security Studies in Honolulu, Hawaii.

17. Banlaoi, p. 64.

18. Gentry White, Lorraine Mazerolle, Michael Porter, and Peter Chalk. "Modeling the Effectiveness of Counter-terrorism Interventions." *Trends & Issues in Crime and Criminal Justice* No. 475 (2014), p. 472.

19. Chalk, p. 144.

20. Dennis Haney, interview, February 2015, at Stanford University.

21. National Consortium for the Study of Terrorism and Responses to Terrorism (START), University of Maryland, Website accessed on December 1, 2014. Number of attacks were documented for each year in both Indonesia and the Philippines.

22. White, p. 461.

23. White, p. 468.

24. Kristen E. Schulze, interview, November 2014, London School of Economics, London, U.K.

25. Chalk, p. 154.

Critical Thinking

1. What can the United States do in order to improve CT in the Philippines?

2. Are deradicalization programs an effective counterterrorism tool?

3. What lessons can the United States learn from counterterrorism efforts in Indonesia and the Philippines?

Internet References

Indonesia's Struggle Against Terrorism
http://www.cfr.org/councilofcouncils/global_memos/p32772

National Strategy for Counterterrorism
https://www.whitehouse.gov/sites/default/files/counterterrorism_strategy.pdf

USDOS: Bureau of Counterterrorism
http://www.state.gov/j/ct

U.S Phasing Out its Counterterrorism Unit in Philippines
http://www.nytimes.com/2014/06/27/world/asia/us-will-disband-terrorism-task-force-in-philippines.html?module=ArrowsNav&contentCollection=Asia%20Pacific&action=keypress&region=FixedLeft&pgtype=article

Majors Scott McKay and David Webb are currently Wayne A. Downing Fellows pursuing Masters of Arts Degrees at Stanford University in International Policy Studies. They have served in a variety of conventional and special operations assignments including and most recently with the 75th Ranger Regiment.

Scott N. McKay & David A. Webb, "Comparing Counterterrosim in Indonesia and the Philippines," *Combating Terrorism Center at West Point,* February, 27, 2015.

Article   Prepared by: Thomas J. Badey, *Randolph-Macon College*

Following the Peshawar School Attack, Pakistan Moves against Domestic Terrorism

Brian M. Perkins

Learning Outcomes

After reading this article, you will be able to:

- Identify key elements of Pakistan's National Action Plan.
- Discuss the use of military courts for terrorist cases.
- Discuss the role of civil society in Pakistan's counterterrorism plan.

The attack by Tehrik-e-Taliban Pakistan (TTP) on the Army Public School in Peshawar on December 16 was a watershed moment in the country's fight against terrorism. The death of 132 children transcended preconceived boundaries between civil and military or Sunni and Shi'a, creating space for concerted action against terrorism and Islamic extremism (*Dawn* [Karachi], December 16, 2014). In its aftermath, the Pakistani government immediately stepped up its war against terrorism through both military and legislative action. The reinstatement of the death penalty and a move to establish military anti-terrorism courts are at the forefront of its 20-point National Action Plan (NAP) (*Express Tribune* [Karachi], December 25, 2014). The military meanwhile intensified Operations Zarb-e-Azb and Khyber-I against the TTP in the country's volatile Federally Administered Tribal Area, with increased air and ground operations (*Express Tribune* [Karachi], February 5). Meanwhile, Pakistan's civil society demonstrated a level of unity unusual in a country divided along ethnic and religious lines. Although implementing the NAP, and maintaining public support of it, is essential to sustaining its momentum, events

nonetheless suggest that the attacks created a new willingness in Pakistan to tackle terrorism.

Implementation

One day after the Peshawar attack, on December 17, Prime Minister Nawaz Sharif lifted the six-year death penalty moratorium, announcing that 500 death row inmates would face execution (*Dawn* [Karachi], December 27, 2014). In a matter of weeks, 24 prisoners were executed at various prisons across Pakistan. The executions sparked a series of reprisal attacks that claimed the lives of 86 individuals. Sunni militant group Jundullah also claimed responsibility for two separate attacks on Shi'a mosques; the first occurred in the Shikarpur district of Sindh Province on January 30, killing 60 people, and the second in Peshawar, on February 13, killed 20. On February 17, TTP splinter group Jamaat ul-Ahrar claimed responsibility for an attack on a Lahore police headquarters that claimed the lives of eight people (*Express Tribune* [Karachi], February 17). Representatives from both groups said the attacks were in retaliation for the execution of militant prisoners, hoping to pressure the government into halting further executions.

Members of the Pakistan Peoples Party and Pakistan Muslim League-Nawaz who were previously ousted by military coups watched nervously as the civil government conceded sweeping authority to the military, as it has done in the wake of previous crises. Despite latent concerns, a measure to establish military courts passed unopposed, with the country's two main Islamic parties, the Jamaat-e-Islami and Jamiat Ulema-e-Islam Fazal, abstaining (*Dawn* [Karachi], January 6). As a result, special military courts are expected to begin functioning by the end of February for a two-year period in order to expedite the trial of suspected terrorists by bypassing the already overburdened civil judiciary (*Express Tribune* [Karachi], February 9). However, members of Pakistan's judicial system have criticized the move as they feel it gives too much power to the military without improving civilian courts (*Dawn* [Karachi], January 30). The structure of these courts and the method of transferring cases from a civil to a military jurisdiction remain unclear. What is clear, however, is that they will drastically alter the requirements needed to secure convictions, as the standard of what constitutes evidence will be up to the discretion of those presiding over the case.

Around a month after the attack, thousands of schools reopened in mid-January with tightened security and improved security features, but many high-risk schools remain closed (*Express Tribune* [Karachi], February 27). The government has formulated a plan to create a new security force comprised of retired military and law enforcement officials to protect the nation's schools. However, it is unclear when it will become operational, and many schools will continue to rely on untrained and poorly armed guards or teachers. Students across the country have demonstrated unprecedented resilience and bravery, with many children openly stating they will not be deterred from returning to school (*Dawn* [Karachi], January 12). The government has, meanwhile, opened terrorism hotlines in every province (*Dawn* [Karachi], December 30, 2014). According to local sources, the hotlines have already received 253 actionable calls, highlighting the public's increased willingness to report incidents (*The Nation* [Lahore], February 25). Figures released by *Dawn News* reported that since the National Action Plan was first introduced, law enforcement officials have arrested more than 10,000 individuals on charges ranging from loudspeaker misuse to direct involvement in terror attacks (*Dawn* [Karachi], February 19). Police officials have also cracked down on hate speech and the distribution of extremist propaganda as well as the use of cellular devices with unregistered SIM cards (*Dawn* [Karachi], January 8).

Response and Outlook

The Peshawar attack has so far unified Pakistan's historically divided civil society and acted as a springboard for public activism across the country. In one notable incident, for example, Sunni and Shi'a Pakistani rallied together against Islamabad's Lal Masjid mosque and its hardline chief cleric Maulana Abdul Aziz for his refusal to publicly condemn the massacre and the militants responsible (*Dawn* [Karachi], December 19, 2014). On the second day of the rally, Aziz threatened to attack the protesters; rather than resorting to violence, the protesters registered a case against Aziz in the form of a First Information Report (FIR) (*Express Tribune* [Karachi], December 19, 2014). A FIR

alone is not damning; however, it prompted the police and civilian courts to file an arrest warrant against Aziz (Pakistan Today, December 26, 2014). The police have done so 22 times previously without taking action, primarily due to the memory of the Musharraf regime's bloody siege of the mosque in 2007, and there is no guarantee of action taking place this time. However, the development does indicate a renewed public willingness to look again at the long-standing problem of Lal Masjid.

While the response from civil society has mostly been in favor of the NAP, civil society is also now, more than ever, critical of every previous counter-terrorism initiative enacted by the government. Repeatedly the Pakistani public has watched as the government hastily responds to a tragedy, only to lose steam after achieving meager or narrow results. Although the director general of Inter-Services Public Relations, Major General Asim Bajwa, purports that nine of the 27 individuals responsible for the Peshawar attack have been killed and 12 others arrested, a considerable segment of the public will not be satisfied until authorities show equal effort in eliminating all terrorist groups, not just the "bad Taliban" (*The Nation* [Lahore], February 13). The success of the NAP will be determined by the government and military's actions, as well as the civil society's will to stand up against terrorism and religious intolerance. The younger generation of activists, like the Pakistan Youth Alliance, is trying to push government action through peaceful demonstrations and social media, with Twitter hashtags such as #ReclaimYourMosque to encourage the public to speak out against radicalization.

Meanwhile, the country's bellicose militant groups will likely alter their tactics in an attempt to break the will of the Pakistani people. Terrorist attacks since December highlight an increased willingness to claim civilian lives and an increased propensity for conducting attacks on "soft targets." For instance, the Lahore police headquarters is the only fortified target attacked since December, but there have been a series of attacks on schools and students. For instance, on February 17 in Wah Cantonment in Punjab (a town with a large army presence), military personnel defused an explosive device outside a school after students reported a suspicious package, potentially saving the lives of their teachers and classmates (*Dawn* [Karachi], February 17). In another incident, armed assailants kidnapped a student in Karachi on February 20, before setting him ablaze and pushing him from a moving van (*Pakistan Today*, February 20). According to local police officials, the kidnappers left a note threatening further attacks against students if military operations continued (*Dawn* [Karachi], February 20). Pakistan's children, students and minority Shi'a community will likely continue to face such terrorist threats as the government grapples with implementing the NAP. Pakistan will not win the war against terrorism without more bloodshed, but the NAP—combined with civil society's increased willingness to stand up to militants—could potentially serve as a stepping-stone towards normalcy.

Critical Thinking

1. What are the key elements of Pakistan's National Action Plan?
2. What are the benefits and drawbacks of the use of military courts?
3. Why is the support of civil society essential to counterterrorism?
4. What are other possible actions the Pakistani government can take to reduce terrorism?

Internet References

The Need for Civil Society in Pakistan
http://www.aljazeera.com/indepth/opinion/2015/02/civil-society-pakistan-150225084535989.html

The National Action Plan: An Overview
http://cpakgulf.org/the-national-action-plan-an-over-view

Who are the Pakistani Taliban?
http://www.cnn.com/2014/12/17/world/asia/pakistan-taliban-explainer

BRIAN M. PERKINS is a South and Central Asia analyst and freelance journalist specializing in terrorism and sectarian violence.

Unit 10

UNIT

Prepared by: Thomas J. Badey, *Randolph-Macon College*

Future Threats

Terrorism will undoubtedly remain a major policy issue for the United States well into this twenty-first century. As the rise of ISIS and attacks in major cities around the world indicate, the killing of Osama bin Laden in May of 2011, while an important political victory for the United States has had only a limited impact on on terrorism as a whole. As al-Qaeda central has weakened, al-Qaeda affiliates and small groups or individuals who claim association with al-Qaeda or Islamic extremism have emerged in various parts of the world.

As the overall appeal of al-Qaeda has declined, organizations like ISIS have garnered international media attention. ISIS has managed to fill the vacuum created by the slow decline of al-Qaeda. Using social media to its advantage, it is effectively recruiting young men and women from around the world to fight in support of an extreme and violent version of Islam which seeks to create a new Caliphate. ISIS has become what al-Qaeda may have aspired to be. It is much larger, more extreme, more sophisticated, better financed, and significantly more deadly. While al-Qaeda killed thousands, ISIS has killed and continues to kill tens of thousands.

While there appears to be a broad consensus among terrorism scholars about terrorism of the past, there is no such consensus about the future of terrorism. David C. Rapoport argued that there have been four waves of modern terrorism, the anarchist wave from the 1880s to the 1920s, the anti-colonial wave from the 1920s to the 1960s, the new left wave which largely dissolved by the 1990s, and a new religious wave which began with the Soviet invasion of Afghanistan and the Iranian revolution in 1979. His theory gives rise to some key questions. Are we seeing a continuation of Rapoport's fourth, religious wave of violence or are we experiencing something fundamentally different? If this is a new wave, how do we describe it? If this is the fourth wave, what will the fifth wave look like? These are fundamental questions which must be addressed when talking about the future of international terrorism.

Opinions as to what future perpetrators will look like and what methods they will use are also subject to controversy. While some argue that the traditional methods of terrorism, such as bombing, kidnapping, and hostage taking will continue to dominate this millennium, others warn that weapons of mass destruction such as biological and chemical weapons, or even radiological or nuclear weapons, will be the weapons of choice for future terrorists. Almost everyone agrees that the Internet and social media will significantly impact the way in which terrorist groups will operate in the future.

While these discussions continue, there are also questions about the broad future trends that will influence international terrorism in the coming years. Some scholars predict that the continuing rise of Islamic extremists and unstable governments in the Middle East and North Africa will give rise to a new generation of violent extremists. Others warn that economic instability in parts of Europe may lead to the reemergence of left-wing terrorism groups in Europe. Still others warn that West Africa and Central Europe are potential new frontiers for international terrorism. Most believe that the tactics employed by terrorists will be more varied. From the use of meat cleavers, as in an attack on British soldiers in the United Kingdom to the potential use of weapons of mass destruction, terrorism will likely continue to cause casualties around the world.

The first article in this section identifies key differences in how two of the foremost experts on terrorism, Bruce Hoffman and Marc Sageman, interpret the nature of the terrorist threat. Picarelli argues that law enforcement agencies can offer valuable insights as key contributors to this debate. In the second article of this section, Anthony N. Celso examines what he describes as the fifth wave of jihadist terror groups. He concludes that ISIS and Boko Haram are likely to implode in the face of popular revulsion, internal dissension, and external resistance Next, Lolita Baldor in "U.S. Eyes Anti-Piracy Effort along West Africa Coast" discusses potential future anti-piracy operations along Africa's west coast. She argues that the United States and its allies are increasingly concerned about potential ties between terrorist organizations and pirates in the region. Finally, William Tupman in "Reflecting on Terror after Charlie Hebdo. What Now?" reflects on the future implications of the Charlie Hebdo attacks in Paris. He believes that more spontaneous acts of violence are likely, conducted by organizations that may break up as quickly as they formed, but also cautions that "the break up will be bloody."

Article   Prepared by: Thomas J. Badey, *Randolph-Macon College*

The Future of Terrorism

Two experts debate the evolving nature of terrorism and its effect on law enforcement.

JOHN T. PICARELLI

Learning Outcomes

After reading this article, you will be able to:

- Explain the importance of when and where radicalism occurs.
- Describe how terrorist groups organize.
- Discuss the potential contribution of law enforcement agencies to the counterterrorist effort.

A future terrorist threat could emerge in Minnesota, Mogadishu, or perhaps both simultaneously.

In a recent case, the FBI investigated what had become of a group of young Somali-American men who lived in the Minneapolis area and disappeared. Relatives said they had abruptly left the country to join a suspected terrorist organization in Somalia. If that is true, the men might train with terrorists and then join local operations in Somalia or return to the United States on their American passports.

This case demonstrates how a sharp debate between two terrorism experts has significant implications for state, local and tribal law enforcement agencies in the United States. Bruce Hoffman and Marc Sageman—two of the nation's preeminent terrorism experts—disagree about the nature of the threat. Hoffman, a professor at Georgetown University and a former senior executive of the RAND Corp., says the primary threat lies with al-Qaida slowly reconstituting itself in Pakistan. Sageman, a scholar-in-residence at the New York Police Department and a former case officer with the CIA, contends that the threat has shifted to radicalized individuals forming groups in the United States and Europe.

Although Hoffman and Sageman focus mainly on the threat from al-Qaida and Islamic terrorism, the issues they raise are not limited to these groups. Both men touch on factors common to all terrorist groups, such as recruitment and organization.

The debate between Hoffman and Sageman presents law enforcement agencies with a challenge and an opportunity. The challenge is deciding which analysis of terrorism is correct.

At its core, the debate concerns terrorist recruitment and organization. Therefore, agencies will form their community protection strategies based on the more accurate point of view. The difference between radicalization within a community and radicalization directed from abroad creates the difference between investing in counterterrorism programs that stress community outreach and those that stress intelligence sharing.

The opportunity, however, is equally great. Law enforcement agencies have a critical role to play in contributing to the debate because their observations of how terrorists recruit, radicalize, organize and train people are prime drivers of how counterterrorism efforts will unfold in the future.

The Nature of the Threat

Both Hoffman and Sageman are prominent, well-published researchers who often consult with security and law enforcement agencies on terrorism issues. Critics and colleagues alike agree that their books are influential, and, in fact, they are among the most often cited in terrorism studies.[1]

Hoffman says the main threat from terrorism lies with the core of al-Qaida, which he believes is gradually rebuilding itself in Pakistan to attack targets in the United States and Europe. "Al-Qaida is much like a shark, which must keep moving forward, no matter how slow or incrementally, or die . . . The group's capacity to survive is also a direct reflection of both its resilience and the continued resonance of its ideology," he said.[2]

Sageman sees the threat of terrorism originating not from a centralized core but from the "bottom up." Although Sageman agrees that al-Qaida's core group in Pakistan remains a danger, he believes it is effectively contained. For Sageman, the future of terrorism is more diffuse, with the primary risk of attack coming from smaller groups of radicalized individuals who find one another in the community (often through the Internet). Sageman believes that al-Qaida's ideology—not its organization—binds these groups. "The threat from al-Qaida and its progeny has evolved over time," Sageman said. "The process of radicalization is still going on but now proceeds in a hostile, post-Sept. 11, wired environment, resulting in a social structure comprised of disconnected groups."[3]

When and Where Does Radicalization Occur?

Radicalization occurs when recruits align their existing world-view with the ideology of a group and commit themselves to using violence to achieve the group's goals. To understand this alignment is to understand what drives a person to commit terrorism.

> **Radicalization occurs when recruits align their existing worldview with the ideology of a group and commit themselves to using violence to achieve the group's goals.**

Hoffman and Sageman agree that understanding radicalization is vital to understanding terrorism. However, they strongly differ on where radicalization takes place. For Hoffman, radicalization occurs in a centralized core of terrorist elites who oversee recruitment and training programs housed in clandestine facilities or in lawless regions of the globe such as the Afghanistan-Pakistan border. Sageman, on the other hand, argues that radicalization is diffuse—or leaderless—and occurs through groups of loosely associated radicals found within American and European communities.

If Hoffman's theory is correct, law enforcement officials would expect to find radicals trained through organized programs, most often overseas. To identify and counter this threat, the best strategy would be to track foreign-born or domestic radicals through intelligence fusion centers or other interagency task forces.

On the other hand, if Sageman's theory is valid—that terror groups form within local communities without the help of organized training programs—law enforcement officials would focus on identifying and countering sources of radicalization within their communities. For example, correctional facilities are one place where radicalization can occur. A 2007 National Institute of Justice study found that prisoner radicalization was indeed happening in prisons, mostly through personal inmate relationships.[4] The study found that radicalization often began with a prisoner's religious conversion and continued with extremist religious teachings, eventually leading individuals to undertake political violence. Similar to what Sageman holds, the NIJ study found the threat arose from small groups of "true believers" who were motivated to commit terrorist acts.[5]

Although Hoffman and Sageman disagree on where radicalization occurs, they believe outreach programs are important in combating radicalization. Community policing builds bridges of trust between community members and police, providing an important link to understanding when potential radicals might be active within a community.

A 2006 NIJ study found that although an increased prevalence of hate crimes against Arab-American communities and heightened levels of alienation within these communities followed the Sept. 11 attacks, outreach programs helped rebuild trust.[6] Community policing served as a bulwark against radicalization. Relationships between community members and authorities helped dampen or remove the grievances that often lead to radicalization, such as perceptions of bias or hate crimes. Such relationships and trust could also yield information on trained radicals arriving in communities.

The study further showed that these communities responded more favorably to outreach efforts from state and local agencies than to those from the federal level. This affirms the critical role of local law enforcement in combating radicalization and terrorism.

> **Communities responded more favorably to outreach efforts from state and local agencies than to those from the federal level. This affirms the critical role of local law enforcement in combating radicalization and terrorism.**

How Do Terrorists Organize?

Another significant dispute between Hoffman and Sageman concerns how terrorist groups organize. Hoffman's analysis suggests the most dangerous terrorist groups organize around a center-periphery model. In this model, the leadership and best-trained cells remain in safe havens such as Afghanistan, drawing information, money and practical assistance from support cells working in target countries. When it is time to strike, the attack cells quickly enter, attack and exit the target country with the aid of the already-embedded support cells. Organizational control remains centralized with the leadership cells, which give orders to the other groups.

Sageman, on the other hand, sees the most dangerous terrorist organizations centered in small groups that provide their own support. The groups do not travel overseas for specialized training; rather, they educate themselves using sources such as Web postings. Sageman's groups are more autonomous than the cells that Hoffman describes in that they conduct their

---

Further Reading on the Debate

Bruce Hoffman's review of Marc Sageman's most recent book in the journal *Foreign Affairs* began the debate regarding the nature of the threat from terrorism. The debate continued in subsequent issues of *Foreign Affairs*. For more on the public policy impact of this issue, see "A Not Very Private Feud Over Terrorism," published in the *New York Times* in 2008. See:

- www.foreignaffairs.org/20080501fareview essay87310/bruce-hoffman/the-myth-of-grass-roots-terrorism.html.
- www.foreignaffairs.org/20080701faresponse87415/marc-sageman-bruce-hoffman/does-osama-still-call-the-shots.html.
- www.nytimes.com/2008/06/08/weekinreview/08sciolino.html?sq=bruce%20hoffman&st=cse&scp=4&pagewanted=all.

preparations and attacks from within the community, keeping their own organizational control.

NIJ's research on organizational learning and the role of the Internet has found merit in both positions, suggesting a complex reality. A 2005 NIJ study examined terror groups' organization, especially how they get, interpret and disseminate information. The study identified evidence supporting both models of terrorist organization, concluding that how these groups adapt to changing conditions will influence which counterterrorism strategies are most effective. If, for example, terrorists responsible for collecting and analyzing information are in the community, law enforcement agencies would have to adopt a more active surveillance and investigation plan than if the terrorists were abroad. Agencies would also have to help identify safe havens that terrorist groups use, such as warehouses, ranches or even houses in suburban areas.[7]

Continuing NIJ studies on extremism on the Internet may also help further clarify this discussion. For example, one study is examining the content of extremist websites to identify the location of people who contribute to the sites.[8]

Meanwhile, state and local law enforcement agencies are already bringing this discussion into sharper focus. Many have collected information about specific terrorist groups and shared it with other agencies. This has led to a better understanding about how terrorist groups organize in communities and how best to counter them. In addition, agencies are paying closer attention to online extremism, another important way to understand terrorist organization. Continued information gathering and vigilance from counterterrorism agencies will inform the Sageman-Hoffman debate and will influence how the nation develops counterterrorism measures.

A Two-Way Street

History will decide who won this debate. Now, however, the differing opinions offer a superb example of how complex issues evolve into policy choices. Whether radicalization happens here or abroad is an important question, but for law enforcement agencies, the academic debate translates into how to provide the most effective community outreach in the effort to prevent terrorist attacks.

Law enforcement agencies are not passive bystanders in the discussion—they are key contributors. Their efforts offer valuable insights into how terrorists recruit and organize. This give-and-take between research and practice will yield greater clarity and improved decision-making for counterterrorism efforts.

Notes

1. Hoffman, B., *Inside Terrorism*, New York: Columbia University Press, 1999 (revised and enlarged in 2006); Sageman, M., *Understanding Terror Networks,* Philadelphia: University of Pennsylvania Press, 2004; and Sageman, M., *Leaderless Jihad: Terror Networks in the Twenty-First Century,* Philadelphia: University of Pennsylvania Press, 2008.

2. Hoffman, B., "The Myth of Grass-Roots Terrorism: Why Osama bin Laden Still Matters," *Foreign Affairs* 87 (2008): 133–138.

3. Sageman, M., and B. Hoffman, "Does Osama Still Call the Shots? Debating the Containment of al Qaeda's Leadership," *Foreign Affairs* 87 (2008): 163–166.

4. Hamm, M.S., *Terrorist Recruitment in American Correctional Institutions: An Exploratory Study of Non-Traditional Faith Groups,* final report submitted to the National Institute of Justice, U.S. Department of Justice, Washington, DC: December 2007 (NCJ 220957), available at www.ncjrs.gov/pdffiles1/nij/grants/220957.pdf.

5. See "Prisoner Radicalization: Assessing the Threat in U.S. Correctional Institutions," *NIJ Journal* 261 (October 2008), available at www.ojp.usdoj.gov/nij/journals/261/prisoner-radicalization.htm.

6. Henderson, N.J., C.W. Ortiz, N.F. Sugie, and J. Miller, *Policing in Arab-American Communities After September 11,* Research for Practice, Washington, DC: National Institute of Justice, U.S. Department of Justice: July 2008 (NCJ 221706), available at: www.ncjrs.gov/pdffiles1/nij/221706.pdf.

7. Jackson, B.A., J.C. Baker, K. Cragin et al., *Aptitude for Destruction, Volume I: Organizational Learning in Terrorist Groups and Its Implications for Combating Terrorism,* Santa Monica, Calif.: RAND Corp., 2005, available at www.rand.org/pubs/monographs/2005/RAND_MG331.pdf.

8. Erez, E., *Jihad, Crime and the Internet,* NIJ Award 2006-IJ-CX-0038.

Critical Thinking

1. What are the conflicting theories put forward by Hoffman and Sageman?
2. Why is it important where radicalization occurs?
3. What can state and local law-enforcement agencies contribute to counterterrorism efforts?

Internet References

How to Look at Homegrown Terrorism
www.time.com/time/nation/article/0,8599,1653566,00.html
Not a Very Private Feud Over Terrorism
www.nytimes.com/2008/06/08/weekinreview/08sciolino.html?sq=bruce%20hoffman&st=cse&scp=4&pagewanted=all&_r=0
Future of Terrorism
www.terrorism-research.com/future/

JOHN T. PICARELLI joined the International Center of the National Institute of Justice in 2008.

Picarelli, John T. From *National Institute of Justice Journal*, November 2009, pp. 26–30. Published by U.S. Department of Justice.

Article   Prepared by: Thomas J. Badey, *Randolph-Macon College*

The Islamic State and Boko Haram: Fifth Wave Jihadist Terror Groups

Anthony N. Celso

Learning Outcomes

After reading this article, you will be able to:

- Identify David Rapoport's four waves of terror.
- Identify the general "hallmarks" of fifth wave terror groups.
- Discuss why, according to Celso, these groups are likely to implode.

Introduction

The rise of Boko Haram (BH) in northern Nigeria and the Islamic State's (IS) dramatic conquest over a third of Iraq and Syria are remarkable. Directed by messianic leaders these groups have unleashed an ultra-violent campaign to construct transnational empires. IS's proclamation of a "caliphate" in Sunni areas of Iraq and northern Syria hopes to erase national borders. Similarly Boko Haram has created an ungovernable space in northeastern Nigeria and the Cameroon border that aspires to resurrect regional Islamic rule.

Driven by hostility toward secular authority and impelled by ethno-religious hatred, they have inspired revulsion and fear. Governments seem incapable of stopping them. BH and IS's capacity to wage terror has grown rapidly. Thousands have perished in these organization's relentless dreams to create a pure Islamic state. IS and BH have made impressive territorial gains with Islamic State forces encircling Baghdad and Boko Haram's wave of violence sharply escalating across Nigeria.

Both networks are characterized by cultish practices and a millenarian ideology associated with smaller organizations. The proposition that terrorism is a rational is widely accepted. Yet this explanation appears poorly suited to account for theologically driven terror organizations. Recently theories that all terror networks are rational have come under vigorous attack. The Islamist takfiri terrorism and millenarian violence it inspires seems particularly resistant to rational explanation.

Past millenarian terror cults like Aum Shinriko, the Shi'ite Assassins, and the Zealots are viewed as anomalies. Much of this analysis relies on psychological effects of intense social bonding. Such cults stretch across religions. Jessica Stein has nicely documented these small scale groups. The building of large millenarian terror organizations seems incongruous when examined within this context.

Yet large organizations have been driven by quasi-religious passions. French Revolutionaries, Bolsheviks and the Nazis are preeminent examples. Bruce Hoffman's work nicely illustrates the association between populist ideology and self-destructive violence. Membership in terror organizations driven by totalitarian impulses is often explained in terms of social climbing and monetary rewards. Some of this is quite true, but [it] is doubtful that it accounts for all of the membership. Ideological affinity for the group's world view must also be [a] driving if not preeminent force.

The traditional preference to analyze Islamist groups from a rational perspective may be misplaced. Numerous authors have critiqued rational analytical models and their applicability to Islamist terrorism. Paul Berman, for example, critiques the rational paradigm for failing to account for the theological imperatives that dominate Islamist groups. Based on the studies of secular terror groups, Robert Nalbandov argues that rational perspectives are poorly designed to analyze Islamic terrorism. While these groups are very capable of short-term operational rationality, their long-range objectives are utopian and unachievable. Jihadism may be a unique form of terrorism with distinct cycles of activity driven by belief in mystical "prophetic" forces.

If rational models explaining "sacred" terror are inappropriate, how can we account for such groups? Fortunately theoretical frameworks exist that may explain large millenarian terror organizations. Jeffery Kaplan argues that such groups belong to a *fifth wave* of modern terror that has its historical precedent in Khmer Rouge.

The organization and sequencing of my argument is as follows. First, Jeffery Kaplan's *fifth wave* of terror theory is presented and discussed. Second, the essay argues that takfiri jihadist groups have tendencies consistent with Kaplan's theory. Third, BH and IS are discussed within Kaplan's essential framework. Finally, Boko Haram and Islamic State are placed within the context of takfiri precursors like the Armed Islamic Group (GIA), Al Qaeda in Iraq (AQI) and Al Qaeda in the Islamic Maghreb (AQIM). Contrary to Kaplan's argument that Islamist groups are not part of the *fifth wave,* this essay concludes that his theory does pertain to takfiri jihadist groups.

Kaplan Fifth Wave Theory

Jeffery Kaplan's *fifth wave* concept refines David Rapoport's *four wave* theory of modern terrorism. According to Rapoport modernity has bred four distinct terror cycles lasting a generation. Rapoport argues that revolutions in communication and travel have accelerated the global reach of terror groups, spreading their ideals among radicalized diaspora communities. The velocity by which ideas are communicated and the destructiveness of modern weaponry facilitate international terror activity with each cycle governed by a core set of ideas. The *four waves* (anarchist, colonial, left-revolutionary and Islamist) have a particular agenda and a core set of enemies. Rapoport argues terrorist waves are short lived as each cycle dissipates due to a combination of internal weakness, generational change and external pressures.

Kaplan clearly admires Rapoport's analysis but critiques his *four wave* theory as static for it does not account for groups that separate from preexisting waves. This disengagement produces a unique millenarian dynamic that begins with Kaplan's Khmer Rouge *fifth wave* prototype.

The Khmer Rouge is a *fifth wave* progenitor because the group in the 1970s broke from the left revolutionary phase. Kaplan argues that the Khmer's combat experience and rural isolation in its brutal struggle were key determinants in its devolution. Such forces contributed to a cult-like organization exacerbated by Maoist principles of localism and a millenarian desire to remake the world. Maoism conjoined with brutalization of war to create an organization committed to the destruction of the old order and the formation of a radical new society. The Khmer viewed themselves as the vanguard of this revolutionary transformation. Their proclamation of a new revolutionary calendar beginning in "year zero" and their forced migration of the urbanites to the countryside exemplified this millenarian dynamic. Multitudes were subject to "revolutionary conditioning" that killed millions.

Based on the Khmer experience and his study of the Ugandan Christian millenarian Lord's Resistance Army (LRA), Kaplan develops his *fifth wave* terrorism theory. Such groups have distinctive qualities. Among these general "hallmarks" are: (1) a devolution from a preexisting terror wave; (2) a "hopeful" extreme idealism; (3) a physical withdraw into the hinterland; (4) a desired aim to recreate a past "Golden Age" by beginning the calendar anew; (5) an intent to destroy the old world and create a pure new society; (6) an inability to compromise and the use of force against internal dissidents; (7) a belief in perfectibility of humans and the creation of a new man; (8) a quest for a new society leading to genocidal violence; (9) violence as a way of group life; (10) an emphasis on the subjugation of women and children; (11) recruitment of child soldiers and child brides; (12) the use of rape as a terror tactic; (13) a continuous cycle of violence engaged by the group across generations; (13) a particularistic emphasis on racial purity and ethno-tribal centrism; (14) pragmatic reliance on foreign allies to enhance group survival; (15) charismatic and authoritarian leadership; and (16) an apocalyptic world view buttressed by intense religious commitment.

While Kaplan sees similarities between *fifth wave* groups and jihadist groups he is reluctant to include them. His rejection of Islamist groups is based on their internationalization that he believes militates against the *fifth wave's* autarkic tendencies. Kaplan argues that Islamist's quest for a united *ummah* prevent their *fifth wave* devolution. He remains, however, open to the prospect of some *fifth wave* Islamist groups.

Kaplan moreover does make exceptions. He argues that the Janjaweed and their violence against Darfur's black population exhibit *fifth wave* hallmarks. He attributes their *fifth wave* behavior to nonreligious forces like environmental factors (drought and civil war) and Arab racism against blacks. The Janjaweed's Islamic ideology he argues is peripheral in its *fifth wave* evolution.

Kaplan's *fifth wave* Janjaweed designation may be applicable to other Islamist groups. The Janjaweed's *fifth wave* brutality has been copied by other Islamist groups. Contrary to Kaplan, most jihadi groups have Muhammad's Medina community as their initial philosophical ideal and only later his successors' caliphate. For jihadists, reconstructing the Prophet's Medina community provides for ample experimentation, localism and autarky.

Historically the quest for a unified *ummah* has been challenged by localism, power struggles and divisions. Efraim Karsh argues that ethnic-tribal divisions have militated against attaining a unified caliphate. The bloody history of caliphate succession has included civil wars and assassinations. Fragmentation and local variation, not unity, has been the norm governing Islamic history. This pattern, moreover, has plagued jihadist movements. Thomas Hegghammer maintains that divisions within radical Islamist groups are endemic as leaders vie for power and failed jihads inspire intra-organizational feuding and persistent reorganizations.

The mix of Arab racialism and Islam, moreover, has been a catalyst for localized ethnic cleansing. Walid Phares argues that Arabic and Islamist animus toward Kurds, Berbers, Coopts, Sudanese black Muslims reflects nostalgia for renewed rule over ethno-religious minorities. Despite their internationalism, jihadi groups are plagued by localism, brutality and divisions galvanized by an opportunity to replicate Muhammad's mythic Medina. These visions have been the basis for much barbarism.

Jihadists often develop rural insurgencies where government authority is weak. Borrowing from Che Guevara's "el foco" insurgency theory, Islamists hope their micro communities will catalyze a populist revolution. Jihadist rebels who seize towns establish Sharia councils frequently imposing drastic versions of Islamic law. Typically they organized religious police in these communities to harshly enforce moral codes.

Critical Thinking

1. What distinctive tendencies are found amongst fifth wave terror groups?
2. Why does the quick geographic expansion of The Islamic State and Boko Haram pose a problem?
3. What are the factors likely to cause Boko Haram and IS to implode?

Internet References

Boko Haram and ISIS Allegiance
http://www.cnn.com/2015/03/12/middleeast/isis-boko-haram
Terrorism's Fifth Wave: A Theory, a Conundrum and a Dilemma
http://www.terrorismanalysts.com/pt/index.php/pot/article/view/26/html
The Four Waves of Modern Terrorism
http://international.ucla.edu/media/files/Rapoport-Four-Waves-of-Modern-Terrorism.pdf

Article   Prepared by: Thomas J. Badey, *Randolph-Macon College*

US Eyes Anti-Piracy Effort Along West Africa Coast

LOLITA C. BALDOR

Learning Outcomes

After reading this article, you will be able to:

- Describe the connection between Boko Haram and al-Qaeda.

- Describe the tactics that the pirates have been using in the Gulf of Guinea.

- Discuss the factors that may influence a future US deployment in this region.

The U.S. and some of its allies are considering plans to increase anti-piracy operations along Africa's west coast, spurred on by concerns that money from the attacks is funding a Nigerian-based insurgent group that is linked to one of al-Qaida's most dangerous affiliates.

Piracy in the Gulf of Guinea has escalated over the past year, and senior U.S. defense and counter-piracy officials say allied leaders are weighing whether beefed up enforcement efforts that worked against pirates off the Somalia coast might also be needed in the waters off Nigeria.

There has been growing coordination between Nigeria-based Boko Haram and al-Qaida in the Islamic Maghreb (AQIM), which was linked to the attack on the U.S. diplomatic mission in Benghazi, Libya, last September that killed four Americans, including the ambassador. Military leaders say AQIM has become the wealthiest al-Qaida offshoot and an increasing terrorist threat to the region.

It has long been difficult to track whether there are terrorist ties to piracy in the waters off Africa. But officials are worried that even if Boko Haram insurgents aren't directly involved in the attacks off Nigeria and Cameroon, they may be reaping some of the profits and using the money for ongoing terrorist training or weapons.

No final decisions have been made on how counter-piracy operations could be increased in that region, and budget restrictions could hamper that effort, said the officials, who spoke on condition of anonymity because they were not authorized to talk about emerging discussions between senior U.S. military commanders and other international leaders.

But officials say the solution could include continued work and counter-piracy training with African nations. The U.S. participated last month in a maritime exercise with European and African partners in the Gulf of Guinea.

"Maritime partnerships and maritime security and safety are increasingly important in the Gulf of Guinea region to combat a variety of challenges including maritime crime, illicit trafficking and piracy," said Gen. Carter Ham, head of U.S. Africa Command.

In recent weeks, Ham and other U.S. military commanders have bluntly warned Congress that the terrorist threat from northern Africa has become far more worrisome.

"If the threat that is present in Africa is left unaddressed, it will over time grow to an increasingly dangerous and imminent threat to U.S. interests, and certainly could develop into a threat that threatens us in other places," Ham told Congress earlier this month. "We've already seen from some places in Africa, individuals that—from Nigeria, for example—attempt to enter our country with explosives."

Piracy in the Gulf of Guinea has escalated from low-level armed robberies to hijackings and cargo thefts and kidnappings. Last year, London-based Lloyd's Market Association—an umbrella group of insurers—listed oil-rich Nigeria, neighboring Benin and nearby waters in the same risk category as Somalia.

Pirates have been more willing to use violence in their robberies, at times targeting the crew for ransom. And experts suggest that many of the pirates come from Nigeria, where corrupt law enforcement allows criminality to thrive and there's a bustling black market for stolen crude oil.

Typically, foreign companies operating in Nigeria's Niger Delta pay cash ransoms to free their employees after negotiating down kidnappers' demands. Foreign hostages can fetch hundreds of thousands of dollars apiece.

Lately, however, the attacks, which had traditionally focused on the Nigerian coast, have spread, hitting ships carrying fuel from an Ivory Coast port. In January pirates made off with about $5 million in cargo from a fuel-laden tanker near the port of Abidjan, and two weeks later a French-owned fuel tanker was hijacked in the same area.

Just days after that, three sailors were kidnapped off a U.K.-flagged ship off the coast of Nigeria, and late in February six foreigners were taken off an energy company vessel in that same region.

The International Maritime Bureau has raised alarms about the Ivory Coast attacks, calling the first January incident a "potential game changer" in piracy in the region because [it] was the farthest ever from Nigeria in the Gulf of Guinea. And U.S. Navy Capt. Dave Rollo, who directed the recent naval exercise in the Gulf of Guinea that involved as many as 15 nations, said piracy in that area is not just a regional crime issue, it's "a global problem."

Meanwhile, over the past year, piracy off Somalia's coast has plummeted, as the U.S.-led enforcement effort beefed up patrols and encouraged increased security measures on ships transiting the region. After repeated urgings from military commanders and other officials, shipping companies increased the use of armed guards and took steps to better avoid and deter pirates.

According to data from the combined maritime force, nearly 50 ships were taken by pirates in 2010 in the Gulf of Aden and Somali Basin and there were another close to 200 unsuccessful attempts. Last year, just seven ships were pirated there along with 36 failed attacks.

Even as defense officials warn about the growing threat, they acknowledge that increasing counter-piracy operations around the Gulf of Guinea presents a number of challenges.

In recent weeks, the U.S. Navy has had to postpone or cancel a number of ship deployments because of budget cuts, including a decision not to send the aircraft carrier USS Harry S Truman to the Persian Gulf. The U.S. has maintained two carrier groups in the Gulf for much of the past two years, as tensions with Iran have escalated.

U.S. Africa Command has no ships of its own, so any U.S. vessels needed for operations would have to come from other places, such as Europe or America.

And defense officials also note that it may be difficult to build as much international interest in the Gulf of Guinea attacks as those in the more heavily traveled shipping lanes on the northeastern side of the continent.

Critical Thinking

1. How could the increase in piracy in the Gulf of Guinea threaten global maritime security?
2. Why has the use of violence by pirates increased?
3. Does the connection between piracy and terrorism pose a future threat to US interests?

Create Central

www.mhhe.com/createcentral

Internet References

African coastal piracy in 2013-the beginning of the end or the end of the beginning?
www.issafrica.org/iss-today/african-coastal-piracy-in-2013-the-beginning-of-the-end-or-the-end-of-the-beginning

Piracy sweeps West African seas
http://gga.org/analysis/piracy-sweeps-west-african-seas

Gulf of Guinea needs regional anti-piracy strategy
www.untogo.org/News/Africa/Gulf-of-Guinea-needs-regional-anti-piracy-strategy

Article   Prepared by: Thomas J. Badey, *Randolph-Macon College*

Reflecting on Terror after Charlie Hebdo. What Now?

WILLIAM (BILL) TUPMAN

Learning Outcomes

After reading this article, you will be able to:

- Identify lessons that can be learned from the Charlie Hebdo attacks.

- Explain the benefits and drawbacks of these types of attacks for ISIS.

- Discuss why new groups are likely to "break up as quickly as they formed."

On 26th January, Abu Mohamed al-Adnani, an ISIS spokesman, praised the Paris attacks, the Sydney siege, the failed plot in Belgium and the gunman who shot a soldier at Canada's national war memorial last October before attacking parliament. ISIS is thereby placing as much importance on such attacks as on going to Syria and Iraq to fight. Why? What does it gain by them? Are such attacks aimed at Western voters, with the intention that they agitate against Western military intervention in the Islamic world, or are they intended to raise morale among the jihadists suffering bomb and drone attacks? Or are they underlining the message that violence is the only way forward for Islam: that democracy is an irrelevance and that every non-Muslim, and even many Muslims, everywhere are legitimate targets? Is this tactic as much derived from Franz Fanon's "the Wretched of the Earth" as it is from the Koran and Islamic scholars? Or are they much less random and more targeted than the media would have us believe?

The reason for raising these question is that recent events appear to be more familiar than unfamiliar to old school academics who have studied terrorism since the 1960s. American academics after 9/11 would have everyone believe that there was something called "New terrorism" which bore no resemblance to "old" terrorism . . . a bit like the myth of Old Europe and New Europe. What's new? The perpetrator wants to be a martyr and has no wish to survive the attack and strike again, although that was true of the long-forgotten Japanese Red Army. The visual images are not particularly aimed at the indigenous population of "Western" countries, which include Russia and probably even China, from the al Qaeda perspective, but at potentially radicalisable young people in the Islamic world broadly defined: not just the Middle and Far East, but the diasporas in the "Western" world too. We may well have our categories wrong.

Looking at what we now know about the actual events as opposed to the contemporary mobile phone images, some of which have brought out the conspiracy theorists, as they did at the time of 9/11 with claims of false flag attacks, picking up on the image of disciplined, merciless killers, who hid behind balaclavas and wore black in imitation of the forces of Islamic State, the murderous terrorists of Iraq and Syria. In one sense the conspiracy theorists were right; the images did not tell the whole truth. In reality, the attackers went to the wrong building first, had to force someone to let them into the offices, escaped but with no safe house established and were without a plan as to what to do next.

It is worth remembering that all that follows are allegations and have not yet been proved in a court of law. There will be a trial of alleged associates of the brothers Cherif and Said Kouachi who are alleged to have been the attackers of the Charlie Hebdo journalists, the killers of a police officer that they had already wounded and the individuals killed in the siege of the printworks at Dammartin en Goele in North eastern France and of Amedi Coulibaly who is alleged to have shot at and wounded a jogger on the same morning as the Charlie Hebdo murders, murdered a policewoman and wounded a man the following morning in Montrouge, proceeding to hold hostages in a kosher supermarket near Porte des Vincennes. The siege of the supermarket ended shortly after the siege of the printworks. Coulibaly's girlfriend is supposed to have left for Syria the week before the attacks, which may or may not suggest an element of planning.

The point to be made here is that with the exception of the jogger, these are not random attacks made on any random Westerner. Even where the attacks do not appear to have been pre-planned, the targets were police officers, a group of journalists who had become a cause celebre for jihadis and, most worryingly, a Jewish supermarket. No-one was shot at the garage where they stole petrol and food and a hostage was actually released at the printworks, where they had told the local media they were prepared for martyrdom. The Kouachi brothers after the Charlie Hebdo murders do not appear to have had a plan as to what to do next, presumably having anticipated a shoot-out with the police that would end with their deaths. The Kouachi brothers claimed to be carrying out the shootings on behalf of al Qaeda in Yemen, Coulibaly on behalf of ISIS, just to muddy the waters a little more.

There is little information about the shootings in Verviers, Belgium, that took place the week after the Paris shootings. The Belgian prosecutors say that a plot to kill police was foiled, and that a shoot-out took place with a group that had returned from Syria. Four Kalashnikovs, bomb-making equipment and police clothing was found. A trial has yet to take place, but raids were carried out on a number of addresses around the country.

In the Canadian shootings, Ottawa, October 2014, a gunman killed a soldier on duty at the national war memorial before attacking the Canadian parliament where he was shot and killed before he could do any harm. Two days previously another soldier had been killed in a hit and run attack. The Australian siege in Sydney involved a fairly disturbed individual and the Lindt chocolate café doesn't seem to be an easily explainable target, so may fall into the category of a copycat attack.

This is a piece for the Newsletter of the Standing Group on Organised Crime, so are there any crime angles? The Kouachi brothers had a Kalashnikov and a rocket launcher purchased from an arms dealer in Belgium. So did the Belgian jihadis. But so did some people in a street fight in London at the weekend. How easy is it to get these weapons? It is much easier than we think. Google Kalashnikovs and London and you will be amazed. It is true that they are easier to get in Belgium and that Belgian firearms law needs attention. But it isn't that difficult for criminals to get hold of them.

The brothers fell off police and intelligence services' radar because they had originally been petty criminals and appeared to have returned to old habits. The division between crime and terrorism is not so clear cut. Terrorist cells in the West have been ordered to be self-financing and crime is an acceptable means of fund raising. Equally, appearing to be an active criminal makes it more likely that weapons will be sold to you by illegal armourers. Remember the existence of the terror organised crime nexus, although in this case it is not clear how "organised" they were.

Finally, it is worth remembering that, horrendous as these attacks are and were, much worse is going on in the Islamic world. In Nigeria, the week of the Charlie Hebdo murders, Boko Haram is supposed to have killed 2,000 people in a massacre in Borno province. The Yemeni government has given in to Houthi Shia tribesmen, possibly giving the initiative to al Qaeda in the Arab Peninsula to lead the Sunni resistance. Syria and Iraq are still in flames. In Libya as I write this on 27th January, a hotel used by foreigners in Tripoli has been occupied by gunmen. I would return to two points from the earlier piece in the Conversation. A generational change may be taking place: as the founding members die, the restrictions they placed on themselves are lifted. Osama bin Laden's long planning of specific symbolic attacks is replaced by more spontaneous acts of what is seen by the new younger less Islamic leaders as acts of revenge. Secondly, there is more that divides these organisations than unites them. They may break up as quickly as they formed. But the break up will be bloody.

Critical Thinking

1. What does ISIS gain from attacks like the Charlie Hebdo attack?
2. What is "new terrorism"?
3. What is the impact of generational change on terrorist organizations?
4. Why are these new groups likely to "break up as quickly as they formed?"

Internet References

The Debate over "New" vs. "Old" Terrorism
http://www.start.umd.edu/publication/debate-over-new-vs-old-terrorism

Lone-operator Terrorism: Tackling a Growing Threat
http://cambridgeglobalist.org/2015/02/12/lone-operator-terrorism-tackling-growing-threat

Understanding Charlie Hebdo
http://www.slate.com/articles/news_and_politics/foreigners/2015/01/charlie_hebdo_cartoons_the_anti_clerical_newspaper_tradition_that_s_as_french.html

---

WILLIAM (BILL) TUPMAN is Visiting Professor in Criminal Justice at BPP University, London; Research Fellow, Department of Criminology at Anglia Ruskin University, Cambridge; Honorary Fellow and retired academic, Department of Politics University of Exeter.